MILITARY
AVIATION
DISASTERS

Other titles by the same author:

Aviation Disasters

Flights of Terror

MILITARY AVIATION DISASTERS

SIGNIFICANT LOSSES SINCE 1908

SECOND EDITION

DAVID B. GERO

Haynes Publishing

First published in 1999 by Patrick Stephens Limited,
an imprint of Haynes Publishing
This 2nd Edition published in 2010 by Haynes Publishing

A catalogue record for this book is available from the British
Library

ISBN 978 1 84425 645 7

Library of Congress control no. 2009936969

Published by Haynes Publishing,
Sparkford, Yeovil, Somerset BA22 7JJ, UK
Tel: 01963 442030 Fax: 01963 440001
Int. tel: +44 1963 442030 Int. fax: +44 1963 440001
E-mail: sales@haynes.co.uk
Website: www.haynes.co.uk

Haynes North America Inc.
861 Lawrence Drive, Newbury Park,
California 91320, USA

Printed and bound in Great Britain

Contents

Acknowledgements

The author wishes to thank the following organisations and individuals for their assistance in the creation of this book:

Accident Reports, contact: Michael T. Stowe; Argentine Air Force, contacts: Guillermo Raul Barreira and Mario Santamaria; Australian Archives, contact: Elyse Boutcher; Australian Department of Defence, contact: Wing Commander J. W. Kindler, David Wilson; Aviation Safety Network website; Belgian Air Force, contact: F. Mabeyt; Canadian Directorate of History and Heritage, National Defence Headquarters, contact: Steve Harris; Dutch Ministry of Defence, contact: Dr P. C. van Royen; French Ministry of Defence, contact: Colonel J. F. Bodere; German Archives, contact: Jansen; German Ministry of Defence, contacts: Kunze, Dr Kruger Gorsdorf; German Naval Air Museum, contact: Fritz Schroder; German War Archives, contact: Dr Bernd-Rudiger Ahlbrecht; Israel Defence Force, contact: Major Avital Margalit; UK Ministry of Defence Air Historical Branch, contacts: L. R. Howard, E. A. Munday; US Air Force, contacts: Colonel Donn Kearns, Rhonda M. Jenkins; US Air Force Inspection and Safety Center, contacts: Louie F. Alley; Colonel Bernard Burklund, Colonel Rolland Moore, Vincent P. Murone; US Air Force Historical Research Center, contacts: Alan Clair, Captain Christopher Cwynar, Lieutenant Robert Guentz, Daniel Haulman, Essie Roberts, A. T. Warnock; US Army Safety Center, contacts: Lieutenant Colonels Thomas Johnson, Johnny Marshall and Marco Torres, Major Joe Cole; US Coast Guard, contact: W. K. Lowry; US Naval Historical Center; US Naval Safety Center, contacts: G. T. Eccles, Lieutenant Commander Mark Enderson, H. W. Raines, T. J. Tucker; US Navy Office of the Judge Advocate General, contacts: Commanders R. N. Fiske, A. K. Llewellyn, J. B. Norman and G. C. Paad, Colonel C. H. Mitchell (USMC); US National Archives, contact: Mary J. Brooke.

Research services provided by Alan Cooper, Terry Denham, Ronan Hubert, Graham K. Salt and Kathryn Powers.

Translation services provided by: Global Language Services, Luis Gonzalez, Giorgio Isella, Piet Moeleker, Julio Puchalt and Claude Seywert.

Introduction

Those familiar with my previous books, *Aviation Disasters* and *Flights of Terror*, which dealt with the subjects of airline disasters and aerial terrorism, will be well aware of the wealth of information that has been amassed on these subjects. Over the years, I have also collected a sizeable amount of material that has been made available, though not necessarily published, on air catastrophes involving the armed forces of the world. The compilation of this information now results in this, my third book, *Military Aviation Disasters*. This second edition completely updates the subject, and includes information on incidents occurring in the first major conflicts of the 21st century, in Afghanistan and Iraq.

Due to the nature of the subject matter in this volume, it should be read with a certain amount of caution. Military censorship has played a major role in what is presented here. Whereas some fighting forces are notably forthright in sharing information, such as the Royal Air Force and the US Navy, this is not usually the rule. Although basic details are invariably available, causative factors are often deleted from official reports. Even less material is made available on disasters occurring in Third World and/or non-democratic nations, although some progress has been made in this area in recent years, with incidents occurring in the former Soviet Union finally coming to light. Difficulty in obtaining information is complicated during wartime, when censorship frequently becomes a matter of national security. For these reasons, absolute accuracy and completeness cannot be guaranteed as it was for my previous books.

Having offered that disclaimer, I am still presenting this book as the most comprehensive reference work on the subject ever published. Using the same format as *Aviation Disasters*, all significant military losses from the earliest days of powered flight are reviewed. I have attempted to include every individual incident with at least 20 fatalities, although certain cases with a fewer number of deaths have also been recounted where they are particularly noteworthy. There are also some accounts of a few significant combat incidents involving heavy loss of life or aircraft. (Collisions between military and civil aircraft have also been included if a significant number of the fatalities were aboard the former, but major airline disasters falling into this category have been previously detailed in *Aviation Disasters*.)

Some controversy is anticipated regarding my classification of a military air disaster, when considering that some of these were combat losses or occurred within a combat environment. Such losses should in no way detract from the success of a military operation. On the other hand, no wartime victory can totally overshadow the losses occurring therein. There may also be some disagreement as to exactly what is a military aircraft. In the former Soviet Union, for example, aircraft belonging to the airline Aeroflot were often used in military transport operations. In South America there exist several military branches that also perform civil aviation flights. Generally, though, if either the operator or the operation were related to the military, they have been included, unless the incident has been dealt with in my previous book.

As always, I shall be interested in hearing from readers, wherever they may be, who possess information that clarifies or corrects any of the material presented here, and who should contact me via the publishers.

David B. Gero
San Gabriel, California
2009

1

1908–1939

Loosely speaking, the first application of 'air power' was the day humans began throwing stones at one another. The first actual use of flying machines in combat is believed to have occurred in ancient China, when kites were employed

The Wright biplane, carrying Orville Wright (in cap) and US Army Lt Thomas Selfridge, photographed prior to the demonstration flight that ended in tragedy. (Smithsonian Institution)

as unmanned bombers. Soldiers took to the air for the first time in the mid-19th century during the American Civil War when Union balloonists were used as forward spotters. True military aviation is a by-product of 20th-century technology, when governments first began using machines that were not bound by the whims of gravity or the wind. Even before its use in commerce, the aeroplane saw application during the First World War as a tool of conflict. During the same war, dirigibles also came into use as vulnerable though deadly offensive weapons. Following the Germans, the British, French and American military forces experimented with airships, with equal misfortune. Larger than today's jet transports and built with the highest hopes, many of these lighter-than-air craft, including the R.38, R.101 and Akron, ended their short careers with disastrous crashes. And with the explosion of the German commercial airship *Hindenberg* in 1937, aviation's affair with dirigibles ended altogether. Non-rigid airships, or blimps, were successfully used on patrol duties during the Second World War and saw a brief revival in the late 1950s, but that chapter also ended with a fatal crash. It is only now, using modern technology, that interest in such craft is being revived. The tremendous size of the early 20th century airships accounts for their prominence in this section, which recounts major military air disasters prior to the Second World War.

17 SEPTEMBER 1908 (c.17:20)

Location	*Near Arlington, Virginia, USA*
Operator	*Orville Wright*
Aircraft type	*Wright Type A*

In what could be described as the first fatal military aeroplane accident, this crash occurred at Fort Myer, just outside

The aftermath of the first fatal aeroplane crash, which occurred at Fort Myer, Virginia, on 17 September 1908. (Smithsonian Institution)

Washington, DC, during a demonstration flight for the US Army. The passenger, Lt Thomas E. Selfridge, suffered a fractured skull in the accident and died about 3 hours later, and pilot Orville Wright, who had made the first successful powered, heavier-than-air flight five years earlier, was seriously injured. The accident sequence began about 4 minutes after take-off, and at an estimated altitude of 150ft (50m) above the ground, when a blade of one of the aircraft's two propellers broke, imbalancing the corresponding blade and causing the latter to tear loose one of the wires bracing the rudder-outriggers to the wing. Distortion of the rudder resulted in a loss of control, and as the pilot was attempting to land, the biplane immediately fell to the ground from an approximate height of 75ft (20m).

9 SEPTEMBER 1913 (c.18:30)

Location	*North Sea*
Operator	*Kriegsmarine (Germany Navy)*
Aircraft type	*Zeppelin L.1*

The first aviation disaster to result in double-figure fatalities would also be the first deadly one in a series of accidents and combat-related losses involving these huge German dirigibles. Flying in a thunderstorm, accompanied by rain and windy conditions, the airship was carried by an air current to a height of about 5,000ft (1,500m), then apparently encountered a severe down-draught and crashed some 20 miles (30km) north of the German island of Heligoland, killing 14 of the 20 men aboard. The survivors were rescued by surface vessels. On impact with the surface of the water, the envelope broke in two, and the control car sank immediately, drowning its occupants. A possible contributing factor in the accident, which occurred around dusk, was that the Zeppelin may have been overloaded.

Little remains of the German Zeppelin L.2, which crashed in flames near Berlin, killing all 28 men aboard. (US Library of Congress)

17 OCTOBER 1913 (c.10:30)

Location   Near Johannisthal, Germany
Operator   Kriegsmarine (German Navy)
Aircraft type   Zeppelin L.2

Aviation experienced its first major disaster, in which the death toll doubled that of the previous worst one, with this fiery destruction of an airship just outside this suburb of Berlin. It was believed that highly-inflammable hydrogen gas being vented from valves on the underside of the hull was sucked into the forward engine and ignited. In seconds, the dirigible was enveloped in flames and exploded at an altitude of approximately 600ft (180m), falling into a field. All 28 men aboard were killed, including one who was removed from the burning hulk alive but died about eight hours later. The victims included both military personnel and representatives of the manufacturer. The accident occurred during a qualifying flight prior to the navy's formal acceptance of the airship.

5 MARCH 1915 (c.01:00)

Location   Near Tienen (Tirlemont), Brabant,
                   Belgium
Operator   Kriegsmarine (German Navy)
Aircraft type   Zeppelin L.8

Attacked the night before by two British and two French aircraft, the dirigible crashed into trees about 25 miles (40km) east-south-east of Brussels as it was attempting to land in darkness. Among the 41 men aboard, 21 were killed and 17 injured.

3 SEPTEMBER 1915 (c.15:20)

Location   Near Cuxhaven, Germany
Operator   Kriegsmarine (German Navy)
Aircraft type   Zeppelin L.10

Reportedly struck by lightning while valving off hydrogen gas in preparation for landing, the airship exploded during a thunderstorm and plummeted into the sea at the mouth of the River Elbe, in the vicinity of Neuwerk Island, killing all 19 men aboard.

28 JULY 1916 (time unknown)

Location	*Near Jambol, Bulgaria*
Operator	*Imperial German Army*
Aircraft type	*Schutte-Lanz S.L.10*

The crash of the dirigible, which occurred for unknown reasons in the vicinity of the Black Sea, claimed the lives of all 20 men aboard the aircraft.

24 SEPTEMBER 1916 (c.01:00)

Location	*Near Billericay, Essex, England*
Operator	*Kriegsmarine (German Navy)*
Aircraft type	*Zeppelin L.32*

Shot down in early-morning darkness by a British fighter, the airship fell in flames some 10 miles (15km) north-east of London, and all 22 men aboard were killed.

1 OCTOBER 1916 (c.23:45)

Location	*Near Potters Bar, Hertford, England*
Operator	*Kriegsmarine (German Navy)*
Aircraft type	*Zeppelin L.31*

All 19 men aboard were killed when the dirigible was shot down by a British aeroplane, falling in flames just outside the northern limits of London from an approximate height of 13,000ft (4,000m).

21 NOVEMBER 1916 (time unknown)

Location	*Near Mainz, Germany*
Operator	*German military forces*
Aircraft type	*'Super' Zeppelin*

The airship reportedly crashed in a wooded area during a storm about 15 miles (25km) south-west of Frankfurt, and all but one of the 28 men aboard were killed.

28 NOVEMBER 1916 (c.23:45)

Location	*Near West Hartlepool, Cleveland, England*
Operator	*Kriegsmarine (German Navy)*
Aircraft type	*Zeppelin L.34*

Hit by British anti-aircraft artillery fire and attacked by British aeroplanes during a night raid, the airship fell in flames into the North Sea about 10 miles (15km) offshore, killing all 20 men aboard.

4 MARCH 1917 (time unknown)

Location	*Near Gent, Vlaanderen, Belgium*
Operator	*German military forces*
Aircraft type	*Dirigible*

The entire crew of an estimated 20 men lost their lives when the airship caught fire in the air and crashed some 30 miles (50km) north-west of Brussels.

One of the L-series Zeppelin dirigibles that were used by Germany as weapons during the First World War.
(British National Archives)

30 MARCH 1917 (time unknown)

Location   Off Northern Germany
Operator   Kriegsmarine (German Navy)
Aircraft type   Schutte-Lanz S.L.9

The dirigible caught fire in flight after apparently being struck by lightning and plunged into the Baltic Sea, killing all 23 men aboard.

14 MAY 1917 (c.05:15)

Location   North Sea
Operator   Kriegsmarine (German Navy)
Aircraft type   Zeppelin L.22

A British Naval Curtiss H.12 flying boat, firing tracer bullets, attacked the airship around dawn after observing it flying in a north-easterly direction at about 3,000ft (1,000m). Catching fire, the Zeppelin fell vertically in a tail-down attitude some 20 miles (30km) north-north-west of the Dutch island of Texel, with two members of its crew who were not wearing parachutes seen jumping out before it struck the water. There were no survivors among the 21 men aboard.

14 JUNE 1917 (c.08:45)

Location   North Sea
Operator   Kriegsmarine (German Navy)
Aircraft type   Zeppelin L.43

As it was flying due north at an approximate height of 1,500ft (500m), the dirigible was attacked and shot down by a British fighter off the Dutch island of Vlieland. Hit by tracer bullets, the Zeppelin fell in flames, its wreckage continuing to burn on the surface of the water after crashing, and all 24 men aboard were killed.

21 AUGUST 1917 (c.07:00)

Location   North Sea
Operator   Kriegsmarine (German Navy)
Aircraft type   Zeppelin L.23

The dirigible was shot down by a British fighter off the western coast of Denmark, and all 18 men aboard were killed.

20 OCTOBER 1917 (c.07:45)

Location   Near Luneville, Lorraine, France
Operator   Kriegsmarine (German Navy)
Aircraft type   Zeppelin L.44

The airship was brought down by anti-aircraft artillery and crashed in flames about 15 miles (25km) south-east of Nancy, killing all 18 men aboard.

7 APRIL 1918 (c.21:30)

Location   Strait of Otranto
Operator   Kriegsmarine (German Navy)
Aircraft type   Zeppelin L.59

Flying in darkness and clear weather conditions, with a visibility of 25–30 miles (40–50km), the airship plunged into the sea off the south-eastern coast of Italy, possibly after a mid-air explosion of unknown causes. All 23 men aboard were killed.

The skeleton of a German Zeppelin, one of many of the huge airships shot down or that crashed during the First World War. (British National Archives)

10 MAY 1918 (c.10:00)

Location	*North Sea*
Operator	*Kriegsmarine (German Navy)*
Aircraft type	*Zeppelin L.62*

Having been attacked and perhaps damaged earlier in the day by a British F.2 fighter, the dirigible crashed off the German island of Heligoland after an apparent in-flight explosion of an undetermined cause. There were no survivors among the 20 men aboard the airship.

5 AUGUST 1918 (c.22:30)

Location	*North Sea*
Operator	*Kriegsmarine (German Navy)*
Aircraft type	*Zeppelin L.70*

All 22 men aboard the dirigible were killed when it was shot down in darkness by a Royal Flying Corps aircraft, falling in flames from a height of around 17,000ft (5,200m) some 40 miles (65km) offshore from King's Lynn, Norfolk, England.

11 AUGUST 1918 (c.10:00)

Location	*North Sea*
Operator	*Kriegsmarine (German Navy)*
Aircraft type	*Zeppelin L.53*

During an air/sea battle between German and British forces, the airship was shot down by a Royal Flying Corps Camel fighter and fell in flames off the Dutch island of Ameland, killing all 19 men aboard.

24 AUGUST 1921 (c.17:40)

Location	*Near Kingston upon Hull, Yorkshire, England*
Operator	*Royal Airship Works*
Aircraft type	*Royal Airship Works dirigible R.38*

The hydrogen-filled airship plummeted into the River Humber some 150 miles (250km) north of London after in-flight structural failure. All but five of its crew of 49 men, most of them British and American military personnel but also including four civilians, lost their lives in the disaster. Additionally, a 55-year-old woman on the ground reportedly died of shock and scores of others suffered injuries, as did two of the survivors. At least two of the men aboard apparently tried to escape by parachute, but unsuccessfully. Most of the victims' bodies were subsequently recovered. Measuring 698ft (212m) long, the dirigible was on a trial flight prior to its planned take-over by the US Navy (as the ZR-2), and had been proceeding in a south-westerly direction at an approximate height of 1,200ft (350m). After initiating a sharp right turn at a speed in excess of 60mph (100kmh), its envelope fractured, with fire erupting in its front section, and the R.38 was then shattered by two explosions, the force of which broke hundreds of windows on the ground. The

weather at the time was fair and apparently not a factor in the accident. The break-up would later be attributed to structural weakness, which was itself blamed on faulty design.

21 FEBRUARY 1922 (c.14:15)

Location	*Near Norfolk, Virginia, USA*
Operator	*US Army Air Service*
Aircraft type	*State Airship Factory dirigible* Roma

The semi-rigid airship crashed in flames in the vicinity of Langley Field, where it had been based, killing 34 of the 45 men aboard, most of whom were American military personnel but also including several civilians. All but three of the survivors were injured. Built in Italy and measuring 410ft (125m) in length, the dirigible had been on a test flight and was proceeding at a speed of around 60mph (100kmh) when it suddenly assumed a nose-down attitude at an approximate height of 600ft (180m) and plunged to earth. Its crew were unable to recover from the uncontrolled descent and the *Roma* ultimately struck high-tension lines. Contact with the broken leads ignited the hydrogen gas in its envelope, resulting in the fire.

According to the report of an army investigative board, the accident was most likely precipitated by the flattening of the upper surface of the metal nose cap on the bow of the airship, which caused the nose-down condition. Resistance from the stern stabilisers would have produced overstressing that probably buckled the keel structure, completely disabling the elevator controls. Italian authorities disagreed with these findings, declaring that after the elevator cable had broken, the natural position of the control surfaces would have automatically caused the rear section of the dirigible to pitch upward, leading to the descent. Following this disaster, hydrogen was discarded as the lifting agent in American airships. The US Army also stopped experimenting with dirigibles, which would remain within the sole domain of the navy.

23 DECEMBER 1923 (c.02:30)

Location	*Mediterranean Sea*
Operator	*Aeronavale (French Navy)*
Aircraft type	*Zeppelin* Dixmunde

Originally built by Germany as the L.72 and taken over by the French after the First World War, this airship had been on a flight from its base near Toulon, France, to Algiers, Algeria, when it crashed in early-morning darkness near Sciacca, Sicily, with 52 men aboard. One of the three bodies later found was that of the commander's; there were no survivors. In its last radio transmission, the hydrogen-filled dirigible was reported to have been nearly out of fuel and battling gale-force winds. Due to the charred condition of some of the recovered wreckage, an investigative commission concluded that it had been set afire by a lightning strike, then fell into the sea 5 miles (10km) offshore from an estimated height of 6,000ft (1,800m).

Onlookers gather at the scene where one section of the US Navy dirigible Shenandoah *fell after the in-flight break-up of the airship during a thunderstorm.* (UPI/Corbis-Bettmann)

3 SEPTEMBER 1925 (c.05:30)

Location	*Near Caldwell, Ohio, USA*
Operator	*US Navy*
Aircraft type	*Naval Aircraft Factory dirigible Shenandoah (ZR-1)*

The helium-filled airship fell to earth in pieces around dawn some 80 miles (130km) south-south-west of Columbus, and 14 of the 41 American servicemen aboard were killed. All but two of those who survived escaped with little or no injury. Measuring 682ft (207m) in length, the ZR-1 had been on a publicity tour of the American Mid-west, the flight originating at Lakehurst, New Jersey, and was headed in a south-westerly direction when it encountered an area of thunderstorm activity. Inadvertantly flying into a line squall, the dirigible rose to over 6,000ft (1,800m), then lost about half that height in a matter of only a few minutes, and subsequently suffered structural failure at an approximate altitude of 3,700ft (1,100m). Its control car broke away after the initial fracture, sending its occupants, among them the commander, plunging to their deaths. The aft part of the airship, containing more than half of the survivors, and two other sections of the envelope descended to earth more slowly.

The break-up was attributed to large aerodynamic forces against the dirigible that were produced by strong upward currents of air associated with the thunderstorm.

5 OCTOBER 1930 (c.02:00)

Location	*Near Beauvais, Picardie, France*
Operator	*(British) Air Ministry*
Aircraft type	*Royal Airship Works dirigible R.101 (G-FAAW)*

During a trip from England to India, the airship crashed in darkness and adverse meteorological conditions about 40 miles (65km) north-north-west of Paris. Killed in the disaster were all but six of the 54 men aboard, including the six who had been designated as passengers on the flight. The survivors, five of whom were among the dirigible's crew of 42, suffered various injuries. Slightly more than 777ft (236m) in length, the R.101 had in fact undergone only one test flight prior to the long voyage that ended in tragedy. Flying on this Sunday morning just under a low overcast and in a south-westerly wind of around 35 to 45 knots, the dirigible was proceeding on a south-south-easterly heading at an approximate altitude of 1,000ft (300m) above the ground when it began to lose height. Levelling off briefly, it then descended into the ground, striking a ridge in a nose-down angle of 15–25 degrees before rebounding back into the air, and finally came to rest on the sloping terrain. Although the impact was not considered violent, fire erupted when the

The majestic R.101 was a true marvel of aeronautical engineering in its day, but its crash ended the British dirigible programme. (Air Ministry)

highly-inflammable calcium flares that were being carried aboard came in contact with the rain-drenched ground, leading to an explosion and a larger blaze that consumed the airship.

Prior to the crash, some hydrogen gas had apparently been lost gradually, either through chafing or chattering of the valves, and considerably more was believed to have escaped from at least one of the forward gas bags, possibly due to the ripping of the forepart of the envelope while still airborne. This condition and an encounter with a down-draught probably led to the uncontrolled descent into the ground. Another significant factor was the intentional reduction of engine power following the initial descent, in order to reduce the speed of the airship, and which would have further contributed to the loss of height. This disaster led to the end of Britain's dirigible industry.

Completely burned out, the hulk of the R.101 rests in the French countryside following the tragedy that claimed 48 lives. (British National Archives)

4 APRIL 1933 (c.00:30)

Location	*Off Barnegat City, New Jersey, USA*
Operator	*US Navy*
Aircraft type	*Goodyear-Zeppelin dirigible* Akron *(ZRS-4)*

The helium-filled airship crashed in the Atlantic Ocean some 20 miles (30km) east-south-east of the Barnegat lighthouse and approximately 70 miles (110km) south of New York City, killing 73 servicemen aboard. Other than a member of the US Army – one of seven occupants not part of the regular crew – the victims were all naval personnel. The three survivors – two navy-enlisted men and an officer – were rescued by a ship. Most of the victims' bodies were lost at sea, but a considerable amount of debris was recovered, and a marine research team located the main wreckage on the ocean floor, in water about 100ft (30m) deep, 53 years after the disaster.

Flying in darkness through an area of thunderstorm activity, accompanied by heavy rain and high winds, the dirigible, which measured 785ft (240m) in length, apparently encountered a severe down-draught that could not be overcome by the crew's use of engine power, elevator controls or ballast release. Ultimately, it ploughed into the sea in a tail-down attitude and broke apart. Some 13 hours later, the US Navy blimp J-3, which had been returning from the *Akron* rescue operations and was battling high winds, itself crashed just offshore from Beach Haven, New Jersey, and two of its seven crewmen lost their lives.

An 'error of judgement' by its commander in flying into the storm despite the observance of lightning in its path was considered to be a contributory factor in the *Akron* disaster. That no altimeter correction had been made to compensate for the drop in atmospheric pressure, which placed the airship about 600ft (180m) below its indicated height of around 1,000ft (300m), may have been an additional factor. However, it could not be determined with certainty whether the uncontrolled descent could have been arrested even had the dirigible been at the correct altitude when it encountered the down-draught.

Individual life preservers and rafts were later added to navy dirigible operations and, perhaps as a result, in the loss of the *Akron*'s sister ship, the *Macon*, which crashed in the Pacific Ocean in 1935, all but two of the more than 80 men aboard survived. However, one additional casualty did result from the second accident, the American dirigible programme itself, which was disbanded.

Right: A portion of the Akron *is raised from the Atlantic Ocean after it crashed in a thunderstorm early on the morning of 4 April 1933.* (UPI/Corbis-Bettmann)

Below: The US Navy's airship Akron *is photographed over Florida a few months before its disastrous crash off the New Jersey coast.* (UPI/Corbis-Bettmann)

2 FEBRUARY 1938 (c.20:40)

Location	*Off Southern California, USA*
First aircraft	
Operator	*US Navy*
Aircraft type	*Consolidated PBY-2 (0462)*
Second aircraft	
Operator	*US Navy*
Aircraft type	*Consolidated PBY-2 (0463)*

In the first 'heavier-than-air' disaster in the history of American military aviation to claim more than ten lives, the two twin-engine amphibious patrol bombers collided in mid-air and plummeted into the Pacific Ocean south of San Clemente Island, some 70 miles (110km) west of San Diego. The accident claimed the lives of 11 servicemen, while three others who managed to parachute from one PBY before it crashed were rescued with injuries. The two aircraft involved in the accident were part of a formation flying in darkness that had entered an area of intense rain, with the visibility reportedly reduced to zero. One of the pilots killed later received a posthumus navy medal of honour for staying at the controls of his aircraft after the collision and allowing some of his crewmen to escape by parachute.

24 JULY 1938 (c.13:00)

Location	*Near Bogotá, Colombia*
Operator	*Ejército de Colombia (Colombian Army)*
Aircraft type	*Curtiss Hawk*

As a squadron of the single-engine fighters were performing

A giant cloud of smoke rises above the grandstand seconds after the Colombian biplane crash, the first 'heavier-than-air' aviation disaster to claim more than 50 lives. (New York Times Pictures)

aerobatics before a crowd of about 50,000 at the Campo de Marte exercise field, one of them crashed into a grandstand, then plummeted into an area where other spectators were standing, and burst into flames. Killed in the disaster were 53 persons, including the pilot (and sole occupant) of the biplane, while more than 100 others on the ground suffered injuries. Though not officially reported, the crash may have resulted from an encounter with a gust of wind or a loss of control by the pilot during a looping manoeuvre.

8 MAY 1939 (c.12:00)

Location	*Guayaquil, Ecuador*
Operator	*Fuerza Aérea Ecuatoriana (Ecuadorean Air Force)*
Aircraft type	*Curtiss C-14 Osprey*

The single-engine fighter was seen performing low-altitude aerobatics over the city before it crashed near a college. Among the 23 persons killed was the pilot (and sole occupant) of the aircraft; 60 others on the ground suffered injuries and numerous buildings and houses were destroyed or damaged. Following a loop, performed at an altitude of less than 500ft (150m) above the ground, the biplane apparently lost flying speed. It then clipped a tree before slamming into a street and erupting into flames.

2

1940–1949

Having relatively little significance during the First World War, the full power of military aviation was truly realised in the Second World War. The war not only saw fierce aerial combat, but also the deaths of millions of civilians due to bombings,

Large, four-engine bombers such as the famed, American-built Consolidated B-24 saw wide action during the Second World War. (General Dynamics)

both conventional and, in two instances, with the use of nuclear weapons. A number of aircraft achieved immortality during this period: the Spitfire, P-51 Mustang, B-17 Flying Fortress, and the C-47. The latter, the famed Douglas transport, which had been originally designed as an airliner during the mid-1930s, was listed by the Allied Supreme Commander and future American President, Dwight D. Eisenhower, as one of the most important military tools of the Second World War.

Air transport changed for ever the nature of ground warfare, making it possible to drop troops behind enemy lines. This technique paved the road to success in the Allied invasion of France in June 1944. Perhaps over-confident from their success at Normandy, the Allies stumbled three months later in Holland. Losses in men and aircraft in the war were heavy on both sides. In 1940, the Battle of Britain alone cost the Royal Air Force about 1,000 aeroplanes, mostly Spitfire and Hurricane fighters, together with 537 aviators. Total British air force losses were nearly 80,000 lives and some 22,000 aircraft. The loss figures were approximately the same for the US Army Air Forces, which represented around one-fifth of the nation's war dead. About half of these fatalities were among members of the Eighth and Ninth Air Forces, which bore the brunt of the heaviest action in the European Theatre. A few of the more noteworthy combat losses are included in this section, but the majority of entries result from accidental causes.

10 MAY 1940

Location	Western Europe
Operator	Luftwaffe (German Air Force)
Aircraft types	Various (total 304)

The heaviest losses experienced in a single-day airborne assault were suffered by German forces in their invasion of Belgium and The Netherlands. Aircraft losses included 157 Junkers Ju 52/3m trimotored transports, 430 in the entire operation. More than 600 Luftwaffe personnel were reported killed or missing, while losses among German airborne troops probably numbered several thousand in what was considered a highly successful campaign that would ultimately lead to the capture of most of Western Europe. Most of the losses were to ground fire or to Belgian, Dutch, French, Norwegian or British air forces.

20/21 MAY 1941

Location	Crete
Operator	Luftwaffe (German Air Force)
Aircraft types:	Various (c.600)

During the invasion of the Greek island, some 270 Junkers Ju 52/3m transports and DFS 320 gliders were lost by German forces, either to hostile action or in accidents. In the air operation alone, a total of 3,748 men were killed or reported missing, and more than 2,600 others wounded. Despite the heavy casualties, Germany conquered Crete and forced the retreat of British forces from the island.

10 AUGUST 1941 (c.20:35)

Location	Arran, Strathclyde, Scotland
Operator	Royal Air Force
Aircraft type	Consolidated Liberator I (AM261)

All 22 persons aboard were killed when the four-engine transport crashed and burned on a ridge near Goat Fell, a mountain located on the island. The victims included both British and American military personnel, although two members of the crew of five were civilians. Impact occurred only about 75ft (20m) below the summit of the terrain, at an approximate elevation of 2,700ft (820m), some 25 miles (40km) north-west of Ayr, from where it had taken off shortly before, on a transatlantic flight to Montreal, Canada. It was dark at the time, and the weather conditions were adverse, with rain and a solid, low overcast. An apparent navigational error had placed the aircraft on a heading of 295 degrees, which at the time of the crash was 12 degrees, or around 10 miles (15km), north of the prescribed track. It was not, however, possible to determine what factors had led to this error.

14 AUGUST 1941 (c.20:40)

Location	Near Ayr, Strathclyde, Scotland
Operator	Royal Air Force
Aircraft type	Consolidated Liberator I (AM260)

The four-engine transport crashed and burned while taking off from Heathfield Aerodrome, killing all 22 persons aboard. Most of the victims were American and British servicemen, including the crew of four. Bound for Canada, the aircraft suddenly swerved off Runway 06, knocking over haystacks, hitting a hut and a telegraph pole and finally slammed into an embankment. It was dark at the time, but the weather conditions were good, with a broken overcast at 2,500ft (750m), a visibility of around 20 miles (30km), and a slight breeze out of the west.

1 JULY 1942 (c.12:00)

Location	Near Premier, West Virginia, USA
Operator	US Army Air Forces
Aircraft type	Douglas C-49E (42-56093)

The twin-engine transport crashed and burned about 5 miles (10km) south-west of Welch, and all 21 American servicemen aboard, including the two-member flight crew, perished. Having taken off earlier from Battle Creek, Michigan, on a domestic flight to Florence, South Carolina, the aircraft was to have landed at Lunken Field, serving Cincinnati, Ohio, an en-route stop. Following three unsuccessful attempts, the C-49 began a fourth approach, at an excessive speed and with its flaps retracted, and as the pilot evidently tried to force the landing, it 'ballooned' about 20ft (6m) into the air, then dropped back on to the runway and bounced before power was applied. The aircraft then proceeded on towards its ultimate destination, which it never reached. Shortly before the crash, 42-56093 was observed flying in and out of a layer of low clouds in an area of thunderstorm activity, yawing with one power plant apparently surging. Plunging out of the overcast in a near-vertical dive, it then pulled up and levelled off at a height of approximately 800ft (250m) above the ground, at which time both wing tips and the outer sections of both ailerons broke off, followed by the starboard wing and engine and both stabilisers and their corresponding elevators. The C-49 then went into a spin and plummeted into a wooded ravine.

According to the investigative report, the pilot exercised 'very poor' flying technique and judgement in subjecting the aircraft to severe, abnormal shock loads in the baulked landing at Cincinnati, and then in continuing the flight without setting down to inspect for possible damage. Subsequently, he proceeded into questionable weather conditions, with turbulence, trying to fly visually and alternating to instrument procedures through an area where the ceiling was low. Prior to the accident, he apparently became lost and circled in the vicinity of Welch in an attempt to land or reorientate himself.

It was concluded that the transport had suffered damage at the wing root fittings and wing structure in both the initial hard landing and from the reversed loads experienced in the bounce. The surging power plant, which may have been related to carburettor icing, coupled with the turbulent air, which led to torsional vibration and created flutter, probably contributed to the failure of the wing that was ultimately overstressed during the pull-up manoeuvre. It was noted in the report that the atmospheric conditions were conducive to such icing, and that the carburettors installed on 42-56093 had shown potentially dangerous characteristics if allowed to ice. Had the engine been subjected to a long period of surging, with backfiring and alternate cutting in and out of full power, it could have shifted the counterweight, creating a misalignment of the crankshaft, resulting in rough running or vibration that could have led to the in-flight break-up, particularly if combined with turbulence or mishandling by the crew.

Heavy loading was an additional factor in the accident, and for that reason one of the recommendations made in the report called for the specification of loading charts and rules for individual aircraft, a procedure that would later become a regular practice in transport flying.

25 AUGUST 1942 (c.14:00)

Location	*Near Braemore, Caithness, Scotland*
Operator	*Royal Air Force*
Aircraft type	*Short Sunderland (W4026)*

Prince George, the Duke of Kent, was among 14 military personnel killed in the crash of the four-engine flying boat, which took place some 35 miles (55km) north-west of Inverness. Only the rear gunner, one of 11 crewmen assigned to the aircraft, survived. Having taken off earlier from the base at Invergordon, bound for Iceland, the aircraft was flying on the wrong track and at an insufficient height when it struck cloud-obscured Eagle's Rock, a hill rising to about 700ft (200m). There was no fire. One theory was that the accident resulted from an incorrect setting on the Sunderland's gyrosyn compass, then a relatively new piece of equipment, which placed the aircraft too far west. The crew then descended to a lower altitude in an attempt to make visual contact with the sea, over which they were thought to have been, resulting in the impact with the terrain.

A Short Sunderland flying boat of the type flown by the RAF that crashed in Scotland, killing the Duke of Kent and 13 others.
(Short Brothers)

1 OCTOBER 1942 (c.09:30)

Location	Near Caomo, Puerto Rico
Operator	US Army Air Forces
Aircraft type	Douglas C-39 (38-524)

The twin-engine transport crashed and burned in a mountainous region approximately 30 miles (50km) south-west of San Juan, which was its destination at the end of an intra-island flight from Losey Field. All 22 persons aboard lost their lives, including three civilians; the rest of the passengers and the crew of five were American military personnel.

Witnesses observed the aircraft making a wide right, descending turn from a north-easterly on to a south-easterly heading when over a small valley, then disappear into low overcast. Shortly thereafter, the C-39 slammed into a hill at high speed, about 200ft (60m) below the crest, and while flying on a heading of 150 degrees. Its throttles were found jammed in the closed position, although this may have occurred on impact. The cloud layer in the area was some 4,000ft (1,200m) thick and extended down to the tops of the hills.

Though uncertain as to the exact cause of the accident, an investigative committee concluded that it either resulted from pilot error alone or in conjunction with mechanical failure. With regard to the first theory, the pilot may have tried to fly beneath the overcast and mistook the blind valley for an open one, resulting in the controlled-flight-into-terrain crash. Regarding the second, a possible power plant failure may have prompted him to turn back towards his departure point, but he was unable to maintain height with the heavy load and instead tried to fly down the valley that lay east of his course, believing it to be open.

15 JANUARY 1943 (c.03:20)

Location	Near Paramaribo, Dutch Guyana (Suriname)
Operator	US Army Air Forces
Aircraft type	Douglas C-54 (41-32939)

All 35 men aboard perished when the four-engine aircraft, which was being operated for the Air Transport Command (ATC) branch by the American commercial airline Transcontinental and Western Air (TWA) and was bound for Africa from the US, crashed and burned some 25 miles (40 km) east-north-east of the capital city. Nearly half of the victims were American civilians, including the nine members of its crew, but the passengers were comprised mostly of US and British service personnel.

A witness had seen 41-32939 proceeding in the early-morning darkness in an easterly direction before he heard a series of loud noises and observed a flare of light. The transport had fallen in water approximately 2ft deep (60 cm) in a tropical forest region, apparently after disintegrating in flight. And due to the close proximity of the debris, it was concluded by an investigative committee that the aircraft must have been flying at a relatively low altitude at the time

of its break-up. But due to the condition of the wreckage, no determination could be made as to the cause of the structural failure. There was no evidence of sabotage.

18 JANUARY 1943 (c.23:00)

Location	South Atlantic Ocean
Operator	US Army Air Forces
Aircraft type	Consolidated C-87 (41-1708)

Operated by the Air Transport Command (ATC) and on a transatlantic service from Accra, Gold Coast (Ghana), to Natal, Brazil, the converted B-24 bomber crashed at sea, probably between Ascension Island and its destination. Subsequently, two life rafts identified as belonging to the C-87 were recovered off the eastern coast of Brazil, but no survivors or bodies were found from the four-engine aircraft. The 26 Allied service personnel aboard included six American crewmen as well as 12 members of the Royal Air Force. It was dark at the time of the crash and the weather along the route of 41-1708 consisted of broken clouds and scattered rain showers.

18 FEBRUARY 1943 (c.12:30)

Location	Seattle, Washington, USA
Operator	Boeing Aircraft Company
Aircraft type	Boeing XB-29 (41-3)

A trial flight of the second prototype of what was then the newest and largest American heavy bomber ended on this day in a major disaster in a heavily urban area. With the intention of testing its power plant performance and cooling, propeller governing and two-engine capability, the XB-29 took off from Boeing Field, Renton. Less than 10 minutes later, a member of the crew radioed that the aircraft was returning due to a fire in its No. 1 power plant, which had been brought under control using the engine fire-extinguishing system. A subsequent transmission reported it at a height of 2,400ft (730m) and descending, and that the same engine was ablaze and the corresponding propeller had been feathered. The radio operator also requested immediate landing clearance, and asked that emergency equipment stand by, but stated that the trouble was not serious; his voice did not indicate any undue stress. But the situation deteriorated rapidly.

In the final message from 41-3, the crewman advised the airport control tower, 'Have fire equipment ready. Am coming in with wing on fire.' Less than a minute later, and while on an approximately southerly heading, the four-engine aircraft struck a high-tension line and then slammed into a packing plant, bursting into flames on impact. Killed in the disaster were all ten civilian crewmen of the aircraft, three of whom jumped out at a low altitude before the crash, and 20 persons on the ground. About a dozen others suffered injuries.

The weather at the time, with a ceiling of around 8,000ft (2,500m) and a visibility of 5 miles (10km), was not considered a factor. The fire was thought to have originated from the leakage of fuel and/or oil into the engine nacelle,

The famed Boeing B-29 Superfortress heavy bomber, whose early testing was marred by the disastrous crash in Seattle, Washington, USA. (Boeing)

ignited by contact with the exhaust pipe or shroud, by the operation of electrical equipment, or by the failure of the accessory section of the power plant, or a particular accessory. Gasoline that leaked into the leading edge, primarily around the filler neck cover and drain, could also have been ignited through contact with the heated nacelle skin or by fire through the nacelle firewall openings. The source of the gasoline was believed to have been overflow from the fuel tank filler necks, through vent holes, and subsequent leakage around the filler cover plates and their fastenings into the leading edge. (The location of the filler neck assembly in the leading edge of the wing, an area of greatly reduced air pressure, and the fact that the filler cap cover and the cap itself did not seal tightly could have allowed gasoline to be sucked out in this manner.) Flames then apparently spread to the leading edge of the port wing prior to the extinguishing of the nacelle fire, without the knowledge of the crew. Through the effect of gravity and the flow of ventilating air, the fire must have progressed through the leading edge to the inboard nacelle, wheel well and into the bomb bay.

As the fire consumed a magnesium wing de-icer valve casting, the force of the air entering the leading edge caused an explosion that was observed by witnesses on the ground. This blast probably tore loose the No. 2 filler neck well and assembly, thereby releasing a large quantity of fuel, producing an inferno that must have led to the failure of both port engines. In the final seconds before the crash, the pilots probably abandoned any hope of reaching the airport, and the aircraft's undercarriage was extended, possibly to allow members of the crew to escape or to throw out important

records of the flight. As the cabin filled with smoke, visibility would have been reduced, preventing them from maintaining control of the bomber.

One of the recommended changes in the B-29 made in the investigative report on this crash was a relocation of the filler necks outside the leading edge and redesign of the caps to prevent the leakage of fuel. Considerable modifications were incorporated in the first production models of the aircraft, and thus the bomber that had such a tentative start would be given much of the credit for bringing an end to the war in the Pacific theatre.

27 MARCH 1943 (c.05:15)

Location	Near Brisbane, Queensland, Australia
Operator	Royal Australian Air Force
Aircraft type	Douglas C-47 Dakota (A30-16)

The twin-engine transport crashed and burned in a wooded area approximately 2 miles (3km) from Archerfield Airfield, from where it had taken off shortly before, the accident occurring in pre-dawn darkness and conditions of poor visibility. All 24 military personnel aboard lost their lives; other than two American officers, the victims were Australian, including the crew of four. Although the cause was not determined with certainty, the crash probably resulted from power plant failure.

7 JUNE 1943 (c.04:00)

Location	*Near Red Springs, North Carolina, USA*
Operator	*US Army Air Forces*
Aircraft type	*Douglas C-47A (42-23512)*

All 20 American servicemen aboard were killed, including the crew of four, when the twin-engine transport crashed and burned some 20 miles (30km) south-west of Fayetteville. The passengers were glider pilots, and the aircraft had been on an intrastate flight from Pope Field to Maxton Army Air Base when the accident occurred, in pre-dawn darkness. Proceeding on a southerly heading at a height of only about 200ft (60m), the C-47 had turned northwards and then back towards the base, located 5 miles (10km) to the south-west, before it slammed to earth moments later in an area of thunderstorm activity, which was accompanied by heavy rain and turbulence.

It was the opinion of the investigative board that the accident resulted from the combination of the following piloting errors: failure of the pilot to obtain a weather briefing; his attempt to maintain visual flight considering the poor visibility, and his failure to maintain a safe altitude and to return to visual weather conditions after encountering the thunderstorm activity. One of the recommendations made in the wake of the crash was to restrict pilots with limited experience from flying in darkness and such adverse meteorological conditions.

14 JUNE 1943 (c.06:00)

Location	*Near Bakers Creek, Queensland, Australia*
Operator	*US Army Air Forces*
Aircraft type	*Boeing B-17C (40-2072)*

The worst aviation disaster in the history of this island continent involved a makeshift transport aircraft carrying personnel back to duty in New Guinea after a period of rest and recreation in Australia. All but one of the 41 American servicemen aboard the four-engine bomber lost their lives in the accident, including six crew members; the surviving passenger was injured. Shortly after it had taken off from the airfield, located about 5 miles (10km) south-south-west of Mackay, the B-17 crashed and burned before dawn and in foggy weather conditions. No determination could be made as to the cause of the accident, which reportedly occurred after a low-altitude turn.

1 AUGUST 1943 (c.15:00)

Location	*Ploesti, Romania*
Operator	*US Army Air Forces*
Aircraft type	*Consolidated B-24*

During an attack on Romanian oil fields, one of the bombers that had been hit by flak crashed into a women's prison, killing its ten crewmen and 63 persons on the ground. Losses were heavy in this mission, designed to stall the German military machine, with 310 American airmen being killed (some on damaged aircraft that returned) and another 128 wounded. About 30 per cent of the B-24s dispatched on the mission – 54 of the 177 aircraft – were lost in combat or accidents, 41 being shot down by fighters or ground batteries over or on their way to the target.

1 AUGUST 1943 (c.16:00)

Location	*St Louis, Missouri, USA*
Operator	*US Army Air Forces*
Aircraft type	*Waco CG-4A (42-78839)*

This Sunday afternoon demonstration to city officials of a locally-produced contribution to the American war effort ended in one of the worst non-combat glider disasters in the history of US military aviation. The glider involved was produced by the St Louis-based Robertson Aircraft Company, under contract to the principal manufacturer, Waco. Towed aloft by a C-47 transport, the CG-4A was to have landed on its own at Lambert Field. The two aircraft arrived over the airport from the south-east at an approximate height of 2,000ft (600m), but just after being released, the glider suffered catastrophic structural failure, its starboard wing folding up and separating from the fuselage completely. It plummeted to the ground, crashing in a grassy area adjacent to the runway. Ten persons aboard lost their lives, including St Louis Mayor William Dee Becker and three US servicemen, two of whom comprised the crew of 42-78839. There were no survivors. The local weather at the time, which was not considered a factor in the accident, consisted of scattered clouds at 2,500ft (750m), a visibility of 3 miles (5km) and light, variable winds.

Examination of the wreckage indicated that the strut of the wing that failed was fractured at the point where it joined the fuselage. The military board investigating the crash expressed the opinion that the fitting that was welded on the lower end of the strut had too thin a wall thickness due either to erroneous specifications or faulty workmanship. Specifically, the machined dimensional limits of the fitting did not conform to the manufacturer's drawing with regard to the thickness of the wall between the inside diameter of the countersink in the fitting barrel and the outside diameter flat in the fitting shank taper. The wall thickness at the failed section was $1/16$in (2mm), or only about 20 per cent of that specified, when considering a tolerance of $1/32$in (1mm). It was obvious that the countersink had been drilled too deep. The failed section further showed evidence of deep tool marks, with both chattering, a surface flaw caused by vibration of the cutting tool, and gouging. Visual inspection would have easily detected these machining errors, while the thickness defect could have been found through the use of a micrometer or a caliper.

According to the investigative report, these flaws indicated that there had been no inspection of the part by either the prime or sub-contractor, or by army personnel. When the fitting broke, the wing was allowed to hinge upwards as far as the wing root attachment fitting would permit, after which

Its right wing completely sheared off, the US Army Waco CG-4A glider is photographed during its plunge to earth. (St Louis Mercantile Library)

the unsupported spar snapped at a point approximately 1ft (30cm) from the fuselage.

It was concluded that the manufacturer Robertson did not have a sufficient force of experienced personnel and did not exercise proper control over work produced by its subcontractors, and that it could guarantee neither quality material nor workmanship or the quality of highly-stressed parts produced at some of its subcontractors' plants. Also, the military inspector in charge was found to have insufficient help to properly exercise his duties with regard to the activities of the contractors. Subsequent to the accident, all gliders produced by Robertson were grounded until a complete inspection of highly-stressed parts used in them could be accomplished. A new inspection procedure was later introduced by the firm, and four civilian inspectors and the aforementioned military official were relieved of their duties.

7 AUGUST 1943 (c.05:20)

Location	*Near Townsville, Queensland, Australia*
Operator	*US Army Air Forces*
Aircraft type	*Douglas C-47 (41-7733)*

The twin-engine transport plunged into Cleveland Bay shortly after its departure on an internal Australian flight to Brisbane. All 27 American military personnel aboard the aircraft (23 passengers and a crew of four) perished. After what was described by witnesses as a normal take-off, both power plants of 41-7733 reportedly 'cut out' before the aircraft plummeted into the water. The crash occurred before dawn, and the local weather at the time was overcast, with a visibility of 10 miles (15km) in patchy ground fog. Only human remains and small fragments of wreckage were recovered, and the cause of the crash was unknown.

10 SEPTEMBER 1943 (c.16:00)

Location	*Gulf of Mexico*
First aircraft	
Operator	*US Army Air Forces*
Aircraft type	*Boeing B-17F (42-4621)*
Second aircraft	
Operator	*US Army Air Forces*
Aircraft type	*Boeing B-17F (42-6031)*

The two four-engine heavy bombers collided in mid-air, then both crashed at sea about 50 miles (80km) south-east of Galveston, Texas, USA, killing 22 crewmen (11 aboard each

The most famous bomber of the Second World War, the Boeing B-17 Flying Fortress, two of which, identical to the one shown here, were involved in a collision over the Gulf of Mexico. (Boeing)

one). There were no survivors. The two B-17s involved were among six bombers flying in a tight formation when the leading edge of the vertical stabiliser of 4621 contacted the trailing edge of the wing of 6031, after which the two aircraft slammed together with considerable force, the collision occurring in good weather conditions.

20 SEPTEMBER 1943 (c.08:50)

Location	*Near Maxton, North Carolina, USA*
Operator	*US Army Air Forces*
Aircraft type	*Douglas C-53D (42-68729)*

All 25 American service personnel aboard were killed, including four crewmen, when the twin-engine transport crashed in a wooded area about 35 miles (55km) south-west of Fayetteville after nearly colliding with another C-53 that was towing a glider. Immediately after it had taken off from Maxton Army Air Base, 42-68729 confronted the other two aircraft nearly head-on, at an approximate height of 300ft (100m), prompting an evasive manoeuvre. However, the crew were unable to recover from the steep bank and resulting stall, and the transport slammed to earth and burst into flames.

22 SEPTEMBER 1943 (c.06:00)

Location	*Near Calcutta, India*
Operator	*US Army Air Forces*
Aircraft type	*Douglas C-53 (42-6471)*

The twin-engine transport crashed and burned immediately after its departure from Dum Dum Airport, on a scheduled passenger/cargo service. Including a crew of five, all 20 American service personnel aboard the aircraft were killed. Taking off in a northernly direction, 42-6471 had become airborne following what appeared to be a longer-than-normal ground run. Its landing lights were turned off just before the C-53 initially clipped trees, then slammed to earth slightly less than a mile (1.5km) from the end of the runway, its undercarriage in the retracted position at the moment of impact. It was still dark at the time of the accident, and the local meteorological conditions consisted of a high overcast, with scattered to broken clouds at 2,000ft (600m), a visibility of 7 miles (11km) and a light wind.

Although the cause of the crash could not be determined, it was the opinion of an investigative board that the take-off technique employed by the pilot had sacrificed height for air speed, which placed the aircraft below a safe altitude. It was believed that as soon as he saw that he was clearing the trees, the pilot turned off the landing lights. In doing so, or for some other reason, he must have become distracted, during which time the C-53 lost height. Considered as contributing factors were the night-time conditions and the lack of adequate lighting at the airport, with the only ground light being provided by flare-pots. No evidence was found of power plant or other technical malfunction, and although the pilot was familiar with the airport, the accident report inferred that this could have created a sense of complacency on his part, leading to the take-off technique that also contributed to the crash.

19 OCTOBER 1943 (time unknown)

Location	*Near Joliette, Quebec, Canada*
Operator	*Royal Canadian Air Force*
Aircraft type	*Consolidated B-24*

The four-engine bomber, which was on a flight to Montreal from a port on Canada's Atlantic coast, crashed some 60 miles (100km) north of its destination, and all 24 Canadian service personnel aboard the aircraft (18 passengers and a crew of six) were killed. Flying in darkness and weather conditions consisting of a low overcast, the B-24 was last heard from after 22:00 local time; its wreckage and the remains of the victims were located nearly three years later.

22 OCTOBER 1943 (c.20:20)

Location	*Near Columbus, Georgia, USA*
Operator	*US Army Air Forces*
Aircraft type	*Douglas C-47 (42-5677)*

All 20 American servicemen aboard lost their lives, including a crew of five, when the twin-engine transport crashed and burned at Fort Benning, during a night parachute exercise. Shortly after 11 soldiers had successfully parachuted from it, the aircraft apparently stalled, then went into a descending turn to the left at the prescribed drop altitude of 800ft (250m) and plummeted to earth.

8 NOVEMBER 1943 (time unknown)

Location	*Poona, Maharashtra, India*
Operator	*Indian Air Force*
Aircraft type	*Unknown*

The aeroplane crashed into the village located some 70 miles (110km) south-east of Bombay, striking huts and bursting into flames. Killed in the accident were 38 persons, including the pilot (and sole occupant) of the aircraft.

7 DECEMBER 1943 (c.11:20)

Location	*Near Pauwela, Territory of Hawaii, USA*
First aircraft	
Operator	*US Navy*
Aircraft type	*Douglas SBD-5 Dauntless (36045)*
Second aircraft	
Operator	*US Navy*
Aircraft type	*Douglas SBD-5 Dauntless (36099)*

This freak accident occurred as the two single-engine dive bombers were providing simulated air support in an exercise involving US Marine Corps ground forces, which was being conducted in the vicinity of Opana Point, on the island of Maui. The two were part of a flight of aircraft in a right echelon formation. With 36045 following, 36099 began its

The wide use of the Douglas C-47 Dakota transport accounts for its involvement in so many accidents and combat losses during the Second World War. (McDonnell Douglas)

descent with its dive flaps extended, making a slight turn to the right to effect alignment with the target. It was at this time that the second SBD, whose pilot had not opened its dive flaps, struck the other aircraft in the area of its baggage compartment and at an angle of approximately 45 degrees. Both dive bombers crashed, 36045 slamming into a hillside and erupting into flames, and a bomb that had been knocked off that aircraft in the collision detonated in the midst of a company of marines.

The accident claimed the lives of 20 marines and two navy crewmen, one from each SBD, with one of the latter being killed after parachuting from his aircraft. Both pilots also bailed out and escaped with only minor injuries. Some two dozen marine personnel were seriously injured in the explosion. The collision was attributed to a combination of poor judgement and faulty flying technique on the part of the navy pilots.

19 DECEMBER 1943 (c.08:50)

Location	*Near Rockhampton, Queensland, Australia*
Operator	*US Army Air Forces*
Aircraft type	*Douglas C-47A (43-30742)*

The twin-engine transport crashed and burst into flames during an internal Australian flight from Townsville to Brisbane, with an en route stop planned at Rockhampton. All 31 persons aboard lost their lives in the accident. Except for a war correspondent, the victims were American military personnel, including the crew of four.

It was determined that the left power plant of 43-30742 had caught fire in the air, after which the pilot must have lost control. The aircraft then entered a spin, and at an approximate height of 100ft (30m) above the ground, a fuel tank exploded, resulting in the separation of the port wing, followed by the vertical stabiliser, rudder and left elevator.

An examination of the wreckage indicated that the fire had been precipitated by an oil leak. The local weather at the time, consisting of a low overcast accompanied by light drizzle, was not considered to have been a contributing factor.

29 DECEMBER 1943 (c.15:00)

Location	*Near Lakeside, Utah, USA*
First aircraft	
Operator	*US Army Air Forces*
Aircraft type	*Consolidated B-24E (42-7183)*
Second aircraft	
Operator	*US Army Air Forces*
Aircraft type	*Consolidated B-24E (42-7408)*

A cross-country formation flight by five heavy bombers ended in tragedy when two of them collided in mid-air, then crashed and burned near the western shore of the Great Salt Lake, 70 miles (110km) north-west of Salt Lake City, killing 25 American servicemen. There were no survivors from either aircraft among the 12 aboard 7183 and 13 aboard 7408.

The group had taken off earlier from Wendover Field, in Utah, bound for Pocatello Army Air Base, in neighbouring Idaho, and proceeded normally until a point where 7183, which was in the No. 3 position, found itself too high and too far back from the formation. In trying to get back in place, it apparently got in the prop wash of the lead aircraft, and was blown downward on top of 7408, which had been in the No. 4 position. In the ensuing collision, which occurred above the cloud layer at an approximate height of 11,000ft (3,400m), the latter's port wing outside the No. 1 power plant was torn off, resulting in a loss of control, while the former was also badly damaged and went into a flat spin. Icing conditions existed in the area at the time within the clouds, the bases of which were down to about 700ft (200m). According to the official report, the accident was entirely attributable to the faulty flying technique displayed by the pilot of 7183.

6 MARCH 1944 (c.13:00)

Location	Near Berlin, Germany
First aircraft	
Operator	US Army Air Forces
Aircraft type	Boeing B-17 (42-31595)
Second aircraft	
Operator	US Army Air Forces
Aircraft type	Boeing B-17G (42-31627)
Third aircraft	
Operator	Luftwaffe (German Air Force)
Aircraft type	Messerschmitt Me410A

In what may have been an accident or an intentional act of ramming, the twin-engine fighter collided with one of the four-engine bombers, 31595, which itself then struck the second B-17, and all three aircraft crashed. Two German and 19 American airmen were killed; the sole survivor of the triple collision was the tail gunner of 31627. This incident occurred during a bombing of Berlin, which was one of the most costly missions of the Second World War, with 69 American bombers being destroyed in combat or from accidents, and more than 200 airmen losing their lives.

30/31 MARCH 1944

Location	Germany
Operator	Royal Air Force
Aircraft type	Various (108)

The single costliest bombing mission in the history of the RAF was this night raid on Nuremberg, which claimed mostly Lancaster and Halifax bombers, and a Mosquito fighter on an intruder flight, the aircraft being lost due to both hostile action and accidents. A total of 545 airmen were killed in this operation.

6 JUNE 1944 (c.01:15)

Location	Near Barneville, Normandy, France
Operator	US Army Air Forces
Aircraft type	Douglas C-47A (42-93095)

Loaded with paratroopers and participating in D-Day, the Allied invasion of Normandy, the twin-engine transport was believed shot down over the Cherbourg Peninsula, 25 miles (40km) north-west of Carentan, while flying in darkness and meteorological conditions consisting of a broken overcast, with a visibility of 5 miles (10km). All 22 American servicemen aboard were killed, including a crew of five.

6 JUNE 1944 (c.01:30)

Location	Near Carentan, Normandy, France
Operator	US Army Air Forces
Aircraft type	Douglas C-47A (42-101025)

During its participation in the Normandy invasion, the twin-engine transport was apparently brought down by anti-aircraft fire before it could drop its load of paratroopers. There were no survivors among the 22 American servicemen aboard the C-47, including a crew of four. Two of the paratroopers, who apparently jumped from the aircraft into the pre-dawn darkness before the crash, were listed as 'missing in action'.

6 JUNE 1944 (c.02:00)

Location	Near Flamanville, Normandy, France
Operator	US Army Air Forces
Aircraft type	Douglas C-47A (42-100905)

The twin-engine transport, which was involved in the Normandy invasion, crashed about 10 miles (15km) south-west of Cherbourg, under unknown circumstances and about 5 minutes before the planned drop of its load of paratroopers. All 22 American servicemen aboard lost their lives, including a crew of four. It was dark at the time the aircraft went down, and the local weather consisted of scattered clouds, with a visibility of between 5 and 10 miles (10 and 15km).

26 JULY 1944 (time unknown)

Location	North Atlantic Ocean
Operator	US Army Air Forces
Aircraft type	Douglas C-54A (42-107470)

Operated by the Air Transport Command (ATC) and carrying 26 persons, the four-engine aircraft vanished while en route from Iceland to Stephenville, Newfoundland, one segment of a scheduled transatlantic flight originating at Prestwick, Scotland, with an ultimate destination of Long Island, New York. A thorough search failed to find any trace of the C-54 or its occupants, and it was concluded that whatever happened to it must have been sudden and without warning. The aircraft was last heard from shortly after 03:00 Iceland time, some 3 hours after its departure, when probably off south-eastern Greenland. The weather along the route taken was reported to have consisted of a broken overcast, with cloud tops of 6,000–7,000ft (1,800–2,000m). The passengers of the aircraft were all American service personnel and except for one, its six crew members were civilian employees of the US airline Transcontinental and Western Air (TWA), working under contract to the army.

27 JULY 1944 (c.16:00)

Location	*Near West Freugh, Argyllshire, Scotland*
Operator	*US Army Air Forces*
Aircraft type	*Douglas C-47A (42-93038)*

All 22 military personnel aboard lost their lives in the crash of the twin-engine transport in the vicinity of Port Logan, on the Mull of Galloway peninsula. Other than one member of the Royal Air Force, the victims were Americans, including a nurse and the five members of the flight crew. Its passengers comprised 13 men wounded in the Normandy invasion the previous month, who were being transported to the US. The C-47 had been en route to Prestwick from Filton Aerodrome, near Bristol, and was proceeding under a low overcast at a minimal altitude so that a following aircraft could keep it in sight. Approaching land, 42-93038 initiated a climb, but did not gain sufficient height to clear a fog-shrouded cliff rising to more than 400ft (120m), which it struck only about 20ft (6m) from its crest, bursting into flames on impact. The second aircraft barely avoided the terrain itself.

3 AUGUST 1944 (c.20:30)

Location	*Near Naper, Nebraska, USA*
Operator	*US Army Air Forces*
Aircraft type	*Douglas C-47A (42-23652)*

The twin-engine transport, which was carrying as passengers Army Air Force pilots on an interstate flight from the air base located near Bruning, Nebraska, to one near Pierre, South Dakota, crashed and burned in a ravine some 200 miles (320km) north-west of Omaha. All 28 American servicemen aboard were killed, including a crew of four. The accident occurred in darkness after the C-47 had flown into an area of thunderstorm activity that contained lightning and, apparently, extreme turbulence. One witness was of the opinion that the storm cloud was of a tornadic variety, although this could not be confirmed.

The condition of the wreckage indicated that 42-23652 broke apart in the turbulent conditions, and possibly after being struck by lightning. Specifically, the evidence pointed to the separation of its right wing tip, after which there was a more general disintegration of the C-47, possibly while the pilot was conducting an emergency descent and either entered an area of greater turbulence or over-stressed the aircraft. It then slammed to earth while apparently in an inverted attitude.

The accident was primarily attributable to error by the pilot, who exercised bad judgement in continuing into the storm. Responsibility was also assigned to an inadequate meteorological forecast, which did not give the pilot an accurate representation of the existing conditions. Considered as contributing factors were the 'lower' standards of weather forecasters during the Second World War; the loading of the transport beyond the weight limit authorised by the manufacturer; and the possible initial effects of the lightning. With regard to the first factor, a policy by which

meteorological forecasts shall 'err on the side of safety' was recommended in the investigative report.

23 AUGUST 1944 (c.10:45)

Location	*Freckleton, Lancashire, England*
Operator	*US Army Air Forces*
Aircraft type	*Consolidated B-24H (42-50291)*

In the worst non-combat aviation disaster of the Second World War, the four-engine bomber crashed while attempting to land at Warton Air Depot, around 7 miles (11km) west of Preston, striking the village school and an adjacent café, a pub and three houses, and bursting into flames. Among the 61 persons killed were the three crewmen (and only occupants) of the aircraft, which had been on a test flight, and 38 children on the ground; about 30 others suffered injuries.

The accident occurred during a thunderstorm, which was accompanied by heavy rain, a ceiling of 400ft (120m) and a horizontal visibility of less than 1,000ft (300m), with a northerly wind of approximately 25 knots and even stronger gusts. During its landing approach, the B-24 must have been forced down by the violent winds and down-draughts associated with the storm, and was unable to gain sufficient speed and altitude to prevent the crash.

28 AUGUST 1944 (c.01:00)

Location	*Prestwick, Strathclyde, Scotland*
Operator	*US Army Air Forces*
Aircraft type	*Douglas C-54A (42-72171)*

Having completed a transatlantic crossing, the four-engine transport, which was operated by American Airlines under contract to the USAAF and flown by a civilian crew, crashed

Rescue workers sift through the remains of the village school and other structures struck by an American B-24 bomber at Freckleton, England. (US National Archives)

and burned in a residential area while attempting to land at Prestwick airport. All 20 persons aboard (14 passengers and a crew of six) and five others on the ground, the latter including a 6-year-old girl who had been sleeping in her home at the time of the accident, were killed.

The crash occurred in darkness and during a low overcast, with the clouds scattered at 700ft (200m), broken at about 1,000ft (300m) and solid at 1,800ft (550m), and a visibility of approximately 1 mile (1.5km) in rain. The wind was out of the east at around 10 knots. The cause of the accident could not be determined, but may have been related to an incorrect altimeter reading and/or pilot error, with the poor weather and wartime blackout regulations considered as contributing factors.

18 OCTOBER 1944 (c.15:40)

Location	*Near Birkenhead, Merseyside, England*
Operator	*US Army Air Forces*
Aircraft type	*Consolidated B-24H (42-50347)*

All 24 American servicemen aboard perished, including a crew of five, when the four-engine bomber crashed in the vicinity of Liverpool during a transatlantic flight. Its passengers were all airmen returning to their base in New York. Proceeding through an area of squally weather conditions, with heavy rain, a broken overcast of 1,000ft (300m), a visibility of 8 miles (13km) and a westerly wind of around 30 knots, the aircraft suddenly disintegrated at an estimated height of 6,000ft (1,800m) after either an explosion or a catastrophic structural failure, the cause of which could not be determined. Investigation revealed no evidence of pre-impact fire or mechanical failure.

19 NOVEMBER 1944 (c.15:10)

Location	*Near Lewes, East Sussex, England*
Operator	*US Army Air Forces*
Aircraft type	*Douglas C-47A (43-15046)*

The crash of the twin-engine transport, which occurred approximately 3 miles (5km) north-east of Brighton, claimed the lives of 25 servicemen aboard the aircraft, including its entire crew of five. All the occupants were American except for two Frenchmen, one of whom was among the five injured survivors. A witness on the ground had observed 43-15046 proceeding under a low overcast, then disappear into the clouds before the aircraft struck the east slope of a hill at an approximate elevation of 600ft (180m), exploding on impact. Some 10 miles (15km) south-east of the scene of the accident, the weather was characterised by a ceiling of only 300–400ft (100–120m), a visibility of about half a mile (0.8km), lower in areas of heavy, intermittent rain, and a south-south-westerly wind of 13 knots. After clearing the top of the hill, the C-47 had initiated a descent in an apparent attempt by the pilot to regain visual contact with the ground. Turbulence and a down-draught over the down-wind side of the terrain were considered as probable contributing factors in the crash.

The investigative report issued on the accident recommended greater emphasis on instrument flight training and the need for pilots to remain at a safe altitude when operating in instrument meteorological conditions, and also improvements in the dissemination of weather information.

2 FEBRUARY 1945 (c.10:15)

Location	*Near Montieri, Toscana, Italy*
Operator	*US Army Air Forces*
Aircraft type	*Douglas C-47 (41-18603)*

Three army nurses were among the 23 American service personnel aboard who were killed when the twin-engine transport, which was on an Italian internal flight from Florence to Rome, crashed and burned about 60 miles (100km) north of its destination. Two passengers and the pilot, one of four crewmen assigned to 41-18603, survived with injuries. Proceeding on a south-westerly heading through a river valley, with hills on either side that were obscured by strato-cumulus clouds and mist, the C-47 encountered a fog bank, necessitating a transition by its crew from visual to instrument flight procedures. The pilot immediately initiated a climb to avoid rising terrain, but not at a sufficient rate to prevent the aircraft from hitting trees, whereupon it slammed to earth. At the time, the ceiling in the area was 2,000–3,000ft (600–1,000m), and the visibility reduced by the fog to less than 1 mile (1.5km).

6 FEBRUARY 1945 (c.10:05)

Location	*Near Hunters Burgh, Sussex, England*
Operator	*Royal Air Force*
Aircraft type	*Douglas C-47 Dakota (KG630)*

The twin-engine transport crashed and burned, killing all 23 British Commonwealth servicemen aboard (19 passengers and a crew of four). Flying too low in clouds, the aircraft struck a hill at an above-sea level elevation of around 500ft (150m), the impact shearing off its starboard wing, after which the C-47 plummeted into a wooded area.

13 FEBRUARY 1945 (c.06:30)

Location	*Near Oakland, California, USA*
Operator	*US Navy*
Aircraft type	*Douglas R4D-6 (50765)*

All 24 American servicemen aboard were killed, including a crew of three, when the twin-engine transport crashed in San Francisco Bay shortly after its departure from Oakland airport. The main wreckage and the bodies of 17 victims were recovered from the water. Among the latter, the cause of death was divided by approximately half between traumatic injury and drowning. Ultimately bound for the US East Coast, the aircraft had taken off from Runway 27 and proceeded towards the west before making a right turn, whereupon its starboard wing struck the surface of the bay. Its undercarriage

still extended, the R4D then slammed into the water. It was dark at the time, being before dawn, and the local weather consisted of a light drizzle, with a ceiling of 700ft (200m) and unlimited visibility under the clouds. The wind was out of the south-east at 5 knots.

The aircraft's gyro horizon was found to be caged, or locked in a fixed position, and this could have been a factor in the crash. Because of this, it was recommended in the investigative report that navy transports be equipped with non-cageable gyro horizon units. Among the other recommendations was for a greater emphasis on the instrument training of pilots, specifically, in the use of rate-of-climb and turn-and-bank indicators, magnetic compass and clock.

27 MARCH 1945 (time unknown)

Location	*Coral Sea*
Operator	*US Army Air Forces*
Aircraft type	*Douglas C-47A (43-16011)*

The twin-engine transport vanished with 24 American military personnel aboard (20 passengers and a crew of four) during a flight to Finschaffen, Netherlands New Guinea, from Townsville, Queensland, Australia. At the time of its loss, 43-16011 had been returning the personnel on leave from Sydney, New South Wales. It was last heard from around 20:20 local time, when flying in darkness, and the circumstances of its disappearance remain a mystery.

The fuselage section of the wrecked US Navy R4D transport is raised from San Francisco Bay following the crash that took 24 lives. (UPI/Corbis-Bettmann)

20 APRIL 1945 (c.06:40)

Location	*Near Sweetwater, Texas, USA*
Operator	*US Army Air Forces*
Aircraft type	*Douglas C-47 (41-18451)*

The twin-engine transport crashed, exploded and burned in a pasture some 50 miles (80km) west of Abilene, and all 25 American servicemen aboard were killed, including a crew of five. Having taken off earlier from Midland Army Air Field, also in Texas, on a domestic interstate flight to Nashville, Tennessee, 41-18451 had been assigned to a cruising altitude of 5,000ft (1,500m), and was believed to have been proceeding in a north-north-easterly direction before it disintegrated in an area of thunderstorm activity. The accident occurred around dawn.

The break-up sequence began with the failure of the aircraft's elevators, which was followed by the separation of the vertical stabiliser and its right wing. The structural failure was probably related to the extreme turbulence encountered by the transport, and action taken after the crash included the inspection of some aircraft in the C-47 fleet and installation on the type of a reinforced wing tip.

23 APRIL 1945 (c.10:30)

Location	Near Ramsey, Isle of Man
Operator	US Army Air Forces
Aircraft type	Boeing B-17G (43-38856)

All 31 American servicemen aboard (26 passengers and a crew of five) were killed when the four-engine bomber struck a mountain on the Isle of Man during a troop transport flight. The aircraft was to have landed at the Nutts Corner airfield, near Belfast, Northern Ireland, and crashed some 300ft (100m) from the top of the mountain while descending through a haze. About half an hour before the accident, the weather over the southern part of the island was reported as mostly clear, with a few cumulus clouds at 1,800ft (550m) and a visibility of around 10 miles (15km). The crew was at the time operating under a contact (visual) clearance. Although the cause was unknown, the crash was believed to have been related to pilot error.

5 MAY 1945 (22:26)

Location	Territory of New Guinea
Operator	US Army Air Forces
Aircraft type	Douglas C-54E (44-9043)

The four-engine transport crashed and burst into flames on Manus, one of the Admiralty Islands in the Bismarck Archipelago region, killing all 21 American servicemen aboard (15 passengers and a crew of six). Having taken off shortly before from the Sorido airstrip, on an intra-island flight, the C-54 slammed into a bluff at an approximate elevation of 500ft (150m). The accident occurred on a dark, moonless

An RAF Avro Lancaster bomber, similar to the aircraft involved in the prisoners-of-war flight tragedy on 9 May 1945. (Philip Jarrett)

night, but the local weather conditions were otherwise good, with a ceiling of around 2,000ft (600m) and unrestricted visibility under the clouds. A slight breeze was blowing out of the north-west. Due to the complete destruction of the aircraft, it was not possible to determine the cause of the crash. However, its direction at the moment of impact indicated that the pilot did not make a turn away from the rising terrain as soon as he reached the minimum safe altitude for such a manoeuvre.

Subsequently, the flight operations officer for the airfield issued a directory that aircraft departing on the same north-westerly heading as had 44-9043 initiate a left turn upon reaching a sufficient height and not more than 45 seconds after take-off. The investigative report also emphasised the importance of attaining a minimum altitude of 1,000ft (300m) before flap retraction in night operations of the C-54, which in this case was apparently not done.

6 MAY 1945 (12:54)

Location	Hindhead, Surrey, England
Operator	US Army Air Forces
Aircraft type	Curtiss C-46D (44-77839)

Loaded with litter patients being brought back from the Continent, the twin-engine transport crashed and burned after striking radar towers located on Gibbets Hill, 25 miles (40km) south-west of London. A total of 31 military personnel lost their lives in the crash, one of them a Canadian who was on the ground in a hut struck by falling debris and the rest aboard the aircraft; except for three British, the latter were all Americans, including the crew of five assigned to 44-77839. There were no survivors. Flying through a valley close to the terrain on account of a low overcast, with 8/10 cloud coverage at 600ft (180m) and a visibility of 3 miles (5km), the aircraft was bound for Newbury, Berkshire, England, when it hit the tops of the towers, which rose to 240ft (70m) above the ground, the impact shearing off the starboard wing.

The accident was attributed to pilot error, specifically, his attempt to maintain contact (visual) flight rules in the instrument meteorological conditions. An additional factor may have been the absence of lights on the towers and the fact that the obstacles were not indicated on regional flight charts.

9 MAY 1945 (c.12:30)

Location	Near Roye, Picardie, France
Operator	Royal Air Force
Aircraft type	Avro Lancaster (RF230)

Only about 12 hours after the end of hostilities in the European theatre, this prisoners-of-war transport flight ended in tragedy. All 31 servicemen aboard lost their lives when the four-engine bomber plummeted into a wooded area and caught fire about 25 miles (40km) south-east of Amiens after going into an uncontrollable spin. The crash occurred during a flight to England from Brussels, Belgium. Other than one American, the victims were British, including the crew of six. At the time, the weather conditions in the area consisted of scattered clouds above 10,000ft (3,000m) and high cirrus, with a visibility of between 5 and 10 miles (10 and 15km) and a slight, south-easterly breeze.

13 MAY 1945 (c.15:00)

Location	*New Guinea*
Operator	*US Army Air Forces*
Aircraft type	*Douglas C-47A (41-23052)*

All but three of the 24 American military personnel aboard were killed when the twin-engine transport crashed and burned in mountainous terrain in the West Irian region of the island. The injured survivors, who included a member of the Women's Army Corps (WAC), were found by a search party nearly two weeks later and taken back to civilisation; two others apparently survived the crash but succumbed to their injuries before they could be rescued.

At the time of the accident, the C-47 was on a navigational training mission, and according to one of the survivors, it had been flying at a low altitude through a canyon when it encountered cloudy conditions, then struck a ridge while trying to climb out of the area and as it proceeded on a south-westerly heading. There was no evidence of any prior mechanical failure in the aircraft.

30 MAY 1945 (c.09:20)

Location	*Near Sassandra, Ivory Coast*
Operator	*US Army Air Forces*
Aircraft type	*Douglas C-47B (44-76406)*

Operated by the Air Transport Command (ATC), the aircraft had been on a scheduled flight from Accra, Gold Coast (Ghana), to Roberts Field, serving Monrovia, Liberia. It carried 21 American service personnel, including three crewmen; its passengers were all members of the Women's Army Corps (WAC). Last reported cruising at an altitude of 8,000ft (2,500m), the C-47 sent out a Mayday distress message before it crashed in the Atlantic Ocean off Drewin. According to a native eyewitness, it plummeted into the water at an angle of approximately 45 degrees. Only an oil slick was found at the crash site; no survivors, bodies or wreckage were recovered.

15 JUNE 1945 (c.07:50)

Location	*Near Swanage, Dorset, England*
Operator	*Royal Air Force*
Aircraft type	*Consolidated Liberator (JT985)*

Flown by Transport Command, the aircraft crashed and burned on a hillside 10 miles (15km) south-south-west of Bournemouth, in conditions of poor visibility and after experiencing engine trouble. All 27 military personnel aboard were killed, including the crew of five.

24 JUNE 1945 (c.06:00)

Location	*Near Pajao, Burma*
Operator	*US Army Air Forces*
Aircraft type	*Curtiss C-46D (42-101205)*

The twin-engine aircraft, carrying as passengers Chinese troops and bound for Luliang, Yunnan, China, crashed and burned in mountainous terrain some 35 miles (55km) north-north-west of the airfield serving Myitkyina, from where it had taken off earlier. All but one of the 27 personnel aboard were killed in the accident, the fatalities including the crew of four American servicemen.

Based on testimony of the survivor, the transport had been flying 'very low' before it struck a ridge and then slammed to earth at an approximate elevation of 8,000ft (2,500m). The crash occurred around dawn, and the meteorological conditions along the route were overcast, with the cloud bases as low as 10,000ft (3,000m) and a visibility of around 3 miles (5km). The wind at 14,000ft (4,300m) was blowing at 20 knots from a direction of 240 degrees. In addition to the weather, the accident was attributed to 'pilot technique'. Subsequently, a directive was sent out to squadrons to set up a check ride system for flight crews employing experienced aviators in order to improve the proficiency of the former, and also a method of briefing pilots to assure their adherence to the procedures necessary to complete a safe flight.

29 JUNE 1945 (time unknown)

Location	*Near Bangalore, Karnataka, India*
Operator	*Royal Indian Air Force*
Aircraft type	*Unknown*

The aircraft crashed into a village where a *jatra* celebration was taking place, killing both crewmen and 36 persons on the ground. About 20 others suffered injuries in the afternoon accident, while the impact explosion and ensuing fires destroyed or damaged numerous houses.

3/4 JULY 1945 (time unknown)

Location	*North Atlantic Ocean*
Operator	*Royal Air Force*
Aircraft type	*Consolidated Liberator (JT982)*

Operated by Transport Command and carrying as passengers delegates returning from a conference in the US, the England-bound aircraft, which had last stopped at Montreal, Canada, vanished with 15 persons aboard. Among the occupants was a crew of six British, American and Canadian service personnel. Search for the transport was abandoned some two weeks later.

11 JULY 1945 (time unknown)

Location	*Near Kisumu, Kenya*
Operator	*South African Air Force*
Aircraft type	*Douglas C-47A Dakota (6812)*

All 28 South African servicemen aboard lost their lives, including a crew of four, when the twin-engine transport

A North American B-25 medium bomber, used extensively during the Second World War and the type that struck the Empire State Building on 28 July 1945. (US National Archives)

The tremendous force of the impact of the B-25 is illustrated by the huge hole left in the side of the skyscraper. (New York Times Pictures)

crashed into an inlet of Lake Victoria. The accident occurred in early-morning darkness shortly after the aircraft, its passengers all former prisoners-of-war returning home, had taken off, although the suspected cause was never released. Night flying from the airport was, however, temporarily suspended in the wake of the crash.

28 JULY 1945 (c.10:00)

Location	*New York, New York, USA*
Operator	*US Army Air Forces*
Aircraft type	*North American B-25D (43-0577)*

This remains, even today, one of the best-known military air disasters in history, due to its involvement with one of the most famous and, at that time, the tallest building in the world. The twin-engine bomber had been on a domestic interstate flight originating at Bedford airfield, Massachusetts, to New York City. It had been operating under a contact (visual) clearance only to La Guardia Airport, on Long Island, but upon reaching that point its pilot requested permission from the La Guardia control tower, and was so granted, to proceed on to Newark Airport, located in New Jersey across the Hudson River from Manhattan Island. Contained within that clearance were instructions to return if the visibility fell below 3 miles (5km).

Apparently becoming uncertain of his position, the pilot turned from a south-westerly to a southerly heading approximately over the Rockefeller Center, and while flying at too low an altitude. Ahead was the giant Empire State Building, towering to 1,250ft (380m), the top third of which was shrouded by fog, with an overcast of approximately 800ft (250m). Pulling up just before impact, the aircraft was in a near-vertical attitude when it struck the skyscraper at its 79th Floor, some 900ft (275m) above 34th Street. The crash resulted in an explosion and fire, with parts of the wreckage completely penetrating the building and dropping on to a near-by roof.

Among the 14 persons killed were the three servicemen aboard the B-25, including a navy-enlisted man, and one victim who was in the building at the time of the accident and succumbed to burns four days later; 25 others suffered non-fatal injuries. But it could have been much worse. This was a Saturday, and many offices were closed, while others had reduced staffs. Also, several floors around the level of the crash were completely unoccupied. Although the clearance given to him was considered a contributing factor, the army primarily blamed the accident on an error in judgement on the part of the pilot for proceeding over Manhattan under the prevailing conditions.

Subsequently, the US Civil Aeronautics Administration (CAA) raised the minimum altitude over lower Manhattan Island from 1,000ft (300m) above all obstructions to 2,500ft (750m) absolute.

10 SEPTEMBER 1945 (c.17:00)

Location	*Near Lin'an, Zhejiang, China*
Operator	*US Army Air Forces*
Aircraft type	*Douglas C-54G (45-526)*

In what was believed to have been the worst aviation disaster prior to 1950, the four-engine aircraft crashed and burned while transporting approximately 70 Chinese troops within their country, to Shanghai from Liuchow, Gangxi. Those killed also included the crew of four American servicemen assigned to the C-54; there were no survivors. The accident took place some 120 miles (190km) south-east of the transport's destination, and in an area where there was at the time heavy rain and a low overcast. After 45-526 had struck the top of a mountain at an elevation of around 2,500ft (750m), its fuselage slid nearly half-way down the slope. It was believed that local inhabitants removed and buried the bodies of the victims not long after the crash, preventing a determination of the exact death toll.

No specific material failure nor a definite causative factor could be identified, although it was noted in the investigative report that the accident occurred in the vicinity where pilots taking the route usually start their let-down, as there was no high terrain depicted on charts covering that area. It was therefore considered possible that the pilot of the C-54 had been at the time attempting to establish visual contact with the ground and could have been uncertain of his position. Also, head winds may have reduced the ground speed of the aircraft, and thus affected its anticipated progress during the trip.

An additional factor was the absence of air-traffic control facilities in the area at the time. Subsequently, a radio

beacon was installed at Nangchow, and an approach control system established at Shanghai. Additionally, pilots were instructed not to descend below 5,000ft (1,500m) when operating in instrument meteorological conditions in the Shanghai area.

14 SEPTEMBER 1945 (c.05:20)

Location	*Chihkiang, Hunan, China*
Operator	*US Army Air Forces*
Aircraft type	*Curtiss C-46D (44-78436)*

The twin-engine aircraft was transporting Chinese troops on an internal flight to Nanking, Jiangsu, and crashed about a minute after its departure from the airfield at Chihkiang. Including its crew of three servicemen, all 39 personnel aboard lost their lives in the accident. According to witnesses, 44-78436 accomplished a normal take-off from Runway 06, but its climb-out appeared unusually slow. After initiating a sharp left turn, the C-46 struck a ridge with its port wing, a portion of which was sheared off, and the aircraft then slammed to earth and burst into flames.

The crash occurred at dawn and in generally good weather conditions, with a ceiling of 8,000ft (2,500m) and a visibility of 7 miles (11km). The wind was calm. Although the cause could not be determined, the accident was probably related to pilot error, specifically, the sharp turn that must have led to a loss of altitude. It was recommended in the investigative report that aircraft not turn from the runway heading until reaching an above-ground altitude of at least 400ft (120m).

15 SEPTEMBER 1945 (00:08)

Location	*Near Kansas City, Missouri, USA*
Operator	*US Army Air Forces*
Aircraft type	*Douglas C-47B (45-1011)*

Flown by the Air Transport Command (ATC), the twin-engine aircraft crashed and burst into flames soon after its departure from Fairfax Field, Kansas City. All but one passenger among the 24 American servicemen aboard were killed, including the crew of three, and the sole survivor was seriously injured. Bound for the US East Coast, the transport lifted off from Runway 35, but then failed to gain sufficient altitude. Initial contact was with trees located on the north bank of the Missouri River, which were about 30ft (10m) tall and approximately 1 mile (1.5km) beyond the end of the runway, with the impact shearing off both wings, and the C-47 then slammed to earth. The accident occurred in darkness and clear meteorological conditions, with a visibility of 10 miles (15km), and a slight breeze.

Examination of the wreckage revealed one blade on the right propeller to be unbent, indicating a considerable reduction in power in the corresponding engine at the moment of impact. This suspected loss of power could have been related to one or a combination of the following factors:

the aircraft's power plants had been fitted with spark plugs whose use was not recommended by the manufacturer; the heat control had possibly been misused by the crew due to dissimilarity with earlier models of the C-47, or, there was excessive dilution and blow-by caused by a sudden increase in oil consumption during a preceding flight.

18 SEPTEMBER 1945 (time unknown)

Location   *Netherlands New Guinea*
Operator   *Royal Australian Air Force*
Aircraft type   *Douglas C-47B Dakota (A65-61)*

All 29 Australian military personnel aboard were killed, including a crew of five, when the twin-engine transport crashed during a medical evacuation flight originating from the island of Morotai, in the Moluccas group, with an ultimate destination of Townsville, Queensland, Australia. Having taken off at around 11:20 local time from Biak Island, which was one of two en route stops, the aircraft was declared overdue about 8 hours later. No radio transmissions from the C-47 were received after its departure.

The transport may have tried to proceed directly over the high terrain and encountered deteriorating weather conditions, although the loss of A65-61 would remain a mystery for more than two decades, when its wreckage was first spotted from the air. The C-47 had slammed into a mountain approximately 100ft (30m) below the crest of the ridge and at an elevation of around 13,500ft (4,100m) some 40 miles (65km) east of the Wissel Lakes region and about 300 miles (480km) west of the border with what is today Papua New Guinea, while apparently on a due-southerly heading. The occupants, who included a nurse and one passenger not officially on the manifest, were mostly comprised of former prisoners-of-war being repatriated to their country; all probably died instantly in the impact, after which the wreckage must have partially burned.

In December 1970, the victims of the crash, consisting of approximately 80lb (36kg) of skeletal remains that probably did not represent all of those killed, were recovered in an operation conducted by Royal Australian Air Force personnel and buried at a war cemetery in Papua New Guinea.

5 OCTOBER 1945 (c.12:50)

Location   *Near Elvetham, Hampshire, England*
Operator   *Royal Air Force*
Aircraft type   *Consolidated Liberator (KG867)*

The four-engine transport crashed and burned 2 miles (3km) south-west of Blackbushe Airfield, from where it had taken off shortly before, bound for Prague, Czechoslovakia. All 23 persons aboard lost their lives, including a crew of five military personnel; the occupants were all Czech refugees returning home. Fire had erupted in the aircraft's No. 2 power-plant nacelle, apparently resulting in a loss of control.

7 OCTOBER 1945 (c.00:30)

Location   *Near Rennes, Brittany, France*
Operator   *Royal Air Force*
Aircraft type   *Short Stirling IV (LJ668)*

Operated by Transport Command, the aircraft crashed less than a mile (1.5km) south of the city while attempting to land at the local airport, an en-route stop during a flight from London to Cairo, Egypt. All 26 British military personnel aboard (20 passengers and a crew of six) were killed. With its undercarriage extended, the four-engine transport lost height while in a turn and then slammed to earth and caught fire as its crew attempted to break through the cloud base, which was down to about only 200ft (60m), the accident occurring in darkness.

13 OCTOBER 1945 (c.20:45)

Location   *Melsbroek, Brabant, Belgium*
Operator   *Royal Air Force*
Aircraft type   *Consolidated Liberator (KL595)*

The four-engine aircraft had been on a Transport Command trooping flight with an ultimate destination of India when it crashed and burned immediately after taking off in darkness from Melsbroek Airport, about 5 miles (10km) north-east of Brussels. All 31 British military personnel aboard were killed, including a crew of six. Apparently failing to obtain sufficient flying speed, the Liberator had gained little height before it struck a small rise beyond the end of the runway.

15 OCTOBER 1945 (c.06:15)

Location   *Near Johor Baharu, Malaysia*
Operator   *Royal Air Force*
Aircraft type   *Short Sunderland V (NJ277)*

All 22 persons aboard were killed in the crash of the four-engine flying boat, which at the time was transporting former prisoners-of-war. The victims also included seven RAF personnel. The aircraft slammed into a hilltop at an approximate elevation of 2,000ft (600m) and burned before dawn and in conditions of poor visibility, which must have prevented the pilots from maintaining contact (visual) flight. It was noted in the investigative report that some technical failure in the aircraft could not be completely eliminated as a causative factor.

16 OCTOBER 1945 (c.11:30)

Location   *Near Peking (Beijing), China*
Operator   *US Army Air Forces*
Aircraft type   *Curtiss C-46F (44-78591)*

Following a flight from Hankou, in the Chinese province of Hubei, the twin-engine transport struck a commercial radio transmission tower while on a south-easterly heading as it approached for a landing at Nanyman Airfield, which served the capital city, then crashed and burned. All 59 military

A US Army Air Forces Curtiss C-46, two of which suffered major
crashes in China during trooping flights in October 1945.
(US National Archives)

personnel aboard lost their lives, including four American
crewmen; the passengers were all Chinese soldiers. At the
time of the accident, the weather in the area was poor, with
an overcast of about only 300ft (100m) and a visibility of
approximately 1 mile (1.5km). As there were no radio beacon
facilities in the area, a commercial broadcasting station was
being used as a navigational aid. But while the pre-flight pilot
briefing mentioned the location of the antenna mast, some
15 miles (25km) west-north-west of the airfield, its height,
which was 800ft (250m) above the ground and approximately
1,000ft (300m) above airfield elevation, had not been given.

30 OCTOBER 1945 (c.19:15)

Location	Near Chihchiang, Hunan, China
Operator	US Army Air Forces
Aircraft type	Curtiss C-46A (43-47228)

The twin-engine transport, carrying a load of Chinese troops
to Shanghai, crashed and burned on a hill about 2 minutes
after it had taken off from the Chihchiang airfield, killing 45
servicemen. Four soldiers and the aircraft's co-pilot, one of
the four American crewmen assigned to 43-47228, survived
with injuries.

A board of investigation expressed the opinion that a
loss of engine power and the possibility of overloading
of the aircraft, due to the fact that the troops had taken
aboard some mortar ammunition that was not part of their

regular equipment, had, in combination, contributed to the
accident. A radiogram from Tenth Air Force headquarters
had authorised this as a daylight operation, but this message
was not received until two days after the crash. Subsequently,
payloads were reduced and night flying abandoned in the
Chinese troop transport operations.

1 NOVEMBER 1945 (c.15:30)

Location	Near Herrenalb, Germany
Operator	US Army Air Forces
Aircraft type	Douglas C-47A (42-93041)

The twin-engine transport crashed some 50 miles (80km)
west of Stuttgart during a flight from England to an air base
near Munich. All but four of the 30 American servicemen
aboard the aircraft lost their lives, including the entire crew
of four, while the surviving passengers suffered serious
injuries. In an apparent attempt to let the navigator check his
position, the C-47 had descended through a low overcast,
and witnesses stated that it then followed a river for several
minutes before beginning to climb back into the clouds. It
subsequently slammed into a wooded mountainside and
burned. According to a local observer, the meteorological
conditions in the area at the time of the accident consisted of
low stratus clouds that extended down to the hilltops, with
a ceiling of around 1,300ft (400m) and a visibility of 2 miles
(3km) in light rain and haze.

The underlying cause of the accident was that the pilot
had been flying on instruments below a safe altitude.
Responsibility was also placed on the navigator, who failed to
warn the pilot of the high terrain in the area. As a result, the
pilot had initiated a descent while uncertain of his position.
And, after determining his location, he should have ascended
using higher engine power settings. Still another factor was
inadequate meteorological information provided to the flight
crew, this due to the absence of weather stations in the area.
For that reason, one recommendation made in the investigative
report was to employ local residents with knowledge of or
backgrounds in weather observation and forecasting.

The accident occurred in darkness, but the local weather
conditions, with a ceiling of 12,000ft (3,700m), were not
considered a factor. Prior to take-off, the co-pilot had
noted that the right engine run-up and magneto checks
were unsatisfactory, but in response to his questioning, the
pilot stated that he knew the terrain very well and that he
considered the power check satisfactory.

3 NOVEMBER 1945 (c.02:00)

Location   Near Chhuka, Bhutan, India
Operator   US Army Air Forces
Aircraft type   Douglas C-54G (45-528A)

During an internal Indian flight to Karachi from the Chabua airfield, located near Dibrugarh, Assam, the four-engine transport slammed into a mountain ridge in the Himalayas at an approximate elevation of 8,000ft (2,500m) and some 50 miles (80km) south of Punakha. Although the wreckage of the aircraft was not located until the following month, all 44 American servicemen aboard (40 passengers and a crew of four) had perished in the crash. It was dark at the time of the accident, with no moon, but the meteorological conditions in the area, consisting of unlimited ceiling and visibility, were apparently not a factor. The location of the crash indicated that 45-528A had flown the direct route between the two cities and off the designated airway.

An investigative board concluded that this action was probably deliberate on the part of the pilot-in-command, in violation of prescribed regulations, and placed the aircraft at an insufficient height to clear the terrain. Villagers reported seeing an aircraft, probably the C-54, proceeding east to west at a low altitude. Initial impact with trees tore off its starboard wing, after which the transport crashed, exploded and disintegrated.

8 NOVEMBER 1945 (c.20:00)

Location   Corpus Christi Bay, Texas, USA
First aircraft
Operator   US Navy
Aircraft type   Martin PBM-3S Mariner (01710)
Second aircraft
Operator   US Navy
Aircraft type   Martin PBM-5 Mariner (69113)

The two twin-engine amphibious patrol bombers collided and crashed about 2.5 miles (4km) north-north-west of Corpus Christi Naval Air Station. Killed in the accident were 22 American servicemen, including all 12 occupants of 69113; the five survivors from 01710 suffered various injuries.

Both aircraft were on training flights, 69113 having taken off from the water on a true heading of 150 degrees, while 01710 was making its approach to a different landing area and on a course of 165 degrees true. Despite taking off behind it, the former overtook the latter due to the differences in speed between the two models of the PBM, flying slightly to starboard but on an approximately parallel course. The tail lights on the Mariner were at best difficult to see, but when 01710 turned on its landing lights, 69113 pulled up and turned left in a futile attempt to avoid the collision, which occurred in darkness at an estimated height of 400ft (120m). The PBM-5 then plummeted straight down, exploding on impact with the water. At the time, the meteorological conditions in the area were good, with an unlimited ceiling and a visibility in excess of 10 miles (15km).

An investigative report attributed the accident to error by the crew of 69113, primarily inattention on the part of its co-pilot, whose role would normally have been relegated to that of 'look-out' during instrument take-offs and landings. Other factors were the judgement displayed by its pilot in pulling up upon the sudden appearance of 01710, which was probably related to confusion on his part, when maintaining the same course could possibly have avoided the collision. It was determined that although the PBM-5 did establish radio contact with the control tower, there were no transmissions subsequent to the initial one. A board of inquiry considered it doubtful that as they were operating in an uncontrolled area, where pilots took off and landed at their own discretion, the crew had heard 01710 receive landing clearance, and also ruled that in its 'touch-and-go' exercise, 69113 had apparently proceeded too far in the traffic pattern before starting its down-wind turn.

9 NOVEMBER 1945 (c.20:00)

Location   Near Boccadi, Sicily, Italy
Operator   US Army Air Forces
Aircraft type   Douglas C-47A (42-24363)

Operated by the Air Transport Command (ATC) and on a scheduled flight to Naples from Athens, Greece, the twin-engine aircraft slammed into a mountain and burned near Palermo. The 24 persons killed in the crash included two civilian passengers and a British serviceman; the rest of the victims were American military personnel, among them the aircraft's four crewmen. The sole survivor, a US Army soldier riding as a passenger, was seriously injured.

About an hour before the crash, the pilot radioed that he was lost. Some 20 minutes after its position had been re-established, 42-24363 flew over, then crashed approximately half a mile (0.8km) north of, Palermo airport. The crew may have seen flares fired from the ground and initiated a climb just before the impact. It was dark at the time, and the weather in the area consisted of an almost solid layer of strato-cumulus clouds at about 2,000ft (600m) and broken fracto-cumulus at 1,000ft (300m), with a light rain and a visibility of around 3 miles (5km). The wind was out of the south-west at around 15 knots.

According to the investigative report, the weather was undoubtedly the cause of the pilot becoming lost, which in turn led to the crash. The ATC division of the USAAF would subsequently discontinue night landings until the development of more sophisticated procedures and facilities.

11 NOVEMBER 1945 (c.12:00)

Location   Near Picinisco, Lazio, Italy
Operator   US Army Air Forces
Aircraft type   Boeing B-17G (43-39197)

One of three bombers of the same type that had taken off earlier from Marignane, France, bound for Athens, Greece, 43-39197 was last heard from when its pilot, in a radio transmission, reported heavy icing and requested permission to divert to Rome. A search failed to find any trace of the aircraft. The loss of the B-17 remained a mystery until the following May, when three shepherds came across its wreckage and the remains of the occupants about 75ft (20m) from the summit of Monte Meta, some 65 miles (105km) east-south-east of the Italian capital. The aircraft had exploded and disintegrated on impact, and it was apparent that all 20 American servicemen aboard (16 passengers and a crew of four) had perished in the crash.

Although the cause of the accident could not be determined, poor judgement on the part of the pilot or navigator coupled with the inclement weather encountered by the bomber, which consisted of cumulus clouds with bases of 4,000ft (1,200m) and tops at about 15,000ft (5,000m), and with conditions conducive to icing, were suspected factors. In accordance with recommendations made in the investigative report, flight crews operating in the area would receive thorough briefings with regard to the dangers of icing and hazards associated with the mountainous terrain.

11 NOVEMBER 1945 (c.23:45)

Location	Near Castel Benito, Libya
Operator	Royal Air Force
Aircraft type	Short Stirling (PJ950)

Flown by Transport Command and on a trooping flight, the four-engine aircraft crashed immediately after it had taken off from Tripoli. Including a crew of seven, all 29 British service personnel aboard were killed. Climbing slowly due to its heavy load, the aircraft reached an approximate height of 150ft (50m) before beginning to descend in a forced

An RAF Short Stirling heavy bomber, which was also used as a transport aircraft, the type involved in the fatal crash in North Africa. (Short Brothers)

landing attempt, with one power plant afire. The Stirling then slammed to earth, disintegrated and burned, the accident occurring in darkness, shortly before midnight.

15 NOVEMBER 1945 (c.09:20)

Location	Territory of New Guinea
Operator	Royal Australian Air Force
Aircraft type	Douglas C-47A Dakota (A65-54)

All 28 Australian and Indian military personnel aboard were killed, including a crew of four, when the twin-engine transport crashed on New Britain Island, in the Bismarck Archipelago region. The site of impact was approximately 150ft (50m) below the crest of a mountain rising to about 7,000ft (2,000m), the accident having occurred in adverse meteorological conditions shortly after the aircraft had taken off from the airfield near Jacquinot Bay, on an intra-island flight to Rabaul. The cause of the crash was unknown.

22 NOVEMBER 1945 (c.10:00)

Location	White's Farm, Chard, Somerset, England
Operator	Royal Air Force
Aircraft type	Consolidated Liberator (KH126)

Operated by RAF Transport Command and on a trooping flight with an ultimate destination of India, the aircraft crashed and burst into flames some 4 miles (6.5km) from the end of the runway at Merryfield airfield, from where it had taken off shortly before. All 27 British and Polish service personnel aboard the four-engine transport (22 passengers and a crew of five) were killed in the accident. The pilot had initiated a left procedural turn before reaching the minimum terrain clearance altitude of 1,500ft (500m), and the aircraft subsequently struck Castle Hill approximately 800ft (250m) above airfield elevation, the accident occurring in cloudy weather conditions.

23 NOVEMBER 1945 (c.11:00)

Location   *Java, Republic of Indonesia*
Operator   *Royal Air Force*
Aircraft type *Douglas C-47 Dakota (KG520)*

The twin-engine transport crash-landed about 5 miles (10km) south-south-east of Jakarta after the failure of a power plant, and although its 25 occupants survived, all were subsequently killed by rebels.

3 DECEMBER 1945 (c.13:30)

Location   *Near Rochefort, Poitou, France*
Operator   *Royal Air Force*
Aircraft type *Consolidated Liberator (KH125)*

During a Transport Command trooping flight from India to Oakington, near Cambridge, England, the aircraft crashed in flames some 20 miles (30km) south-east of La Rochelle. All 28 British servicemen aboard were killed, including a crew of five. Apparently due to severe turbulence, the left outboard wing section broke off as the four-engine transport was flying through a thunderstorm.

5 DECEMBER 1945 (c.20:00)

Location   *Off Florida, USA*
Operator   *US Navy*
Aircraft types *(5) Grumman TBM Avenger (23307)*
                (45714) (46094) (46325) (73209) and
                (1) Martin PBM-5 Mariner (59225)

This multiple crash, which would later become the centre of the Bermuda Triangle legend, began as a routine over-water navigational training flight out of the US Naval Air Station at Fort Lauderdale, on Florida's eastern coast. The five torpedo bombers had been assembled into a group designated as Flight 19. Its leader, Lt Charles Taylor, was a qualified instructor with recent combat experience; his students had between 350 and 400 hours in the air, more than 50 hours each in the type. Aboard the five aircraft were a total of 14 men, with one carrying two rather than the normal three-member crew.

As part of the exercise, the group was to fly a triangular-shaped course over the Atlantic Ocean that would end back at the base. Following take-off, they proceeded almost due east for a distance of more than 100 miles (150km), with the initial leg including some low-level practice bombing at about the half-way point. The first hint of trouble came at around 16:00 local time, or some 2 hours into the mission, after the flight was to have turned left and continued on the second leg, on a heading of 346 degrees, when a radio conversation between two of its pilots was heard by the leader of another group of aircraft, indicating that they had become lost.

Over a period of at least 3 hours, the group zigzagged over the sea, changing their direction several times, the flight leader trying to lead them to safety. Apparently over the northern Bahamas, Lt Taylor, who had reported both his compasses inoperative, probably thought he had been over the Florida Keys, located off the southern tip of the state and with which he was more familiar. In the process, he disregarded the suggestions of his students to fly west, which, had he been correct, would have taken the aircraft out over the Gulf of Mexico, with no chance of reaching land. By using directional bearings obtained from different ground stations, the approximate position of the group was determined to have been in an area some 150 miles (250km) east of New Smyrna Beach, Florida. This information was relayed to the aircraft, but as attempts to contact them had been unsuccessful due to interference from Cuban radio broadcasting stations, static and atmospheric conditions, it probably never got through.

An air/sea search that would continue for five days began after the bombers were reported in trouble, and during this operation a sixth aircraft was lost. The Mariner, with a crew of 13 men aboard, went missing after being dispatched from Banana River Naval Air Station, near Merritt Island. At around 19:50, a crewman on a ship observed an aircraft, presumably 59225, burst into flames in the air, then plunge into the sea and explode at a position 30 miles (50km) west of New Smyrna Beach. The vessel reported passing through a pool of oil where the twin-engine amphibian had fallen, but recovered no survivors, bodies or solid pieces of debris from the water, which was about 80ft (25m) deep at the crash site. Nor was any trace found of the five TBM Avengers in what, to this day, remains as one of the biggest media-embellished incidents in the history of military aviation. The suspected causes were, however, far more mundane.

An investigative report attributed the loss of Flight 19 to temporary mental confusion resulting in faulty judgement on the part of Lt Taylor, who allowed himself to become disorientated relative to the Florida peninsula, and his failure to use all the navigational facilities available to him. He also failed to take into account the strong winds that carried the aircraft further east than expected, and did not switch to the emergency radio band, perhaps fearing that in changing frequencies, the pilots might lose contact with each other. There was no evidence that any of the pilots had used their ZBX homing devices designed to receive a special land-based transmitter. The aircraft would have exhausted their supply of fuel by 20:00, but the flight leader was heard to tell his fellow pilots that when any aircraft got down to 10 gallons (35 litres) of gasoline, they would all ditch together. But by then darkness would have fallen, the sea was rough, and there could have been some unexpected development in the local weather, which as forecast, consisted of rain showers, with reduced visibility and a lower overcast within the areas of precipitation, and surface winds of 20 knots, gusting to more than 30. These factors and the relative inexperience of all but the lead pilot would have made a successful water landing unlikely.

The apparent mid-air explosion of the Mariner, an aircraft that had become known as the 'flying gas tank' because of its fuel capacity, could have resulted from structural failure due to severe turbulence, power plant malfunction or the ignition of fumes by an electrical spark, or merely the lighting of a cigarette by a member of the crew in violation of smoking regulations. It was recommended in the report pertaining to the loss of the five Avengers that greater emphasis be placed on the importance of proper navigation and lost-aircraft procedures in such over-water flights.

19 DECEMBER 1945 (time unknown)

Location	Timor Sea
Operator	Royal Australian Air Force
Aircraft type	Douglas C-47B Dakota (A65-83)

The twin-engine transport vanished with 25 Australian military personnel aboard, including a crew of four, during an ambulance flight from the Indonesian island of Ambon, in the Moluccas group, to Darwin, Australia. Having taken off shortly before 12:00 local time, A65-83 was last heard from approximately an hour later. A search for the aircraft that went on for more than two weeks proved fruitless, and the cause of the disappearance remains a mystery.

9 JANUARY 1946 (time unknown)

Location	Changchun, Jilin, China
First aircraft	
Operator	Chinese Air Force
Aircraft type	Unknown
Second aircraft	
Operator	Chinese Air Force
Aircraft type	Unknown

The two transports, carrying as passengers army soldiers, collided in mid-air over the city. Among the 36 service personnel killed in the accident were six airmen, presumably the crews of the aircraft, while others were reported injured. One or both of the transports may have been Douglas C-47 or Curtiss C-46 models.

15 JANUARY 1946 (18:25)

Location	Provence, France
Operator	Royal Air Force
Aircraft type	Douglas C-47B Dakota (KN557)

Operated by Transport Command and returning British prisoners-of-war home from Singapore, the aircraft slammed into a hillside at an approximate elevation of 1,000ft (300m) some 5 miles (10km) south of Marseilles, the accident occurring in darkness and during a snow shower. All but two of the 25 servicemen aboard lost their lives in the fiery crash, including the four members of the aircraft's crew. Both survivors were injured.

5 FEBRUARY 1946 (c.09:00)

Location	The Philippines
Operator	US Army Air Forces
Aircraft type	Douglas C-47A (42-23619)

The twin-engine transport, which was operated by the Philippine Air Force branch of the USAAF, vanished in adverse

A formation of US Navy TBM Avenger torpedo bombers, identical to the aircraft lost off the coast of Florida in December 1945. (US Navy)

weather conditions during an inter-island flight to Cebu from Iloilo, located on Panay. Its wreckage and the remains of the 21 persons aboard, all of whom had apparently been killed in the crash, were found in mountainous terrain on the island of Negros more than seven months later. The victims included nine American civilian entertainers riding as passengers and a crew of five military personnel. The aircraft had taken off at 08:40 local time, with inoperative radio-navigational equipment.

17 MARCH 1946 (time unknown)

Location	Near Nanking, Jiangsu, China
Operator	Chinese Air Force
Aircraft type	'Transport'

At least one high-ranking Chinese official was among the 20 persons killed when the aircraft, on an internal flight from Shanghai to Nanking, crashed in mountainous terrain, reportedly during a low overcast. There were no survivors. The aircraft may have been a Douglas C-47.

19 MARCH 1946 (c.11:45)

Location	*Near Hobart Mills, California, USA*
Operator	*US Army Air Forces*
Aircraft type	*Douglas C-47B (45-1085)*

Operated by the Air Transport Command (ATC), the twin-engine aircraft crashed in the Sierra Nevada region, not far from the Nevada border, and all 26 men aboard were killed, including a crew of three; some of the passengers had recently been discharged from the military. Having taken off earlier from Stockton, California, and subsequently landed at McClellan Army Air Base, near the state capital of Sacramento, 45-1085 had been on a domestic US flight with an ultimate destination of Denver, Colorado, and another planned stop at Hill Field, near Ogden, Utah. Proceeding towards the east, the C-47 was last reported over Donner Summit at 13,000ft (4,000m) before it began to disintegrate. The separation of its right wing and empennage was followed by a more general break-up of the aircraft, which scattered wreckage and bodies across the mountainous terrain over an area of some 2sq miles (3sq km). There was no evidence of in-flight or post-impact fire or explosion.

Although the cause of the accident could not be determined with certainty, the theory considered most probable by military investigators was that the pilots of 45-1085 had been displaced or even injured by turbulence encountered by the aircraft due to the fact that they did not have their seat belts fastened, which led to a loss of control. The over-stressing that precipitated the break-up probably resulted from excessive speed, an unusual attitude or a spin or spiral manoeuvre, or from the attempted recovery from this condition. Subsequently, pilots would be informed as to the importance of properly using seat belts when flying.

10 MAY 1946 (c.10:25)

Location	*Near Munson, Florida, USA*
First aircraft	
Operator	*US Navy*
Aircraft type	*Consolidated-Vultee PB4Y-2 Privateer (59437)*
Second aircraft	
Operator	*US Navy*
Aircraft type	*Consolidated-Vultee PB4Y-2 Privateer (59721)*

The two four-engine patrol bombers collided in mid-air and crashed some 30 miles (50km) north-north-east of Pensacola, killing all 28 military personnel aboard both aircraft. At the time, the two aircraft directly involved were part of a formation and engaged in manoeuvres with a Grumman F-6F Hellcat fighter, which was making practice dives on the bomber flight, and during a turn, one PB4Y struck another. The collision occurred at a height of 6,000ft (1,800m), after which both Privateers plummeted to earth and exploded. Blamed for the accident was faulty judgement on the part of at least one of the two bomber crews, combined with a lack of experience in formation flying. Subsequently, a restriction was placed on pilots in such fighter 'affiliation' operations as to how close the smaller aircraft could approach the group.

1 JUNE 1946 (c.07:40)

Location	*Off Amalfi, Campina, Italy*
Operator	*US Army Air Forces*
Aircraft type	*Douglas C-54 (44-9078)*

Operated by the Air Transport Command (ATC), the four-engine aircraft had been en route to Ciampino Airport, serving Rome, from Payne Field, near Cairo, Egypt, when fire of an undetermined origin erupted in the cockpit, to the left of the pilot's seat. An emergency bail-out by the occupants was initiated, but shortly thereafter the transport plummeted into the Gulf of Salerno, 30 miles (50km) south-south-east of Naples. Among the 38 men aboard, all US service personnel except for two civilians riding as passengers, only eight who parachuted from the aircraft were rescued, the survivors including four members of the crew of eight. The bodies of seven victims were retrieved from the water; the main wreckage of the aircraft sank and could not be recovered.

Attempts to put out the blaze prior to the crash had been unsuccessful, and the flight crew was in fact forced from the cockpit by the smoke, fumes and gases produced by the fire extinguisher used in a small area, having left the C-54 on autopilot. Shortly afterwards, the aircraft went into a flat spin. The passengers and most of the crew did not know how to use the British, quick-release-type parachutes that were provided. The meteorological conditions in the area, which were not considered a factor in the accident, consisted of scattered cumulus clouds, with bases of 2,000ft (600m), high cirrus and a visibility of 5 miles (10km).

8 JUNE 1946 (c.13:15)

Location	*Near Abeokuta, Nigeria*
Operator	*Royal Air Force*
Aircraft type	*Douglas C-47 Dakota (KG747)*

The twin-engine transport crashed about 70 miles (110km) north-east of Lagos, the accident occurring in poor weather during an internal Nigerian flight from Kano to Ikeja. A total of 23 persons lost their lives in the crash, including four civilian passengers. There were no survivors. Most of the victims were British military personnel, including the crew of six, although one of them, whose body could not be identified, may have been a ground fatality. The Dakota had deviated from the direct track and had descended to a low altitude in an apparent attempt to avoid the turbulent conditions, and was flying through a low overcast when it struck trees. It was noted in the investigative report that the chart being used by the pilots did not accurately depict the height of the terrain in the area.

9 JUNE 1946 (c.10:15)

Location	*Taboga Island, Panama*
Operator	*US Army Air Forces*
Aircraft type	*Douglas C-54D (43-17231)*

The four-engine transport crashed and exploded about 10 miles (15km) south of Albrook Field, in the Canal Zone, near Balboa, where it was to have landed at the end of an Air Transport Command (ATC) flight from the US mainland. All 23 American service personnel aboard perished; except for one civilian passenger, the victims were American service personnel, including the crew of six. Executing a radio range instrument let-down procedure, the aircraft had been advised to remain above 1,000ft (300m). The subsequent crash occurred about 50ft (15m) below that height, near the summit of the island, and after the pilot estimated his position as 5 miles (10km) south of the airfield. The local weather at the time consisted of a low overcast, with the clouds covering the top quarter of the island, and a visibility within that area of about 300ft (100m) in light rain.

It was the opinion of the investigative board that the pilot had sighted Otoque Island and mistook it for Taboga before initially reporting he was about 15 miles (25km) south-east of the airfield. At the time of the last message, he must have believed he was past Taboga, and probably thought that by descending lower, he could achieve contact (visual) flight. The south leg of the Howard radio range was found to be 'entirely unreliable' two days later, and it was suspected that the same condition existed at the time of the crash. Another factor was that various maps and navigational facility charts showed the radio range course to be in a different location with respect to Taboga Island.

It was also noted in the accident report that the pilot of 43-17231 had filed an instrument flight plan despite the fact that he did not have an effective instrument pilot certificate, which was in violation of Army Air Forces regulations. And significantly, no system of airway traffic control existed in the area at the time to handle instrument flight operations. The establishment of such a system was one of the recommendations made in the report.

9 JULY 1946 (c.20:10)

Location	*Near Ware, Massachusetts, USA*
Operator	*US Army Air Forces*
Aircraft type	*Boeing B-17G (43-39136)*

All 25 persons aboard perished when the converted four-engine bomber crashed 8 miles (13km) north-west of Westover Field, where it was to have landed, and which was an en-route stop during a flight originating in Labrador and ultimately bound for Mitchell Field, Long Island, New York, USA. Except for one civilian, the occupants were US Coast Guard or service personnel, including the crew of four. Cleared to descend, but possibly not at the correct time, the aircraft struck a slope of Mount Tom at an approximate elevation of 1,000ft (300m), or some 200ft (60m) below its summit, bursting into flames on impact. It was dark at the time, and the local weather consisted of thundershower activity, with a ceiling of 3,000ft (1,000m) and a visibility down to around 5 miles (10km). The wind was out of the south at 10 knots.

20 JULY 1946 (c.12:15)

Location	*Off Panama*
First aircraft	
Operator	*US Army Air Forces*
Aircraft type	*Boeing B-17G (44-85624)*
Second aircraft	
Operator	*US Army Air Forces*
Aircraft type	*Boeing B-17G (44-85626)*

The two four-engine bombers were participating with another B-17 in a search for three missing P-47 fighters when they collided, and both then plummeted into the Pacific Ocean about 20 miles (30km) north of the Panamanian island of Coiba. Among the 20 crewmen, ten aboard each aircraft, searchers recovered the bodies of five victims; there were no survivors.

Due to deteriorating weather conditions, 85624 had closed in on the lead aircraft, 85626, while the third B-17 came into position on the leader's left wing. Suddenly, the leader and

An Avro York transport of the type flown by the RAF that crashed from unknown causes in the Strait of Malacca. (British Aerospace)

the No. 2 aircraft simultaneously sighted what appeared to be a life-raft in the water and both then initiated a slight turn to the left, after which their wings interlocked. The collision, which occurred at an approximate height of 250ft (75m), severed the empennage of 85624 and the starboard wing of 85626. The exact cause of the accident could not be determined. However, in accordance with an earlier briefing, the sighting aircraft was supposed to have climbed to a higher altitude and circled to allow the others to fly lower and identify the object.

25 JULY 1946 (time unknown)

Location	*Near Bassein, Burma*
Operator	*Royal Air Force*
Aircraft type	*Douglas C-47 Dakota (KN585)*

The twin-engine transport crashed soon after taking off from Mingaladon, killing all 22 British military personnel aboard (18 passengers and a crew of four). Bound for Kanpur, India, the aircraft had been flying in adverse meteorological conditions when it plummeted into a swamp about 100 miles (150km) west of Rangoon after the structural failure of its left wing, attributed to overloading.

15 SEPTEMBER 1946 (c.10:20)

Location	*Near Estevan, Saskatchewan, Canada*
Operator	*Royal Canadian Air Force*
Aircraft type	*Douglas C-47A Dakota (962)*

All 21 Canadian and American servicemen aboard lost their lives when the twin-engine transport crashed and burned in

the vicinity of Estevan Airport, where it was to have landed. Except for one, the victims of the accident were pilots. Having nearly completed a flight from Minot Air Base, in North Dakota, USA, 962 was observed to abandon its landing approach, and after its undercarriage was raised, the C-47 plummeted to the ground. It was determined that, prior to the flight, a control lock had apparently not been removed from the aircraft's starboard elevator, which must have led to a loss of control during the go-around manoeuvre.

19 SEPTEMBER 1946 (c.06:45)

Location	*Near Tripoli, Libya*
Operator	*Royal Air Force*
Aircraft type	*Avro Lancaster (NX690)*

Flown by Transport Command and en route from St Mawgan, Cornwall, England, to Almaza Airfield, near Cairo, Egypt, the four-engine aircraft plunged to earth in a steep angle about 5 miles (10km) west of Homs, in the province of Tripolitania, disintegrating on impact. All 25 British servicemen aboard (19 passengers and a crew of six) perished in the crash, which occurred around dawn. The transport may have been struck by lightning.

6 OCTOBER 1946 (c.07:30)

Location	*Strait of Malacca*
Operator	*Royal Air Force*
Aircraft type	*Avro York (MW125)*

For unknown reasons, the four-engine transport crashed approximately 100 miles (150km) south-west of Penang, Malaya. There were no survivors among the 21 British military personnel aboard the aircraft (15 passengers and a crew of six), which had been on a Transport Command flight originating in England, with an ultimate destination of Singapore, and searchers recovered none of the victims' bodies from the water.

A Fairey Firefly of the type flown by the Netherlands Naval Air Service that crashed into a Dutch school. (Westland Aircraft)

7 OCTOBER 1946 (c.11:20)

Location	*Apeldoorn, Gelderland, The Netherlands*
Operator	*Marine Luchtvaartdienst (Royal Netherlands Naval Air Service)*
Aircraft type	*Fairey Firefly Mk 1 (PP526)*

Having taken off on a solo flight from Valkenburg Air Base, near The Hague, the pilot proceeded without authorisation towards Apeldoorn, where his parents lived. Subsequently, PP526 was observed making low-altitude turns over the city, the pilot throttling his power plant in an apparent attempt to get the attention of those on the ground. Minutes later, the single-engine fighter suddenly lost height during a manoeuvre, its starboard wing hitting the roof of the main building at a high school as it tried to level off. The initial impact knocked off an external fuel tank, which fell on top of the school gymnasium and ruptured, spreading its flaming contents over the building where 27 students and their instructor had just begun an exercise. The Firefly itself then crashed into some trees. In addition to the pilot, 22 teenage boys on the ground lost their lives in the fiery holocaust, while about a dozen other persons suffered injuries. An additional indirect casualty of the crash was the mother of the young aviator, who died of a heart attack after watching her son crash to his death.

16 NOVEMBER 1946 (c.23:30)

Location	*North Pacific Ocean*
Operator	*US Army Air Forces*
Aircraft type	*Curtiss C-46F (44-78691)*

All 24 American military personnel aboard (19 passengers and a crew of five) lost their lives when the twin-engine transport

crashed some 10 miles (15km) east of Central Field, on the island of Iwo Jima, where it was to have landed. Having nearly completed an inter-island flight from Guam, 44-78691 had been offered a ground-controlled (GCA) approach, which the pilot declined, and was given the latest weather, which as reported consisted of an unlimited ceiling and a visibility of 15 miles (25 km). The C-47 was observed to turn on to a heading of 35 degrees before radar contact was lost. Subsequently, a small amount of personal effects and seven damaged life-rafts were found floating in the sea, but none of the victims' bodies were recovered.

The accident occurred in darkness, and the meteorological conditions in the immediate area were reported by the crew of a search aircraft to have been considerably different from those reported, with a ceiling of only 1,000ft (300m) and the visibility having been restricted by mist. There was no evidence of technical failure in the aircraft, and considering his experience and proficiency, pilot error was considered 'very improbable'. No contributing factors were identified by the investigative board, and the cause of the crash was considered unknown.

10 DECEMBER 1946 (c.13:10)

Location	*Near Osaka, Japan*
Operator	*US Army Air Forces*
Aircraft type	*Curtiss C-46F (44-78604)*

The twin-engine transport crashed and burned approximately 3 miles (5km) south-west of Itami Air Base, from where it had taken off about 2 minutes earlier, killing all 24 persons aboard. Except for three American civilians travelling as passengers, the victims were US service personnel, including the crew of five. One of the victims was found alive in the wreckage but died nearly a week later.

Having lifted off from Runway 28 on an internal Japanese courier flight that had originated at Tachikawa Air Base, near Tokyo, and ultimately destined for Konaya Air Base, the C-46 was observed by one witness to yaw to the right, which would indicate a malfunction in the starboard power plant. A shallow turn to the left was then begun, with the aircraft continuing to settle, after which it stalled, rolled back to the right and finally slammed into a rice field, coming to rest inverted. The local weather at the time consisted of scattered clouds at 3,000ft (1,000m), a visibility of 15 miles (25km) and a westerly wind of around 20 knots.

Due to the condition of the wreckage, no positive determination could be made as to which engine had failed, if either. Nevertheless, an investigative board concluded that the crash must have been precipitated from a loss of power, probably in the right engine. Considered as contributory were the fact that the C-46 would have been near the maximum gross weight for a single-engine operation, and the presence of high-tension wires directly in the path of the flight, which could have prompted an evasive manoeuvre.

It was noted in the accident report that both power plants of 44-78604 had been changed prior to its last flight. Among the recommendations made in the report were that aircraft be restricted to 5 hours of local flying following an engine change, and that pilots be cautioned to drain fuel pumps after refuelling.

10 DECEMBER 1946 (time unknown)

Location	*Southern Washington, USA*
Operator	*US Marine Corps*
Aircraft type	*Curtiss R5C-1 (39528)*

The twin-engine transport, carrying 32 American servicemen (29 passengers and a crew of three), vanished during a domestic interstate flight originating at Miramar Naval Air Station, near San Diego, California, and destined for Sand Point Naval Base, at Seattle. In the last radio transmission from 39528, received at 16:16 local time, the pilot reported being at a position of 30 miles (50km) south of the airport serving the town of Toledo, about 30 minutes flying time from his destination and at a height of 9,000ft (2,700m). He also reported picking up ice, and asked permission to fly 500ft (150m) above the overcast. An attempt to contact the aircraft 20 minutes later was unsuccessful. Darkness was falling at the time, and strong winds, in excess of 40 knots, would have been blowing out of the north-west at its cruising altitude.

Despite an extensive search over the wooded, mountainous terrain, no trace of the R5C was found, and due to the lack of evidence, no determination could be made as to the cause of its disappearance. Significantly, 39528 had not been equipped with de-icer boots.

14 JANUARY 1947 (c.09:00)

Location	*Near Puebla, Mexico*
Operator	*Fuerza Aérea Mexicana (Mexican Air Force)*
Aircraft type	*Lockheed C-60 Lodestar (60-03)*

All 21 Mexican servicemen aboard perished, including a crew of four, when the twin-engine transport crashed and burst into flames moments after it had taken off from a military base, on an internal flight to the city of Oaxaca. The passengers were all troops engaged in a practice manoeuvre. There were indications that the aircraft's right power plant had malfunctioned and that the pilot had lost control while trying to return to the airfield.

21 FEBRUARY 1947 (c.16:00)

Location	*Near Chungking, Sichuan, China*
Operator	*Chinese Air Force*
Aircraft type	*Douglas C-47*

The twin-engine transport, which was on an internal flight from Kunming, Yunnan, crashed while approaching to land, killing all 21 persons aboard. According to an unofficial report, the accident may have resulted from an encounter with severe icing conditions.

29 MAY 1947 (c.22:45)

Location   *Near Atsugi, Kanagawa, Japan*
Operator   *US Army Air Forces*
Aircraft type *Douglas C-54D (42-72553)*

All 40 persons aboard perished when the four-engine transport crashed some 20 miles (30km) south-south-west of Tachikawa Air Base, where it was to have landed, and around 30 miles (50km) south-west of Tokyo. With the exception of four civilians, the victims were American military personnel, including the seven members of the aircraft's crew.

As it neared the end of a flight from Kimpo Air Base, near Seoul, South Korea, 42-72553 was cleared for descent to 4,000ft (1,200m). Inexplicably, it assumed a north-westerly heading, and after initiating a right turn, struck a mountain at an approximate elevation of 5,000ft (1,500m), bursting into flames on impact. At the moment of impact, its heading was around 40 degrees, or some 10 degrees too far to the north of the correct course to its intended destination. The accident occurred in darkness, and the weather along the route was cloudy, with 3 to 6/10 cumulus clouds between 3,000 and 4,000ft (1,000 and 1,200m) and at about 8,000ft (2,500m) and broken altostratus above that, with a visibility of between 5 and 10 miles (10 and 15km). The winds in the vicinity of Tokyo and Nagoya were approximately 40 knots.

Although the cause could not be determined with certainty, the disaster apparently resulted from faulty navigation and poor piloting technique on the part of the crew, with the meteorological conditions considered as contributory. It was believed that the accident could have been prevented had attempts been made to contact the aircraft when a radar operator observed its target disappear about 4 minutes before the crash. Procedural changes were made in this area after a similar C-54 accident three years later (see 21 April 1950).

31 JULY 1947 (time unknown)

Location   *Near Yumen, Gansu, China*
Operator   *Chinese Air Force*
Aircraft type *Douglas C-47*

The twin-engine transport disappeared during an internal Chinese flight from Tihua (Urumqi), Xinjiang, to Lanzhou, Gansu, and its wreckage was later found about 400 miles (650km) north-west of its destination, with no survivors among the 26 people aboard. Among the passengers were at least one American and one British civilian.

6 AUGUST 1947 (time unknown)

Location   *US Territory of Alaska*
Operator   *US Navy*
Aircraft type *Consolidated-Vultee PBY-5A Catalina (34032)*

During an intra-Alaskan flight from Kodiak to Dutch Harbor, located in the Aleutian Island chain, the twin-engine

The route of the US Army Air Forces C-54, including the deviation in a north-westerly direction that led to the disaster in Japan. (US Air Force)

amphibian vanished with 20 American servicemen aboard. Its occupants included members of an army/navy softball team. Cleared to proceed in accordance with contact (visual) flight rules (CFR), the aircraft had encountered instrument meteorological conditions along the way. Nevertheless, the pilot continued at a height below the recommended instrument flight altitude, off airways and with no positive radio fixes. In its last message, received at 10:45 local time, 34032 was reported at 4,000ft (1,200m) and crossing the south-east leg of the Randall radio range, or some 150 miles (250km) from its destination. The weather at Fort Randall, located at Cold Bay, had remained below minimums throughout the day, with ceilings reported as low as 200ft (60m).

A search that went on for days failed to find any trace of the Catalina or its occupants. It was assumed that 34032 had experienced a sudden occurrence that prevented the crew from sending a distress message. The possibility of a power plant malfunction was considered doubtful, as such an emergency should have afforded the time to make such a transmission. One possibly significant factor was that the weather forecaster did not fill in the meteorological section of the flight clearance form in sufficient detail to indicate whether the entire flight should have been conducted under CFR. It was also noted in the investigative report that Dutch Harbor had no radio-navigational aids for aircraft.

A US Navy Consolidated Catalina amphibious patrol aircraft of the type lost over the Aleutian Island region of Alaska. (General Dynamics)

31 OCTOBER 1947 (time unknown)

Location	*Near Srinagar, Jammu and Kashmir, India*
Operator	*Royal Indian Air Force*
Aircraft type	*Douglas C-47 (MI1965)*

The crash of the twin-engine transport in the Pir Panjal Range of mountains claimed the lives of all 25 persons aboard the aircraft. No further details about the accident, including phase of flight and possible cause, are known.

28 NOVEMBER 1947 (c.14:10)

Location	*Near Demonte, Piemonte, Italy*
Operator	*US Air Force*
Aircraft type	*Douglas C-47B (43-48736)*

The twin-engine transport crashed and burned about 20 miles (30km) south-south-west of Cuneo, killing all 20 persons aboard. Except for one civilian, the victims were all American military personnel, including the crew. As evidenced by the heavy clothing they were wearing and the use of makeshift medical applications, two men must have survived the impact, but one died soon after, probably of shock, and the other apparently succumbed to exposure within 8 hours of the crash. The wreckage and remains of the victims were not located until the following August.

Bound for Frankfurt, Germany, the aircraft slammed into an eastern slope of Mount Carbone in the Maritime Alps, some 150 miles (250km) west-north-west of Pisa, from where it had taken off earlier, and at a position approximately 30 miles (50km) off the prescribed route. At around the time of the accident, the meteorological conditions in the area were adverse, with snowstorms, solid altocumulus clouds reaching all the way down to the mountaintops, and a 25-knot wind blowing from a west-south-westerly direction. Other pilots had reported strong south-westerly winds at an altitude of 2,000ft (600m), which were in excess of the forecasted 50 knots.

10 DECEMBER 1947 (c.00:20)

Location	*Near Goose Bay, Labrador*
Operator	*US Air Force*
Aircraft type	*Douglas C-54D (42-72572)*

Operated by the Air Transport Command, the four-engine aircraft crashed and burned 8.5 miles (13.5km) north of Goose Bay Air Base, from where it had taken off shortly before, bound for Westover Field, Massachusetts, USA. Among the 29 persons aboard the aircraft, all of whom were American military personnel except for one civilian, 23 lost their lives. The six servicemen who survived, all with injuries, included one member of the crew. About a minute after its departure, the crew requested an emergency landing, but the C-54 subsequently slammed into a wooded area in what appeared to be a 'power stall' attitude. It was dark at the time and the weather was overcast, with a ceiling of 2,500ft (750m) and a visibility of 10 miles (15km). Although it had stopped before 42-72572 took off, about ½in (12mm) of snow had fallen while the aircraft was on the ground, raising speculation as to its contribution to the accident.

11 DECEMBER 1947 (c.18:10)

Location   Near Memphis, Tennessee, USA
Operator   US Air Force
Aircraft type Douglas C-47D (44-76366)

All 20 American service personnel aboard perished, including a crew of four, when the twin-engine transport crashed and exploded in a wooded area some 3.5 miles (6km) south-south-east of Memphis Municipal Airport, where it was to have landed at the end of a US domestic flight from Biggs Field, near El Paso, Texas. After its crew reported descending out of 3,000ft (1,000m), the C-47 went into a right-hand spiral and plummeted to earth. The accident occurred in darkness, and the meteorological conditions in the area shortly beforehand were described as 'marginal', with an overcast of 1,700ft (520m) and a visibility of about 4 miles (6.5km) in smoke. The wind was from a north-north-easterly direction at approximately 10 knots.

No significant turbulence had been reported, and despite slight evidence of icing conditions, the weather was not considered to have been a factor in the crash. Nor was there any indication of prior technical failure in the aircraft, of altimeter error or in-flight fire or explosion. Although it was considered possible that the pilot had experienced vertigo during or after completion of the letdown, resulting in the uncontrolled descent, the cause of the accident could not be determined.

27 FEBRUARY 1948 (time unknown)

Location   Near Belem, Para, Brazil
Operator   Força Aérea Brasileira (Brazilian Air Force)
Aircraft type Douglas C-47A (2040)

The twin-engine transport, its passengers comprising Brazilian service personnel and their dependants, crashed and burst into flames during a flight that had originated at Rio de Janeiro, with an intended destination of Cayenne, French Guiana. Among the 26 persons aboard the aircraft, including a crew of six, there were only three survivors – an army man, a woman and a child. No further details about the crash, including the possible cause, were released.

17 JANUARY 1949 (c.09:50)

Location   Near Lochgoilhead, Argyllshire, Scotland
Operator   US Air Force
Aircraft type Boeing B-29 (44-62276)

All 20 American servicemen aboard perished in the crash of the four-engine bomber, which occurred 30 miles (50km) north-west of Glasgow. One of two B-29s to have taken off earlier from Scampton, Lincolnshire, England, on a transatlantic flight to the US, 44-62276 had, about half an hour before the accident, requested, and been granted, clearance to ascend from 8,500ft to 14,500ft (2,600m to 4,400m).

At the time of the request, the aircraft was believed to have been encountering heavy icing conditions. Subsequently, the heavily-iced bomber slammed into a mountain at an approximate elevation of 700ft (200m), or about a third of the way to its summit, in a steep diving attitude and an air speed indicator reading of nearly 300mph (500kmh). The surface weather, which was otherwise not a factor in the crash, consisted of rain, with an overcast of around 1,000ft (300m) and a visibility of about 1.5 miles (2.5km). The wind was from a west-south-westerly direction at approximately 35 knots.

24 FEBRUARY 1949 (c.08:00)

Location   Near Cuzco, Peru
Operator   Cuerpo de Aeronáutica del Perú (Air Arm of Peru)
Aircraft type Douglas C-47

Operated by the military airline Transportes Aéreos Militares, the twin-engine aircraft crashed and burned as it was taking off from the city's airport, on an internal flight to Lima, killing 22 persons aboard. Two passengers, both of whom were seriously injured, and two members of the aircraft's crew of four military personnel, who escaped unscathed, survived the accident. Reportedly, the left main undercarriage leg of the C-47 had collapsed during the ground run, resulting in a fire that swept through the passenger cabin.

7 JUNE 1949 (c.14:00)

Location   Near Florianpolis, Santa Catarina, Brazil
Operator   Força Aérea Brasileira (Brazilian Air Force)
Aircraft type Douglas C-47B (2023)

The twin-engine transport, which was carrying as passengers Brazilian service personnel and their dependants, slammed into a mountainside and burned shortly after taking off from the city's airport, an en-route stop during an internal flight originating at Rio de Janeiro, with an ultimate destination of Porto Alegre, Rio Grande do Sul. Including a crew of six, all 27 persons aboard were killed. The crash occurred in adverse weather conditions, which may have been a primary or contributing causative factor.

21 AUGUST 1949 (c.23:30)

Location   Near Bigstone Lake, Manitoba, Canada
Operator   Royal Canadian Air Force
Aircraft type Consolidated Canso (11057)

During an internal mercy flight from Churchill to Winnipeg, the twin-engine amphibian crashed and burned in a wooded area some 270 miles (435km) north-north-east of its destination, the accident occurring in darkness and adverse meteorological conditions consisting of thunderstorm activity, with rain and a low overcast. All 21 persons aboard perished; the passengers were civilians, the crew of seven being Canadian military personnel. No further details about the accident, including the possible cause, were released.

3

1950–1965

Simmering since the end of the Second World War, hostilities between the East and West reached a boiling point when, on 25 June 1950, Soviet and Chinese-backed North Korean ground troops invaded South Korea. After three years of fighting, an

The size of the Douglas C-124 Globemaster accounted for its involvement in several major crashes in the early 1950s, including the North Atlantic disaster. (McDonnell Douglas)

American-led United Nations coalition managed to bring about an uneasy truce, one that exists to this day. The Korean War witnessed the first aerial dogfights between jet fighters and also extensive use, primarily in search-and-rescue and medical evacuation duties, of rotary-wing aircraft. This was also the period that multi-engine piston-powered transports reached the peak of their development. Their size accounted for their involvement in a number of major crashes, including the Korean airlift disaster of 1953, the first aviation catastrophe to have claimed more than 100 lives. The Cold War brought about the introduction of strategic nuclear forces, with such delivery systems as the 10-engine Convair B-36 and the famed eight-jet Boeing B-52.

Of course, every aircraft has its own learning curve, which often means the loss of some in accidents before their optimum operational efficiency can be achieved. This section deals with incidents occurring during the Korean War and the height of the Cold War, from 1950 to 1965.

20 JANUARY 1950 (c.12:00)

Location	*Near Vacas, Cochabamba, Bolivia*
Operator	*Fuerza Aérea Boliviana (Bolivian Air Force)*
Aircraft type	*Douglas C-47 (TAM-10)*

The twin-engine transport, which was on an internal flight from Valle Grande to the city of Cochabamba, crashed in the Andes Mountains about 20 miles (30km) from its destination, during a thunderstorm. All 32 Bolivian military personnel aboard, including a crew of four, lost their lives; the passengers were soldiers. The weather was undoubtedly a factor in the accident, although the probable cause was not disclosed.

26 JANUARY 1950 (time unknown)

Location	*Yukon Territory, Canada*
Operator	*US Air Force*
Aircraft type	*Douglas C-54D (42-72469)*

Operated by the Strategic Air Command (SAC), the four-engine transport disappeared while flying between two air bases, from Elmendorf, near Anchorage, Territory of Alaska, to Great Falls, Montana, USA, with 44 persons aboard, including a crew of eight. All were American military personnel except for two passengers, a civilian dependant and her infant son. In its last position report, transmitted shortly after 14:00 local time, the aircraft was in the vicinity of Snag. There were no indications of what could have happened to the C-54. The weather along the route ranged from clear to partly cloudy, except in the vicinity of Whitehorse, where there was a solid overcast at 7,500ft (2,300m), and a slight possibility of icing.

21 APRIL 1950 (c.23:25)

Location	*Near Atsugi, Kanagawa, Japan*
Operator	*US Air Force*
Aircraft type	*Douglas C-54D (42-72704A)*

All 35 persons aboard perished, including an eight-member crew of US Air Force personnel, when the transport crashed and burned on Mount Tanzawa. The accident occurred about 20 miles (30km) south-west of Tachikawa Air Base, located on the western outskirts of Tokyo, where the aircraft was to have landed during a scheduled service originating at Clark Air Base in the Philippines, with en-route stops on Okinawa and O-shima Island.

After he reported being over the O-shima radio range station, the pilot was cleared to proceed towards Tokyo and to descend to 5,000ft (1,500m), and the C-54 was at approximately that altitude when it initially struck trees while on an east-north-easterly heading. It was dark at the time, with intermittent rain and stratiform clouds obscuring the mountains. Light to moderate turbulence within the clouds had also been reported. Despite the pilot's position report of being over it, the aircraft had turned at a point some 25 miles (40km) south-west of the navigational aid, and from this point began its initial let-down.

The crash was primarily attributed to pilot error, although the reason for navigational error that led to the descent from the wrong position could not be determined. Minutes before the crash, a radar facility other than the one responsible for its immediate control had observed it to have been to the left of the prescribed course and proceeding in an almost due northerly direction towards the high terrain. However, a subsequent transmission from the Tokyo control centre instructing 42-72704A to reverse its course and climb came too late. It was noted in the investigative report that false automatic direction finder (ADF) indications had previously been reported by other flights in the area. Positive radar identification would become part of the revised procedure for aircraft operating under instrument flight rules (IFR) in this region, in accordance with one of the recommendations made in the report.

30 JUNE 1950 (time unknown)

Location	*Suwon, South Korea*
Operator	*US Air Force*
Aircraft type	*Douglas C-54D (42-72648)*

At the beginning of the Korean War and the involvement of the US military in the conflict, the four-engine transport was destroyed in a bombing by North Korean aircraft while either airborne or on the ground at the Suwon airstrip, some 20 miles (30km) south-south-west of Seoul. All 23 American servicemen aboard the C-54D (18 passengers and five crew members) were killed in the combat loss.

23 JULY 1950 (c.10:20)

Location	*Near Myrtle Beach, South Carolina, USA*
Operator	*US Air Force*
Aircraft type	*Curtiss C-46D (44-77577)*

The twin-engine transport, which was carrying as passengers US National Guard personnel, crashed some 10 miles (15km) north-west of Myrtle Beach Airport, from where it had taken off shortly before, on a domestic US flight to Nashville, Tennessee. Including a crew of four, all 39 American servicemen aboard perished.

Witnesses had observed 44-77577 turn on to an easterly course, back towards its departure point, before seeing parts fall from the aircraft. The C-46 then spiralled to the ground from an estimated height of 1,000–2,000ft (300–600m), exploding on impact. It was determined that after the centre section of its left aileron had torn loose, the entire control surface separated from the transport, and during the subsequent uncontrolled descent, both its wings failed due to overstressing. An investigative board expressed the opinion that the initial failure of an aileron hinge fitting had created a vibration that prompted the pilot to return to the airport, despite the absence of a distress message from the crew.

The underlying cause of the structural failure was unknown. The weather, consisting of scattered clouds at around 5,000ft (1,500m) and a visibility of 10 miles (15km), was not considered a factor. It was recommended in the accident report that the C-46 fleet be inspected in order to detect any defects in their aileron hinges and fittings.

27 JULY 1950 (c.04:30)

Location	Off Eastern Japan
Operator	US Air Force
Aircraft type	Douglas C-47D (44-76439A)

The twin-engine transport crashed in the Pacific Ocean some 10 miles (15km) south of the Island of O-shima and about 65 miles (105km) south-south-west of Tokyo. Among the 26 persons aboard, including a crew of three air force personnel, only one passenger was rescued. Four of those killed were American civilian war correspondents. None of the victims' bodies were found, and the wreckage sank in water more than 5,000ft (1,500m) deep and was not recovered.

Having taken off some 20 minutes earlier from Haneda Air Base, near the Japanese capital, and bound for the island of Kyushu, the C-47 had penetrated an overcast while climbing in pre-dawn darkness and was believed to have reached an altitude of about 3,500ft (1,050m) before its sudden and unexplained descent into the water. The army soldier who survived said that prior to impact the aircraft hit two moderate bumps, and that the cabin lights went dim, then went out, came back on and then dimmed again.

5 AUGUST 1950 (c.23:00)

Location	Near Fairfield, California, USA
Operator	US Air Force
Aircraft type	Boeing B-29MR (46-87651)

This crash and subsequent explosion involving a four-engine bomber, which was operated by the Strategic Air Command (SAC), wreaked havoc at Fairfield-Suisun Air Force Base and the surrounding community, some 40 miles (65km) north-east of San Francisco. The first hint of trouble came during the pre-flight run-up, when the two in-board propellers did not return to normal speed when the master control was decreased. The discrepancy was dismissed by the pilot and flight engineer as merely incorrect propeller settings. Nor did the aircraft commander express concern when his radio malfunctioned during the taxi phase, as the pilot was not experiencing the same difficulty.

Take-off began, but after the B-29 had used approximately three-quarters of Runway 21 and reached an indicated air speed of 125mph (200kmh), the No. 2 propeller started to overspeed. An attempt to correct the anomaly was unsuccessful, so the commander activated the feathering switch. The No. 2 propeller feathered just as the 46-87651 became airborne and, additionally, the aircraft's undercarriage would not retract. Soon afterwards, the No. 3 propeller began to overspeed, but was brought under control through a reduction in manifold pressure.

With the bomber unable to climb due to its configuration and reduced power, and with rising terrain ahead, the commander elected to make a 180-degree turn to the right, back towards the base. Upon completion of the turn, he experienced difficulty in holding up the left wing and asked the co-pilot for assistance with the controls. Shortly thereafter, the flight engineer advised the pilots that the No. 3 was running away again, and the aircraft began to shudder. Realising a crash was imminent, the commander allowed it to slide to the left to avoid a trailer park directly in its path, and the B-29 finally stalled and slammed into the ground along the boundary of the military installation. Impact was at a speed of around 120mph (190kmh), with the left wing slightly down and the nose raised, upon which the aircraft broke apart and caught fire.

Some 25 minutes later, after crash personnel and equipment had arrived on the scene, the load of bombs being carried aboard 46-87651 detonated. A total of 19 American servicemen were killed in the disaster, including 12 of the 20 who had been aboard the aircraft. About 180 others suffered injuries, among them the eight survivors of the crash and several dozen civilians. Numerous trailer caravans and vehicles were damaged, as the second explosion threw debris and burning gasoline over an area of some 2sq miles (3sq km).

It was dark at the time, but the weather conditions were not considered a factor. It was of the opinion of personnel investigating the accident that a fault existed in the electrical circuit of the undercarriage that prevented the gear from being retracted, but the nature or identity of the problem could not be determined. Significantly, the radio trouble experienced before take-off could have been a manifestation of this fault. It was further ruled that the No. 2 propeller may have oversped due to the improper adjustment of the propeller control brush block assembly. Brush tracks revealed they had been rubbing against one side of the slip ring separators. Examination also revealed badly burned decrease, feather and common slip rings, with the automatic decrease ring indicating the worst damage. As the No. 3 engine/propeller assembly had been destroyed, no similar examination on it was possible. However, in view of the condition of the No. 2 slip rings, the same condition may have also brought about its malfunction.

An important operational factor in the crash was the failure of the pilot to follow standard operating procedures in the event of a runaway propeller, in that he left the propeller selector switch in the automatic position. Had he placed it in the fixed position, it would probably not have run away

A scene of devastation is left by the crash and subsequent explosion of the Boeing B-29 bomber at Fairfield-Suisun Air Force Base. (Wide World Photos)

a second time. Alternatively, his placement of the No. 2 feathering switch in the off position could have had similar adverse consequences by allowing an increase in propeller rotation commensurate to the increase in air speed. He probably could have maintained control of that propeller by intermittently actuating the switch, instead of letting it feather completely.

Following this accident, an order was issued requiring all aircraft equipped with Curtiss Electric propellers, as was 46-87651, to be test flown after any corrective maintenance. Significant to this issue was the fact that the same B-29 had experienced overspeeding of the No. 2 propeller only five days earlier, and as a result the ground crew had been instructed to install new contactor leads. There was no way of knowing whether this had been done, as the same crewmen were killed in the crash.

In accordance with another recommendation made in the accident report, the number of persons allowed aboard on any B-29 flight operation was reduced to 16. Overloading of men, baggage and equipment and an insufficient number of safety belts probably contributed to the loss of life, since ten of the occupants killed had been trapped in the rear cabin section. Also killed was the aircraft and base commander, Brigadier General Robert F. Travis. The installation where the disaster occurred on that summer night in 1950 was later renamed in his honour, becoming Travis Air Force Base.

20 SEPTEMBER 1950 (c.05:20)

Location	*North Pacific Ocean*
Operator	*US Navy*
Aircraft type	*Douglas R5D-3 (56496)*

The four-engine transport crashed at sea and exploded about 3 minutes after taking off from the US naval air station on Kwajalein, one of the Marshall Islands, an en-route stop during a flight from Hawaii to the Far East. There were no survivors among the 26 American military personnel aboard the aircraft, who included a crew of seven; among the passengers were 11 navy nurses. Sharks were later observed molesting the bodies of victims in the water. Four unidentified female victims were recovered and debris was found floating in the general vicinity of the crash, approximately 1.5 miles (2.5km) from the easterly end of Runway 07, which the aircraft had used. Due to the depth of the ocean in the area, the main wreckage could not be salvaged.

An investigative board was unable to determine the specific cause of the crash, which had occurred in pre-dawn darkness. Possible causes listed in the accident report, in the order of probability, were as follows:

1. The pilot-in-command experienced vertigo at a time when the co-pilot's attention was directed to shifting radio frequencies or something else in the cockpit and away from monitoring the flight instruments.
2. The malfunctioning of instruments that resulted from the improper intermediate positioning of the vacuum selector control.
3. A sudden loss of power in one engine and the unintentional feathering of the propeller of another power plant on the same side.

4. The inadvertent engagement of an unaligned autopilot by a member of the crew other than the pilots at the controls.

5. A loss of lateral control due to an asymmetrical wing flap condition resulting from the malfunction of either the interconnecting or operating mechanism.

6. Malfunctioning of one or more of the primary flight controls.

7. Partial structural failure leading to the loss or misalignment of a certain component, such as the outer wing panel or a part of the empennage.

8. Any reasonable combination of the aforementioned items. The weather was not a factor.

Among the recommendations appearing in the report was one designed to improve the manner by which maintenance information on a particular aircraft is collected and made available, and one that called for a review of search-and-rescue (SAR) procedures. The latter was in response to what the board considered as an unreasonable delay in the dispatch of SAR aircraft, with the first surface vessel not reaching the scene until more than 80 minutes after the R5D had gone down. It was noted in the report, however, that since the impact with the water was apparently non-survivable, this delay did not cost any lives in this particular instance.

26 SEPTEMBER 1950 (c.04:00)

Location	*Near Kita-Kyushu, Fukuoka, Japan*
Operator	*US Air Force*
Aircraft type	*Douglas C-54D (42-72457)*

Bound for Kimpo Air Base, near Seoul, South Korea, the four-engine transport crashed in the Korea Strait, off the island of Kyushu, shortly after taking off from Runway 30 at Ashiya Air Base. Killed in the accident were 23 of the 51 American military personnel aboard, including five members of its crew of eight. All of the survivors, who were rescued by fishing boats, suffered injuries. The crash occurred approximately 1 mile (1.5km) from the end of the runway that the aircraft had used, in darkness and meteorological conditions consisting of a high overcast, with a visibility of 2 miles (3km) in ground fog.

The C-54 had been loaded in haste, so that the passengers received no briefing whatsoever regarding life vests, rafts or ditching procedures. Furthermore, 42-72457 was determined to have been improperly loaded prior to departure, and possibly even at the time of take-off. After becoming airborne, the aircraft's tail dropped suddenly and its air speed decreased. Lowering its nose to regain speed, the pilot inadvertently allowed the C-54 to descend into the water. (The pilot had apparently rolled forward the trim wheel, but did not apply additional power.) There was also the possibility that condensation in the aircraft's pitot tube system had resulted in erroneous air speed indications.

Procedural changes made in the wake of this accident included additional instruction to C-54 pilots pertaining to the aircraft's stall characteristics. And since the pilot of 42-72457 had been in the aircraft's right seat, all take-offs conducted at night or while under instrument flight rules (IFR) were required to be carried out from the left (pilot's) seat.

19 DECEMBER 1950 (c.07:30)

Location	*Near Kabayan, Benguet, the Philippines*
Operator	*US Air Force*
Aircraft type	*Douglas C-54G (44-9096)*

Operated by the Military Air Transport Service (MATS) and on a scheduled flight between two US air bases, from Naha, on the island of Okinawa, to Clark, near Angeles, the Philippines, the aircraft crashed on Luzon some 30 miles (50km) north-east of Baguio and about 100 miles (150km) north of its destination. Its burned wreckage was located two days later, on Mount Tabayoc, with no survivors among the 38 persons aboard. With the exception of two Filipino passengers, the victims were all American servicemen, including the crew of seven.

Proceeding under instrument flight rules (IFR), the aircraft was probably in and out of clouds at its assigned height of 8,000ft (2,500m) prior to the accident, although witnesses had reported a solid overcast at the time and location of the crash. The C-54 had struck the mountain at that altitude, or some 1,500ft (500m) below its peak. At the moment of impact, it was in a left wing-low attitude, which was an indication that the pilot apparently saw the terrain seconds beforehand and turned to the left in an attempted evasive manoeuvre. After initially striking trees, the transport continued rolling to port until it slammed into the slope in a nearly inverted attitude.

An investigative board attributed the accident to a navigational error made by one or both of the aircraft's two navigators, both of whom satisfied the rigid requirements of MATS. In its report, the board noted that about 400 miles (650km) from Naha, the winds had shifted from the west to the east, which could have caused 44-9096 to drift off course. The pilot of another C-54 that had flown the route approximately 5 hours earlier in fact reported that his aircraft had drifted more than 30 miles (50km) off course and required a course correction of 40 degrees. Furthermore, the cloud coverage in the area would have prevented the crew of 44-9096 from determining their position visually.

It was not known whether the Long-Range Aid (Loran) navigational equipment with which the C-54 was equipped had been used. One of the recommendations made in the report was a requirement for an aircraft to immediately climb to a minimum safety altitude if at any time its position could not be established.

28 JANUARY 1951 (c.08:40)

Location	*Near An-tung, Taiwan*
Operator	*Royal Air Force*
Aircraft type	*Short Sunderland (PP107)*

The four-engine flying boat crashed in mountainous terrain during a flight to Hong Kong from Iwakuni, Japan. The burnt wreckage was later found at an approximate elevation of 5,000ft (1,500m) with no survivors among the 16 British servicemen aboard, including a crew of five; two of the victims were not on the original manifest. The cause was probably related to the bad weather conditions in which the accident occurred.

22 MARCH 1951 (c.23:50)

Location	*North Atlantic Ocean*
Operator	*US Air Force*
Aircraft type	*Douglas C-124A (49-244)*

Although the exact circumstances of this disaster could not be determined, a mid-air explosion or catastrophic structural failure was suspected in the loss of the four-engine transport, which in its last position report had been 750 miles (1,200km) west of Limerick, Ireland. Searchers recovered pieces of floating wreckage from the aircraft approximately 600 miles (965km) off Ireland's south-west coast. Among the 53 American servicemen aboard (40 passengers and a crew of 13), no survivors were found.

Operated by the Strategic Air Command, the C-124 had last stopped at Loring Air Force Base, near Limestone, Maine, during a transatlantic flight originating at Walker Air Force Base, near Roswell, New Mexico. Its ultimate destination was RAF Mildenhall, Suffolk, England. The aircraft had been flying in darkness, and the weather along the route consisted of extensive formations of cumulus clouds, with bases of 2,500–3,000ft (750–1,000m) and tops generally at 7,000–8,000ft (2,000–2,500m), and scattered build-ups to 13,000ft (4,000m), the latter being accompanied by showers. Examination of the recovered debris revealed that a post-crash blaze had occurred, although no further conclusions could be made.

8 APRIL 1951 (c.11:35)

Location	*Near Charleston, West Virginia, USA*
Operator	*US Air Force*
Aircraft type	*Douglas C-47D (43-48298)*

The transport crashed and burst into flames about 5 miles (10km) north-east of Kanawha County Airport, which served Charleston, and where it was to have landed. Including a crew of three, all 21 American servicemen aboard were killed; one of the passengers succumbed to his injuries nine days later. Most of the victims had been on their way from Godman Air Force Base, in neighbouring Kentucky, to attend a funeral for a fellow flyer killed in a previous crash.

Prior to the accident, 43-48298 had been cleared from 5,000ft to 3,500ft (1,500m to 1,050m), and in his last radio message, the pilot announced the initiation of a procedural turn shortly after he reported being over the locator beacon at 2,300ft (700m) while on the outbound track during the automatic direction finder (ADF) instrument procedure approach to Runway 23. Subsequently, the C-47 struck a wooded hillside at an approximate elevation of 1,200ft (350m) and while proceeding on an approximate heading of 200 degrees with its undercarriage down and flaps retracted, the impact with the trees shearing off both wings. The local weather at the time consisted of an overcast estimated at 1,000ft (300m), with scattered clouds down to

The flaming wreckage of the US Air Force C-47, which crashed during an attempted landing at Charleston, West Virginia, USA. (UPI/Corbis-Bettmann)

200ft (60m), a visibility of 3 miles (5km) and a west-south-westerly wind of 10 knots. There was also fog and light rain in the area.

The most probable cause of the accident was the decision of the pilot to continue the approach in the adverse meteorological conditions and for trying to fly by visual reference, in the process failing to maintain the minimum safe altitude and to adhere to the proper pattern approved for an ADF procedure landing, coupled with a possible misreading of his altimeter. With regard to the latter theory, one of the occupants who initially survived the accident reported seeing the airport prior to the crash, and when considering the known height of the overcast, this would indicate that the aircraft was actually 1,000ft (c.300m) lower than the altitude reported by the pilot. The time lapse of only 2 minutes from his position report over the inner locator beacon and the beginning of the procedural turn further suggested that the actions of the pilot were what the investigative report described as 'distinctly hurried'.

Although the aircraft's instrument landing system indicator was inoperative, which would have prevented him from making a precision approach, this was not considered to have contributed to the accident, since the pilot was aware of this fact and thus able to plan his approach accordingly.

6 MAY 1951 (c.12:30)

Location	Near Albuquerque, New Mexico, USA
Operator	US Air Force
Aircraft type	Convair B-36D (49-2660)

The 10-engine strategic bomber crashed at Kirtland Air Force Base, killing 23 of its 25 crewmen. Both survivors, who had been seated in the rear part of its fuselage, were injured. A lack of lateral control was an apparent factor in the accident, which occurred as the aircraft attempted to land on Runway 08 during a 30-knot east-south-easterly wind, with gusts of up to 35 knots, and a visibility of 8 miles (13km) in blowing dust.

The pilot appeared to have difficulty maintaining the correct flight path, making constant corrections to keep the wings level and remain aligned with the runway centreline. Passing over the threshold with its wings level but to the left of the centreline, the B-36 banked to the right for correction, whereupon its starboard jet pod and No. 6 propeller struck the ground some 500ft (150m) down the runway. Following the initial impact, which tore off the propeller blades of the piston power plant, the pilot undoubtedly decided to go around. The aircraft climbed to about 200ft (60m) above airfield elevation with the No. 6 engine afire, then slammed to earth on a northerly heading and in a right wing-down attitude and burst into flames, its undercarriage extended at the time of the crash. A Douglas C-54 four-engine transport, a twin-engine Lockheed Lodestar and a single-engine Beechcraft Bonanza that had been parked at the air base were damaged by flying debris and/or fire.

27 OCTOBER 1951 (c.19:00)

Location	Near Flores, Peten, Guatemala
Operator	Fuerza Aérea Guatemalteca (Guatemalan Air Force)
Aircraft type	Douglas C-47 (FAG-0961)

The twin-engine transport, carrying Guatemalan radio stars who had been touring the country, crashed and burst into flames in a jungle area some 150 miles (250km) north-north-east of Guatemala City and approximately 1 mile (1.5km) from Santa Elena Airport, serving Flores, from where it had taken off shortly before. The accident occurred in darkness. All but two of the 29 persons aboard were killed, including the entire crew of four military personnel, and both survivors suffered serious injuries. Though not reported officially, authorities initially suspected that one of the passengers may have started a fire in the aircraft's cabin with a cigarette.

13 NOVEMBER 1951 (c.13:00)

Location	Near Besse-St-Anastaise, Auvergne, France
Operator	US Air Force
Aircraft type	Fairchild C-82A (45-57801A)

All 36 American servicemen aboard (32 passengers and four crew members) perished in the crash of the twin-engine transport about 30 miles (50km) south-west of Clermont-Ferrand, where its wreckage was located two days later. The aircraft had been en route from Rhein-Main Air Base, near Frankfurt, (West) Germany, to Bordeaux, France, when it struck a mountain peak at an approximate elevation of 5,600ft (1,700m), exploded and burned.

Around the time of the accident, the meteorological conditions at Clermont-Ferrand consisted of a low ceiling, with 6/8 cumulus clouds at around 3,000ft (1,000m), a visibility of 25 miles (40km) below the overcast and a west-south-westerly wind of 12 knots. Winds of up to 30 knots had been forecast in the area from Dijon to Bordeaux. At the time of impact, 45-57801A was both off course and 60 miles (100km) to the left of the proposed route. It was also some 400ft (120m) below the assigned cruising altitude, which probably resulted from the fact that it was being flown by hand at the time, with the autopilot found in the off position.

The accident was ascribed to improper operation of the aircraft by the pilot while under an instrument flight rules (IFR) clearance, with inadequate planning and his failure to compensate for the prevailing wind conditions and to properly utilise the available navigational aids in establishing his position considered as contributing factors.

30 DECEMBER 1951 (c.15:40)

Location	Near Roosevelt, Arizona, USA
Operator	US Air Force
Aircraft type	Douglas C-47D (44-76266)

The transport crashed and burned on a mountain 60 miles (100km) north-east of Phoenix, and all 28 American military personnel aboard perished, including four crew members. Most of the passengers were army cadets returning to the US Military Academy at West Point, New York, USA. The aircraft was to have landed at Williams Air Force Base, located about 25 miles (40km) south-east of Phoenix, while en route to Texas from Hamilton Air Force Base, in California, one segment of the transcontinental flight.

Cleared down to 6,000ft (1,800m) during the instrument let-down, the crew had last reported leaving 7,000ft (2,000m), which was the approximate elevation of the crash site. The local weather at the time was overcast, with a ceiling of 6,000ft (1,800m) and a visibility of 15 miles (25km) under the cloud base, accompanied by fog, and a south-westerly wind of 45 knots reported at Phoenix.

At the time of impact, 44-76266 was proceeding on a magnetic heading of 70 to 75 degrees, after having flown past its destination. The C-47 had in fact been some 50 miles (80km) further east of where the pilot believed he was when he initiated his descent, the navigational error apparently resulting from his failure to compensate for the wind conditions, which increased its ground speed, combined with the probable failure of the aircraft's radio compass.

26 AUGUST 1952 (c.07:00)

Location   Near Khewra, West Pakistan
Operator   Royal Pakistan Air Force
Aircraft type Bristol 170 (G783)

The twin-engine transport crashed and burned about 100 miles (150km) north-west of Lahore, from where it had

A US Air Force Fairchild C-82 transport, identical to the aircraft that crashed into a mountain in France. (Fairchild Aircraft)

taken off earlier, killing all 18 persons aboard. Except for one civilian, the victims were all Pakistani military personnel. The aircraft had been on an internal flight to Peshawar when it plummeted into hilly terrain, possibly after a power plant malfunction, although officially no cause was given.

6 SEPTEMBER 1952 (c.15:40)

Location   Near Aldershot, Hampshire, England
Operator   de Havilland Aircraft
Aircraft type de Havilland 110 (WG236)

As it was performing at the Farnborough Air Show, the jet fighter disintegrated about 1.5 miles (2.5km) from the public enclosure area, and one of its two engines then plummeted into a crowd of spectators. Thirty persons were killed in the disaster, including both crewmen of the aircraft; about 60 others on the ground suffered injuries. The accident sequence began with a supersonic dive from an approximate height of 40,000ft (12,000m). After civilian test pilot John Derry levelled off and made a low pass along the runway, the aircraft circled in a tight left-hand, high-speed bank. As it returned to level flight from this turn and then began an upward roll, the break-up occurred at an approximate height of 500ft (150m) above the ground and at an estimated speed of 650mph (1,050kmh).

An examination of the distribution of the wreckage, which

A spectator's snapshot captures the moment of impact of a section of the de Havilland 110, the crash of which killed both crewmen and 28 persons on the ground. (Associated Press)

was supported by the analysis of an amateur motion picture taken of the accident, showed that the starboard outer wing failed first, followed by the separation of the port outer wing section. The subsequent rapid pitch-up of trim caused a more general disintegration, with the aircraft's cockpit section, power plants and tailplane breaking away due to abnormal gravitational forces.

The initial failure was believed to have resulted from heavy 'suction' loading on the upper and lower wing surfaces, combined with vibration or wing 'flutter'. (It was noted in the investigative report that intermittent wing vibration had been noted previously in both flying prototypes of the de Havilland 110.) Considerable modification was made on the type, including thicker ribs and reinforced stringers in the wing, before its acceptance as a carrier combat jet. A new set of rules was also introduced to guarantee greater safety in exhibition flying events taking place in the UK, and since that action, no member of the public has been killed at a British air show.

16 OCTOBER 1952 (time unknown)

Location	*Near Kangnung, Kangwon-do, South Korea*
Operator	*US Air Force*
Aircraft type	*Curtiss C-46D (44-77538)*

The twin-engine transport crashed in the Sea of Japan with 25 American servicemen aboard, including a crew of four. A massive search failed to locate any trace of the aircraft, and only two bodies were found, one, which had washed ashore,

being identified as a passenger; both victims wore life vests. There were no survivors from the crash, the circumstances of which were unknown. Having taken off from a military base shortly before 01:00 local time, on an internal South Korean flight that should have lasted about 40 minutes, the C-46 was last observed by the control tower operator as it climbed into the early-morning darkness. The weather along the route was clear, but the winds were believed to have been strong at higher altitudes.

7 NOVEMBER 1952 (c.03:00)

Location	*Near Summit, Territory of Alaska, USA*
Operator	*US Air Force*
Aircraft type	*Fairchild C-119C (51-2560A)*

During an intra-territorial Alaskan flight from Elmendorf Air Force Base, near Anchorage, to the town of Big Delta, the twin-engine transport crashed in the vicinity of Mount McKinley, some 150 miles (250km) south-west of Fairbanks. The wreckage was located about a week later at an approximate elevation of 12,000ft (3,700m), with no survivors among the 19 American military personnel aboard (14 passengers and a crew of five).

Occurring in darkness and local weather conditions consisting of an overcast of 5,000ft (1,500m), a visibility of 15 miles (25km) and a gentle breeze from a north-north-westerly direction, the accident apparently resulted from a navigational error. The course deviation that led to the crash may have resulted from the confusion between two radio range stations associated with precipitation static. A possible contributing factor was the absence on the aircraft of an additional automatic direction finder (ADF) or a high-frequency receiver, which could have been used for obtaining immediate fixes, coupled with insufficient navigational aids on the ground.

14 NOVEMBER 1952 (c.14:45)

Location	*Near Songch'on-ni, Kyonggi-do, South Korea*
Operator	*US Air Force*
Aircraft type	*Fairchild C-119C (51-2551A)*

All 44 American servicemen aboard (37 passengers and a crew of seven) were killed in the crash of the twin-engine transport, which took place some 20 miles (30km) east of Seoul. En route from Ashiya Air Base in Japan, the aircraft struck a mountain and burned while approaching to land at a US military base, designated K-16, using automatic direction finder (ADF) instrument procedures. Its undercarriage still retracted, the C-119 was on a west-south-westerly heading and flying level longitudinally, though banked slightly to the right, when it crashed at an elevation of about 2,000ft (600m).

The base weather at the time of the accident was overcast, with solid coverage at approximately 3,000ft (1,000m) and scattered clouds down to around 1,500ft (500m), which obscured the tops of the surrounding mountains, including the one hit by 51-2551A. The visibility was about 7 miles (11km). Some 3 minutes before the crash, the pilot reported initiating a procedural turn, and witnesses on the ground reported seeing the aircraft tracking back towards the homing beacon. The correct procedure required the initiation of a turn at 3,500ft (1,050m) about 5 miles (10km) from the navigational aid. There was no evidence of inaccuracy in the aircraft's pressure altimeter reading or any indication of power plant failure. It was recommended in the investigative report that pilots conducting an ADF letdown strictly adhere to prescribed procedures.

15 NOVEMBER 1952 (time unknown)

Location	*Territory of Alaska, USA*
Operator	*US Air Force*
Aircraft type	*Fairchild C-119C (51-2570)*

One in a formation of five aircraft on an intra-territorial flight from Elmendorf Air Force Base, near Anchorage, to Kodiak Naval Air Station, the twin-engine transport vanished with 20 American military personnel aboard (15 passengers and five crewmen). The search for 51-2570 was finally abandoned one month later. The C-119 had been cruising at 8,000ft

A US Air Force C-119 transport, two of which crashed fatally in Alaska and a third in South Korea during the month of November 1952. (Fairchild Aircraft)

(2,500m) under an instrument flight rules (IFR) clearance. A radar plot of an aircraft, probably 51-2570, was established on a course parallel to the airway until 12:16 local time, while the targets of the other transports in the group were tracked approximately on course. The error had been detected by air defence surveillance radar, but reports received from the pilot stating that he was on course led to the assumption from the Elemendorf air-traffic controller monitoring the flight that the echo had been that of another aircraft.

The loss of 51-2570 was believed to have resulted from precipitation static that caused confusion between two different radio range stations. Subsequent to this and the previous C-119 accident, the US Civil Aeronautics Board agreed to replace the low-frequency facilities extensively used in Alaska with more reliable very-high-frequency omni-directional range (VOR) installations.

22 NOVEMBER 1952 (c.20:15)

Location	Territory of Alaska, USA
Operator	US Air Force
Aircraft type	Douglas C-124A (51-107A)

All 52 American servicemen aboard (41 passengers and a crew of 11) perished when the four-engine transport, which was bound for Elmendorf Air Force Base, near Anchorage,

struck the south slope of Mount Gannett some 50 miles (80km) east of its destination. The aircraft was being flown by the Military Air Transport Service (MATS) and was en route from McChord Air Force Base, in Washington state, when it crashed at an approximate elevation of 9,000ft (2,700m), or about 1,000ft (300m) below the top of the mountain, disintegrated and burned.

Located a few days later and subsequently identified, its wreckage lay buried in snow, and neither it nor the remains of the victims could be recovered. It was dark at the time of the accident, and the weather conditions in the area consisted of an indefinite ceiling of 600ft (180m), with a visibility of 2 miles (3km) in fog. The crosswinds encountered by 51-107A following its passage of Middleton Island may have been between 60 and 80 knots, more than double that forecast. Under the circumstances, the course correction made by the pilot would have been insufficient to compensate for the northward drift of the aircraft, which would account for its deviation from the proper track by some 30 miles (50km).

The crew had been operating under an instrument flight rules (IFR) clearance, but static and terrain features could

The aftermath of the disastrous C-124A accident at Larson Air Force Base, which claimed the lives of 87 servicemen. (Wide World Photos)

have interfered with signals from the Elmendorf radio range station, and the crew had also faced icing conditions. Subsequently, the minimum height along the portion of the route where the disaster occurred was raised from 9,000ft to 11,000ft (2,700m to 3,400m).

28 NOVEMBER 1952 (c.00:50)

Location	Near Tacoma, Washington, USA
Operator	US Air Force
Aircraft type	Douglas C-54G

The four-engine aircraft, which was on a Military Air Transport Service (MATS) flight from Alaska and carrying American servicemen and their dependants, crashed in early-morning darkness and conditions of poor visibility, with fog and a low overcast, killing 37 persons aboard. Among the fatalities were the seven members of the crew, all air force personnel. Two passengers, including an 8-year-old boy whose family was killed, survived with injuries. After abandoning a ground-controlled approach to land at McChord Air Force Base due to the weather, the pilot announced his intention to proceed to Great Falls, in neighbouring Montana, but the aircraft's No. 3 power plant failed. Subsequently, the C-54 struck trees, slammed into a clearing approximately 1 mile (1.5km) south-west of the airfield and burst into flames.

20 DECEMBER 1952 (c.06:30)

Location	Near Moses Lake, Washington, USA
Operator	US Air Force
Aircraft type	Douglas C-124A (50-100)

Operated by the Tactical Air Command (TAC) and on a joint operation to carry personnel on Christmas leave to US air bases in Texas, Tennessee, South Carolina and Florida, and to pick up a helicopter and aircraft parts, the four-engine transport crashed and burned at Larson Air Force Base about a minute after it had taken off. Killed in the disaster were 87 of the 115 American servicemen aboard; among the survivors, who included five members of the aircraft's crew of ten, all but six suffered injuries.

The crash occurred in pre-dawn darkness and as a light snow was falling. The sky was overcast, with an indefinite ceiling of 500ft (150m) and a visibility of 2 miles (3km), and the wind blowing out of the north at 13 knots. It was determined that the aircraft's rudder and elevator gust locks, designed to keep these control surfaces fixed in windy conditions while on the ground, had not been disengaged by the crew before take-off (the activating handle only having been advanced enough to release the throttle and aileron locks). This would have prevented free movement of the flight controls and thus the transport from gaining height after becoming airborne, accounting for the fact that it never got higher than approximately 100ft (30m) above the ground before it slammed into a snow-covered field beyond the end of the runway. Following the accident, a directive was sent out to all US Air Force commands flying the C-124

emphasising strict compliance with the existing requirement that pilots take steps to assure free movement of the control surfaces before taking off.

15 JANUARY 1953 (c.04:50)

Location	Mediterranean Sea
First aircraft	
Operator	Royal Air Force
Aircraft type	Vickers Valetta Mark 1 (VX562)
Second aircraft	
Operator	Royal Air Force
Aircraft type	Avro Lancaster (TX270)

The twin-engine transport and the four-engine bomber collided at an approximate altitude of 1,500ft (500m), and both then crashed some 100 miles (150km) north-west of the island of Malta. A total of 26 British service personnel lost their lives in the accident, including the Lancaster's seven crewmen; there were no survivors from either aircraft. The Valetta, carrying 16 passengers and a crew of three, had been en route from Malta to England and the Lancaster was on an anti-submarine exercise at the time of the collision, which occurred in pre-dawn darkness and thunderstorm activity, with heavy rain and hail having reduced the visibility to zero.

9 FEBRUARY 1953 (c.19:00)

Location	Near Cairo, Egypt
Operator	Egyptian Air Force
Aircraft type	Curtiss C-46 (1001)

During an internal flight from Al 'Arish to Almaza Airport, near Cairo, the twin-engine transport crashed into a hill east of its destination, the accident occurring in darkness and during a sandstorm. Among the 40 Egyptian military personnel aboard the aircraft, 29 were killed, the survivors suffering various injuries. Though not officially reported, the accident may have been related to mechanical failure.

18 MARCH 1953 (04:10)

Location	Random Island, Newfoundland, Canada
Operator	US Air Force
Aircraft type	Convair RB-36H (51-13721A)

Operated by the Strategic Air Command (SAC), the 10-engine strategic reconnaissance bomber had been on a simulated combat mission that originated in the Azores and was to have terminated at Rapid City Air Force Base, South Dakota, USA, when it crashed and burned near Smith Sound, and its 23 crewmen perished. Operating under instrument flight rules (IFR), the aircraft had flown at a low altitude over the Atlantic Ocean and was to have initiated a climb 20 miles (30km) from land. However, position reports received from the crew and known changes in the weather indicated that it encountered an unexpected tail-wind during the last half of the leg and reached landfall about 1½ hr before the navigator's estimated time of arrival.

The resulting accident occurred in darkness and during a low overcast, with a ceiling estimated at only 50–100ft (15–30m), which was accompanied by sleet, freezing drizzle and fog, conditions that had reduced the horizontal visibility from less than 700ft (200m) to zero. Its ground speed estimated to have been around 230mph (370kmh), 51-13721A was in level flight when it struck a hill at an approximate height of 800ft (250m), only about 100ft (30m) below its crest, the initial impact shearing off the left wing. Later that same day, a US Air Force B-29 that was searching for the missing RB-36 itself crashed in St George's Bay, between Nova Scotia and Cape Breton Island, and its ten crewmen were also killed. The installation where 51-13721A had been based was later named in honour of its then-commanding officer, Brigadier General Richard Ellsworth, one of the victims of the RB-36 accident.

18 JUNE 1953 (c.16:30)

Location	*Near Kodaira, Japan*
Operator	*US Air Force*
Aircraft type	*Douglas C-124A (51-137A)*

The first aviation disaster known to have claimed more than 100 lives occurred near the end of the Korean War and during the movement of troops back to duty status following a five-day leave in Japan. All 129 American servicemen aboard, including a crew of seven, were killed when the four-engine transport crashed some 25 miles (40km) west of Tokyo and approximately 3.5 miles (6km) north-east of Tachikawa Air Base, from where it had taken off earlier. Originally bound for Kimpo Air Base, near Seoul, South Korea, the aircraft had turned back towards its departure point, the pilot reporting that its No. 1 power plant was shut down and the corresponding propeller feathered. Giving his height

The first known aviation disaster to claim more than 100 lives was this crash of a US Air Force C-124A near Tokyo, Japan, on 18 June 1953. (UPI/Corbis-Bettmann)

as 1,200ft (350m), he then accepted an offer for a ground-controlled approach; later, the tower controller heard over the radio the pilot, in intra-cockpit conversation, excitedly request 'More power, more power'.

The C-124 was on the down-wind leg of the airfield circuit and proceeding in a due northerly direction when it faded from the radar scope. At the time and location of the accident, the weather consisted of a broken overcast at around 1,000ft (300m), a visibility of 1 mile (1.5km) and a south-easterly wind of 6 knots. There was fog and light rain in the immediate area, with broken clouds down to only 400ft (120m). The power plant failure that indirectly led to the disaster was attributed to a sheared generator shaft, but the subsequent crash was blamed on the crew's premature application of full flaps during the three-engine let-down, which apparently resulted in a loss of flying speed. Its undercarriage still retracted, the aircraft plummeted into a field in a nose and left wing-down attitude, on a heading of 140 degrees and with no forward velocity, exploded and burned. The flight had lasted about 5 minutes.

17 JULY 1953 (c.23:15)

Location	*Near Milton, Florida, USA*
Operator	*US Marine Corps*
Aircraft type	*Fairchild R4Q-2 (131663)*

The twin-engine transport crashed and burned about 20 miles (30km) north-north-east of Pensacola, moments after it had taken off from Whiting Naval Air Station, on a domestic US flight to the Norfolk naval base in Virginia, carrying as passengers members of the Reserve Officer's Training Corps (ROTC). All but two of the 46 American servicemen aboard lost their lives in the accident, while the survivors, one a passenger and the other a member of the aircraft's crew of six, suffered injuries.

Its undercarriage and flaps fully retracted, the R4Q slammed into a wooded area in a wings-level attitude approximately 4,000ft (1,200m) from the departure end and to the left of the extended centreline of Runway 31, which it had used. The crash occurred on what was described as an 'extremely black' night, and there were patches of fog in the area despite an unlimited ceiling and a visibility of 10 miles (16km). The co-pilot, who was flying the aircraft at the time of the take-off, must have been unable visually to denote obstacles in his flight path or to adequately discern his attitude owing to the absence of both a distinguishable horizon and reference lights in his forefront, and had apparently failed to maintain a sufficient rate of climb during the crucial phase of operation after becoming airborne.

A retired marine aviator with experience in the type later noted that the faster acceleration of such aircraft as the R4Q affected its gyros and could result in an instrument indication opposite to what was happening, i.e. climbing instead of descending, which led pilots to change procedures during instrument take-offs. It was not known, however, whether this factor contributed to the crash of 131663.

17 DECEMBER 1953 (c.06:50)

Location	Guam, Mariana Islands
Operator	US Air Force
Aircraft type	Boeing B-29MR (44-87741)

Flown by the Strategic Air Command (SAC), the bomber crashed into an officer's housing area at Anderson Air Force Base, located near the tip of the island and some 15 miles (25km) north-east of Agana, while attempting an emergency landing with one of its four engines out. Among the 19 persons killed were five of the 16 American servicemen aboard the aircraft and eight civilians on the ground, six of them children. Eight others suffered injuries, four of whom were survivors from the B-29.

About 15 minutes after 44-87741 had taken off from the island of Kwajalein, its No. 2 power plant developed high oil and cylinder temperatures and was smoking and throwing sparks from around the cowl flaps; the power plant was then shut down and the crew diverted to Guam. As it was turning left on the base leg of the circuit, the B-29 overshot the final approach course to Runway 07-Right. Its bank angle increased to about 80 degrees, whereupon the bomber stalled, plunged into the residential area and exploded. The weather, which at the time consisted of a broken overcast at 800ft (2,500m), with a visibility of 8 miles (13km) and a west-south-westerly wind of 8 knots, was apparently not a factor as the aircraft had been under the clouds while in the traffic pattern of the base.

6 JANUARY 1954 (c.17:20)

Location	Near Aldbury, Hertfordshire, England
Operator	Royal Air Force
Aircraft type	Vickers Valetta (WJ474)

All but one of the 17 British servicemen aboard were killed, including the entire crew of four, when the twin-engine transport crashed in a wooded area some 30 miles (50km)

All but one of the 17 occupants lost their lives in the crash of the RAF Valetta transport, which took place on 6 January 1954. (UPI/Corbis-Bettmann)

north-west of London. The surviving passenger was seriously injured. The accident occurred in darkness and during a snow shower, with an estimated visibility of only 100ft (30m), about 4 minutes after the aircraft had taken off from Bovingdon airfield on a communications flight to RAF Thorney Island, near Portsmouth. For unknown reasons, the aircraft had lost height and descended into the ground, with no evidence being found of power plant or other mechanical failure.

1 FEBRUARY 1954 (c.13:50)

Location	Off Hokkaido, Japan
Operator	US Air Force
Aircraft type	Curtiss C-46D (44-78027A)

Operating on a scheduled internal Japanese service originating at Tachikawa Air Base, near Tokyo, and carrying 35 American servicemen (30 passengers and a crew of five), the twin-engine transport had last taken off from Misawa, the second of two en-route stops, bound for its ultimate destination of Chitose Airport, located near Sapporo. It had nearly completed this last leg of the flight when the pilot reported a fire in the cargo compartment, and that he may have to ditch. Two minutes later, in his last message, he radioed, '. . . I've lost control of the aircraft . . . we're going in!'

The C-46 crashed in the Pacific Ocean, approximately 20 miles (30km) south of Tomakomai, and in meteorological conditions consisting of a low overcast, with scattered clouds at 2,000ft (600m), a visibility of about 10 miles (15km) beneath them and a wind out of the north at 5 knots. Searchers recovered the bodies of two victims; there were no survivors.

4 MARCH 1954 (c.14:30)

Location	*Near St Etienne-de-Tinée, Provence, France*
Operator	*US Air Force*
Aircraft type	*Douglas C-47A (42-24096A)*

The transport crashed in the Alps some 60 miles (100km) north of Nice, and all 20 American servicemen aboard, including its two pilots, were killed. Proceeding on a heading of about 305 degrees while on a flight with an ultimate destination of Hahn, (West) Germany, which had originated at Wheelus Field, near Tripoli, Libya, and last stopped at Rome, Italy, the aircraft struck a mountain at an approximate elevation of 8,000ft (2,500m), disintegrated and burned. Much of the wreckage was then carried down the slope in an avalanche.

Only receiving an oral briefing about the weather, the pilot had not requested a cross-sectional forecast for the intended route. The subsequent accident occurred in instrument meteorological conditions, with falling snow and a low overcast. Only winds of 60 to 75 knots, twice that reported by pilots flying the same route on the day of the crash, could account for the distance that 42-24096A had drifted off the prescribed course. The required velocity would have been slightly less had no wind drift correction been made.

19 MARCH 1954 (c.22:30)

Location	*Near Lothian, Maryland, USA*
Operator	*US Air Force*
Aircraft type	*Fairchild C-119F (51-7993)*

All 18 American servicemen aboard (12 passengers and a crew of six) were killed in the crash of the twin-engine transport, which took place some 15 miles (25km) west of Andrews Air Force Base, and just east of the Potomac River. The aircraft, on a domestic US flight from Oklahoma to Mitchell Field, on Long Island, New York, slammed to earth and burned about 20 minutes after its departure from Bolling Air Force Base, near Washington, DC, which was an intermediate stop. Before the crash it had been circling over a radio beacon under visual flight rules (VFR) procedures, awaiting instrument flight rules (IFR) clearance before proceeding on towards its destination. Factors apparently contributing to the accident were: an attempt to maintain VFR flight at night and in rain (although the exact weather conditions at the time and scene of the crash were not known), and possible crew fatigue.

2 JULY 1954 (c.12:00)

Location	*Near Salvador, Bahia, Brazil*
Operator	*Força Aérea Brasileira (Brazilian Air Force)*
Aircraft type	*Lockheed C-28 (2901)*

After completing an internal flight from Fortaleza, Ceara, the twin-engine transport crashed while attempting to land at the Salvador military base, killing all 20 persons aboard. The passengers included some civilian dependants, five of them children; the rest of the victims were military personnel, among them the aircraft's four crewmen. Though not officially reported, the accident was believed to have resulted from power plant failure, which occurred during the landing approach, after which the C-28 plummeted to earth and burst into flames.

27 AUGUST 1954 (22:11)

Location	*Near Rapid City, South Dakota, USA*
Operator	*US Air Force*
Aircraft type	*Convair RB-36H (51-13722)*

Having already completed five landing approaches to Ellsworth Air Force Base, using ground-controlled (GCA) and plan-position indicator (aerial mapping) procedures, the strategic reconnaissance bomber, operated by the Strategic Air Command, was making a sixth when it crashed and burned about 2 miles (3km) north-north-west of the military installation. All but one of the aircraft's 27 crewmen lost their lives, including two who succumbed within five days of the accident; the seriously injured survivor was the designated first pilot.

Configured with its undercarriage retracted and flaps set at 20 degrees, the RB-36 was proceeding on a south-south-easterly heading towards Runway 12 in a near-level attitude at an indicated air speed of 145mph (230kmh) when it slammed into the ground some 9,000ft (2,700m) from its threshold and approximately 200ft (60m) to the right of its extended centreline. The impact point was on a bluff around 150ft (50m) above airfield elevation. It was dark at the time, although the weather conditions were good, with the sky cloudless and a visibility of 15 miles (25km). The wind was out of the south at 6 knots.

It was concluded that fatigue had apparently played a role in the accident, with most of the members of the crew having not received adequate sleep prior to their mission. The investigative report also noted that despite being 'extremely capable', the crewman at the controls of 51-13722 when it crashed was relatively inexperienced as a B-36 pilot, and was possibly not being properly monitored by the commander just beforehand. Additional factors mentioned in the report were that the airfield approach lights were inoperative, as were the obstruction lights on the hills to the north-west of the base, although the crew had been advised of the latter situation by the GCA unit.

24 OCTOBER 1954 (c.17:50)

Location	*Near Limone Piemonte, Cuneo, Italy*
Operator	*US Air Force*
Aircraft type	*Douglas C-47A (43-16044)*

The transport was bound for Lyon, France, from Rome, Italy, when it crashed in the Maritime Alps near the border of the two countries. Its wreckage was located nearly a week later, with no survivors among the 21 American servicemen aboard (18 passengers and a crew of three).

An error in planning on the part of the pilot proved to be the primary factor in this accident. Specifically, the instrument flight plan he had filed indicated a cruising height that was lower than the authorised minimum altitude on the portion of the route wherein the accident occurred. The flight plan also contained a bearing error of 13 degrees, possibly resulting from confusion between the Poretta radio beacon and Bastia, which is also located on the island of Corsica but some 15 miles (25km) further north. Proceeding on a north-westerly track at a height of 8,500ft (2,600m), the C-47 slammed into the mountainous terrain and disintegrated. There was no post-impact fire.

The weather at Lyon, about 175 miles (280km) north-west of where the crash occurred, was forecast to have consisted of broken cloud layers at 8,000ft (2,500m) and at 2,000ft (600m), with a visibility of around 5 miles (10km) in light rain. The winds encountered by the aircraft, which may have been an additional contributing factor in the accident, were blowing from a south-westerly direction and may have reached a velocity of 45 knots.

A giant, 10-engine Convair B-36 bomber of the US Air Force, similar to the aircraft that crashed near Ellsworth Air Force Base in South Dakota. (General Dynamics)

30/31 OCTOBER 1954 (time unknown)

Location	*North Atlantic Ocean*
Operator	*US Navy*
Aircraft type	*Lockheed R7V-1 (128441)*

The four-engine transport had taken off from Patuxent River Naval Air Station, in Maryland, USA, bound for Kenitra (Port Lyautey), Morocco, with a planned stop in the Azores. Most of the 42 persons aboard were American service personnel, including 21 on and off-duty crew members, although the passengers also included seven civilian dependants, nearly all of them children. Proceeding in darkness and 'intermittent' instrument meteorological conditions, the aircraft was last heard from when at a position of approximately 300 miles (480km) east of Ocean City, Maryland.

Within 90 minutes of that radio transmission, sent at 23:30 local time, a possibly sudden and catastrophic event of an unknown nature claimed 128441 and its occupants. A search by aircraft and ships, which began after the transport was reported overdue, went on for four days, but failed to find any survivors, bodies or wreckage.

A US Navy Lockheed R7V-1, a military version of the Super Constellation airliner and the type lost during a transatlantic flight. (US Navy)

16 NOVEMBER 1954 (time unknown)

Location	*Near Huayllay, Pasco, Peru*
Operator	*Fuerza Aérea del Perú (Peruvian Air Force)*
Aircraft type	*Douglas C-47 (403)*

Operated by the military airline Transportes Aéreos Militares and on a domestic passenger flight to Lima from Pucallpa, Loreto, the aircraft disappeared over the Andes Mountains with 24 persons aboard, including a crew of three military personnel. No survivors were found at the crash site, which was located four days later, about 100 miles (150km) north-east of the transport's destination.

11 JANUARY 1955 (c.21:00)

Location	*North Atlantic Ocean*
First aircraft	
Operator	*Royal Air Force*
Aircraft type	*Avro Shackleton Mark 2 (WG531)*
Second aircraft	
Operator	*Royal Air Force*
Aircraft type	*Avro Shackleton Mark 2 (WL743)*

Both four-engine patrol aircraft were on training flights out of St Eval air base, in Cornwall, England, when lost with a

total of 18 crewmen aboard (nine assigned to each). Though never proven, there was speculation that they had collided in darkness and possibly during a rain shower. The accident could have happened less than 5 minutes after the last radio message from one of them. More than a decade later, the No. 4 power plant identified as belonging to WL743 was inadvertently found by fishermen off the southern coast of Ireland, between the Skelligs and Bull Rock.

22 MARCH 1955 (c.02:00)

Location	*Oahu, Territory of Hawaii, USA*
Operator	*US Navy*
Aircraft type	*Douglas R6D-1 (131612)*

All 66 persons aboard perished when the four-engine transport crashed and burned in the Waianae Mountain range, some 15 miles (25km) north-west of Honolulu. Most of the victims were American servicemen, including the nine members of the crew, although the passengers included two civilian dependants – the wife and 3-year-old daughter – of a navy-enlisted man who was also on the aircraft.

Operated by the Military Air Transport Service (MATS)

An RAF Avro Shackleton patrol bomber, two of which were lost off the coast of England during training manoeuvres. (British Aerospace)

and originally bound for Travis Air Force Base, in California, the R6D was returning to land at Hickam Field, from where it had taken off earlier, because its high-frequency radio transmitters were inoperative. Communications were not affected when the aircraft came within close proximity to the islands. Cleared for landing, the transport was last reported descending out of 3,000ft (1,000m) before it slammed into the slope and exploded at an approximate elevation of 1,200ft (350m), or some 750ft (230m) below the peak of the mountain. Just prior to impact, its landing lights were turned on and it had banked to the right in what might have been an evasive manoeuvre.

Due to apparent navigational miscalculations by the flight crew as to their position and direction, the transport was at the moment of the crash some 8 miles (13km) north of the proper approach pattern and flying at an insufficient height to clear the terrain. It was dark at the time, and the meteorological conditions in the area, which were considered a contributing factor in the disaster, consisted of scattered clouds and rain showers, with a visibility of around 7 miles (11km). The wind was calm. No deficiencies were found in the Honolulu radio range or very-high-frequency omni-directional range (VOR) stations or other facilities.

11 AUGUST 1955 (c.14:20)

Location	*Near Edelweiler, (West) Germany*
First aircraft	
Operator	*US Air Force*
Aircraft type	*Fairchild C-119G (53-3222)*
Second aircraft	
Operator	*US Air Force*
Aircraft type	*Fairchild C-119G (53-7841)*

The two aircraft involved in this disaster were members of a flight of nine Flying Boxcar transports participating in a joint US military exercise out of Echterdingen Air Base, located near Stuttgart, their passengers all army soldiers. Proceeding in a westerly direction in good meteorological conditions, with a visibility of more than 10 miles (15km) and layers of scattered clouds at 3,000ft (1,000m) and at 20,000ft (6,000m), the group had begun a left turn back towards the east at a height of 4,000ft (1,200m), or about 2,000ft (600m) above the terrain, when 3222 reported losing its left power plant and that it was leaving the formation. Shortly afterwards, 3222 collided with 7841. Both transports plummeted to the ground some 30 miles (50km) west of the city of Stuttgart, disintegrated and burned. A total of 66 American servicemen perished in the accident, 46 aboard 7841 and 20 aboard 3222; among the victims were ten air force personnel, the two five-member crews assigned to each aircraft. There were no survivors.

After its final message had been acknowledged by

7841

3222

The diagram illustrates the formation of C-119 transports, indicating the two involved in the disastrous mid-air collision on 11 August 1955. (US Air Force)

the lead aircraft, which then cleared it to a heading of 80 degrees, 3222 started a descending turn to the left, but as it was passing under 7841, the latter inexplicably also began to descend in a left bank, resulting in the collision. The underside of the nose section of 7841 struck the left vertical stabiliser of 3222, the impact severing the latter's starboard boom and tail section. The collision could have rendered the controls of 7841 inoperative, and/or sent flying debris into the cockpit, incapacitating the two pilots. Falling into a spin, 3222 crashed into a wooded area in a flat attitude, while 7841 continued straight-and-level for a few seconds before going into a right turn, finally crashing into a field in a steep nose-down, inverted attitude. Whereas 3222 used the correct procedures in exiting the group, 7841 had failed to maintain its position in the formation.

A soldier stands guard at the crash site of one Flying Boxcar. (Associated Press)

17 FEBRUARY 1956 (c.13:45)

Location	*Near Niles, California, USA*
Operator	*US Marine Corps*
Aircraft type	*Douglas R5D-2 (39116)*

All 40 American servicemen aboard (35 passengers and a crew of five) perished when the four-engine transport crashed about 20 miles (30km) south-east of Oakland. Operating under an instrument flight rules (IFR) clearance, the aircraft had been en route from El Toro Marine Air Station, in Southern California, and was to have landed at Alameda Naval Air Station, located on the east side of San Francisco Bay.

After receiving instructions from Oakland approach control to maintain at least 1,000ft (300m) above the clouds, it entered a holding pattern and circled for about half an hour before being cleared for a straight-in radio range approach from the Newark fan-marker beacon. It was observed by a ground witness proceeding in a westerly direction under a low overcast, and in a level or slight nose-down attitude, and to disappear into the clouds. Moments later, and while on a magnetic heading of approximately 270 degrees, the R5D slammed into Sunol Ridge at an approximate elevation of 1,500ft (500m), or almost 200ft (60m) below the crest of the hill, exploded and burned. The cloudy conditions in the area were accompanied by occasional squalls, containing light to moderate rain, one of which obscured the terrain struck by 39116.

Examination of the wreckage revealed no evidence of material failure in the aircraft, nor any indication of altimeter mis-setting. The accident was attributed to the non-adherence of the flight crew to the holding pattern, and to their departure from the radio beacon and let-down in an unprescribed manner. These irregularities may have resulted from one or more of the following factors: improper instrument procedures; misinterpretation of radio-navigational signals; an incorrect automatic direction finder (ADF) indication; miscalculation of time while on the outbound leg of the circuit; or an attempt to proceed in the instrument meteorological conditions under visual flight rules (VFR) procedures.

Apparently unable to descend in a standard four-minute pattern to 3,500ft (1,050m), the specified final approach initiation altitude, the pilots extended the outbound leg in order to reach the Newark radio beacon at that height. This took the aircraft to an area where the ground was visible, which must have been misidentified as the flat terrain in the vicinity of Niles and nearby Irvington, located to the west of its actual position. The descent continued to 1,500ft (500m), with the R5D flying in and out of the clouds, the pilots firmly convinced they would clear all obstacles at this height as they

The crash of the US Marine Corps R5D into a ridge claimed 40 lives during a landing approach to Alameda Naval Air Station in California. (UPI/Corbis-Bettmann)

A Douglas C-118A transport of the type that crashed after taking off from McGuire Air Force Base on a MATS flight. (McDonnell Douglas)

proceeded towards the Oakland radio range station (their belief would have been reinforced by the high background signals of the navigational aid that they would have been receiving at this location). It was also possible that the aircraft had been in or near the correct pattern and that the crew elected to make an unprescribed left-hand turn back to the Newark homing beacon when VFR conditions were observed to the south-east.

It was noted in the investigative report that the area where the crash took place had a history of pilot disorientation and several major accidents. The standard instrument approach chart used by pilots flying into the Alameda base lacked an annotation with regard to the minimum altitude at the point of the final approach fix, which was actually 2,000ft (600m) higher than that indicated, and a procedural change was one of the recommendations made in the report.

13 JULY 1956 (c.15:35)

Location	Near Browns Mills, New Jersey, USA
Operator	US Air Force
Aircraft type	Douglas C-118A (53-3301A)

This scheduled Military Air Transport Service (MATS) flight ended in disaster shortly after the aircraft had taken off from Runway 24 at McGuire Air Force Base, located on the grounds of the Fort Dix Military Reservation, some 20 miles (30km) south-west of Lakewood. Bound for Harmon Air Force Base, Newfoundland, Canada, the first segment of a transatlantic service with an ultimate destination of England, the four-engine transport had been airborne for approximately 2

The wreckage of the US Air Force C-118 is scattered among the trees following the crash that occurred in a thunderstorm. (Wide World Photos) minutes before it slammed into a wooded area some 2 miles (3km) from the end of the runway and shattered into pieces, although there was no post-impact fire. The crash claimed the lives of 46 persons, including all but two of the aircraft's ten air force crew members; though mostly comprised of US military personnel, the passengers included six American and British civilians who were among those killed. All 20 survivors suffered serious injuries.

Shortly before the accident, the weather in the area consisted of thunderstorm activity, with 'sheets' of rain, a ceiling of about 2,000ft (600m) and scattered clouds at 500ft (150m), and a visibility of 1 mile (1.5km). The wind was blowing out of the west at 10 knots, gusting to almost 30. Severe down-draughts were believed to have been present, and although no official cause was announced by air force authorities, an encounter with one or more of these vertical air currents apparently led to the uncontrolled descent of the aircraft into the ground. The fact that the C-118 had rear-facing passenger seats may have saved lives in this crash.

10 OCTOBER 1956 (c.22:00)

Location	North Atlantic Ocean
Operator	US Navy
Aircraft type	Douglas R6D-1 (131588)

Operated by the Military Air Transport Service (MATS), the aircraft had taken off from Royal Air Force Lakenheath, Suffolk, England, with an ultimate destination of McGuire Air Force Base, New Jersey, USA. It was carrying 59 American servicemen, including a crew of nine navy personnel; all the passengers were members of the US Air Force. With a planned stop at Lajes Air Base, in the Azores, the four-engine transport was on the first segment of the transatlantic flight when it met with disaster, the circumstances of which will probably for ever remain a mystery. Its last known position report was sent at 20:55 local time, at which time, and in accordance with its flight plan, the aircraft would have been cruising in darkness at an approximate height of 15,000ft (5,000m).

A search that began after it was reported missing failed to

A US Air Force Boeing RB-52B, serial number 52-8716, the same aircraft that crashed during a night training flight in November 1956. (Boeing)

find any survivors or victims' bodies. Subsequently, wreckage identified as belonging to the R6D, a life-raft and a main undercarriage gear leg, with the two wheels still attached, were recovered 250 miles (400km) south-west of Land's End, England, and examination of the tyres revealed traces of post-impact fire. Two aircraft that had flown the same course before and after 131588 described the weather along the route as consisting of a scattered to broken overcast, with cloud tops at around 5,000ft (1,500m). With regard to the possibility of a malicious act, it was noted in the investigative report that normal security measures had been in effect at the Lakenheath air base before the departure of the transport.

28 OCTOBER 1956 (c.22:00)

Location	Mediterranean Sea
Operator	Egyptian Air Force
Aircraft type	Ilyushin Il-14 (1101)

The Soviet-built twin-engine transport, its passengers including both military personnel and civilians, was shot down in darkness by an Israeli Meteor jet fighter during a flight to Cairo from Damascus, Syria, and all 16 persons aboard the Il-14 were killed. Not among the victims was the supreme commander of Egyptian armed forces, who had been misidentified by Israeli authorities as being a passenger on the aircraft and was the target of the attack.

30 NOVEMBER 1956 (c.22:00)

Location	Near Ballico, California, USA
Operator	US Air Force
Aircraft type	Boeing RB-52B (52-8716)

The worst-ever B-52 crash involving a single aircraft occurred about a year and a half after the first of the eight-engine jet bombers had entered service with the Strategic Air Command (SAC). A little less than 3 minutes after it had taken off from Castle Air Force Base, on a combat training mission, 52-8716 plunged to earth and disintegrated in a fiery explosion some 15 miles (25km) north-north-west of Merced, and all ten crewmen were killed. The accident occurred in darkness, but the weather was clear, with a slight breeze out of the west. At the moment of impact, the cleanly-configured aircraft was descending at an angle of about 5 degrees from the horizontal, in a slight right wing-down attitude and on an almost due northerly heading.

Investigation revealed no evidence of in-flight fire, explosion or structural failure, and that the crash apparently resulted from an abnormal nose-down trim condition which the pilots could not or did not correct due to an unknown malfunction or distraction. Subsequent to this accident, the minimum altitude for flap retraction in B-52 operations was raised to 1,000ft (300m), and pilots flying the type would also receive expanded training to include the importance of maintaining a positive rate of climb when retracting the flaps.

11 JANUARY 1957 (c.09:00)

Location	Near Buenos Aires, Argentina
Operator	Fuerza Aérea Argentina (Argentine Air Force)
Aircraft type	Vickers Viking 1B (T-11)

Operated by the military airline Lineas Aéreas del Estado (LADE) and on a scheduled domestic passenger flight bound for Mar del Plata, with an ultimate destination of Mendoza, the twin-engine transport crashed and burned immediately after taking off from Jorge Newbury Airport. The accident claimed the lives of 18 persons, one of whom was on the ground and the rest aboard the aircraft. Among the 16 injured survivors was the co-pilot, one member of the transport's crew of four military personnel. With the operation out of this airport by an aircraft the size of a Viking judged 'critical' even under normal circumstances due to runway length, T-11 had been attempting to take off during a crosswind that exceeded the maximum allowed, apparently resulting in a loss of control.

22 FEBRUARY 1957 (c.20:00)

Location	Near Yanggong-ni, Kyonggi-do, South Korea
Operator	US Air Force
Aircraft type	Douglas C-124A (51-141A)

Heavily laden with passengers, the four-engine transport had taken off from Runway 32 at Kimpo Air Base, bound for Japan. After reaching an approximate height of 800–1,000ft (250–300m), the No. 3 power plant backfired, and an emergency was then declared. As it was returning to the airfield, the same engine exploded, with flying debris disabling the No. 4 power plant and tearing a hole in the fuselage. Despite the application of maximum power on the two port engines, level flight could

not be maintained, and the C-124 continued descending until finally touching down, with its undercarriage still retracted, in a channel of the Han River, about 10 miles (15km) north of the base and 25 miles (40km) north-west of Seoul, coming to a stop on an ice-littered sand bar.

Among the 159 American service personnel aboard, 22 lost their lives, including three of the aircraft's ten air force crew members, one of them the co-pilot. The survivors, 24 of whom suffered varying degrees of injury, were evacuated from the crash scene by helicopter. Fire, which had erupted in the wing areas an estimated 15 minutes after the crash, eventually consumed most of the wreckage.

The cause of the initial power plant failure was not disclosed by military authorities. The resulting forced landing was carried out in darkness, but the meteorological conditions in the area were good, with the sky clear and a visibility of more than 10 miles (15km).

5 MARCH 1957 (c.11:00)

Location	Drayton, Berkshire, England
Operator	Royal Air Force
Aircraft type	Blackburn Beverley C Mark 1 (XH117)

Operated by Transport Command, the four-engine aircraft crashed about half an hour after it had taken off from Abingdon airfield, located some 75 miles (120km) north-west of London. All but three of the 18 British servicemen aboard, plus two persons on the ground, were killed in the accident; one other civilian and the three survivors from the aircraft, including two members of the crew of five, suffered injuries. Also killed on the Beverley were eight RAF police dogs.

Originally bound for Cyprus, the transport had turned back after the crew detected a serious fuel leak near the No. 1 power plant, which was feathered. During the let-down procedure, the corresponding gauge indicated an unusual loss of fuel from the No. 2 tank, and so the fuel cocks and boosters for that tank were turned off. The cocks and boosters for the No. 1 tank remained on. When power was increased on the remaining three engines, the No. 2 failed to respond, and with the loss of power, the aircraft began to lose height and air speed until the point that it became uncontrollable, striking power lines and trees before it ploughed into two farm buildings and caught fire. The base weather around the time of the crash consisted of a low overcast, with 8/8 cloud coverage at around 500ft (150m), visibility down to less than 1,000ft (300m) and easterly winds of nearly 10 knots.

Opposite top: An RAF Blackburn Beverley transport, the type that crashed following multiple power plant failure linked to faulty maintenance. (British Aerospace)

Opposite bottom: The remains of the Beverley beside one of the badly damaged farm buildings that it struck in Drayton, Berkshire, England. (UPI/Corbis-Bettmann)

The four fuel tanks on the port side of the Beverley were designed to feed into a collector box, from which gasoline would be provided to both left-hand engines. Investigation revealed that on XH117, the non-return valve between the No. 1 tank and the collector box had been fitted in reverse, and that the No. 2 power plant malfunctioned due to fuel starvation resulting from this maintenance error, to the fact that the fuel supply from the other main tank had been turned off after the No. 1 engine was feathered, and because the fuel supply from the two smaller port tanks had been turned off throughout the flight. The latter action, which was that of the pilot's, did not conform to proper handling of the aircraft's fuel system. However, it was noted in the investigative report on the accident that as the amount of fuel in the two smaller tanks was not large, he would have had no reason to believe that the two port engines could not operate satisfactorily off the two main tanks alone.

As a result of this accident, an RAF mechanic was court-martialled for negligence, but his punishment was later reduced to only a reprimand. Additionally, a requirement was implemented requiring that tests be carried out after this type of maintenance had been performed on an aircraft.

17 MARCH 1957 (c.01:30)

Location	*Near Asturias, Cebu, the Philippines*
Operator	*Philippine Air Force*
Aircraft type	*Douglas C-47A (2100925)*

Ramon Magsaysay, the President of the Philippines, was among 25 persons killed when the twin-engine transport crashed and burned on a jungle-covered mountain on the island of Cebu, about 20 miles (30km) north-west of the city of Cebu, from where it had taken off shortly before, on an internal flight to Nichols Field, located near Manila. The victims also included the aircraft's five crewmen, all military personnel. One seriously injured passenger survived the accident, which occurred in early-morning darkness. Prior to the crash the pilot had reported no difficulties and that the weather conditions were clear. According to an official statement, the C-47 had experienced a loss of power in its starboard engine while climbing, attributed to a carburettor malfunction.

22 MARCH 1957 (c.01:00)

Location	*North Pacific Ocean*
Operator	*US Air Force*
Aircraft type	*Boeing C-97C (50-702A)*

The aircraft was on a scheduled Military Air Transport Service (MATS) flight from Travis Air Force Base, in California, USA, to Tokyo, Japan, with three en-route stops, the last of these on Wake Island, when it vanished during the final segment of the transpacific crossing. With the exception of three civilians, including a female dependant, the 67 persons aboard the C-97 were American servicemen, including the crew of ten.

Operating under an instrument flight rules (IFR) clearance, with a cruising altitude of 8,000ft (2,500m), the

A US Air Force Boeing C-97, virtually identical to the aircraft that vanished during a MATS transpacific flight from California to Japan. (Boeing)

four-engine transport was last heard from around 00:40 local time, or about 20 minutes before the unexplained disaster was believed to have occurred, at an approximate location of 200 miles (320km) south-east of its intended destination. Search was abandoned eight days later, with no trace of it having been found. The pilot of a commercial airliner, who had flown the Wake Island–Tokyo route some 30 minutes ahead of the 50-702A, reported cloudy weather in the area where the latter was believed lost, with bases of 5,000ft (1,500m) and tops at 10,000ft (3,000m), light icing and light-to-moderate turbulence. He also observed lightning in the night sky some distance to the north of his position.

17 APRIL 1957 (c.08:30)

Location	*Near El Quweira, Jordan*
Operator	*Royal Air Force*
Aircraft type	*Vickers Valetta C Mark 1 (VW832)*

The twin-engine transport crashed and burned some 25 miles (40km) north-east of Aqaba, from where it had taken off about 5 minutes earlier. All 27 British servicemen aboard (24 passengers and a crew of three) were killed. As the aircraft was proceeding in a north-easterly direction through a mountain pass at an estimated height of 5,000ft (1,500m), its left wing broke, and evidence indicated that the structural failure resulted from the imposition of loads that exceeded its designed strength. It was considered probable that the break-up was precipitated by a loss of control in conditions of clear-air turbulence and the attempted recovery from the resulting high-speed dive.

An RAF Vickers Valetta transport, one of which crashed in Jordan after turbulence-related in-flight structural failure. (Martin W. Bowman)

23 DECEMBER 1957 (c.16:00)

Location	*North Pacific Ocean*
Operator	*US Navy*
Aircraft type	*Lockheed WV-2 (143197)*

A simulated emergency led to a real disaster about 30 miles (50km) north of Kahuku Point, on Oahu, one of the Hawaiian islands, in this first major crash of one of the early-warning/radar-intelligence aircraft designed to protect US coastlines. The WV-2 was on a training syllabus flight and had descended beneath a low overcast when the aircraft commander and designated check pilot instituted the drill, a simulated fire in the forward cargo compartment.

As part of this exercise, the commander instructed the pilot to turn off the aileron boost during the drill, then to return his aileron booster control to the 'on' position. In attempting to regain elevator boost, one of the men in the cockpit – the pilot, check pilot or one of the two flight engineers – moved the emergency shut-off levers in the wrong direction, to the 'blast air, fuel and hydraulic off' position. This error deprived all four engines of their fuel supply, resulting in a total loss of power. Its propellers windmilling, 143197 rapidly descended from an approximate height of 1,000ft (300m) and finally slammed into the water with its undercarriage and flaps in the retracted position and with its nose and left wing slightly low, breaking into at least

two major sections on impact. Fire then erupted and burned for a while on the surface of the ocean.

Among its 23 crewmen, four injured survivors were rescued, including the commander. Searchers recovered only two bodies, but several of those killed were known to have survived the impact. Around the time of the accident, the cloud base was down to less than 1,000ft (300m) and the visibility only about half a mile (0.8km) where it had been raining, higher outside of the area of precipitation. With the wind blowing from an east-north-easterly direction at 15 to 25 knots, the sea was rough.

It was ruled that the check pilot had failed to initiate remedial action when the WV-2 began to lose altitude and while at the relatively slow indicated air speed of around 180mph (290kmh) during the fire drill, and also failed to exercise authority when a real emergency developed. Neither did he activate the emergency warning bell when the ditching was imminent.

1 FEBRUARY 1958 (c.19:15)

Location	Norwalk, California, USA
First aircraft	
Operator	US Air Force
Aircraft type	Douglas C-118A (53-3277A)
Second aircraft	
Operator	US Navy
Aircraft type	Lockheed P2V-5F (127723)

The two aircraft collided at an approximate height of 3,000ft (1,000m), scattering wreckage over residential and business areas of suburban Los Angeles. Killed in the disaster were a total of 47 American military personnel, all 41 aboard 53-3277A (35 passengers and six crew members) and six of the eight crewmen of 127723, one of whom died on the way to hospital, plus one civilian on the ground who was struck by a piece of falling debris outside her house. The two navy men who survived suffered serious injuries.

Operated by the Military Air Transport Service (MATS), the C-118 had taken off from Long Beach Municipal Airport about 5 minutes before the accident, on a domestic transcontinental flight with a destination of McGuire Air Force Base, in New Jersey. Although it was to have continued under instrument flight rules (IFR) upon reaching its cruising altitude of 17,000ft (5,200m), the four-engine transport had been cleared to climb to that height under visual flight rules (VFR) procedures.

Meanwhile, the twin-engine patrol bomber had been

Opposite top: A US Navy Lockheed P-2V Neptune, similar to the aircraft involved in the collision with a MATS transport over suburban Los Angeles. (Lockheed Martin)

Opposite bottom: The empennage of the US Air Force C-118 and the badly damaged service station following mid-air collision with the Navy patrol bomber. (UPI/Corbis-Bettmann)

on an instrument training exercise, also being conducted under VFR. At the moment of the collision, 53-3277A was on an easterly heading and banked to the right, and 127723 northbound, and the former then burst into flames. Its empennage fell on top of a service station and the main portion of its wreckage crashed in the nearby car park of the Norwalk Sheriff's Department sub-station, with some 30 civilian or patrol vehicles being destroyed or damaged in the impact or ensuing fires. The P2V fell into a rock quarry about 2.5 miles (4km) to the north of the C-118 crash site. It was dark at the time of the accident, although the meteorological conditions were good to excellent, with a high, thin ceiling and a visibility of 15 miles (25km).

The probable cause of the collision was the failure of both crews to 'see-and-avoid' the conflicting traffic, although in accordance with civil air regulations, when two aircraft are on crossing paths, the one on the right (in this case the P2V), would have had the right-of-way. Procedural changes made in the wake of this accident included restrictions on VFR flights over metropolitan Los Angeles by US Navy aircraft.

20 FEBRUARY 1958 (c.05:35)

Location	North Atlantic Ocean
Operator	US Navy
Aircraft type	Lockheed WV-2 (141310)

In the early years of the Cold War, before satellites and sophisticated ground-based systems, WV-2 early-warning aircraft played an important role in the defence of the US coastline. This particular aircraft, with 22 crewmen aboard, and which was part of the so-called Atlantic Barrier fleet, vanished for reasons unknown while flying along a rhumb line orientated on a true heading of 113 degrees that stretched from Argentia, Newfoundland, Canada, to Lajes Air Base, on the island of Terceira, in the Azores. A navy board of inquiry concluded that 141310 had been 'suddenly and catastrophically' destroyed approximately 100 miles (150km) west of Corvo, another island in the Azores, in such a manner as to prevent any distress message from being transmitted. It was dark at the time, but there were no indications of any thunderstorm activity or other adverse weather conditions in the area.

Numerous conjectures were considered by the navy as to the cause of its disappearance, among them catastrophic material failure and the clandestine action of a foreign aircraft, but the following were considered the most likely:
1. A strike of lightning or a static discharge causing total electrical failure.
2. The explosion of an accumulation of fuel vapour in some part of the aircraft.
3. A loss of a single propeller blade or an entire propeller.
4. A loss of control resulting from an error or failure by the crew.

There was, however, evidence that seemed to contradict some of these theories. One endorsement to the investigative report noted that the operating history of the WV-2 and its close relative, the R7V-1 transport, did not support the probability of an in-flight explosion, and that such an event would be expected to distribute some buoyant items that searchers should have found floating on the surface of the ocean. And a fire in the aircraft should have afforded the crew ample time for an emergency radio transmission. It was also noted that the failure of an entire propeller or individual blade, though not unknown to piston-engine aircraft, would probably be progressive in nature and not result in an instantaneous loss of control. Nevertheless, some six months after the loss of 141310, a Super Constellation airliner, very similar to the WV-2, crashed off the coast of Ireland, the sudden nature of which prevented the crew from sending a distress message, and an investigative board concluded with a high degree of probability that the disaster resulted from the overspeeding of an outer propeller.

7 MARCH 1958 (c.19:45)

Location	Off Okinawa, Ryukyu Islands
First aircraft	
Operator	US Marine Corps
Aircraft type	Fairchild R4Q (128741)
Second aircraft	
Operator	US Marine Corps
Aircraft type	Douglas AD-6 Skyraider (135350)

Both propeller-driven aircraft had flown from Subi Point, in the Philippines, the twin-engine Flying Boxcar transport escorting the single-engine attack bomber because of the former's superior navigational equipment. After having entered a holding pattern, both were descending in darkness through a broken to solid layer of clouds when they collided and plummeted into the Philippine Sea approximately 4 miles (6.5km) from the south end of one runway at Naha Air Base, where they were to have landed, and slightly to the left of its extended centreline.

A total of 26 American servicemen lost their lives in the accident, including the transport's crew of six and the pilot (and sole occupant) of the bomber. There were no survivors. Searchers were able to recover all the victims' bodies and the main wreckage of the two aircraft from the water, which was about 50ft (15m) deep at the crash site.

Investigation revealed that the initial contact was between the left side of the fuselage of 135350 and the right wing tip of 128741, after which the former's propeller struck the latter's starboard power plant. The collision apparently resulted from the failure of the AD-6 pilot to maintain his correct position as wing man in a formation during a descending left-hand turn due to several factors, either alone or in combination with others:

1. Disorientation on his part while manoeuvring through moderate turbulence.
2. Loss or impairment of visibility because of the clouds, aggravated by the darkness.

3. Possible vertigo caused by these conditions, aggravated by flashing navigational lights.
4. Moderate fatigue and slight hypoxia affecting the pilot.

A board of inquiry did not totally discount the possibility that the pilot of the transport had himself become disorientated and executed a manoeuvre that was too sudden for successful evasive action by the smaller aircraft. He also erred in failing to request clearance to make a visual flight rules (VFR) procedure let-down earlier or, having elected to remain above the overcast, in failing to break formation and, utilising available navigational aids and ground radar, penetrate the clouds separately.

It was recommended in the investigative report that except in emergency situations, such joint flights as the one here be permitted only in VFR conditions and daylight hours, and that the aircraft involved maintain a horizontal separation of 1,000ft (300m) at all times. The Commanding General of the Marine Corps' Pacific and Atlantic fleets was requested to ensure that their standard operating procedures relative to the transport escort of tactical aircraft be clear and concise in matters related to safety.

27 MARCH 1958 (c.16:15)

Location	Near Bridgeport, Texas, USA
First aircraft	
Operator	US Air Force
Aircraft type	Douglas C-124C (52-981A)
Second aircraft	
Operator	US Air Force
Aircraft type	Fairchild C-119C (49-195A)

Both operating under instrument flight rules (IFR) and cruising along designated airways, the two transports collided over a very-high-frequency omni-directional range (VOR) station some 40 miles (65km) north-west of Fort Worth, and both crashed in farmland, with the wreckage of 52-981A burning after ground impact. A total of 18 American servicemen were killed in the accident, with no survivors from either aircraft.

The four-engine C-124 had been on a north-north-easterly heading, en route from Kelly Air Force Base, near San Antonio, Texas, to Tinker Air Force Base, in neighbouring Oklahoma, and carrying five passengers and a crew of ten. The twin-engine C-119 was on a south-easterly heading and on an intra-state flight from Sheppard Air Force Base, near Wichita Falls, to Carswell Air Force Base, near Fort Worth, with three crewmen aboard. The collision was determined to have occurred at an approximate height of 6,000ft (1,800m), in the midst of an overcast, with a visibility of around 5 miles (10km) but down to zero within the clouds. There was also haze and fog in the area.

Although 52-981A had been cleared by the Fort Worth air-traffic control centre to maintain 7,000ft (2,000m), the height at which it collided with 49-195A, which had been assigned to 6,000ft, indicated that it was flying at the wrong altitude at the time of the accident.

The blackened area near the top of the photograph marks the scene
of the multiple Nike-Ajax explosion at a US Army missile launching
facility. (UPI/Corbis-Bettmann)

22 MAY 1958 (c.13:15)

Location   *Near Middleton, New Jersey, USA*
Operator   *US Army*
Aircraft type   *(8) Douglas Nike-Ajax*

Ten persons were killed, four of them civilians and the rest
servicemen, in a massive explosion that destroyed the eight
anti-aircraft missiles at Battery B of the AAA Missile Battalion,
an army launching facility located about 25 miles (40km)
south-south-east of Newark. Three others suffered injuries
in the blast, which occurred as a team of civilian ordnance
specialists, aided by several soldiers, were installing a new
arming mechanism on one of the missiles (the modification
involving the removal of the warhead). According to the
investigative report, the most probable cause of the disaster,
the worst in the history of US military rocket forces, was
the rupturing of a detonating cap. New safeguards were
announced for the next generation of anti-aircraft missile, the
Nike Hercules.

27 JUNE 1958 (c.00:30)

Location   *Near Chicopee Falls, Massachusetts, USA*
Operator   *US Air Force*
Aircraft type   *Boeing KC-135A (56-3599A)*

Taking off from Runway 23 at Westover Air Force Base, on an
attempted record-breaking transatlantic flight to London and

*A US Air Force Boeing KC-135, the first jet tanker/transport, which
suffered its first major accident during an attempted record-
breaking flight. (Boeing)*

then back to the US, the Strategic Air Command (SAC) jet tanker crashed just north of Springfield. All 15 men aboard perished, including six journalists and two other civilians riding as passengers; the seven members of the crew were air force personnel.

Since mission requirements called for the maximum permissible fuel load, surface air temperature and its effect on the aircraft's take-off performance were critical. Through calculations made by both the mission and the aircraft commander, it was determined that a flap setting of 40 degrees would provide for a take-off roll of the desired length. There would be a penalty in decreasing the ground roll, however, namely a shallower climb-out path. It was suspected that the pilots had concentrated on monitoring their air speed and failed to detect that the KC-135 had gone into a slight descent after becoming airborne, initially striking tree tops with its left wing and engines, at a point some 4,000ft (1,200m) from the end of the runway. The tanker then cut several power cables and finally slammed to earth in a near-vertical left bank and burst into flames, scattering wreckage across the Massachusetts Turnpike.

It was dark at the time of the crash, and the meteorological conditions consisted of a high overcast, with scattered clouds at 700ft (200m) and a runway visual range of 1.5 miles (2.5km) in fog. The wind was from a south-westerly direction at 9 knots. Investigation ruled out in-flight fire or pre-impact structural failure, power plant or other mechanical malfunction. It was therefore concluded that the accident must have resulted from complications in aircraft handling technique, associated with the high gross weight and the marginal weather and night-time visibility conditions, which were compounded by flight instrument limitations.

2 SEPTEMBER 1958 (c.06:10)

Location	*North Pacific Ocean*
Operator	*US Air Force*
Aircraft type	*Douglas C-124C (52-1081A)*

Operated by the Military Air Transport Service (MATS), the aircraft crashed approximately 35 miles (55km) west of Agana Naval Air Station, on the island of Guam, from where it had taken off earlier on a cargo flight to Clark Air Base in the Philippines. Around 4 hours later, floating wreckage was spotted and, subsequently, the bodies of two victims were recovered, but none of the 19 American servicemen aboard 52-1081A (12 passengers and a crew of seven) survived. There were indications of an in-flight fire, the origin of which remained undetermined.

Airborne around dawn, the four-engine transport had been cleared to its cruising altitude of 8,000ft (2,500m) prior to the crash, which occurred some 20 minutes after its take-off. The weather in the area at the time was good, with a high overcast and scattered cumulus clouds at around 1,200ft (350m), and a visibility of at least 5 miles (10km).

2 SEPTEMBER 1958 (c.15:00)

Location	*Near Talin, Armenia, USSR*
Operator	*US Air Force*
Aircraft type	*Lockheed C-130A-II (56-0528)*

All 17 American servicemen aboard were believed to have perished when the highly-modified four-engine turboprop transport crashed and burned about 35 miles (55km) north-west of Yerevan. Some three weeks later, the remains of six airmen were returned to American authorities in Turkey; these were reportedly the only victims found in the wreckage. The US later released the recording of a conversation among Soviet fighter pilots as they attacked the unarmed aircraft, which it was claimed had strayed off course while ostensibly being used to study the propagation of radio waves transmitted by US broadcast stations, at a reported height of 10,000ft (3,000m).

More than 30 years later, the true nature of the mission came to light with the release of previously-classified documents. The C-130 had in fact been sent to identify Soviet radar defences and test their capabilities, and must have been located and shot down not long after passing into Soviet airspace at an altitude of around 25,000ft (7,500m). It was to have remained at least 100 miles (150km) from the Soviet border, but the crew may have become confused by navigational beacons within the USSR that had frequencies similar to the facilities in Turkey that they were using.

8 SEPTEMBER 1958 (c.19:20)

Location	*Near Airway Heights, Washington, USA*
First aircraft	
Operator	*US Air Force*
Aircraft type	*Boeing B-52D (56-661)*
Second aircraft	
Operator	*US Air Force*
Aircraft type	*Boeing B-52D (56-681)*

This remains as the worst disaster in the history of the US Strategic Air Command's jet bomber operations. Both aircraft had been on pilot proficiency flights and were preparing to land on Runway 23 at Fairchild Air Force Base when 681 was advised to pull up and break to the right after dropping below the glide path during a ground-controlled (GCA) procedure approach. After being advised by the control tower of what the other B-52 was doing, 661 radioed back, 'Roger tower, tell him to turn the other way', and the latter then steepened its bank to the right. Seconds later, the bombers collided at an approximate above-ground height of 900ft (275m) some 2.5 miles (4km) north-east of the base and about 5 miles (10km) west of Spokane, and both plunged to earth and exploded.

Killed in the accident were a total of 13 airmen, eight from 661 and five from 681. Among the three survivors, who bailed out with three others who did not survive, one crewman from 661 was slightly injured, while one of the co-pilots assigned to 681 suffered serious injuries and that aircraft's tail gunner escaped unscathed. The collision occurred at dusk, and the weather conditions in the area consisted of a broken overcast at 10,000ft (3,000m), with a visibility under the clouds of 20 miles (30km) and a slight breeze from a north-north-easterly direction. Prior to the collision, the instrument flight rules clearances of both aircraft had been cancelled.

9 OCTOBER 1958 (c.18:25)

Location	*Near New Plymouth, Idaho, USA*
Operator	*US Air Force*
Aircraft type	*Fairchild C-123B (55-4521A)*

The twin-engine transport crashed and exploded on flat terrain some 7 miles (11km) east of Payette, and all 19 persons aboard were killed. Other than two civilian passengers, the victims were all American servicemen, including the crew of five. Operated by the Tactical Air Command and designated as the support aircraft for the Thunderbirds, the US Air Force precision flying team, 55-4521A had been en route from Hill Air Force Base, in Utah, to McChord Air Force Base, near Tacoma, Washington – one segment of a transcontinental flight originating in North Carolina – when it appeared to stall at an approximate height of 500ft (150m) above the ground, apparently after experiencing uncontrolled phugoid, or 'porpoising' motions.

At the time of the accident, around dusk, the local weather was good, with an estimated ceiling of 9,000ft (2,700m) and a visibility of 30 miles (50km). The wind was calm. It was believed that the C-123 had collided with a flock of geese, resulting in the incapacitation of one or both of the pilots and/or the loss of control.

15 OCTOBER 1958 (time unknown)

Location	*Near Villa Montes, Tarija, Bolivia*
Operator	*Fuerza Aérea Boliviana (Bolivian Air Force)*
Aircraft type	*Douglas C-47A (TAM-03)*

Operated by the military airline Transportes Aéreos Militares on a non-scheduled domestic passenger flight from Fortin Campero to the city of Tarija, the aircraft was reported missing at 17:30 local time, possibly having been diverted by bad weather conditions. Wreckage was later found on a mountain about 100 miles (150km) north-east of its destination, with no survivors among the 20 persons aboard, which included a crew of four military personnel.

10 MARCH 1959 (c.08:30)

Location	*Near Curralinho, Para, Brazil*
Operator	*Força Aérea Brasileira (Brazilian Air Force)*
Aircraft type	*Consolidated OA-10 Catalina (6513)*

All 23 persons aboard lost their lives when the twin-engine amphibian crashed in the River Para some 100 miles (150km) west-south-west of Belem, from where it had taken off earlier, on a domestic interstate flight to Manaus, Amazonas. Most of the victims were military personnel, including the crew

of five, but the passengers also included five civilians, two of them children. The aircraft was apparently attempting an emergency landing due to an on-board fire when it reportedly 'exploded' at a height of around 60ft (20m).

30 JUNE 1959 (c.10:35)

Location	*Okinawa, Ryukyu Islands*
Operator	*US Air Force*
Aircraft type	*North American F-100D (55-3633A)*

Afire and having been abandoned by its pilot, the jet fighter crashed in a residential area in the village of Ishikawa, 40 miles (65km) north-east of Naha, exploding on impact and hurling debris into a school compound. Five of the 17 persons killed on the ground were children, as were most of the other 169 who suffered injuries.

The aircraft, which was on a functional check flight following a time-compliance technical order (TCTO) modification, had taken off from Kadena Air Base, and after climbing to an approximate height of 1,200ft (350m) and accelerating to nearly 300mph (480kmh) with the afterburner on, the power plant compartment fire-warning light illuminated. The pilot then jettisoned two empty fuel tanks and a bomb rack, which fell into the sea, and retarded power, whereupon the light went out. After turning back and while approaching to land, he initiated a go-around for reasons that were not disclosed, but at that instant an explosion occurred in the aircraft. Although it was headed towards an unpopulated area when he ejected, the fighter subsequently veered to the right, and following the accidental deployment of its drag chute and a second explosion, it slammed into some houses.

The pilot landed safely by parachute, without injury. In

A North American F-100 Super Sabre, the US Air Force's first operational supersonic jet fighter and type that crashed into the village on Okinawa. (AP/Wide World Photos)

all, 27 dwellings were destroyed or badly damaged. The local weather at the time consisted of scattered clouds at 1,000ft (300m), with a visibility beneath them of 40 miles (65km) and a slight breeze from the west.

25 FEBRUARY 1960 (c.13:00)

Location	*Rio de Janeiro, Brazil*
First aircraft	
Operator	*US Navy*
Aircraft type	*Douglas R6D-1 (131582)*
Second aircraft	
Operator	*Consorcio REAL Aerovias Nacional*
Aircraft type	*Douglas DC-3 (PP-AXD)*

Diagram showing the flight paths of the US Navy transport and the Brazilian airliner that collided over Guanabara Bay. (International Civil Aviation Organisation)

Both aircraft were approaching to land, the military transport at Galeao Airport and the Brazilian airliner at Santos-Dumont Airport, when they collided in mid-air, and both then plummeted into the entrance of Guanabara Bay. The disaster claimed the lives of 61 persons, all but three passengers among the 38 American servicemen aboard the R6D, including the crew of seven, and all 26 aboard the DC-3 (22 passengers and four crew members). Among the victims from the former aircraft were members of a US Navy band who were to have played for the visiting American President, Dwight D. Eisenhower.

Operating under instrument flight rules, the military transport was en route from Buenos Aires, Argentina, and the commercial one, operating under visual flight rules, was near the end of a scheduled domestic service from Vitoria, Espirito Santo. The local weather at the time consisted of a broken layer of strato-cumulus clouds at about 2,300ft (700m) and a solid overcast at approximately 10,000ft (3,000m). As it converged with the eastbound DC-3, the northbound R6D

A US Navy airship of the Goodyear ZPG-3W class, one of which went down off the New Jersey coast on 6 July 1960. (UPI/Corbis-Bettmann)

was believed to have emerged from a cloud just before the accident, which did not give its crew sufficient time to initiate evasive action. The airline pilots probably never saw the navy aircraft. In the subsequent collision, which occurred at an estimated altitude of 5,000ft (1,500m) and some 2.5 miles (4km) south of Santos-Dumont Airport, both the right wing of PP-AXD and the aft fuselage section of 131582 were severed. The three men who miraculously survived without serious injury were in the rear-facing seats in that part of the R6D, which dropped into the water in an oscillating motion similar to a falling leaf. Most of the wreckage from the two aircraft was subsequently recovered from the bay, as were the bodies of those killed.

Brazilian authorities attributed the disaster to 'improper piloting procedure' by the crew of the military transport, who reportedly disobeyed the instructions of approach control to descend before reaching the Ilha Rasa non-directional beacon. Conducting its own investigation, the US Navy came to a different conclusion, blaming the actions of the air-traffic controller, specifically, his uncertainty as to the original position of the commercial flight; under-estimation of time factors, including that related to aircraft reaction; and a lack of appreciation of communications difficulties and the increasing seriousness of the situation, which it said created the conditions that ultimately led to the collision.

Other factors that it said could have played a role in the accident included the absence of modern navigational aids and air-traffic control facilities on the ground, and the role of language differences. With regard to the latter, Naval authorities noted that while English was used in air/ground communications, pilots and controllers often had difficulty understanding one another because of their accents. Furthermore, in this particular case, the controller's instructions to PP-AXD were given in Portuguese, preventing the American crew from determining the height and anticipated flight path of the airliner. According to the navy

report, its conclusion reportedly based on his own testimony, the controller believed that the R6D was considerably higher than the DC-3 and intentionally reversed his earlier instructions, i.e. for the former to descend and the latter to remain at 6,000ft (1,800m).

6 JULY 1960 (c.14:30)

Location	*Off New Jersey, USA*
Operator	*US Navy*
Aircraft type	*Goodyear ZPG-3W (144242)*

The helium-filled blimp crashed in the Atlantic Ocean about 10 miles (15km) east of Barnegat City, killing 18 men. Three other members of the crew, all of whom suffered injuries, were rescued. Searchers later recovered the bodies of 13 victims, all but one of whom had drowned, and most of the airship's wreckage, which had sunk in water some 75ft (20m) deep.

According to a navy investigative report, the accident resulted from the failure of a seam in the envelope, which was apparently related to some factor that degraded the cement adhesion, and the subsequent shearing of the stitching of the fabric. Starting at the top of the envelope, the tear occurred about a third of the way from the front, and after its forward section collapsed, the blimp plunged nose-first into the ocean from an approximate height of 800ft (250m). The weather, which at the time consisted of a broken overcast, a visibility in excess of 10 miles (15km) and a south-south-easterly wind of around 15 knots, was not considered a factor.

One of the ZPG-3W class airships designed for the mission of airborne early-warning, the 400ft (120m) long 144242

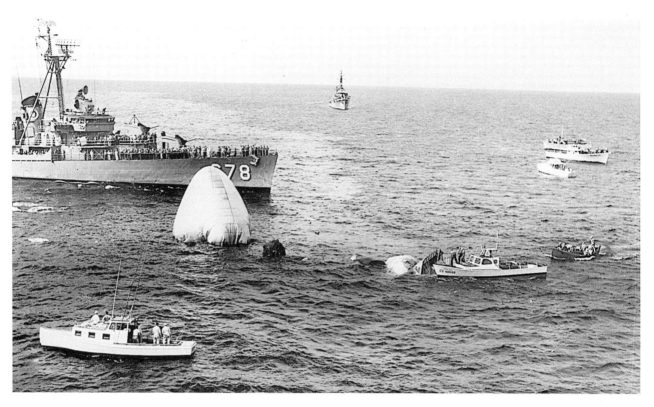

Surface craft converge on the scene where the Navy blimp fell into the Atlantic Ocean after envelope failure, killing 18 crewmen. (UPI/Corbis-Bettmann)

had been delivered to the navy less than six months earlier. At the time of the accident it was searching for two missing yachts, both of which were later found safe. Lighter-than-air operations in the US Navy would end soon afterwards, with the rest of its blimps being retired the following year.

11 JULY 1960 (c.11:45)

Location	Near Quito, Ecuador
Operator	US Air Force
Aircraft type	Douglas C-47E (45-1109A)

Its passengers comprised mostly of American military dependants and Ecuadorean civilians, the twin-engine transport crashed and burned on Mount Pichincha about 10 miles (15km) west-north-west of the Ecuadorean capital, where it was to have landed during a flight from Bogotá, Colombia. All 18 persons aboard, including four US Air Force crewmen, were killed. The aircraft struck the volcano at an approximate elevation of 13,000ft (4,000m). Although the meteorological conditions in the area were generally good, the Pichincha Pass was heavily overcast, with one patch of rain, and the mountain itself cloud-obscured. The air force did not disclose its findings as to the probable cause of the crash, but the investigative report did note, significantly, that at the time the crew had been operating under visual flight rules (VFR) procedures.

19 JULY 1960 (c.13:45)

Location	Near Goma, Kivu, Belgian Congo (Zaire)
Operator	Force Aérienne Belge (Royal Belgian Air Force)
Aircraft type	Fairchild C-119G (CP-36)

The twin-engine transport crashed and burned on a mountain north of Lake Kivu, and all but four of the 41 Belgian military personnel aboard were killed, including the crew of four. All of the survivors suffered injuries. Flying from Belgium, the aircraft had experienced the failure of a power plant, and considering the mountainous terrain and high temperature factor, it was unable to maintain altitude on the remaining engine. Contributing to the accident were the adverse weather conditions, with clouds obscuring the terrain.

17 AUGUST 1960 (c.23:45)

Location	Near El Kelaa, Morocco
Operator	Aéronavale (French Naval Aviation)
Aircraft type	Avro Lancaster Mark 1 (WU-26)

All 20 French servicemen aboard were killed in the crash of the four-engine bomber, which occurred in darkness some 100 miles (150km) south of Casablanca. The aircraft had been en route to Agadir, Morocco, from Istres, France, the final segment of a flight originating at Le Bourget Airport, near Paris, when the pilot reported one power plant was afire and that he had turned back in an attempt to reach Casablanca.

22 SEPTEMBER 1960 (time unknown)

Location	North Pacific Ocean
Operator	US Marine Corps
Aircraft type	Douglas R5D-3 (56541)

The four-engine transport, carrying 29 American servicemen (23 passengers and a crew of six), had been en route from the naval base near Atsugi, Japan, to the installation at Subi Point, in the Philippines, when it sent a radio message reporting a fire in the No. 3 power plant and that it was diverting to Okinawa. In its last transmission, sent shortly after 14:00 local time, the aircraft was reported maintaining a height of 6,500ft (1,980m) and on a heading of 339 degrees, and also requested air/sea rescue assistance. Less than 2 hours later, floating debris was sighted from the air, the R5D having crashed at sea approximately 180 miles (290km) south of Naha, the capital of the island.

Some 770lb (350kg) of wreckage from 56541 was subsequently recovered, much of it showing signs of flash burning, but no survivors or bodies were found. An investigative board could not determine the cause of the crash with certainty. According to available evidence, the most probable sequence of events was that the blaze reported in the No. 3 engine nacelle had been extinguished, but that a residual fire continued to burn, igniting one or both tyres on the right main undercarriage leg, and that one or both then exploded, rupturing the adjacent integral wing fuel tank. Fuel from the breached tank could then have created a combustible fuel/air mixture, resulting in a second explosion that either led to the break-up of the aircraft or significantly affected its airworthiness. The R5D probably disintegrated when it struck the surface of the water, with a flash fire possibly occurring on impact.

The in-flight blaze was believed to have originated from an unidentified electrical or mechanical malfunction or from the detonation of an incendiary device that had been planted aboard prior to take-off. No unusual weather conditions were known to have existed along the route taken by 56541.

11 DECEMBER 1960 (c.19:50)

Location	Near San Andres de Giles, Buenos Aires, Argentina
Operator	Fuerza Aérea Argentina (Argentine Air Force)
Aircraft type	Avro Lancastrian 4 (T-102)

Operated by the Correo Aereo Militar al Exterior (CAME) courier branch on a passenger/mail service to the city of Buenos Aires from Lima, Peru, the four-engine transport crashed and exploded about 100 miles (150km) west-north-west of its intended destination, the accident occurring around dusk and during a heavy rain and low overcast. All 31 persons aboard, including a crew of eight military personnel, were killed. The primary cause of the crash was pilot error, specifically, the continuation under visual flight rules (VFR) procedures into the adverse meteorological conditions, coupled with instrument failure. A contributing factor was considered to be the weather itself.

17 DECEMBER 1960 (c.14:10)

Location	Munich, (West) Germany
Operator	US Air Force
Aircraft type	Convair C-131D (55-291)

Nearly all of the passengers on this flight to England were college students, the children of American military personnel, who had been returning to their families for the Christmas holiday. Bound for RAF Northolt, London, the twin-engine transport had been airborne for only about a minute when the co-pilot radioed that it was returning to Riem Airport, serving Munich, from where it had taken off, its left propeller having been feathered. Shortly thereafter,

A US Air Force Convair C-131 transport, the type involved in the disastrous Munich crash on 17 December 1960, which claimed 53 lives. (General Dynamics)

The wrecked German streetcar continues to smoulder after being struck by the crashing American military aircraft. (AP/Wide World Photos)

in response to a request by the radar controller to ascend to 3,000ft (1,000m), the same crewman reported that the aircraft, then at a height of 2,200ft (670m), was unable to climb. His voice sounding excited, he also requested the airport crash crew to stand by.

Subsequently, and while on an approximate heading of 320 degrees and at a height of about 470ft (140m) above the ground, 55-291 struck, with its port wing, a steeple of St Paul's Cathedral church, then plummeted into a business section of the city, crashing in an almost inverted, left wing-low attitude, exploded and burned. The disaster claimed the lives of 33 persons on the ground, nearly half of whom had been riding in a tram that was struck by an engine and gutted by fire, and all 20 occupants of the aircraft. Among the latter, one passenger and the seven crew members were American military personnel. About a dozen others suffered injuries.

At the time, the weather in the area was characterised by an indefinite ceiling of 100–150ft (30–50m), with a visibility of approximately half a mile (0.8km) and a 7-knot wind from an east-north-easterly direction. And with the temperature below freezing, the conditions were conducive to carburettor icing, which could have caused a power loss.

Significantly, examination of the power plant that was reported to have malfunctioned revealed a collection of water in the inlet side of the left fuel tank booster pump, and disassembly of the pump disclosed even more water. It was further noted in the investigative report that difficulty had been experienced in starting both engines. However, the exact cause of the crash was not disclosed by military authorities.

26 JANUARY 1961 (time unknown)

Location	*North Atlantic Ocean*
Operator	*US Air Force*
Aircraft type	*Douglas C-118A (51-17626)*

Operated by the Military Air Transport Service (MATS), the aircraft crashed while en route from the Azores to the air base at Argentia, Newfoundland, Canada, one segment of a transatlantic flight originating at Kenitra (Port Lyautey), Morocco, with an ultimate destination of Norfolk Naval Air Station, in Virginia, USA. The crew of another American military aircraft flying in the area had spoken with the C-118 at 03:10 local time, and about 35 minutes later witnessed a mid-air explosion in the pre-dawn darkness some 25 miles (40km) north-east of Argentia, although this may have been a flare. A subsequent search found no trace of the four-engine transport or any of the 23 persons aboard, most of whom were American servicemen, including a crew of ten navy personnel. Due to certain classified aspects of this particular operation, no further details were released concerning the loss of the 51-17626.

25 MARCH 1961 (time unknown)

Location	*Near Natal, Rio Grande do Norte, Brazil*
Operator	*Força Aérea Brasileira (Brazilian Air Force)*
Aircraft type	*Douglas C-47 (2055)*

The twin-engine transport crashed as it was attempting to land at the local airport, and 22 persons aboard were killed, including the two-member flight crew, both military personnel. Seven other passengers on the internal flight from Rio de Janeiro to Belem survived the accident with serious injuries.

10 OCTOBER 1961 (c.20:30)

Location	*Near El Adem, Libya*
Operator	*Royal Air Force*
Aircraft type	*Handley Page Hastings C Mark 2 (WD498)*

Operated by Transport Command, the four-engine aircraft crashed and burned while taking off from the El Adem airfield, located some 10 miles (15km) south of Tobruk, on a troop flight. The accident killed 17 of the 55 military personnel aboard the Hastings, including one member of its RAF crew of six; all but one of the passengers who lost their lives were Maltese. Another 15 passengers suffered injuries, although the surviving crewmen were among those who escaped unscathed. The crash occurred in darkness and visual meteorological conditions after the aircraft had apparently become airborne prematurely, resulting in a stall. Considered as contributing factors were the unnecessary 'handing over' of the controls from the second to the first pilot during the take-off, the poor method by which this was accomplished, and the incorrect remedial action then taken by the captain in recovering from the stall. Still another factor was the disobedience of orders by the captain in allowing the second pilot to attempt a take-off considering the latter's qualifications.

6 APRIL 1962 (c.15:00)

Location	*Near Villavicencio, Meta, Colombia*
Operator	*Fuerza Aérea Colombiana (Colombian Air Force)*
Aircraft type	*Douglas C-47 (FAC-563)*

The twin-engine transport, which had last stopped at Araracuara during an internal flight originating at Bogotá, crashed on a mountain some 60 miles (100km) from the Apiay military base, located near Villavicencio, where it was to have landed. All 31 persons aboard perished, including a crew of five military personnel; the passengers included prison officials and five inmates on parole. The wreckage of the aircraft was located the following day at an approximate elevation of 11,500ft (3,500m). Proceeding in adverse meteorological conditions, the C-47 was some 10 degrees off the prescribed course at the time of impact, the deviation probably attributable to the easterly winds it had encountered. An additional significant factor was the absence of ground navigational aids along the route.

8 MAY 1962 (time unknown)

Location	*Eastern Burma*
Operator	*Union of Burma Air Force*
Aircraft type	*Douglas C-47 (UB-BG707)*

All 32 persons aboard lost their lives when the twin-engine transport crashed and burned in a ravine about 400 miles (650km) north-east of Rangoon and approximately 5 miles (10km) north-west of Mong Pa Liao, from where it had taken off shortly before on an internal flight with an ultimate destination of Mandalay. The passengers included 11 civilians; the rest of those killed in the afternoon accident were Burmese military personnel, including the four members of the aircraft's crew. According to a military source, power plant failure was suspected as the cause of the crash.

22 MAY 1962 (c.11:40)

Location	*Near Markt Schwaben, (West) Germany*
Operator	*US Navy*
Aircraft type	*Lockheed WV-2Q (131390)*

The four-engine radar-intelligence aircraft, which was on a navigational training exercise, crashed and burned about 10 miles (15km) east of Munich, after experiencing catastrophic structural failure. All 26 American servicemen aboard, including four army personnel designated as observers, perished. Departing earlier in the morning from Rhein-Main Air Base, near Frankfurt, the WV-2 had last acknowledged ascending out of flight level 170 before twice broadcasting the message, 'Munich, 131390 . . . Request emergency landing at your field, immediately! Over.' The aircraft began to disintegrate at an approximate altitude of 18,000ft (5,500m). The break-up, which was almost instantaneous, involved the separation of the empennage, followed by the left wing and all but one power plant. Major components were scattered over an area of approximately 10sq miles (16sq km), although the dispersal of classified documents that were being carried aboard it extended more than 40 miles (65km).

It was of the opinion of an investigative board that the

A US Navy WV-2 radar intelligence/early warning aircraft, similar to the one that crashed following catastrophic break-up over (West) Germany. (UPI/ Corbis-Bettmann)

initial fracture in the fuselage of 131390 resulted from a combination of a large-sized force imposed on the aft section at a time the cabin had been substantially pressurised. This led to an explosive decompression and the more general disintegration of the aircraft. The nature of the emergency that occurred prior to the break-up, and which prompted the distress message, could not be determined, but was definitely not related to a control system malfunction. Possible reasons for the original emergency included an in-flight fire in the

A swath was cut in the forest by the KC-135 jet tanker, which crashed while approaching to land at Fairchild Air Force Base. (AP/Wide World Photos)

forward fuselage area, or an uncontrollable propeller. It was noted in the accident report, however, that the latter would be expected to have caused some internal damage to the power plant, which should have been evident upon examination. The weather was not a factor.

In the recommendations portion of the report, it was noted that administrative procedures of the squadron that operated the WV-2 were considered lacking to assure the required inspections of aircraft, and that 84 discrepancies in 131390 had been recorded in pilots' and maintenance forms, even though no definite trends towards a possible cause or factor in the crash could be made from this information. It was further noted that while also not a precipitating element in its loss, the WV-2 had been some 2,300lb (1,050kg) overweight.

10 SEPTEMBER 1962 (11:05)

Location	*Near Milan, Washington, USA*
Operator	*US Air Force*
Aircraft type	*Boeing KC-135A (60-0352)*

Operated by the Strategic Air Command (SAC), the jet tanker crashed in mountainous terrain about 30 miles (50km) north-east of Fairchild Air Force Base, located near Spokane, where it was to have landed. All 44 men aboard perished, including a crew of four; with the exception of one civilian passenger, the victims were air force personnel.

The accident occurred near the end of an internal US passenger flight from Ellsworth Air Force Base, in South Dakota. Its undercarriage down and flaps retracted, the aircraft was longitudinally level but banked slightly to the right when it slammed into a wooded slope at an approximate elevation of 4,400ft (1,350m), exploded and burned during the approach to Runway 23 utilising very-high-frequency omni-directional range (VOR) and instrument landing system (ILS) procedures. At the moment of impact, it was completing a right turn in order to effect alignment with the 20-degree radial of the Mead VOR station, and proceeding on a magnetic heading of 195 degrees, having failed to level off at the proper altitude. The local weather at the time of the accident consisted of a scattered to broken overcast at around 1,000ft (300m) and another cloud layer at 8,000ft (2,500m), with a visibility of 25 miles (40km).

Although specific details were not disclosed by the air force, the primary cause of the crash was believed to have been an error by the navigator of 60-0352, which led to the deviation from the published approach procedure and the descent below the minimum safe height.

30 JANUARY 1963 (c.02:00)

Location	*North Atlantic Ocean*
Operator	*US Navy*
Aircraft type	*Lockheed P-3A (149672)*

One of the first of the then new four-engine turboprop patrol aircraft to be delivered to the navy, 149672 had been in service only about half a year and was participating in an anti-submarine warfare (ASW) training exercise when it crashed approximately 250 miles (400km) east-south-east of Atlantic City, New Jersey, USA, in an area where the depth of the water was around 12,000ft (3,700m). Searchers recovered some wreckage and the body of the aircraft commander, but there were no survivors among the 14 crewmen assigned to 149672.

As part of the exercise, the P-3 was to have conducted a mock search and attack on an American submarine, although the location of the accident indicated that the crew may have been pursuing a false contact. No distress message from 149672 was heard, and examination of recovered debris indicated a post-impact fire or explosion, but no such in-flight occurrence. Nor was there evidence that the survival equipment found floating in the ocean had been

used. It was dark at the time, and the weather in the area consisted of scattered clouds, with bases of 2,500–3,000ft (750–1,000m) and a visibility of 10 miles (15km). The moon and stars could not be seen due to the overcast, and there was no visible horizon or any outside visual references. The aircraft had been engaged in low-altitude ASW tactics when it crashed, but neither the cause nor its final manoeuvres before impact could be determined. Though the pilot may have flown it into the water, when considering his experience

The Lockheed P-3A Orion anti-submarine/patrol aircraft suffered its first major crash about half-a-year after the type became operational with the US Navy. (Lockheed Martin)

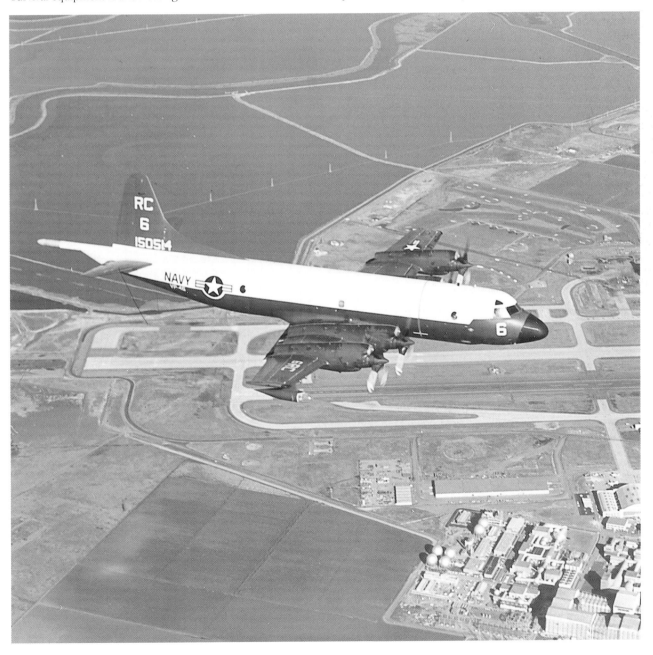

and qualifications, a navy board of inquiry considered it more likely that some extenuating circumstances came into play.

Perhaps significant were a number of shortcomings identified in the aircraft type. Tests indicated performance limitations with respect to weak static longitudinal stability that resulted in poor trim characteristics during ASW operations, when accurate manoeuvering close to the water is required. Experience also showed that the altitude hold feature of the automatic flight control system had a tendency to disengage without apparent warning at low altitudes due to fluctuating signals in its APN-117 radar altimeter. And if electrical power were to be lost, the altimeter would continue to indicate the last reading without a system failure warning to the crew. Since standard operating procedures for most pilots was to fly with the autopilot on and the altitude hold engaged, such a situation could create a false sense of security in the event of such a power loss, a fact about which most P-3 crews were found to be unaware.

Subsequent modifications were made in the type to correct oscillations of the altimeter, provide red flashing lights to warn of altimeter disengagement and of masking the drive pointer of the APN-117 when the altitude hold feature is engaged. Such changes were incorporated into aircraft in production, and retrofit kits used to modify those already in service. Until these corrective actions were completed, the type was restricted to a minimum height of 500ft (150m) at night or in instrument flight rules conditions during ASW missions.

26 JUNE 1963 (c.12:00)

Location	Near Augustdorf, (West) Germany
Operator	Force Aérienne Belge (Royal Belgian Air Force)
Aircraft type	Fairchild C-119 (CP-45)

The twin-engine transport, its passengers all Belgian Army paratroopers, crashed in flames about 5 miles (10km) south-west of Detmold after a freak case of 'friendly fire', and 38 servicemen aboard were killed, including the crew of five Belgian Air Force personnel. Nine paratroopers jumped from the stricken aircraft and survived.

Following a flight originating at Melsbroek Air Base, near Brussels, Belgium, the C-119 was to have landed at Gutersloh Air Base, but during a ground-controlled approach, it passed over the Sennelager military camp and firing range and was hit accidentally on one wing by a phosphorus mortar shell fired by a British Army unit. The splash of the incandescent agent immediately set the aircraft afire, both externally and internally, and the intensity of the blaze was increased by the fact that its fuel tanks and crew oxygen supply system were also struck. Rendered uncontrollable by the fire, CP-45 ultimately plummeted to the ground from an approximate height of 2,500ft (750m). At the time, the local weather was cloudy, with 4/8 coverage at 3,000ft (1,000m) and a visibility of about 15 miles (25km). According to a British military spokesman, aircraft flying over the firing range were to remain above an altitude of 10,000ft (3,000m) to ensure their safety.

28 AUGUST 1963 (c.12:30)

Location	North Atlantic Ocean
First aircraft	
Operator	US Air Force
Aircraft type	Boeing KC-135A (61-0319)
Second aircraft	
Operator	US Air Force
Aircraft type	Boeing KC-135A (61-0322)

The two Strategic Air Command (SAC) jet tankers had just finished refuelling three B-47 jet bombers, whose crews reported that they had turned west before losing sight of them when their own aircraft entered a deck of cirrus clouds. Nothing further was heard from either KC-135, and the following day searchers sighted flier-type life jackets floating in the water some 700 miles (1,125km) north-east of Homestead Air Force Base, in Florida, USA, itself located about 25 miles (40km) south-west of Miami and where both were stationed. Some debris identified as belonging to both tankers was subsequently recovered from the water, but no trace could be found of the 11 crewmen assigned to the two aircraft, six from 0319 and five from 0322. In an investigative report, the loss of the two tankers was ascribed to an 'apparent' mid-air collision, the exact circumstances of which were unknown.

18 OCTOBER 1963 (time unknown)

Location	Near Aswan, Egypt
Operator	Soviet Air Force
Aircraft type	Antonov An-12

During an attempted landing at Aswan Airport, in evening darkness and conditions of reduced visibility due to blowing sand, the four-engine turboprop transport crashed and burned, killing all 31 military personnel aboard, including a Soviet crew. The passengers were all Egyptians. No additional information about the accident was disclosed.

6 MARCH 1964 (time unknown)

Location	Near Barrackpore, West Bengal, India
Operator	Indian Air Force
Aircraft type	Fairchild C-119

All 22 occupants were killed when the twin-engine transport reportedly 'exploded' in flight and then crashed shortly after its departure from Barrackpore Air Base, located some 10 miles (15km) north of Calcutta.

8 MAY 1964 (c.20:20)

Location	Near Santa Rosa, Lima, Peru
Operator	Fuerza Aérea Argentina (Argentine Air Force)
Aircraft type	Douglas C-54 (T-47)

The four-engine transport, which was operated by the Correo Aereo Militar al Exterior (CAME) courier branch, had been on a regular service originating at Buenos Aires, Argentina, and was carrying as passengers both military personnel and civilians when it crashed and burned some 20 miles (30km) north of the city of Lima, where it was to have landed. All but three of the 49 persons aboard the aircraft lost their lives; the survivors, consisting of two children and a member of the crew of seven, suffered serious injuries. Its undercarriage extended, the C-54 slammed into a sand dune during the final phase of the approach to the Lima-Callao airport, the crash occurring in darkness and instrument meteorological conditions, with heavy fog. The accident was attributed to improper instrument flight rules (IFR) procedures on the part of the pilot.

11 MAY 1964 (c.19:20)

Location	*Near Angeles, Papanga, the Philippines*
Operator	*US Air Force*
Aircraft type	*Boeing C-135B (61-0332)*

Operated by the Military Air Transport Service (MATS) and carrying mostly US Air Force and Navy-enlisted men, the jet transport crashed and burned while attempting to land at Clark Air Base, located about 50 miles (80km) north-west of Manila, in the process hitting a taxi-cab that had been travelling along Mitchell Highway. Other than two Chinese Nationalist passengers, the 79 military personnel killed in the disaster were Americans, including five of the aircraft's ten crew members and one riding in the vehicle. The five survivors from the C-135, including the pilot and co-pilot, and the other two occupants of the taxi suffered serious injuries.

Having completed a transpacific flight from the USA, which had originated at Travis Air Force Base in California and stopped at Hickam Air Force Base in Hawaii, the aircraft began a precision radar (PAR) approach to Runway 02 in darkness

and adverse meteorological conditions, with thunderstorm activity, heavy rain showers and an indefinite ceiling of 300ft (100m). Just before the accident the winds, which were blowing at around 20 knots, had shifted from a north-easterly direction to almost due north. At a point some 3 miles (5km) from the threshold, it first descended below the glide path, and this deviation continued despite three advisories from the PAR controller. About 2 miles (3km) out, it exceeded the PAR lower safety limit, whereupon the controller advised the crew to initiate a go-around. Almost immediately, however, the co-pilot reported the runway in sight. The transport was then given the radio frequency of the control tower, which in turn transmitted the latest wind information and gave it landing clearance. Its extended undercarriage initially struck the top of a base perimeter fence approximately 7ft (2m) above the ground and some 3,500ft (1,050m) from the threshold of the runway but on its extended centreline, and the aircraft then clipped a tower with its left wing and finally slammed to earth. Crossing the highway, it broke apart, ultimately coming to rest around 2,000ft (600m) from the end of the runway and approximately 300ft (100m) to the left of the extended centreline.

The factors leading to the unstabilised approach and the crash itself were not disclosed by the air force, although the attempt by the pilot to complete the landing visually undoubtedly contributed to the accident. It was noted in the investigative report that just before the crash, the visibility had improved slightly, to about 1.2 miles (2km).

A US Air Force Boeing C-135B Stratolifter jet transport, identical to the aircraft that crashed at Clark Air Base in the Philippines, with a loss of 79 lives. (Boeing)

3 SEPTEMBER 1964 (c.19:00)

Location   Near Vaong Nong, Thailand
Operator   Royal Thai Air Force
Aircraft type   Douglas C-47D (L2-2902)

The twin-engine transport, carrying Thai military personnel and their dependants, crashed and burst into flames 200 miles (320km) north-east of Bangkok and approximately 1.2 miles (2km) from the airport serving Ubol, where it was to have landed. Killed in the accident were 28 of the 34 persons aboard the aircraft; the survivors suffered various injuries. Having nearly completed an internal flight from Lop Buri, the C-47 struck a tree and slammed to earth during its landing approach, the crash occurring in darkness and conditions of poor visibility. No information regarding the probable cause of the accident was disclosed.

19 OCTOBER 1964 (c.11:35)

Location   Near Belgrade, Yugoslavia
Operator   Soviet Air Force
Aircraft type   Ilyushin Il-18V (SSSR-75668)

The four-engine turboprop transport crashed while attempting to land at Surcin Airport, located 10 miles (15km) west of Belgrade, following a flight from Moscow, USSR. All 33 persons aboard were killed, including a crew of 11; among the passengers were seven high-ranking Soviet military officers, one of them the nation's army Chief of Staff, Marshal Sergei S. Biryuzov. Instructed by the control tower to approach from the west, the aircraft was reportedly 'too low and not on course' when it struck 1,700ft (520m) Avala Hill, approximately 120ft (35m) below its peak, exploding on impact. The weather at the time consisted of rain and fog, with winds of around 25 knots. This aircraft may have been part of the fleet of the Soviet airline Aeroflot.

11 DECEMBER 1964 (time unknown)

Location   Near Da Nang, (South) Vietnam
Operator   (South) Vietnamese Air Force
Aircraft type   Fairchild C-123

All 38 servicemen aboard lost their lives when the twin-engine transport slammed into a mountain north of Da Nang Air Base, from where it had taken off shortly before. Except for two American passengers, the victims were South Vietnamese military personnel, including the crew of six. The crash occurred in evening darkness and during what was described as a 'secret' mission, but no further details were made available.

16 JANUARY 1965 (c.09:30)

Location   Wichita, Kansas, USA
Operator   US Air Force
Aircraft type   Boeing KC-135A (57-1442)

The Strategic Air Command (SAC) jet tanker crashed and exploded in a residential section of the city approximately 5 miles (10km) north-north-west of McConnell Air Force Base, from where it had taken off about 3½ minutes earlier, on an aerial refuelling mission. All seven crewmen of the aircraft and 22 persons on the ground, the latter including a pregnant

A number of houses were levelled or set ablaze by the crash of the US Air Force KC-135 in a neighbourhood of Wichita, Kansas, USA. (AP/Wide World Photos)

woman, perished in the disaster, while 17 others suffered injuries. In the impact and resulting fires, 14 houses were demolished. The scene of the tragedy was ten blocks west of Wichita State University.

Following its departure from Runway 36-Left, the aircraft had climbed to an approximate height of 500–700ft (150–200m) above the ground before it started to descend. A Mayday distress message was transmitted from the tanker, and the crew escape hatch had been jettisoned prior to the crash, further indication of an in-flight emergency. According to witnesses, the KC-135 initiated a left bank while proceeding in a southerly direction, trying to return to the base, and completed a rotation of about 180 degrees as it plunged to earth in a steep nose-down attitude. The weather at the time was clear and cold, with high cirrus clouds and a north-north-easterly wind of 5 knots.

Remains of a parachute were found in the No. 1 engine of 57-1442, which could have resulted in an asymmetrical thrust condition. The control difficulties that may have factored in the crash would have been even worse had it also become entangled in one of the aircraft's ailerons. Furthermore, the crew could have become distracted with a loss of directional control and allowed the tanker to stall during the steep turn.

15 JUNE 1965 (c.09:50)

Location	Near Columbus, Georgia, USA
First aircraft	
Operator	US Army
Aircraft type	Bell UH-1D (63-8760)
Second aircraft	
Operator	US Army
Aircraft type	Bell UH-1D (63-8840)

During a tactical troop lift operation, the two turbine-engine helicopters collided in mid-air and crashed at the Fort Benning military base about 5 miles (10km) north-north-west of the town of Cusseta, killing 18 American servicemen. There were no survivors among the occupants of either aircraft, ten aboard 8760 and eight aboard 8840; the victims included a three-member crew assigned to each helicopter.

The two involved in the accident were among eight UH-1D helicopters flying in two groups of four aircraft each. After the pilot of the lead helicopter of one approximately diamond-shaped formation decided to leave the flight for a weather check, he radioed his intentions to the No. 2 aircraft, 8760, in front of which he would make his turn, assuming that the No. 3, 8840, which was to his left rear, would remain in position. But when the flight leader accelerated and initiated a climbing right turn, the No. 3 inexplicably turned in the same direction, as if to follow, while the No. 2 made a slight left turn. The resulting collision occurred at an above-ground height of approximately 300–350ft (100–105m), despite an evasive bank by 8840. Both helicopters lost their main rotor blades and plummeted to earth, and 8760 burned after its impact with the ground. The fourth UH-1D in the group banked to the right and managed to avoid the flying debris.

Despite rain showers in the vicinity, the meteorological conditions were apparently good at the time and location of the accident.

25 JUNE 1965 (01:46)

Location	Near Santa Ana, California, USA
Operator	US Air Force
Aircraft type	Boeing C-135A (60-0373)

Operated by the Military Air Transport Service (MATS) and bound for Okinawa, with a planned stop at Hickam Air Force Base, in Hawaii, USA, the jet transport crashed some 40 miles (65km) south-east of Los Angeles, about a minute after its departure from El Toro Marine Corps Air Station. All 85 American servicemen aboard perished, including a crew of 12 air force personnel; the passengers were members of the Marine Corps.

After taking off from Runway 34R, the aircraft struck Loma Ridge at an approximate elevation of 1,000ft (300m), or only about 200ft (60m) below its crest, some 3 miles (5km) north-north-west of the base, exploding on impact. The crash occurred in darkness, and the meteorological conditions in the area at the time consisted of light drizzle, fog and a low overcast, with broken clouds at 500ft (150m) and solid coverage at 900ft (275m), and a visibility of 3 miles (5km). The wind was from due south at 4 knots.

For undetermined reasons, 60-0373 had failed to make a left procedural turn following take-off, and as a result flew

One engine of the US Air Force C-135A jet transport lies on the ridge struck by the aircraft following take-off from the El Toro Marine Corps Air Station. (UPI/Corbis-Bettmann)

Opposite top: An RAF Transport Command Handley Page Hastings of the type that crashed near Oxford, England, on 6 July 1965. (British Aerospace)

Opposite bottom: A helicopter swoops low over the smouldering wreckage of the RAF transport after the accident that killed 41 servicemen. (AP/Wide World Photos)

into the rising terrain. The climb rate required for terrain clearance was apparently in excess of the performance capabilities of the aircraft. Significantly, a hazard report concerning operations at the El Toro base had previously been issued because the departure requirements there were known to exceed those of a C-135.

6 JULY 1965 (c.16:00)

Location	Near Oxford, England
Operator	Royal Air Force
Aircraft type	Handley Page Hastings C Mark 1 (TG577)

The four-engine transport, which was on a paratroop dropping sortie, crashed some 35 miles (55km) north-west of London, and all 41 British servicemen aboard perished, including a crew of six. The passengers consisted of both Army and RAF personnel. Soon after it had taken off from RAF Abingdon, a member of the flight crew reported control difficulties and that the aircraft needed to return for an immediate landing. Granted such clearance, TG577 was south-east of the base when it abruptly climbed to an approximate height of 2,000ft (600m), then turned to the left, plummeted to earth and exploded.

The accident was attributed to the fatigue fracture of the two upper bolts that attached the right outer elevator out-rigger to the drag member of the horizontal stabiliser. As a result, the outer portion of the elevator became uncontrollable. It was the opinion of a board of inquiry that abnormal friction in the bearings due to the distortion of the hinge line, coupled with the drooping of the outer half of the elevator, produced the abnormal pitch-up and subsequent stall. The weather at the time was good and did not factor in the crash. A temporary grounding of the entire RAF Hastings fleet was necessary in order to complete inspections and required modifications.

7 JULY 1965 (time unknown)

Location	Near Cairo, Egypt
Operator	Soviet Air Force
Aircraft type	Antonov An-12

The four-engine turboprop transport, its passengers all Egyptian Army soldiers, crashed and burned shortly after taking off from Almaza Airport, on a flight to Yemen. All but one of the 31 servicemen aboard the aircraft were killed, the sole survivor being one member of the crew of nine Soviet air force personnel.

25 JULY 1965 (c.07:40)

Location	Near Libacao, Aklan, the Philippines
Operator	Philippine Air Force
Aircraft type	Douglas C-47 (777)

All 37 persons aboard perished when the twin-engine transport, on a domestic flight to San Jose Buenavista, Antique, from Nichols Air Base, located near Manila, crashed and burned on Panay Island, 60 miles (100km) north-north-east of its destination. The victims included seven military crewmen, but more than half of the passengers were civilians.

Last reported cruising at 7,000ft (2,000m), the southbound aircraft had struck a wooded, north-eastern slope of Mount Madiac, the accident occurring in adverse weather conditions consisting of low clouds and rain. Wreckage was located three days later at an approximate elevation of 6,000ft (1,800m), which was no less than 1,000ft (300m) from the top of the mountain. At the time of impact, it was slightly off course, and although this deviation may have resulted from the winds it encountered, estimated to have been as high as 30 to 40 knots, no official findings pertaining to the cause of the crash were released by the Philippine Air Force.

24 AUGUST 1965 (c.10:10)

Location	Hong Kong
Operator	US Marine Corps
Aircraft type	Lockheed KC-130F (149802)

The four-engine turboprop tanker/transport crashed in Kowloon Bay immediately after it had taken off from Hong Kong (Kai Tak) International Airport, bound for Da Nang and Saigon, (South) Vietnam. Killed in the accident were 59 American servicemen aboard the aircraft, including one passenger who succumbed to his injuries about a week later and two members of the crew of six. The 12 survivors, among them both the pilot and co-pilot, suffered various injuries.

This was a disaster that had its origin in material failure, but which ultimately resulted from what a board of investigation report would later deem as 'the negligence, inefficiency and exercise of poor judgement' on the part of a marine captain, who was the designated aircraft commander of this particular flight. Some two weeks before the crash, 149802 had been grounded due to a malfunction in its No. 1 power plant; two days later, that engine was changed, but not the corresponding propeller. Difficulties with it persisted, however, right up to the take-off that ended in tragedy.

With the No. 1 developing only partial power, the commander, who was in the right seat on the flight deck, announced to the pilot, in the left seat, that they would proceed on three engines. He also instructed the pilot, who had limited experience in the type, to fly the aircraft. The crew neither feathered the propeller of the malfunctioning power plant, nor trimmed the KC-130 Hercules for a three-engine take-off. When all four power levers were advanced as the No. 1 remained under only partial power, it created an asymmetrical condition. Despite the use of nosewheel

One wing is raised from Kowloon Bay near Hong Kong's international airport, the scene of the US Marine Corps KC-130 crash that claimed 59 lives. (Associated Press)

steering, the pilot could not maintain directional control, and the transport began to drift to the left of Runway 13, after reaching a speed of about 100mph (150kmh). Just before it departed the runway, the flight engineer called 'Abort', and the pilot tried to reduce power, but immediately the commander blocked the power levers and commenced rotation. Rolling across an area of grass in a nose-high attitude, the aircraft became airborne and flew in a semi-stalled condition at a height of around 100–200ft (30–60m), while banked to the left, until its port wing struck a sea wall, which was 6ft (2m) high, some 500ft (150m) to the left of the runway. After traversing a distance of approximately 800ft (250m) in the air, the Hercules finally plunged into the water and caught fire about 400ft (120m) beyond the sea wall, its undercarriage and flaps still extended at the moment of impact. All of the victims' bodies were subsequently recovered, their deaths attributed to drowning and/or the effects of the fire. Some of the occupants who managed to escape from the wreckage could not be rescued. At the time of the accident, the local weather conditions were good, the wind calm.

Procedures outlined in the KC-130 pilot's handbook dictated that in a three-engine take-off, wherein an outboard power plant is inoperative, the opposite outboard one be placed at the flight idle position, while both inboard engines

be advanced to take-off power. The operating outboard engine is then to be given increased power during the ground roll as directional control becomes available. Three-engine take-offs were prohibited on passenger flights, but as the No. 1 power plant of 149802 was not totally inoperative, neither this restriction nor the engine-out procedure would have been technically applicable. Compounding the error by the aircraft commander was the fact that he had not been seated in the pilot's position, i.e. to the left on the flight deck, which initially deprived him of recognising the difficulty in controlling the direction of the take-off roll through contact with the nose wheel steering; and in surrendering operation of the power levers, he made possible what may well have been a critical reduction in power when his subordinate crewmen decided to abandon the take-off.

Prior to the attempted take-off, the aircraft's No. 1 engine was determined to have been overspeeding slightly, and not developing enough power to offset the drag produced by the corresponding propeller. After switching to mechanical governing and shifting several times had no corrective effect on this condition, the commander elected to proceed on three engines. The board considered it possible that the same propeller had gone into reverse at a critical point, but this could not be proven because neither it nor the power plant itself were recovered from the bay, as was most of the wreckage. Among the recommendations made in the accident report was one that action be taken within the squadron to which 149802 had belonged to promulgate and require compliance with Naval Air Training and Operating Procedures Standardization (NATOPS) policies.

2 NOVEMBER 1965 (time unknown)

Location	Obock, French Somaliland (Djibouti)
Operator	L'Armée de l'Air (French Air Force)
Aircraft type	Douglas C-47B (316410)

Operated by the Commandement du Transport Aérien Militaire branch and having completed a short flight from the city of Djibouti, the aircraft crashed and exploded while attempting to land at the local airport. All 30 French servicemen aboard the twin-engine transport, including a crew of five, lost their lives in the afternoon accident; the passengers were members of a hand-ball team. No further details about the crash or suspected cause were released.

3 NOVEMBER 1965 (c.07:30)

Location	Off Northern Panama
Operator	Fuerza Aérea Argentina (Argentine Air Force)
Aircraft type	Douglas C-54 (TC-48)

The four-engine transport crashed in the Caribbean Sea with 68 persons aboard, including a military crew of nine. No survivors or bodies were found, and searchers recovered only personal effects – clothing and life vests – floating in the Gulf of Mosquitos near the mouth of the Miguel River. Most of its passengers were Argentine Air Force cadets. The aircraft had been en route from Howard Air Force Base, in the Panama Canal Zone, to San Salvador, El Salvador, its first refuelling stop during a flight with an ultimate destination of the United States, when the pilot sent a distress message, reporting a fire in the No. 3 power plant, and announced he was diverting to Limon, Costa Rica. No determination was made as to the cause of the reported blaze.

11 DECEMBER 1965 (c.15:00)

Location	Near Tuy Hoa, (South) Vietnam
Operator	US Air Force
Aircraft type	Fairchild C-123B (56-4376)

All 85 servicemen aboard perished when the twin-engine transport, which was on a South Vietnamese internal flight from Pleiku to the Tuy Hoa airfield, crashed about 20 miles (30km) west of its destination and some 250 miles (400km) north-east of Saigon. The victims included a crew of four US Air Force personnel; the passengers were all troops of the Army of South Vietnam.

Apparently proceeding on a south-easterly heading and probably descending, the aircraft initially hit trees on top of a mountain at an approximate elevation of 4,000ft (1,200m). After continuing airborne a short distance further, it fell vertically some 1,000ft (300m), and appeared to have struck the ground in a flat spin, with no forward velocity, then disintegrated and burned. The weather in the area at the time was characterised by low ceilings, which could have varied from 50–1,000ft (15–300m), as well as rain showers and variable winds. These conditions hampered the search for 56-4376 for nearly two weeks, after which its positive identification was made. Due to the fact that the crash occurred in hostile territory, in which there were concentrations of Viet Cong troops, neither recovery nor a ground examination of the aircraft's wreckage was possible.

A US Air Force Fairchild C-123 transport, two of which were involved in fatal crashes in South Vietnam during the winter of 1965–66. (Fairchild Aircraft)

4

1966–1990

Introduced during the Second World War and refined in Korea, the helicopter would finally make its mark as a useful military tool during the conflict in South-east Asia. Used primarily by US and South Vietnamese military forces, rotary-wing

aircraft would prove their value by transporting troops into and evacuating them out of battle areas and, coupled with improved medical techniques, saving the lives of countless wounded soldiers. But the aircraft and their crews also paid a heavy price, with the US alone losing nearly 5,000 helicopters during its long involvement in the conflict. Large turboprop and jet transports also saw extensive use in the war. The two worst US military aviation disasters in fact took place in South Vietnam, one a combat loss and the other resulting from

The Bell Iroquois, this model the UH-1D, became synonymous with the US involvement in South East Asia, with both heavy use, and heavy losses. (Bell Helicopter Textron)

accidental causes; the second of these was the tragic C-5A babylift crash occurring in the final days before the collapse of South Vietnam.

The former Soviet Union experienced its own Vietnam-type debacle in Afghanistan, suffering its own share of aircraft losses due to accidents or hostile action. Other 'brush' wars flared up during this period in Africa and Central America. And the invasion of Kuwait by Iraq in 1990 and involvement by Western military forces opened the door to still more losses of aircraft and personnel, although the subsequent combat operation was of remarkably short duration. Due to their willingness to share information, the majority of the accounts covered in the 25-year span of this section involved US military forces.

25 JANUARY 1966 (c.10:15)

Location	Near Binh Khe, (South) Vietnam
Operator	US Air Force
Aircraft type	Fairchild C-123B (54-0702)

The twin-engine transport crashed and burned some 300 miles (480km) north-east of Saigon and approximately 5 miles (10km) east of the An Khe airfield, from where it had taken off less than 10 minutes earlier. All 46 American servicemen aboard, including a crew of four air force personnel, were killed.

The accident occurred as the aircraft was on a (South) Vietnamese internal flight to Bong Son, its passengers comprising army troops. Banked slightly to the right, the C-123 initially struck trees on top of a 2,000ft (600m) hill, which sheared off about 20ft (6m) of its starboard wing and half of its horizontal stabiliser/elevator assembly. It then rolled uncontrollably to the right and slammed to earth inverted. At the time of the crash, the weather in the area consisted of broken clouds at 1,000ft (300m) and an overcast of 2,500ft (750m).

Operating under a visual flight rules (VFR) clearance, 54-0702 had last been observed proceeding normally in an easterly direction and at a low altitude below a ragged layer of clouds prior to the crash. An examination of the No. 2 power plant revealed that an in-flight magnesium fire had consumed the carburettor, accessory and blower sections, and that at the moment of impact the corresponding propeller was windmilling under little or no power. Of unknown significance was that the same engine had stopped twice on the ground before the transport took off.

The exact cause of the blaze could not be determined, but all the components from the firewall to the point that the fuel entered the blower case to the fuel feed valve were suspected. Whatever maintenance or operating factors may have led or contributed to the accident were not disclosed by air force authorities. Noted in the investigative report were the hazards faced by such Vietnam-era flights, including hostile action, inadequate navigational aids and the fact that they were often conducted under VFR in marginal meteorological conditions.

4 MAY 1966 (c.08:00)

Location	Near Di Linh, (South) Vietnam
Operator	US Army
Aircraft type	Boeing/Vertol CH-47A (64-13138)

All 21 American servicemen aboard (17 passengers and a crew of four) were killed when the twin-rotor, turbine-engine helicopter crashed around 15 miles (25km) north-west of Nhon Co, from where it had taken off earlier, on a re-supply mission. As the aircraft approached its intended landing site, located 110 miles (175km) north-east of Saigon, some US military personnel on the ground observed smoke and flames emanating from its aft portion. It then executed a series of turns to the left before plummeting vertically into a wooded area while banked steeply to port, then exploded and burned. A portion of an aft main rotor blade measuring 12ft (3.5m) in length was found to have separated in flight. Blamed for the accident was the material failure of the aircraft's No. 2 pinion drive shaft thrust bearing. The weather was not considered a factor.

17 AUGUST 1966 (c.13:40)

Location	Near Da Nang, (South) Vietnam
Operator	US Marine Corps
Aircraft type	Chance Vought F-8E (150321)

Immediately after taking off from the north/south runway at Da Nang Air Base, on a combat mission, the bomb-laden jet fighter crashed into a village, reportedly following engine failure. Although its pilot (and only occupant) ejected safely, 33 persons on the ground were killed and about 20 injured in the impact and ensuing explosions.

11 NOVEMBER 1966 (c.01:30)

Location	North Atlantic Ocean
Operator	US Air Force
Aircraft type	Lockheed EC-121H (55-5262)

The airborne early-warning and control aircraft crashed some 140 miles (225km) east-south-east of Chatham, located on the eastern tip of the Cape Cod peninsula, Massachusetts, USA, in an area where the depth of the water was about 175–200ft (55–60m). Among its 19 crewmen, searchers found no survivors nor any of the victims' bodies.

None of the recovered wreckage showed evidence of in-flight fire, explosion or mechanical failure. However, shortly before the crash, 55-5262 was observed at a height of only about 200ft (60m), on a north-north-easterly heading and apparently in a level attitude while emitting smoke or vapour. After passing over a fishing vessel with at least one of its four engines back-firing, the aircraft struck the surface of the ocean, apparently extremely hard and in a nose-up, right-banking attitude, with its undercarriage retracted, exploding on impact and leaving flames burning on top of the water. The crash occurred in early-morning darkness, but the weather in the area at the time was clear, with a visibility of around 5 miles (10km) and winds out of the south ranging from approximately 10 to 20 knots.

26 NOVEMBER 1966 (c.19:20)

Location	*Near Saigon, (South) Vietnam*
Operator	*US Air Force*
Aircraft type	*Douglas C-47D (44-76574)*

The twin-engine transport crashed and burst into flames in a rice paddy, killing all 25 persons aboard. With the exception of one American civilian, the victims were all US servicemen, including the crew of six. Due to a malfunction in the left power plant, the aircraft was returning to Tan Son Nhut Airport, from where it had taken off shortly before, ultimately bound for Korat Air Base in Thailand.

The first approach, to Runway 07, ended in a go-around manoeuvre because the undercarriage could not be extended. The crash occurred as the C-47 was proceeding on a north-easterly heading with its left propeller feathered, the pilot having radioed his intention to circle back and land on the same runway. It was dark at the time of the accident, but the meteorological conditions in the area were good, with a broken overcast and a visibility of around 10 miles (15km). No information was released pertaining to the cause of the engine trouble or the crash itself.

10 MARCH 1967 (c.16:20)

Location	*Near Phan Rang, (South) Vietnam*
Operator	*US Navy*
Aircraft type	*Douglas C-47J (99844)*

All 25 American servicemen aboard were killed when the twin-engine transport, which had been on an internal (South) Vietnamese flight to Saigon from Cam Ranh Bay Air Base, crashed and exploded about 170 miles (275km) east-north-east of its intended destination. No further details, including the suspected cause of the crash, were released.

8 APRIL 1967 (c.11:00)

Location	*Seoul, South Korea*
Operator	*Republic of Korea Air Force*
Aircraft type	*Curtiss C-46*

The twin-engine transport, which had been on an internal South Korean flight to Taegu, Kyongsang Pukto, crashed and burst into flames in a residential area in the Seoul suburb of Chonggu-dong. A total of 59 persons lost their lives in the disaster, all 15 South Korean service personnel aboard the aircraft (12 passengers and a crew of three) and the rest on the ground; 23 others suffered injuries. According to an official statement, the accident, which occurred minutes after the C-46 had taken off from Yoido Air Base, was precipitated by a malfunction in the left power plant, after which the pilot must have lost control in the inclement weather conditions, which consisted of fog and drizzling rain.

17 APRIL 1967 (c.17:40)

Location	*Near Ma'muniyeh, Tehran, Iran*
Operator	*Imperial Iranian Air Force*
Aircraft type	*Lockheed C-130B (5-107)*

During a domestic flight from Shiraz to the city of Tehran, the four-engine turboprop transport crashed and burned approximately 50 miles (80km) south-west of its destination, and all 23 persons aboard were killed. Most of the victims were Iranian military personnel, including the crew of nine, but the passengers included some civilian dependants. The aircraft had been cruising in an area of thunderstorm activity and reportedly 'exploded' in mid-air after being struck by lightning.

15 JUNE 1967 (c.05:00)

Location	*Near Coari, Amazonas, Brazil*
Operator	*Força Aérea Brasileira (Brazilian Air Force)*
Aircraft type	*Douglas C-47B (2068)*

The twin-engine transport had been on an internal flight originating at Belem, bound for the military base at Cachimbo, when the pilot reported the failure of its radio compass. Turning back, he was, in the darkness, apparently unable to locate Jacareacanga, also in Para, where it had last stopped for refuelling. He then reported proceeding on towards Manaus. In his last radio transmission, the pilot said he would attempt a forced landing in the jungle. About ten days later, the wreckage of 2068 was found submerged in a swamp, the aircraft having struck trees and lost a wing before plunging into the water. Among the 25 persons aboard the transport, all of whom were military personnel except two civilian passengers, five survivors were located, the latter including one member of the crew of five. It was believed that the C-47 had been forced down before dawn by fuel exhaustion.

17 JUNE 1967 (c.19:30)

Location	*An Khe, (South) Vietnam*
Operator	*US Air Force*
Aircraft type	*Lockheed C-130B (60-0293)*

Operating on a scheduled (South) Vietnamese internal passenger service originating at and ultimately destined for Tan Son Nhut Airport, serving Saigon, the four-engine turboprop transport crashed after an aborted take-off at An Khe Airfield, one of seven en-route stops. Among the 56 persons aboard the aircraft, 35 passengers lost their lives; the victims included US, (South) Vietnamese and South Korean service personnel and five civilians, one an American. The survivors, ten of whom suffered injuries, included the seven-man US Air Force crew.

The aircraft was bound for Qui Nhon, one segment of the flight, when it began its take-off on Runway 21, its elevator control being held back intentionally in order to aerodynamically lighten the load on the nose wheel strut due to the rough surface. Except for extremely hot air entering the cargo compartment of the aircraft, where the air-conditioning system was inoperative, indications were normal during the ground roll until the occurrence of a bright flash of light on the port side, whereupon the C-130 veered to the left and departed the runway at a point approximately 2,400ft (730m) from the point of brake release. Nosewheel steering was effective in returning it to the runway, at which time the crew applied reverse power. Crossing it diagonally, the transport went off the right side of the runway and down a 25ft (7.5m) embankment, coming to rest 400ft (120m) from the end of the hard surface. The impact was not severe, but fire that erupted on the right wing subsequently consumed much of 60-0293. The weather at the time was good and not considered a factor in the accident, which occurred at dusk. No information pertaining to the cause of the crash or the events leading up to it was released by military authorities.

23 JUNE 1967 (c.09:00)

Location	Near Jacksonville, North Carolina, USA
First aircraft	
Operator	US Marine Corps
Aircraft type	Bell UH-1B (638572)
Second aircraft	
Operator	US Marine Corps
Aircraft type	Sikorsky CH-53A (153305)

The two turbine-engine helicopters collided in mid-air, and both then crashed and burned at the New River Marine Corps Air Facility, located on the grounds of Camp LeJeune. Including both pilots (and the only occupants) of the smaller UH-1 and two members of the crew of four assigned to the twin-engine CH-53A Sea Stallion, 22 American servicemen were killed in the accident. With the exception of one victim who succumbed to the effects of the post-crash fire, the fatalities resulted from impact trauma. The 13 survivors from the CH-53, among them the pilot and co-pilot, suffered various injuries.

At the time of the collision, 638572 was engaged in a syllabus instructional flight, and 153305 on a troop-lift exercise. The crew of the former, planning a touch-and-go landing, received authorisation to turn down-wind and also acknowledged a traffic advisory from the control tower concerning the latter, which was preparing to land, but the pilot apparently took no action in response to this information. He evidently was not ready to make the turn at that point, however, and chose to continue straight ahead

The path of the US Air Force C-130 that crashed after an aborted take-off from the An Khe airstrip on 17 June 1967. (US Air Force)

until a more advantageous position could be attained. The UH-1 was on or near the ground about 2 minutes before it proceeded in accordance with the original clearance, flying parallel to Runway 23, while starting to ascend. Meanwhile, the CH-53, which had been authorised for a straight-in landing approach, similarly flew parallel to the same runway and started to descend with its undercarriage extended. As indicated by an evasive roll to the right initiated by the aircraft, one or both pilots of 638572 probably saw 153305 at the last instant, but the helicopters nevertheless collided at an approximate height of 500ft (150m). Losing its tail rotor, the UH-1 fell to the ground immediately, while the CH-53 descended to about 100ft (30m) before plunging out of control after losing its tail boom and rotor.

Considered as the primary factor in the accident was the inexperience and lack of perception on the part of the tower controller, who, not fully aware of the inherent dangers associated in the controlling aircraft with a wide variation in speed, did not accurately perceive the impending conflict until it was too late. Aggravating this shortcoming was the fact that the pilots involved in the disaster had developed confidence in tower personnel to exert strict supervision of air traffic operating within the control zone.

Additionally, tower personnel did not at first realise that the landing site the CH-53 pilot had intended to utilise was directly off the end of the runway, believing it to be some 1,000–1,500ft (300–500m) off to its right side, with the aircraft thus following a corresponding line of flight. Neither was the pilot of the UH-1 himself aware of the landing zone to be used by the CH-53; such knowledge might have led to a different reaction on his part.

The lack of available information on the zone made available to flight crews was considered a contributing factor in the accident. The pilot of 153305 was aware of 638572, but he assumed the tower controller would maintain adequate clearance through timely traffic advisories, since he had been cleared directly into the landing zone. Neither crew apparently had visual contact with each others' aircraft in the final seconds before the accident until it was too late. The weather was not a factor in the collision.

Noted in the investigative report was that the delay

between its clearance and the time 638572 proceeded on the originally planned touch-and-go landing had been too long for such an authorisation to be considered still valid, and that a simple clearing turn on the spot from a hover would have been the minimum effort by its crew to maintain a safe level of flight. It was therefore recommended in the report on this accident that a definite regulation be established and published concerning the length of time a helicopter may remain on or near the ground when cleared for such a procedure. Another recommendation was to clearly describe and label in the Marine Corps' air operations manual the landing sites within the control zone of the New River facility.

29 JULY 1967 (c.11:00)

Location	Gulf of Tonkin (USS Forrestal)
Operator	US Navy
Aircraft type	McDonnell F-4B (153061)

This aviation/marine disaster occurred during the height of the American involvement in the war in South-east Asia. On this day, the naval aircraft carrier USS *Forrestal* (CVA-59) was operating off the coast of (North) Vietnam, preparing for an air strike against targets in that nation. Its location at the time was approximately 175 miles (280km) north of Da

More than a score of aircraft were destroyed in explosions and fire on the flight deck of the US Navy carrier USS Forrestal *in a disaster off the Vietnamese coast.* (UPI/Corbis-Bettmann)

Nang, (South) Vietnam. The vessel had turned into the wind on a launch course of almost due north when a Zuni rocket mounted on 153061 was accidentally fired from its launcher.

Crossing the flight deck, the Zuni struck another combat jet, an A-4E, which was located on the port side of the carrier, some 100ft (30m) away, also being readied for launch. That aircraft's 400-gallon (1,500-litre) fuel tank was ruptured, touching off a fire and the beginning of a holocaust. The burning fuel was spread aft and fanned by a 32-knot wind as well as the exhausts of three other jets that had their engines running. The first of seven explosions that further spread the flames occurred about 90 seconds after the start of the blaze, when a bomb that had fallen from an aircraft detonated. The conflagration was fed by some 40,000 gallons (150,000 litres) of JP-5 jet fuel. The last of the flames on the deck were extinguished in less than an hour, but scattered fires continued to burn in other parts of the ship until early the following morning.

The final toll in the disaster was 134 men killed, including the pilot of the aircraft hit by the rocket, and 161 injured. Miraculously, all but four of the 20 men who jumped, fell or got thrown overboard were rescued. Of the 21 jets destroyed – three RA-5Cs, seven F-4Bs and 11 A-4Es – four had to be jettisoned over the side of the vessel because they were afire or leaking fuel. Another 40 aircraft sustained damage. Total costs exceeded US$70 million.

An investigation revealed that the initial firing of the Zuni rocket resulted from simultaneous material failures of aircraft and armament components of 153061 and its loaded ordnance stores, in conjunction with human error. Specifically, the pilot of the F-4B may have triggered the firing by superimposing enough transient voltage upon the existing stray voltage when he switched from external to internal electrical power preparatory to starting the aircraft's left engine, having already started the right one. Alternatively, two members of the weapons loading team could have been responsible for it by either arming the safety switch while checking whether the safety pin was securely in place or by mistakenly placing the three-point home/step toggle switch located at the rear of the triple ejector rack in the 'stepping' rather than 'homing' position after the rocket launchers had been plugged in and the shorting device on one of the other two launchers been faulty. Contributing to the unplanned rocket launch was the defective design of the pylon electrical disconnect, which proved to be susceptible to shorting by moisture, and the poor and outdated doctrinal and technical documentation of both ordnance and aircraft equipment and procedures, which were evident at all levels of command.

One endorsement in the investigative report concluded that the Zuni would probably not have fired had the rocket harness cable that made the electrical connection between it and the launcher not been plugged in until 153061 was on the catapult, in accordance with prescribed regulations, although this was considered a vague directive. Among the recommendations made in the report was the immediate discontinuation of use of the type launcher involved until modifications could be carried out and the issuance of directives outlining precise procedures for conducting rocket firing circuit stray voltage checks.

8 OCTOBER 1967 (c.09:40)

Location	*Near Huong Thuy, (South) Vietnam*
Operator	*US Air Force*
Aircraft type	*Lockheed C-130B (61-2649)*

In what was classified as a scheduled tactical re-supply mission, the four-engine turboprop transport had been on an internal (South) Vietnamese flight to Da Nang when it crashed some 15 miles (25km) east-south-east of the Hue/ Phu Bai airfield, from where it had taken off about 10 minutes earlier. All 23 American servicemen aboard (18 passengers and a crew of five) perished.

Proceeding under visual flight rules (VFR) procedures in meteorological conditions consisting of a low overcast, with a visibility of around 5 miles (10km) and ground fog in the area, the aircraft struck a mountain at an approximate elevation of 1,700ft (520m), or only about 150ft (50m) below the summit, while on an east-north-easterly heading. Impact was determined to have been with the aircraft in a level attitude and at a speed of approximately 290mph (465kmh), whereupon the C-130 exploded and disintegrated. The wreckage of 61-2649 was located two days later, but due to its location and the difficulty in maintaining security in an area of hostile action, no items could be removed from the site for further examination.

30 NOVEMBER 1967 (c.14:30)

Location	*Near Qui Nhon, (South) Vietnam*
Operator	*US Air Force*
Aircraft type	*de Havilland C-7A Caribou (62-4175)*

All 26 persons aboard were killed, including four US Air Force crewmen, when the twin-engine transport crashed and burned on the eastern slope of a mountain. Its passengers included two American civilians. The accident occurred at an approximate elevation of 1,850ft (565m) and 5 miles (10km) south of Qui Nhon Air Base, where the aircraft had been scheduled to land, after the pilot radioed that he was proceeding to Nha Trang Air Base, located 125 miles (200km) to the south, upon being advised that the weather at the former had fallen below the visual flight rules minimums. In the area at the time, the meteorological conditions consisted of a low overcast, with a visibility of 1.5–2.5 miles (2.5–4km) in drizzle or light rain. The wind was blowing from a north-easterly direction at 17 knots. As the crash occurred in hostile, inaccessible territory, no wreckage from 62-4175 was recovered.

8 JANUARY 1968 (c.17:00)

Location	*Near Quang Tri, (South) Vietnam*
Operator	*US Marine Corps*
Aircraft type	*Sikorsky CH-53A (153710)*

The turbine-engine helicopter was on an internal (South) Vietnamese flight originating at the Marble Mountain Air Facility when it slammed into a mountain and burned some 20 miles (30km) south of Dong Ha airfield, where it had last stopped before proceeding on towards its intended destination of Hue. All 42 American servicemen aboard (37 passengers and a crew of five) perished.

Having apparently lifted off under visual flight rules (VFR) procedures on what was presumed to have been an instrument flight rules (IFR) short-range clearance, with directions from the control tower to contact the Dong Ha ground-controlled approach (GCA) radar facility, the rotorcraft continued under the control of Dong Ha and later the Hue GCA without such a clearance ever being confirmed or its limits defined. Subsequently, 153710 was cleared to the 10 nautical mile fix on the 360-degree radial of the Hue tactical air navigation (TACAN) facility, via the 25 nautical mile fix on the 330-degree radial, and to maintain an altitude of 3,000ft (1,000m). Just before these instructions were given to the helicopter, the Dong Ha GCA controller advised the pilot of a slight right drift in its course, but the reception was reported to have been garbled and thus not understood. As the helicopter continued to track southwards, its target disappeared from the radarscope due to the 'shadow effect' of the surrounding terrain, and around this time radio contact was also lost. Wreckage was located two days later on the 186-degree radial of the Dong Ha TACAN, the CH-53 having crashed approximately at its assigned flight level and about 200ft (60m) below the peak of the mountain. At the time of its take-off, the weather at Dong Ha consisted of a low ceiling, with scattered clouds at 300ft (100m) and solid coverage at 1,000ft (300m), and a visibility of 3 miles (5km) in fog and light rain.

It was ruled that the pilot had erred in judgement in accepting a clearance containing no limit and then proceeding towards the hazardous terrain with both inoperative distance-measuring equipment and poor radio communications. With regard to the primary cause, one endorsement of the investigative report noted that the control tower failed to provide a complete clearance even though one had been requested. The combat environment under which the aircraft and the controlling agencies had been operating was considered a factor in the deviation from established operating procedures that contributed to the disaster. A possible contributing factor was the use of non-standard procedures by the Dong Ha agency due to its lack of communications with the Hue approach control facility.

Other factors identified in the report were the instrument meteorological conditions encountered by 153710 and the 'operationally deficient' ultra-high-frequency reception characteristics of the earlier model of the CH-53, with a significantly reduced range whenever the aircraft was flying away from the transmitting station. In order to ensure safety, the short-range clearance from Dong Ha began to share with the one used by Quang Tri Marine base, and improvements were also made in the land line communications between air-traffic control agencies in the region.

The charred hulk of the US Marine Corps C-54 transport where it came to rest after crashing into a mountain in turbulent conditions. (AP/Wide World Photos)

10 JANUARY 1968 (c.14:00)

Location	*Near Copper Canyon, Nevada, USA*
Operator	*US Marine Corps*
Aircraft type	*Douglas C-54P (50850)*

The four-engine transport crashed and burned some 30 miles (50km) south-west of Battle Mountain, and all 19 servicemen aboard were killed. The victims, including the crew of seven, were all US service personnel except for one passenger, a British Royal Marine who survived the impact but succumbed to the extremely cold temperature. The downed aircraft was located the following morning on the east side of Mount Tobin, which rises to nearly 10,000ft (3,000m). Impact had occurred about 300ft (100m) from its peak, after which the wreckage slid some 1,000ft (300m) down the mountain.

The C-54 was en route from Buckley Air National Guard Base, near Denver, Colorado, to the Naval Air Station at Seattle, Washington, on the final segment of a domestic transcontinental flight originating at the Marine Corps Air Station at Quantico, Virginia. It had been proceeding along a prescribed airway when a member of the flight crew reported difficulty maintaining a cruising height of 12,000ft (3,700m). A request was granted by the Salt Lake City Regional Air Traffic Control Centre to descend to 10,500ft (3,200m), but some time later, the aircraft reported being in icing conditions and requested vectoring around them. Turning down an offer from the control centre to ascend to a higher altitude, the crew then radioed that it was out of the icing conditions. Around 20 minutes later, in its final transmission, the transport reported losing altitude and requested clearance down to 10,000ft (3,000m), which was about 2,000ft (600m) below the minimum height for terrain clearance in this area.

Although the possibility of moderate to heavy icing and snow showers over western Nevada had been included in a pilot briefing, the Salt Lake control centre had, in response to its vector request, informed 50850 that there were no storm cells and no reports of icing along the airway being used. As a result, the pilot of the aircraft involved in the accident was unaware that the turbulence actually encountered would be hazardous, worse than that predicted at the time of the take-off. These turbulent conditions apparently caused the uncontrolled descent of the C-54 into the ground. It was further noted in the investigative report on the crash that the pilot was not technically qualified in the type aircraft, and that had he been aware of the existing weather conditions, he should have discontinued the flight.

7 FEBRUARY 1968 (c.15:00)

Location	*Northern India*
Operator	*Indian Air Force*
Aircraft type	*Antonov An-12BP (BL534)*

During an internal flight from Leh, Kashmir, to Chandigarh, Punjab, the Soviet-built turboprop transport vanished over the Himalayas with 98 persons aboard. Except for one civilian passenger, the occupants were Indian military personnel, including the crew of six. More than 35 years later, in August 2003, the first trace of the missing aircraft turned up when the remains of one of its occupants was located some 125 miles (200km) north of its destination. Two years after that discovery, more victims and wreckage from the An-12 were found on a mountainside at an approximate elevation of 18,000ft (5,500m), buried under nearly 30ft (10m) of snow, and dispersed around an area of 5sq miles (10sq km). The aircraft had apparently encountered a snowstorm in the vicinity of Rohtang Pass and initiated a premature descent.

6 MARCH 1968 (c.08:00)

Location	*Near Khe Sanh, (South) Vietnam*
Operator	*US Air Force*
Aircraft type	*Fairchild C-123K (54-0590)*

The transport, which had nearly completed an internal (South) Vietnamese flight from the Hue/Phu Bai airfield, bringing in a load of US Marine Corps troops, was shot down by enemy forces as it prepared to land at the Khe Sanh garrison, located some 400 miles (650km) north of Saigon. All 49 men aboard, one a civilian photographer riding as a passenger and the rest American service personnel, including a four-member air force crew, were killed. Forced to abandon its approach to the airstrip by a light military aeroplane landing in front of it, the C-123 was hit by ground fire during a go-around manoeuvre. Apparently struck in the right turbine, one of two auxiliary jet engines supplementing its two piston power plants, the transport then plummeted to earth in flames into enemy territory.

A US Army Bell UH-1H, the type of helicopter involved in two disastrous collisions over South Vietnam during a two-month period in 1968. (Bell Helicopter Textron)

9 MARCH 1968 (c.23:20)

Location	*Near St-Denis, Réunion*
Operator	*L'Armée de l'Air (French Air Force)*
Aircraft type	*Douglas DC-6B (43748)*

Operated by the Commandement du Transport Aérien Militaire branch and bound for Paris, the aircraft struck a hill and burst into flames soon after taking off from the airport on this Indian Ocean island, the accident occurring in darkness and rain. Among the 19 persons killed were General Charles Aillerett, the Chief of Staff of the French military and its highest-ranking officer, his wife and daughter; the sole survivor, a hostess and member of the crew assigned to the DC-6B, was seriously injured. Though not officially reported, the cause of the crash was apparently operational in nature, with the four-engine transport having not followed the correct departure procedure of turning out towards the sea after take-off, instead turning right and proceeding inland.

19 APRIL 1968 (c.10:45)

Location	*Near Cheo Reo, (South) Vietnam*
First aircraft	
Operator	*US Army*
Aircraft type	*Bell UH-1H (66-16441)*
Second aircraft	
Operator	*US Army*
Aircraft type	*Bell UH-1H (67-17255)*

The two turbine-engine helicopters, carrying as passengers (South) Vietnamese troops, collided in mid-air, then crashed and burned about 60 miles (100km) south-west of Qui Nhon. All 26 servicemen aboard both aircraft were killed, including a crew of four US Army personnel assigned to each one. Having taken off earlier from the Cheo Reo airfield, the two helicopters were flying on an approximate westerly heading when 16441, which was to the right rear of 17255, struck the lead aircraft, only their main rotor blades making contact. The collision occurred at an altitude estimated at 1,000–1,500ft (300–500m). Five of the victims must have either jumped or fallen out before the impact with the ground. Examination of the bodies and wreckage indicated that the mid-air crash probably did not result from hostile action.

30 APRIL 1968 (time unknown)

Location	Near Islamabad, (West) Pakistan
Operator	Pakistani Air Force
Aircraft type	Lockheed L-100-10 (64145)

All 22 persons aboard were killed in the crash of the four-engine turboprop transport. The victims of the morning accident were both civilians and military personnel, the latter including the crew. Few other details were released, although a preliminary report indicated a possible in-flight break-up of the aircraft, which may have been turbulence-related.

12 MAY 1968 (c.16:00)

Location	Near An Hoa, (South) Vietnam
Operator	US Air Force
Aircraft type	Lockheed C-130B (60-0297)

The four-engine turboprop transport, carrying approximately 150 South Vietnamese military personnel and their dependants and five US Air Force crewmen, was shot down some 350 miles (560km) north-east of Saigon. There were no survivors. Hit by unknown ground fire, the aircraft fell in flames about 2.5 miles (4km) east of Kham Duc, from where it had taken off shortly before.

22 JUNE 1968 (time unknown)

Location	Near Yukhnov, Russian Soviet Federative Socialist Republic, USSR
First aircraft	
Operator	Soviet Air Force
Aircraft type	Antonov An-12
Second aircraft	
Operator	Aeroflot (USSR)
Aircraft type	Ilyushin Il-14

A mid-air collision between the four-engine turboprop transport and the twin-engine piston-powered airliner, which occurred some 110 miles (175km) south-west of Moscow, claimed the lives of 120 persons, the victims including the 24 passengers and crew members of the latter. The An-12, carrying 91 passengers and a crew of five, presumably all military personnel, was one of three aircraft of the type flying from Kaunas, Lithuania, to Ryazan, RSFSR. It was reported that the Il-14, on a scheduled service from Moscow to Gomel, Belarus, had descended without authorisation after repeated requests to change its altitude due to turbulence had been denied by air-traffic control personnel. The resulting collision

occurred at 13,000ft (4,000m), with the tail fin of the military transport slicing into the lower fuselage section of the airliner.

25 JUNE 1968 (c.07:30)

Location	Near Bearcat, (South) Vietnam
First aircraft	
Operator	US Army
Aircraft type	Bell UH-1H (66-16206)
Second aircraft	
Operator	US Army
Aircraft type	Bell UH-1H (66-16592)
Third aircraft	
Operator	US Army
Aircraft type	Bell UH-1H (66-16601)

This triple crash occurred some 15 miles (25km) south-east of Saigon and in conditions of restricted visibility, with clouds obscuring nearly half of the sky as well as fog and haze. Two of the three turbine-engine rotorcraft involved were among ten helicopters engaged in a combat assault mission. A total of 29 service personnel lost their lives in the accident, including four US Army crewmen assigned to each aircraft; the passengers were troops belonging to the Royal Thai Volunteer Regiment. There were no survivors.

With the group having descended to 900ft (275m), where the weather was better, and turned on to a heading of 60 degrees, the flight leader had just entered and then emerged from a cloud when he observed an unidentified helicopter approaching from his immediate right and at the same altitude. The latter was later identified as 16601, the command and control aircraft, which had gone ahead of the group for a weather check. The leader successfully initiated an evasive manoeuvre, breaking down and to the left, but in pulling up and to the left, 16601 collided with 16592, with the latter's main rotor blades severing the former's tail rotor/boom section. The other rotorcraft in the group avoided the resulting fireball except for 16206, which was directly behind 16592 and flew into the explosion and mass of debris. Two of them exploded on impact with the ground and burned, but not 16592, which fell into a swamp after losing its main rotor and transmission assemblies in the collision. The meteorological conditions were considered a contributing factor in the accident.

3 OCTOBER 1968 (c.16:10)

Location	Near Camp Evans, (South) Vietnam
First aircraft	
Operator	US Air Force
Aircraft type	de Havilland C-7A Caribou (63-9753)
Second aircraft	
Operator	US Army
Aircraft type	Boeing/Vertol CH-47A (66-19041)

This mid-air collision between the twin-engine, fixed-wing transport and the twin-rotor, turbine-engine helicopter, which occurred about 10 miles (15km) north of Hue, claimed the lives of 25 servicemen, all but one of them American. There were no survivors from either aircraft.

Carrying ten passengers and a crew of four and on an internal (South) Vietnamese flight to Hue, the C-7 had taken off from Runway 36 at Camp Evans airfield, then made a climbing right turn on to a heading of approximately 130 degrees. Meanwhile, the CH-47 had been on a heading of around 170 degrees and in a shallow descent as it prepared to land at the camp helipad, located east and 1,000ft (300m) south of the approach end of the same runway, and which was an en-route stop during a scheduled passenger and mail service. Aboard were 11 men, including a crew of five. Converging at a shallow angle, with the speed of the aeroplane estimated at around 120mph (190kmh) and that of the helicopter about 100mph (150kmh), they collided at an altitude of approximately 1,100ft (335m).

In an apparent evasive manoeuvre, 63-9753 had initiated a roll to the right before the rear rotor blades of 66-19041 sliced into its cockpit section, killing the former's two pilots. The C-7 then went into a steep descending turn to the right and plunged to earth; there was no post-impact fire. All three of the rear rotor blades having been severed in the collision and its rear rotor pylon separating thereafter, the CH-47 fell to the ground with virtually no forward speed and exploded. Two victims actually fell from the helicopter before it crashed. The local weather conditions at the time were good, with a visibility of more than 5 miles (10km), broken cumulus and altocumulus clouds above the collision altitude and high cirrostratus, and a 5-knot wind from a north-easterly direction.

Though not officially reported by either military branch, there were indications that the army rotorcraft did not conform to the prescribed airfield circuit procedures during its approach. Specifically, it did not follow the traffic pattern of fixed-wing aircraft and had remained above the maximum height of 600ft (180m) required for helicopters. Additionally, its crew had failed to radio the control tower for clearance to land.

21 OCTOBER 1968 (c.06:00)

Location	*Near Ban Me Thuot, (South) Vietnam*
Operator	*US Air Force*
Aircraft type	*Douglas C-47D (45-0934)*

All 23 persons aboard were killed in the crash of the twin-engine transport, which occurred in mountainous terrain 110 miles (175km) north-east of Saigon. With the exception of two civilian passengers, both Americans, the victims were all US military personnel, including the crew.

Having taken off earlier from Saigon, the aircraft was to have stopped for refuelling at Da Nang, also in (South) Vietnam, during a flight with an ultimate destination of Hong Kong. It was last reported at its assigned cruising altitude of 9,000ft (2,700m) before transmitting a Mayday distress message, the pilot reporting the failure of its No. 2 power plant and that the corresponding propeller could not be feathered. Also stating that he could not maintain altitude,

the pilot requested vectors to Ban Me Thuot airfield that would provide adequate terrain clearance.

Radio and radar contact with 45-0934 was subsequently lost, the C-47 having crashed about 20 miles (30km) south of the airfield, at an approximate elevation of 2,300ft (700m) and in pre-dawn darkness and overcast weather conditions, with broken altocumulus clouds at 7,000ft (2,000m) and scattered stratus down to 1,000ft (300m). The visibility in the area was around 5 miles (10km). No further details pertaining to the cause of the initial engine malfunction nor the subsequent accident were released.

14 JANUARY 1969 (c.08:20)

Location	*North Pacific Ocean (USS* Enterprise*)*
Operator	*US Navy*
Aircraft type	*McDonnell F-4J (155804)*

Started by the detonation of some Zuni rockets mounted on the jet fighter, a series of explosions rocked the flight deck of the nuclear-powered aircraft carrier USS *Enterprise* (CVAN-65), which at the time was proceeding on a true course of 90 degrees and at a position some 75 miles (120km) south-west of Honolulu, Hawaii, USA. Killed in the disaster were a total of 27 servicemen, while nearly 350 others suffered varying degrees of injury. Damage exceeded US$50 million, including the destruction of eight F-4J, six A-7B and one EKA-3B jet aircraft.

Investigation revealed that as the ship was preparing to launch a group of aircraft, an MD-3A starting unit had been positioned adjacent to 155804, and jet exhaust gasses emanating from the unit were, or had been, impinging on the Zuni launcher that was mounted on the fighter's starboard wing and contained four rockets. The exhaust outlet of the MD-3A was found to have been within 2ft (60cm) of the launcher, and tests indicated that under similar circumstances, a Zuni warhead would deflagrate in only a little more than a minute. The shrapnel from the initial blast damaged the fuel tanks of the F-4J and four other jets, and the resulting fire rapidly spread across the carrier's flight deck, detonating bombs being carried by some of the aircraft. The fires were brought under control within 40 minutes, and completely extinguished about 2½ hours after the initial explosion.

The primary cause of the accident was determined to have been in the design of the starting unit. It was noted in the investigative report that properly applied design and safety criteria would not have allowed the use of a piece of flight deck support equipment that was capable of detonating a weapon. A significant contributing factor was considered to be the failure at many levels of responsibility to recognise the inherent hazards of the unit. The operating instructions for the MD-3A, for example, did not include specific reference to its potential threat to explosives. Other factors were related to the training, experience and knowledge of personnel and the environment in which they worked. The investigation revealed that at least four of the vessel's crewmen were apparently aware and concerned about the position of the unit relative to the aircraft, but the launcher exploded before any action could be taken. New operating procedures and safety precautions were implemented within a month of the disaster and were to remain in effect until replacement or modification of the MD-3A units could be completed.

5 FEBRUARY 1969 (c.11:45)

Location	*North Pacific Ocean*
Operator	*US Air Force*
Aircraft type	*Lockheed HC-130H (65-0990)*

In searching for 17 crew members from a sunken Japanese ship, the aircraft itself met with disaster, crashing in Bashi Channel, north of the (Philippine) Batan Islands and some 50 miles (80km) south-east of the southern tip of Taiwan. Among its 14 crewmen, only one seriously injured survivor was found.

Having arrived from Clark Air Force Base in the Philippines, 65-0990 was among three aircraft participating in

Two separate crashes in South Vietnam of US Army Boeing/Vertol CH-47 Chinook helicopters, such as this one, claimed more than 50 lives in the spring of 1969. (Boeing Helicopters Division)

the search and rescue operation. The four-engine turboprop had been flying in a wings-level attitude at a low altitude when it slammed into the surface and caught fire. The weather in the area at the time consisted of an overcast at 1,500ft (500m) and a visibility of 7 miles (11km). The wind was from a direction of 30 degrees at 30–35 knots, which contributed to ocean swells estimated at 20–30ft (6–10m). There was no evidence of severe turbulence or wind shear, or that down-draughts could have contributed to the crash. It was not raining in the area, but the crews of the other aircraft reported that salt spray was reducing visibility at low altitudes. It was also noted in the investigative report that while the air pressure remained relatively constant, the common altimeter setting was believed to have been 30–60ft (10–20m) higher than the pressure at the surface level; this would have produced an incorrect height indication. The type of accident was described as 'inadvertant contact with the water' during low-level flight over open sea.

2 APRIL 1969 (c.12:40)

Location	*Near Quang Tri, (South) Vietnam*
Operator	*US Army*
Aircraft type	*Boeing/Vertol CH-47C (67-18523)*

Laden with (South) Vietnamese Army troops, the turbine-engine helicopter crashed about 110 miles (175km) north-west of Da Nang, and 24 of the 78 military personnel aboard were killed, including one of the aircraft's five US Army crewmen. Among the survivors, only one soldier escaped unscathed, the rest suffering varying degrees of injury.

As the CH-47 was climbing out following a vertical take-off and after it had assumed forward flight, the pilots noted a loss in rotor velocity. Its commander then took over the controls, bringing the aircraft into a hover and, by lowering the collective pitch, initiating a descent. Touching down almost vertically on the right side of a ravine 150ft (50m) from its take-off point, the helicopter then slid down the embankment and rolled to the left, at which time its rotor blades hit the ground. Fire erupted seconds after it had come to a rest, and explosions occurred 3 to 5 minutes later, ultimately resulting in the destruction of 67-18523. There being no safety belts or other restraints in the cabin, occupants had been thrown on top of each other when the aircraft rolled over. The cause of the power loss was not disclosed by army authorities.

15 APRIL 1969 (c.13:50)

Location	*Off Chongjin, North Korea*
Operator	*US Navy*
Aircraft type	*Lockheed EC-121M (135749)*

The four-engine radar-intelligence aircraft, with a crew of 31 men aboard, was shot down over the Sea of Japan by two North Korean MiG-21 jet fighters. Searchers recovered the bodies of only two of the victims; there were no survivors.

At the time of the attack, 135749 was believed to have been approximately 90 miles (145km) off the North Korean coast, over international waters. American President Richard Nixon announced three days later that the reconnaissance flights would continue, with fighter escorts.

25 APRIL 1969 (c.16:00)

Location	Near Nakhon Ratchasima, Thailand
Operator	US Air Force
Aircraft type	Lockheed EC-121R (67-21493)

Ten days after hostile action claimed the US Navy EC-121, this aircraft was lost accidentally to adverse meteorological conditions. All 18 crewmen were killed, and a girl on the ground was slightly injured, when 67-21493 crashed on flat terrain some 150 miles (250km) north-east of Bangkok and around 4 miles (6.5km) west-south-west of the Korat Air Base, from where it had taken off about a minute earlier, on a combat tactical mission.

Lifting off from Runway 24, the four-engine aircraft had climbed to an approximate height of 500ft (150m) above the ground before it plunged to earth, exploded and burned, its undercarriage in the retracted position at the moment of impact. The accident took place in an area of thunderstorm activity, with an overcast of 3,000ft (1,000m) and a visibility that had been reduced to 2 miles (3km) by rain showers and blowing dust. The EC-121 was believed to have entered an area of severe wind shear, flying into a head wind of 20 knots and then a tail wind reaching near-hurricane velocity, leading to the uncontrolled descent, with full recovery not being begun in time to prevent the crash.

6 MAY 1969 (c.13:20)

Location	Near Chon Thanh, (South) Vietnam
Operator	US Army
Aircraft type	Boeing/Vertol CH-47A (66-19029)

The turbine-engine helicopter, its passengers mostly (South) Vietnamese Army troops, crashed and burned about 75 miles (120km) north-east of Saigon. Thirty-nine servicemen aboard lost their lives in the accident, including one member of the aircraft's crew of five US Army personnel; all but two of the 44 survivors were injured.

On lifting off from Song Be airfield, on an approximate heading of 96 degrees, the helicopter experienced a loss of rotor speed. As the aircraft approached a precipice, the commander elected against aborting the take-off, but its rear undercarriage became entangled in a strand of copper wire and the CH-47 was dragged down, then skidded along the ground and finally tumbled over the cliff. Although the cause was not given, the investigative report noted that due to the intensity of the post-crash fire, physical examination of the wreckage could not be considered reliable in attempting to determine what led to the accident. A fluctuating tachometer was apparently not a factor, and both combat damage and maintenance error were ruled out.

5 JUNE 1969 (time unknown)

Location	Bering Sea
Operator	US Air Force
Aircraft type	Boeing RC-135E (62-4137)

Operated by the Strategic Air Command (SAC) and flying between two Alaskan air bases, from Shemya, in the Aleutian Islands, to Eielson, near Fairbanks, the four-engine reconnaissance jet vanished with 19 crewmen aboard. A search that began within hours after it was reported missing ended nine days later, with no trace of the aircraft or its occupants having been found.

Cleared to a cruising altitude of 25,000ft (7,500m), the RC-135 had last reported being at a position about 200 miles (320km) north of the Amchitka Pass, a passageway between the Rat and Andreanof Islands, before a member of the crew radioed, at 07:36 local time, that they were experiencing vibration. Though uncertain of the emergency, he stated that the aircraft was under control. In response to the ground controller's query, 'You say you're not declaring an emergency,' the crewman responded 'Roger'. After a long pause, he was heard to say, 'Crew go to oxygen.' There were no further verbal communications from 62-4137, but there was evidence, through the keying of its transmitter, of continued attempts to send a message, which were heard until 08:42.

Communications were probably stifled by a malfunction in the aircraft's transmitter. At the time and place of the disappearance, the weather was cloudy, with tops at 7,000–8,000ft (2,000–2,500m). The visibility was otherwise good, with no reported turbulence and a 20-knot north-north-easterly wind.

2 SEPTEMBER 1969 (c.11:15)

Location	Near Pakse, Laos
Operator	Royal Lao Air Force
Aircraft type	Douglas C-47

The twin-engine transport crashed in the vicinity of the Mekong River, and all 35 persons aboard were killed. The passengers included some civilians. Having nearly completed a domestic flight from Savannakhet to Pakse, the aircraft was apparently unable to land due to an obscuring of the airport and surrounding terrain by low clouds, and it must have run out of fuel.

8 SEPTEMBER 1969 (c.14:00)

Location	Near Medina, Cundinamarca, Colombia
Operator	Fuerza Aérea Colombiana (Colombian Air Force)
Aircraft type	Douglas C-47 (FAC-685)

All 32 persons aboard were killed when the twin-engine transport crashed some 30 miles (50km) north-east of Villavicencio, Meta, where it was to have landed. The victims included a pregnant woman passenger and three military

A US Navy Grumman C-2A Greyhound carrier-based transport, the type lost over the Tonkin Gulf after suspected catastrophic mechanical failure. (Northrop Grumman)

crewmen. Operated by the military airline Servicio de Aeronavegación a Territorios Nacionales (SATENA) and on a scheduled domestic service that had originated at Bogotá and last stopped at Monterrey, the aircraft may have been diverted from its intended destination by strong winds and rain associated with a severe storm before it clipped a mountain peak, crashing on a ranch. The weather was believed to have been the primary factor in the accident.

2 OCTOBER 1969 (c.07:10)

Location	Gulf of Tonkin
Operator	US Navy
Aircraft type	Grumman C-2A (152796)

The twin-engine turboprop transport, which was bound for an aircraft carrier on station in the Tonkin Gulf from Subi Point, in the Philippines, went down less than 30 miles (50km) from the ship. With the exception of one passenger, who was an American civilian, the 26 men killed in the crash were US Navy personnel, including the crew. There were no survivors.

Salvage operations went on for more than a month, but proved unsuccessful in locating the main wreckage due to the adverse and frequently hazardous environmental and weather conditions, and so the cause of the tragedy remained unknown. Of the possible causes, the one considered the most probable was a sudden and catastrophic power plant failure involving a reduction gear, a propeller or the engine truss (support). (Subsequent instrumented flight tests confirmed the truss and gearbox assemblies as primary failure suspects in the loss of 152796 and a previous, though far less serious, C-2 accident that occurred three months earlier.)

Steps taken to prevent a recurrence of the suspected failure were: the imposition of interim time limits on power plant components; certain operating restrictions; increasing the frequency of oil sample analyses; the establishment of balancing and post-flight propeller inspection criteria; a requirement for the identification of any existing weaknesses, evaluation of material conditions and corrections of all deficiencies noted; and the redesign of the engine gearbox and mounting structure of the aircraft type to increase its strength as required to meet design limit sink rates and abnormal landing conditions. The US Navy grounded its C-2 fleet pending these corrective actions.

22 DECEMBER 1969 (c.10:30)

Location	Near San Diego, California, USA
Operator	US Navy
Aircraft type	LTV F-8J (150879)

Following engine failure and the successful ejection of its pilot (and sole occupant), the jet fighter crashed at the Miramar Naval Air Station. The accident claimed the lives of 14 men on the ground, one of them a civilian worker and the rest US Navy personnel. Numerous others were injured, nine seriously.

Having taken off earlier from the base, the aircraft was on a combat manoeuvring practice flight over the Pacific Ocean when the pilot noted an instrument indication of zero engine oil pressure and turned back. Cleared to land at the base, it was at a position of approximately 1 mile (1.5km) from the threshold of Runway 24-Right and a height of about 500ft (150m) above the ground when it experienced a complete flame-out, prompting the pilot to eject. He landed by parachute without injury, but after his abandoning of it, the F-8 veered from the approach heading of 240 degrees and into a descending right turn. Its undercarriage extended and tail hook raised, the fighter then struck an aircraft hangar and burst into flames. Besides 150879, three navy F-4J jet fighters parked in the building were destroyed and four other aircraft of the same type substantially damaged.

Investigation revealed that due to an oil pressure discrepancy occurring 2½ weeks before the accident, the oil pressure relief valve on 150879 had been replaced. The very next day, the new valve was removed by someone else, but not properly re-installed; specifically, it had not been safety-wired in accordance with existing directives. This maintenance error resulted in the separation of the upper support housing of the valve from its lower support housing, causing oil starvation in the bearings and, in turn, the power plant seizure that led to the crash. The proper functioning of the emergency ram-air turbine prevented a complete control systems failure. However, a loss of electrical power occurring concurrent with the engine seizure returned the roll and yaw stabilisation system actuators to a neutral position, resulting in a rather abrupt control shift that the pilot interpreted as a loss of control. His decision to bail out was possibly influenced by his lack of knowledge as to the position of the ram-air unit.

It was noted in the investigative report that in ejecting, the pilot had been following prescribed procedures. Nevertheless, in the wake of this accident, all Naval Air Training and Operating Procedures Standardization (NATOPS) programme flight manuals were expanded with respect to flight crews faced with emergencies involving unusual circumstances. Specifically, they were changed to indicate that the decision to abandon an aircraft must be influenced by the concern for the safety of persons on the ground.

With regard to the underlying cause of the accident, the report noted that the maintenance personnel were not familiar with the proper installation procedures, and neither did they consult the appropriate publications prior to doing the work. Furthermore, the individual who inspected it was

not familiar with the configuration of a properly-installed relief valve. A revision in the procedure for changing such valves on F-8 engines was one of the recommendations made in the report. The weather was not a factor in the crash.

12 JANUARY 1970 (c.12:00)

Location	*Near Villia, Attiki, Greece*
Operator	*Royal Hellenic Air Force*
Aircraft type	*Douglas C-47*

The twin-engine transport, its passengers consisting of paratroopers, crashed and burned on a mountain some 45 miles (70km) west-north-west of Athens, the accident occurring in foggy weather conditions. Killed in the crash were 23 Greek servicemen aboard the aircraft, but three paratroopers and one of the aircraft's five crewmen survived with injuries. No details regarding the suspected cause of the crash were disclosed.

16 MARCH 1970 (c.11:30)

Location	*Near Da Nang, (South) Vietnam*
Operator	*US Navy*
Aircraft type	*Lockheed EC-121M (145927)*

Its No. 4 power plant having been shut down and the corresponding propeller feathered due to generator over-temperature, the reconnaissance aircraft crashed at Da

Little damage is visible outside but much was done inside the hangar struck by the crashing F-8 jet fighter at Miramar Naval Air Station. (AP/Wide World Photos)

Nang Air Base, where it was to have landed at the end of a flight from Taiwan. Killed in the accident were 23 of its 31 crewmen, one of whom succumbed to cardiac arrest; six of the survivors and two other US military personnel on the ground suffered injuries.

During the otherwise normal three-engine, visual landing approach to Runway 35L, the first 1,000ft (300m) of which, significantly, had been closed, the pilots apparently tried to 'stretch' their approach to avoid the overrun area where workers and equipment were present. In the process, however, the aircraft commander allowed 145927 to descend to about 50ft (15m) above the ground, which was half the minimum height prescribed for the initiation of a missed approach procedure, and its air speed dropped too low. A go-around was nevertheless begun, but the aircraft assumed a slight nose-high, banking attitude, with the latter increasing to about 90 degrees, never gained altitude and ultimately struck a concrete revetment, broke into three major sections and burst into flames, its undercarriage down and flaps extended on impact. Several structures, two trucks and a US Navy F-4D jet fighter were also destroyed.

The accident was attributed not only to the error by the aircraft commander, but also to the actions of the co-pilot, who had been at the controls of 145927 and, according to the investigative report, placed it in 'an inherently hazardous position'. The meteorological conditions at the time were comparatively good, with a visibility of 7 miles (11km), scattered clouds at 1,500ft (500m) and a broken overcast at 3,000ft (1,000m), but the winds, blowing from the north at 16 knots and gusting to 22, were considered a minor contributing factor.

In view of the fact that seven of the occupants who suffered fatal head injuries might have survived had they been wearing helmets, one of the recommendations made in the investigative report was for all EC-121 flight personnel to use such protective headgear during take-offs and landings. Another recommendation was for the redesign and/or reinforcement of seats and stations to provide adequate crash protection for crews flying this type of aircraft.

18 JULY 1970 (time unknown)

Location	*North Atlantic Ocean*
Operator	*Soviet Air Force*
Aircraft type	*Antonov An-22 (SSSR-09303)*

The four-engine turboprop transport, which belonged to the fleet of the Soviet airline Aeroflot and was carrying a field hospital to earthquake-ravaged Peru, vanished with 23 persons aboard. Having last stopped at Keflavik, Iceland, the aircraft was to have landed at Halifax, Nova Scotia, Canada, one segment of a flight originating at Moscow. It was officially reported missing at 17:00 Halifax time. Search for the aircraft was finally abandoned about a month later, and the Soviet relief mission, which had been suspended for a week after the loss of the An-22, subsequently ended completely after only nine more flights.

26 AUGUST 1970 (time unknown)

Location	*Near Tam Ky, (South) Vietnam*
Operator	*US Army*
Aircraft type	*Boeing/Vertol CH-47B (67-18445)*

The turbine-engine helicopter was shot down during the afternoon by enemy ground forces about 300 miles (480km) north-north-east of Saigon. All but two of the 32 American servicemen aboard the aircraft, which had been struck by a rocket grenade, and two others on the ground in the area where it crashed were killed. The pilot, who was a member of the aircraft's crew of five, the sole surviving passenger and five men on the ground suffered injuries.

2 OCTOBER 1970 (14:07)

Location	*Northern Taiwan*
Operator	*US Air Force*
Aircraft type	*Lockheed C-130E (64-0536)*

All 43 American servicemen aboard (37 passengers and a crew of six) perished when the four-engine turboprop transport crashed some 20 miles (30km) south-south-west of Taipei, about 6 minutes after its departure from the city's international airport, on an internal Taiwanese flight to Ching Chuan Kang. The aircraft, which was operating under instrument flight rules (IFR) procedures, made a right turn after taking off and entered a low overcast during its climb-out. Subsequently, it was instructed to ascend to 6,000ft (1,800m) and report when over the second radio fix, but it did not acknowledge this transmission. Wreckage was located nearly a week later, the C-130 having struck a mountain ridge only about 30ft (10m) below its crest, at an approximate elevation of 6,150ft (1,875m) and while on a heading of around 210 degrees, exploded and burned.

At the time and location of the accident, the visibility was believed to have been zero, with the cloud tops extending to at least 20,000ft (6,000m). Had 64-0536 assumed its planned course, i.e. to a heading of 252 degrees, it would have cleared the terrain along the route by no less than 3,000ft (1,000m). The reason for its deviation to the south, if known, was not disclosed by air force authorities.

24 NOVEMBER 1970 (c.09:30)

Location	*Near Can Tho, (South) Vietnam*
First aircraft	
Operator	*(South) Vietnamese Air Force*
Aircraft type	*Bell UH-1H (560)*
Second aircraft	
Operator	*US Army*
Aircraft type	*de Havilland RU-6A Beaver (53-7324)*

A mid-air collision and resulting crash of the two aircraft, which occurred about 5 miles (10km) south-east of Can Tho army airfield and 80 miles (130km) south of Saigon, claimed the lives of 18 persons. The victims included a Vietnamese infant, who had been a passenger on the turbine-engine helicopter, and the three occupants, all US servicemen, of the single-engine aeroplane; there were no survivors.

Having taken off shortly before on an avionics test flight, the RU-6 was apparently in a right-hand turn and on a heading of between 240 and 260 degrees, while the UH-1, on an internal resupply mission from Soc Trang to Binh Thuy, was flying in a north-north-westerly direction and probably in a straight climb, when they collided at an approximate height of 1,200ft (350m) above the ground. The impact with the helicopter's main rotor blades sheared off the aeroplane's empennage and left wing, close to the fuselage. At the time, the local weather consisted of a layer of scattered clouds at 1,500ft (500m). Other than the fact that the US Army pilot would have been operating under the 'see-and-be-seen' rules associated with visual flight rules (VFR), an investigation revealed no factors that could have contributed to the collision.

The versatile Lockheed C-130 Hercules turboprop transport, one of which, similar to this earlier model, crashed on Taiwan. (Lockheed Martin)

27 NOVEMBER 1970 (c.13:30)

Location	*Near Nha Trang, (South) Vietnam*
Operator	*US Air Force*
Aircraft type	*Fairchild C-123K (55-4574)*

The transport, which was on an internal (South) Vietnamese flight from Saigon to Nha Trang Air Base, crashed into a mountain 15 miles (25km) south-west of its destination. All 79 servicemen aboard perished, including a crew of six US Air

The flight path of the US Air Force C-123 that crashed in (South) Vietnam indicates collision with trees prior to impact on the mountainside on 27 November 1970. (US Air Force)

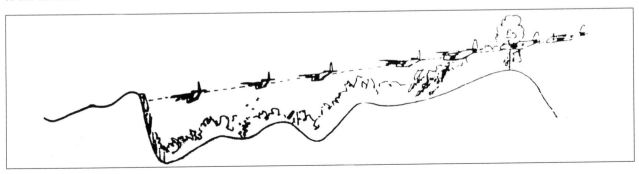

Force personnel; the passengers were troops belonging to the Army of (South) Vietnam.

Airborne for around 10 minutes, the aircraft, which had two auxiliary jet engines to supplement its twin piston power plants, was on a heading of 220 degrees and in a wings-level attitide when it struck some trees that were about 80ft (25m) tall at an approximate elevation of 4,600ft (1,400m), or some 500ft (150m) below the crest of the ridge. Its burned wreckage was found nine days later. At the time and location of the disaster, the meteorological conditions consisted of an overcast, which was variable at 1,000ft (300m) and broken at 2,000ft (600m), with a visibility of 1 mile (1.5km). The wind was from a direction of 30 degrees at 10–15 knots. No distress message had been received from 55-4574, and no proven or suspected causative factors were disclosed in this apparent controlled-flight-into-terrain accident.

29 NOVEMBER 1970 (c.07:35)

Location	Near Cam Ranh, (South) Vietnam
Operator	US Air Force
Aircraft type	Fairchild C-123K (54-0649)

The transport, with 44 US and (South) Vietnamese servicemen aboard, slammed into a dense jungle area and burned some 165 miles (265km) north-east of Saigon and about 15 miles (25km) south-west of Cam Ranh Bay Air Base, where it was to have landed. Wreckage was located five days later with only two of the occupants alive, both of them American passengers who had suffered injuries in the crash. Among those killed were the five members of the crew, all US Air Force personnel.

Less than 10 minutes before the accident, the twin piston-engine aircraft, which was also fitted with two auxiliary jets, had taken off from Phan Rang, along the coast of (South) Vietnam. It was last observed heading for the North Pass, a valley about 2 miles (3km) wide and 10 miles (15km) long, with high terrain on both sides. The pilot had reported proceeding along a prescribed airway that extended on a heading of 30 degrees before requesting a precision radar (PAR) approach. In its last message, 54-0649 acknowledged instructions to a change of course to 100 degrees and an ascent to 2,700ft (820m), and the C-123 was on that heading, at that approximate height and in level flight at the time of impact. The weather at the scene of the crash was poor, with a ceiling estimated at only 300ft (100m), light rain and zero visibility. The wind was from an east-north-easterly direction at 30 knots. No information regarding possible or probable causative factors in this accident were released by air force authorities.

19 DECEMBER 1970 (time unknown)

Location	Near Panagarah, West Bengal, India
Operator	Soviet Air Force
Aircraft type	Antonov An-22 (SSSR-09305)

All 17 persons aboard lost their lives when the four-engine turboprop heavy-lift transport crashed and burned about 100 miles (150km) north of Calcutta while attempting

an emergency landing at the Panagarah airstrip. Some 40 minutes after the aircraft had taken off from Dacca, (East) Pakistan, bound for New Delhi, India, one of its propellers disintegrated, which disabled its power plant control cables. After initiating an emergency descent, the crew was unable to extend the undercarriage or the flaps, and the An-22 flew above the airport runway at a height of only about 3ft (1m) until its starboard wing tip struck the ground.

20 JANUARY 1971 (c.14:30)

Location	Near Harmapuqui, Junin, Peru
Operator	Fureza Aérea del Perú (Peruvian Air Force)
Aircraft type	Curtiss C-46 (FAP-381)

The twin-engine transport, on an internal Peruvian flight from Mazamari to Lima, crashed and burned on a mountain in the Andes range some 35 miles (55km) north-west of Tarma. All 35 persons aboard perished; most of the victims were Peruvian military personnel, including the crew of five, but some had been accompanied by their dependants. Though not officially reported, mechanical failure was believed to have been a factor in the accident, as the aircraft appeared to be experiencing power plant difficulties just beforehand, according to witnesses on the ground.

21 JANUARY 1971 (c.10:00)

Location	Near Privas, Rhône-Alpes, France
Operator	L'Armée de l'Air (French Air Force)
Aircraft type	Nord 262A (44)

The twin-engine turboprop transport slammed into a mountain at an approximate elevation of 3,600ft (1,100m), or only about 700ft (200m) from its peak, west of the Rhône River. All 21 persons aboard were killed, including a crew of four military personnel; the passengers included seven top French civilian nuclear research experts. The crash occurred during a snowstorm as the aircraft was preparing to land following an internal flight from Paris to the Pierrelatte nuclear facility. When considering the adverse weather conditions, there was speculation that the pilots became disorientated, resulting in a controlled-flight-into-terrain accident. There was no evidence of instrument failure, and the absence of a distress message seemed to rule out icing or some other in-flight emergency. The official cause was not released, however.

15 APRIL 1971 (c.07:00)

Location	Near San Jose, Pampanga, the Philippines
Operator	Philippine Air Force
Aircraft type	Douglas C-47A (293246)

The twin-engine transport crashed in a rice field about half a mile (0.8km) from Basa Air Base, near Floridablanca, from where it had taken off moments earlier. Most of the 40 persons killed in the accident were Philippine military personnel, including the aircraft's four crewmen;

one of the passengers, a 3-year-old boy, succumbed to his injuries three days later, leaving no survivors. Bound for Nichols Air Base, near the Philippine capital of Manila, the C-47 reportedly climbed to a height of approximately 200ft (60m) above the ground before it banked to the left, stalled and plummeted to earth. Although no official report was released, there were indications that the crash had been precipitated by the failure of the aircraft's right power plant, after which the crew apparently tried to return to the base.

26 MAY 1971 (c.15:00)

Location	*Near Capetown, South Africa*
Operator	*South African Air Force (3 aircraft)*
Aircraft types	*Hawker Siddeley HS 125-400B (01)*
	Hawker Siddeley HS 125-400B (02)
	Hawker Siddeley HS 125-400B (03)

As they were practising for a forthcoming exhibition, the three twin-engine jets struck Devil's Peak and exploded, and all 11 men aboard them perished. The victims included the flight crews and ground personnel. According to eyewitnesses, the aircraft were flying in a V-formation through a thick mist when they slammed into the mountain. No additional information was released regarding the probable cause of the apparent controlled-flight-into-terrain accident.

13 JUNE 1971 (c.13:30)

Location	*North Pacific Ocean*
Operator	*US Air Force*
Aircraft type	*Boeing C-135B (61-0331)*

Assigned to the classified Project III, with the intention of monitoring French above-ground nuclear testing in the South Pacific, the modified jet transport had, the previous day, successfully completed a test mission from Hickam Air Force Base, in Hawaii, USA, to Pago Pago, American Samoa. On the return flight, however, it met with what was described as a 'catastrophic event', leading to an uncontrolled plunge into the sea about 700 miles (1,100km) south-south-west of its destination. By the time search operations were terminated four days later, only pieces of secondary aircraft structure and the undamaged crash position indicator had been recovered; no trace of its 24 crewmen, who comprised both military personnel and civilians, was found.

Last reported at an altitude of 33,000ft (10,050m), while on a probable true heading of 20 degrees and flying at an estimated air speed of around 540mph (870kmh), 61-0331 had apparently begun a radio transmission that could not be deciphered and which ended abruptly at approximately 13:25 local time. The C-135 was believed to have subsequently struck the surface of the ocean at a high speed and a steep angle of descent, and the absence in the water of helmets, clothing and other personal effects indicated that it had

The spots on the aircraft diagram illustrate the small amount of aircraft structure that was recovered from the downed C-135B. (US Air Force)

been intact until the moment of impact, whereupon it must have disintegrated. There was no evidence of either in-flight or post-crash fire or explosion. The weather in the area at the time was generally clear, with scattered cumulus clouds well below the flight level of the aircraft and a south-south-westerly wind of 25 knots.

There was no evidence that the modifications in 61-0331, which included 11 additional windows and, significantly, a canoe-shaped fairing with radome atop its fuselage, had in any way affected the structural integrity of the aircraft. Nevertheless, nine years later a US federal court ruled that the 12 civilian victims of the tragedy were entitled to wrongful death damages from LTV, which had attached the radome.

30 JULY 1971 (c.15:00)

Location	*Near Pau, Aquitaine, France*
Operator	*L'Armée de l'Air (French Air Force)*
Aircraft type	*Nord 2501 Noratlas (49)*

Operated by the Commandement du Transport Aérien Militaire and carrying as passengers army paratroopers and three jump masters, the twin-engine aircraft crashed in flat terrain along the base of the Pyrenees. All 37 French servicemen aboard, including a crew of three air force personnel, were killed. After a reported electrical fire, the pilot requested clearance to land immediately at Pau-Uzein Air Base, but as it was turning on to the final approach

A French Air Force Nord Noratlas transport, the type that crashed near Pau-Uzein Air Base, killing all 37 military personnel aboard. (Philip Jarrett)

A front main gear assembly is the only easily recognisable part of the US Army CH-47A helicopter that crashed in (West) Germany after in-flight rotor failure. (UPI/Corbis-Bettmann)

leg the transport plummeted to earth and exploded. Two paratroopers managed to jump safely from the aircraft before the start of the in-flight emergency.

18 AUGUST 1971 (c.09:40)

Location	Near Pegnitz, (West) Germany
Operator	US Army
Aircraft type	Boeing/Vertol CH-47A (66-19023)

All 37 American servicemen aboard perished, including a crew of five, when the turbine-engine helicopter, which was flying between two military installations, to the training area near Grafenwohr from Dolan Barracks, near Ludwigsburg, crashed and burned some 20 miles (30km) north-west of its intended destination, and about 25 miles (40km) north-east of Nurnberg. The aircraft had been cruising under visual flight rules (VFR) procedures at an estimated air speed of around 115mph (185kmh) and on a north-easterly heading when an aft main rotor blade separated at the root, the structural failure occurring at an altitude of 2,700ft (820m), or approximately 1,000ft (300m) above the ground. It then plunged into the rolling terrain in a nose-first, inverted attitude, with its fuselage at an angle of around 45 degrees.

The rotor failure was attributed to a fatigue fracture of the subject blade root, which originated on the bottom side and extended in a chordwise direction for about 7in (18cm). Although its age was unknown, the crack must have existed for a sufficient period of time to allow a considerable amount of corrosion to accumulate in about half the area of the fracture face.

23 OCTOBER 1971 (time unknown)

Location	*Near Qui Nhon, (South) Vietnam*
Operator	*(South) Vietnamese Air Force*
Aircraft type	*Douglas C-47*

The crash of the twin-engine transport, which occurred in adverse weather conditions associated with a typhoon, claimed the lives of 22 persons aboard the aircraft. There was only one survivor from the accident, further details about which were not made available.

9 NOVEMBER 1971 (c.05:45)

Location	*Near Livorno, Toscana, Italy*
Operator	*Royal Air Force*
Aircraft type	*Lockheed C-130K Hercules C1 (XV216)*

In the worst peacetime accident in the history of the RAF, all 52 servicemen aboard were killed when the four-engine turboprop transport plunged into the Ligurian Sea about 20 miles (30km) south-west of Pisa and less than 5 miles (10km) offshore. The accident occurred in predawn darkness about 5 minutes after the aircraft, carrying 46 Italian Army paratroopers and six British military personnel, including a parachute instructor, had taken off from Pisa's San Giusto Airport, on a low-level formation flight, in which it was to be in the No. 3 position. The wreckage was located and the bodies of the victims were recovered after an extensive search.

During the grouping phase of the flight, the pilot of the second section leader had XV216 in sight, observing the aircraft to be slightly further behind and to the left of its leader, but not sufficiently to cause alarm. He then took a few seconds for an instrument scan, whereupon he witnessed a large orange flash or glow. The cause of the crash remains unknown, although the investigation found no evidence of significant technical failure or malfunction, nor any indication that the Hercules had been operating any way other than normally until the moment of impact with the ocean.

28 NOVEMBER 1971 (c.13:30)

Location	*Near Hue, (South) Vietnam*
Operator	*US Army*
Aircraft type	*Boeing/Vertol CH-47C (68-15866)*

During a (South) Vietnamese internal flight from Da Nang to Camp Eagle, the turbine-engine helicopter crashed and burned 12 miles (20km) north-west of the Hue/Phu Bai airfield. Wreckage was located a few days later on a jungle-covered mountainside, with no survivors among the 34 American servicemen aboard, including a crew of five.

Operating under visual flight rules (VFR) procedures, the aircraft had proceeded up the coastline before turning inland, in an apparent attempt to fly through a lowland region, probably due to deteriorating weather along the regular route. It then assumed an approximately due westerly course to avoid mountainous terrain, which would have been at its 2 o'clock position.

During this time the aircraft inadvertantly entered instrument meteorological conditions, with a ceiling of 1,000ft (300m), a broken overcast at 600ft (180m) and scattered clouds down to only 300ft (100m), and a visibility of 1 mile (1.5km) or less. Declaring an emergency to Hue approach control, the crew started a left turn away from the mountains. During this 180-degree turn a north-westerly wind apparently caused the helicopter to drift southwards and into another area where the terrain was higher. At the moment of impact, 68-15866 may have been in a slight descent as the crew tried to break through the lowest layer of clouds.

21 JANUARY 1972 (c.10:30)

Location	*Near Betania, Choco, Colombia*
Operator	*Fuerza Aérea Colombiana (Colombian Air Force)*
Aircraft type	*Douglas C-47 (FAC-661)*

All 39 persons aboard were killed, including a crew of four military personnel, when the twin-engine transport slammed into a mountain and exploded. The accident occurred during a thunderstorm and rain about 60 miles (100km) from Medellin, Antioquia, from where the aircraft, which was operated by the military airline Servicio de Aeronavegación a Territorios Nacionales (SATENA), had taken off earlier, on a non-scheduled domestic passenger flight to Quibdo, Choco. No details as to the suspected cause were released, although the weather may have played a significant role in the crash.

10 MAY 1972 (c.10:25)

Location	*Near Gia Dinh, (South) Vietnam*
Operator	*US Army*
Aircraft type	*Boeing/Vertol CH-47A (64-13157)*

The turbine-engine helicopter crashed and exploded in a jungle area some 20 miles (30km) north-east of Saigon while on a (South) Vietnamese internal flight from Bien Hoa to Vung Tau. All 34 American servicemen aboard the aircraft, including its two-member flight crew, perished. Proceeding on a compass heading of 190 degrees at an indicated air speed of approximately 90mph (145kmh), the CH-47 had been at a height of 2,000ft (600m) when a main blade was slung from the aft rotor head. The aft pylon was then torn from the airframe, landing some 300ft (100m) from the main wreckage. The accident was attributed to metal fatigue of the spar in the blade that failed.

16 MAY 1972 (time unknown)

Location	*Svetlogorsk, Soviet Federative Soviet Socialist Republic, USSR*
Operator	*Soviet Navy*
Aircraft type	*Antonov An-26*

The twin-engine turboprop crashed into a kindergarten in this town near the Finnish border, some 100 miles (150km) north-west of Leningrad (St Petersburg). All eight occupants of the aircraft and 25 persons on the ground lost their lives in the accident; all but two of the victims on the ground were children. Having completed a weather research flight over the Baltic Sea, the An-26 was on its way back to Kaliningrad, but its crew apparently failed to set the altimeters correctly, i.e. to the correct airfield pressure. After entering an area of thick fog, it descended to a dangerously low altitude, resulting in the accident.

13 JUNE 1972 (time unknown)

Location	*Near An Loc, (South) Vietnam*
Operator	*(South) Vietnamese Air Force*
Aircraft type	*Boeing/Vertol CH-47*

All 47 persons aboard were killed, including a military crew, when the turbine-engine helicopter was shot down about 60 miles (100km) north of Saigon, shortly after it had taken off. The aircraft was brought down by ground fire while transporting refugees out of the besieged area.

11 JULY 1972 (time unknown)

Location	*Near Quang Tri, (South) Vietnam*
Operator	*US Marine Corps*
Aircraft type	*Sikorsky CH-53D (156658)*

Approximately 50 South Vietnamese Army troops and two US Marine Corps crewmen lost their lives when the turbine-engine helicopter was reportedly shot down. Five other members of the aircraft's crew and ten troops survived.

11 JULY 1972 (c.16:00)

Location	*Near Harstad, Norway*
Operator	*Kongelige Norske Luftforsvaret (Royal Norwegian Air Force)*
Aircraft type	*de Havilland DHC-6 Twin Otter Series 100 (67-056)*

The twin-engine turboprop crashed into a mountain and burned on the island of Hinnoya, some 50 miles (80km) north-west of Narvik, while preparing to land at the Stokmarknes airport, which was an intermediate stop during an internal service from Bardufoss to Bodoe. All 17 persons aboard the aircraft lost their lives, including a two-man military flight crew. A number of civilians, four of them children, were among the passengers. The accident occurred in rain and fog, which had greatly reduced the visibility.

According to a military summary report, the crash was attributed to 'navigational errors and miscalculations of the prevailing conditions'. About a month later, however, it was revealed that the pilot of the Twin Otter, a Norwegian Air Force major, had at the time been under the influence of alcohol, which undoubtedly led to these mistakes. An autopsy performed on his body found his blood level to be more than twice that allowed under Norwegian law. He had apparently consumed alcoholic beverages the night before, although no other pilots reported any indication he was drunk on the day of the accident. Also, there was no evidence of recent alcohol

consumption on the part of the co-pilot. This disturbing finding led to the creation of a military committee to study the issue of alcohol regulations and rest periods for pilots, as fatigue may have been an additional contributing factor in this particular crash.

12 AUGUST 1972 (c.04:00)

Location	*Near Soc Trang (Khanh Hung), (South) Vietnam*
Operator	*US Air Force*
Aircraft type	*Lockheed C-130E (62-1853)*

The four-engine turboprop transport was shot down in predawn darkness over the Mekong Delta region about 100 miles (150km) south-west of Saigon. Thirty-five of the 46 persons aboard the aircraft were killed, one of whom was a civilian and the rest (South) Vietnamese and American military personnel, including all but one of its eight US Air Force crewmen; the survivors suffered various injuries. The C-130 had been hit in a power plant by small arms ground fire shortly after it had taken off from Soc Trang Air Base, on a support mission.

28 AUGUST 1972 (c.14:30)

Location	*Papua New Guinea*
Operator	*Royal Australian Air Force (RAAF)*
Aircraft type	*de Havilland Canada DHC-4 Caribou (A4-233)*

The twin-engine transport was on an intra-island flight from Lae to Port Moresby, carrying mostly Papua New Guinea Army cadets. Twenty-five minutes after it had taken off, the aircraft was reported at 6,500ft (1,980m) over the town of Wau, but no further radio transmissions were heard. Three days later, the five injured cadets who had survived the crash of the Caribou were found, one at the accident site, but the latter succumbed in hospital after his rescue. The final toll in the accident was 25 persons killed, including the aircraft's crew of three RAAF personnel.

Evidence indicated that the southbound transport had entered a region known as the Kudjeru Gap at its reported altitude. At the location where the valley narrows, however, the weather deteriorated down to 6/8 stratus clouds with a base of only 600ft (180m) above the ground and isolated areas of precipitation. The cloud tops were at 10,500ft (3,200m). Confronted with the lowering overcast, which prevented him from maintaining visual flight within the mountainous terrain, the pilot reversed his direction and initiated a climb. During this sharp right turn, at which time A4-233 may have entered the clouds, its starboard wing clipped trees at an approximate elevation of 5,000ft (1,500m), or only about 50ft (15m) below the crest of the ridge, resulting in a loss of control. The Caribou then slammed into the woods, broke apart and burned. The scene of the crash was some 20 miles (30km) south of Wau.

The accident was attributed to 'error of skill' on the part of the pilot-in-command. Although he had flown between Lae and Port Moresby a total of 20 times, twice earlier on the day of the crash, there was strong evidence to suggest that on none of these occasions had he attempted to negotiate the Kudjeru Gap below a low overcast. His decision to enter the valley was probably influenced by the clear weather in the Wau area. It was noted in the investigative report, however, that a pilot with more experience in Papua New Guinea operations would have, under the prevailing conditions, expected clouds in the valley and elected to fly above them. Likewise, one with more experience who had planned to fly below the cloud level would have probably turned back earlier. The report labelled as 'speculative' the suggestion that a pilot with more knowledge of the local area would not have made the same error.

13 SEPTEMBER 1972 (c.12:00)

Location	*Near Dhulikhel, Nepal*
Operator	*Royal Nepalese Army*
Aircraft type	*Douglas C-47 (9N-RF10)*

The twin-engine transport was on a paratroop training mission, flying internally from Panchkhal to Tribhuvan Airport, serving Kathmandu, when it crashed some 25 miles (40km) east of the capital city after reportedly striking an electric power pole. All 31 Nepalese servicemen aboard were killed, including a crew of four.

13 OCTOBER 1972 (c.15:30)

Location	*Near El Sosneado, Mendoza, Argentina*
Operator	*Fuerza Aérea Uruguaya (Uruguayan Air Force)*
Aircraft type	*Fairchild Hiller FH-227D (T-571)*

The twin-engine turboprop, operated by the Transporte Aéreo Militar Uruguayo (TAMU) branch, had taken off the previous day from Montevideo, Uruguay, on a non-scheduled

A de Havilland DHC-4 Caribou of the type flown by the Royal Australian Air Force, and which crashed in Papua New Guinea. (de Havilland/Boeing Canada)

The flight path in the final moments of the RAAF Caribou, including the sudden reverse of direction that preceded the impact with high terrain. (RAAF Directorate of Flying Safety)

A photograph taken by one of the survivors of the others huddled around the wreckage of the Uruguayan Air Force FH-227 that crashed in the Andes. (Sygma)

international service to Santiago, Chile. The passengers included 16 members of the 'Old Christian Brothers', an amateur Uruguayan rugby team, five of who would live through what would become an epic story of survival.

The aircraft had landed at the city of Mendoza, due to adverse meteorological conditions, before proceeding over the highest part of the Andes Mountains on this Friday the 13th with 45 persons aboard. During the second leg of the flight, T-571 had encountered a strong headwind after turning from a south-westerly on to a north-westerly direction, which reduced its ground speed by about 35mph (55kmh). Over the Andean Cordillera, and in accordance with their planned route, the crew turned back on to a north-north-easterly heading. But although the pilot had reported reaching Curico, where the turn was supposed to have been made, the FH-227 had in fact still been some 50 miles (80km) from that point. After giving his position, he was cleared to begin a slow descent in preparation for landing at Pudahuel Airport, serving Santiago.

Minutes later, the aircraft entered a cloud bank, then encountered down-draughts, which may have prevented the crew from climbing out of the area. After emerging from the overcast it clipped a mountain, the impact shearing off most of the right wing, which in turn struck and severed the tail assembly. Some of the occupants were at this time tossed out at the point of the fuselage break. Miraculously, the main fuselage section landed and slid to a stop on a snowy down-slope, coming to rest at an approximate elevation of 12,000ft (3,700m) near the Tinguiririca Volcano. The scene of the crash was about 120 miles (190km) south-east of its destination.

The transport was still missing when two of the passengers who had hiked out were found four days before Christmas, and one of them helped guide helicopters to the crash site, locating 14 other survivors, who had sustained themselves during their two-month ordeal by eating the flesh of the dead. Among the 29 persons who lost their lives were the five members of the aircraft's crew, all military personnel, and eight killed in an avalanche at the crash site on 30 October. A navigator who was aboard T-571 had reportedly been in the passenger cabin during the passage through the mountains, thus preventing any chance to correct the errors by the flight crew that led to the accident.

23 OCTOBER 1972 (time unknown)

Location	*Near Tula, Russian Soviet Federative Soviet Socialist Republic, USASR*

First aircraft

Operator	*Soviet Air Force*
Aircraft type	*Antonov An-12*

Second aircraft

Operator	*Soviet Air Force*
Aircraft type	*Antonov An-12*

A heavy toll of perhaps 50 to 100 fatalities may have resulted from a mid-air crash between the two four-engine turboprop transports, one of which was carrying military personnel bound for Tula, some 120 miles (190km) south of Moscow, for an exercise. The aircraft was approaching to land when it collided with the other An-12, which had been on a local training flight, reportedly with a crew of six aboard. There were no survivors. Due to the failure of surveillance radar, the controller had not been aware of the exact position of the aircraft.

31 OCTOBER 1972 (c.18:00)

Location	*Near My Tho, (South) Vietnam*
Operator	*US Army*
Aircraft type	*Boeing/Vertol CH-47*

The turbine-engine helicopter was apparently shot down around nightfall over the Mekong Delta region about 35 miles (55km) south-west of Saigon, and all 22 military personnel aboard the aircraft, mostly Americans but also including several (South) Vietnamese, were killed.

28 FEBRUARY 1973 (c.23:50)

Location	*Near Szczecin, Poland*
Operator	*Polska Wojska Lotnicze (Polish Air Force)*
Aircraft type	*Antonov An-24B (012)*

The twin-engine turboprop transport crashed and burned while attempting to land, killing all 15 persons aboard, including a military crew. During its landing approach to a combined military/civil airport, which was being conducted in darkness and conditions of poor visibility, the aircraft had apparently encountered a severe down-draught.

12 APRIL 1973 (c.15:00)

Location	*Near Sunnyvale, California, USA*
First aircraft	
Operator	*(US) National Aeronautics and Space Administration (NASA)*
Aircraft type	*Convair 990A (N711NA)*
Second aircraft	
Operator	*US Navy*
Aircraft type	*Lockheed P-3C (157332)*

As they were approaching to land at Moffett Field Naval Air Station, the NASA research jet, a modified airliner known as the 'flying laboratory', and the turboprop patrol aircraft collided in mid-air about 10 miles (15km) north-west of San Jose, and both then crashed and burned on a golf course. Among the 16 persons killed were eight scientists and technicians plus the three-member flight crew aboard the NASA jet, and five navy personnel from the patrol aircraft. A sixth navy crewman, the sole survivor of the accident, was seriously injured.

A Moffett Field ground controller had mistakenly authorised both aircraft to land on the same runway. The Convair 990, which was originally cleared to use Runway 32-Right, had been given the wrong instructions, which were not questioned by the pilot. Subsequently, the aircraft settled on top of the P-3, its extended nose gear striking the tail fin and upper fuselage of the latter. The collision occurred in good weather conditions at an approximate height of 300ft (100m) above the ground.

28 AUGUST 1973 (c.21:45)

Location	*Near Huete, Cuenca, Spain*
Operator	*US Air Force*
Aircraft type	*Lockheed C-141A (63-8077)*

Operated by the Military Airlift Command (MAC), the jet transport crashed and burned some 40 miles (65km) east of Madrid, and about 25 miles (40km) east of Torrejon de Ardoz Air Base, where it was to have landed, killing 24 persons aboard. Only the navigator, one of the eight air force crewmen assigned to the aircraft, survived, but he was seriously injured. The passengers included some civilian dependants, but most were also American military personnel.

Having nearly completed a flight from Athens, Greece, 63-8077 was cleared by Madrid approach control to proceed to the Torrejon non-directional beacon and for descent to 5,000ft (1,500m). The return transmission from the C-141, 'Understand . . . clear to descend to three thousand and Castejon radio beacon', which contained two significant errors, was, however, blocked out by another aircraft calling the same ground facility. The transport then received authorisation for a ground-controlled (GCA) radar-monitored instrument landing system (ILS) approach to Runway 23, but simultaneous with its radio message '. . . passing five for three thousand', the controller was issuing instructions to another military aircraft, an F-4 jet fighter, and hearing from the former only 'MAC-38077', requested the crew to 'Stand by'. Following a 30-second delay, radio transmissions to the C-141 resumed, but it failed to respond, and its target was no longer observed on radar.

Cleanly-configured, the aircraft had slammed into a mesa at an approximate elevation of 3,000ft (1,000m), while on a heading of 292 degrees and at a ground speed of 250mph (400kmh), according its flight data recorder (FDR) read-out. It then became airborne, and after passing over a ravine it rolled over and crashed inverted. The accident occurred on a moonless night, but the weather was clear, with a visibility of

The main wreckage area of the US Air Force C-141 that crashed near Madrid, Spain, with the arrow pointing to the inverted tail assembly. (US Air Force)

at least 10 miles (15km). The wind was from a north-easterly direction at 11 knots.

Evidence indicated that the aircraft's radar altimeter had been functioning, but it was also revealed that the crew did not set their barometric altimeters to the correct pressure, an error apparently related to their failure to use the descent checklist. In addition to the interrupted radio communications, fatigue of the flight crew was probably a factor in the crash.

21 DECEMBER 1973 (time unknown)

Location	*Near Saigon, (South) Vietnam*
Operator	*(South) Vietnamese Air Force*
Aircraft type	*Boeing/Vertol CH-47*

The turbine-engine helicopter, which was loaded with ammunition, exploded while apparently on the ground in the Mekong Delta region. Most or all of the 20 persons killed and 17 injured were believed to have been (South) Vietnamese military personnel.

9 JANUARY 1974 (16:36)

Location	*Near Neiva, Huila, Colombia*
Operator	*Fuerza Aérea Colombiana (Colombian Air Force)*
Aircraft type	*Hawker Siddeley HS 748-2A (FAC-1103)*

All 31 persons aboard perished, including a crew of three military personnel, when the twin-engine turboprop,

Hawker Siddeley 748-2A (FAC-1103) of the military airline SATENA, the actual aircraft that crashed during an internal Colombian flight. (Philip Jarrett)

which was operated by the military airline Servicio de Aeronavegación a Territorios Nacionales (SATENA) and on a scheduled domestic service to Bogotá, crashed and burned on a mountain some 15 miles (25km) north of Florencia, from where it had taken off shortly before. The late afternoon accident was attributed to a sudden change in the weather, but Colombian aviation authorities provided no further details. Significantly, the crew had continued under visual flight rules (VFR) procedures.

10 JANUARY 1974 (time unknown)

Location	*Northern Bolivia*
Operator	*Fuerza Aérea Boliviana (Bolivian Air Force)*
Aircraft type	*Douglas C-54 (TAM-52)*

Operated by Transportes Aéreos Militares and on a non-scheduled domestic service of the Bolivian military-owned airline to La Paz, the four-engine aircraft vanished with 24 persons aboard (21 passengers and a crew of three). Having departed shortly before 16:00 local time from Santa Rosa, Beni, the aircraft was to have arrived at the capital city about an hour later.

18 AUGUST 1974 (time unknown)

Location	*Near Kisangani, Haut-Zaire, Zaire*
Operator	*Force Aérienne Zairoise (Zairean Air Force)*
Aircraft type	*Lockheed C-130H (9T-TCD)*

The crash of the four-engine turboprop transport claimed the lives of all 31 persons aboard the aircraft (24 passengers and a crew of seven). No further details about the accident were known.

The worst German peacetime military air disaster involved a
Luftwaffe-operated Transall C-160 turboprop transport, identical to
this one. (Philip Jarrett)

12 DECEMBER 1974 (time unknown)

Location	Near Moc Hoa, South Vietnam
Operator	(South) Vietnamese Air Force
Aircraft type	Boeing/Vertol CH-47

All 54 South Vietnamese military personnel aboard were
killed when the turbine-engine helicopter was shot down 50
miles (80km) west of Saigon. The aircraft was engaged in a
troop movement when hit by a surface-to-air missile.

8 JANUARY 1975 (c.08:30)

Location	Near Doncello, Caqueta, Colombia
Operator	Fuerza Aérea Colombiana (Colombian Air Force)
Aircraft type	Douglas DC-3 (FAC-688)

The vintage transport, which was operated by the
Colombian military airline Servicio de Aeronavegación a
Territorios Nacionales (SATENA), crashed and burned in a
mountainous region while en route from San Vicente del
Caguan to Florencia, one segment of a domestic passenger
service that had originated at Neiva, Huila. All 21 persons
aboard were killed, including a crew of four military
personnel. Using an inadequate flight plan, the pilot-in-
command of FAC-668 had proceeded over the mountains
in adverse meteorological conditions, which had reduced
visibility along the route.

9 FEBRUARY 1975 (c.17:30)

Location	Near Souda, Crete
Operator	Luftwaffe (West German Air Force)
Aircraft type	Transall C-160D (50+63)

In the worst peacetime aviation disaster in the history of
German military forces, all 40 servicemen aboard were killed,
including a crew of five, when the twin-engine turboprop
transport crashed about 5 miles (10km) south-east of Canea,
where it was to have landed. The aircraft slammed into a
mountain at an approximate height of 5,000ft (1,500m)
during an instrument approach that was being conducted
around dusk and in the midst of a snow shower. No
information regarding the probable cause of the accident was
disclosed by German military authorities.

This is the Argentine Air Force Fokker F.27 Mark 400M (TC-72), operated by the military airline LADE, involved in the accident on 16 March 1975. (Philip Jarrett)

16 MARCH 1975 (13:40)

Location	Near Barito, Rio Negro, Argentina
Operator	Fuerza Aérea Argentina (Argentine Air Force)
Aircraft type	Fokker F.27 Troopship Mark 400M (TC-72)

Operated by the military airline Lineas Aéreas del Estado (LADE), the twin-engine turboprop transport crashed and burned some 25 miles (40km) west of San Carlos de Bariloche, where it was to have landed. All 55 persons aboard were killed, including the five air force crewmen. The accident occurred near the end of a domestic flight that had originated at El Palomar Air Base, near Buenos Aires. Other than two Uruguayans, its passengers were Argentine military personnel and their dependants.

During the final phase of the instrument landing system (ILS) approach, which was being conducted in adverse meteorological conditions, the aircraft struck a mountain after the pilots had apparently descended below the minimum safe altitude before obtaining reliable navigational signals. A possible contributing factor was the crew's lack of knowledge of the winds at their flight altitude.

20 MARCH 1975 (c.23:00)

Location	Near Quilcene, Washington, USA
Operator	US Air Force
Aircraft type	Lockheed C-141A (64-0641)

Flown by the Military Airlift Command (MAC), the jet transport crashed, exploded and burned in Olympic National Park around 25 miles (40km) south-south-east of Port Angeles, and all 16 American servicemen aboard perished. Among the victims were six navy personnel riding as passengers.

The aircraft had been on its assigned heading of 150 degrees when it struck a ridge of Mount Constance at an approximate elevation of 7,000ft (2,000m), or only about 150ft (50m) below the terrain level, some 60 miles (100km) north-west of McChord Air Force Base, where it was to have landed at the end of a transpacific cargo flight originating at Clark Air Base, in the Philippines, with an en-route stop in Japan. The impact triggered an avalanche that buried much of the wreckage in the valley below. It was dark at the time, and the weather in the area consisted of clouds that extended from the ground to 15,000ft (5,000m), with a visibility of only about a quarter of a mile (500m). The wind was blowing from due south at 25 knots.

In its last recorded radio transmission, 64-0641 had acknowledged authorisation by the Seattle air-traffic control (ATC) centre for descent from 10,000ft (3,000m), actually the minimum altitude at the scene of the accident, to 5,000ft (1,500m). This faulty clearance resulted from the controller's mis-identification of the C-141 with another aircraft, a US Navy A-6 jet, which had been at the same height but flying in a northerly direction. It was noted in the investigative report that pilots deviating from the airway structure usually have no way of verifying their altitudes for the basis of challenging ATC height assignments.

4 APRIL 1975 (c.16:30)

Location	Near Saigon, (South) Vietnam
Operator	US Air Force
Aircraft type	Lockheed C-5A (68-0218)

During the final days before the collapse of South Vietnam, the United States was engaged in a frantic effort to evacuate civilians and military personnel from the war-torn nation it had supported for more than a decade. One series of missions, dubbed Operation Babylift, involved the transport of hundreds of Vietnamese orphans, many the children of American service personnel, for relocation in the US. This particular flight would be conducted by the largest fixed-wing aircraft in use by the American forces, and would end in the worst single non-combat US military aviation disaster.

Flown by the Military Airlift Command (MAC), the C-5A had taken off from Saigon's Tan Son Nhut Airport, bound for the Philippines. Besides the children, the passengers included nurses and a number of other American civilians serving as escorts. Less than a quarter-of-an-hour into the flight, at 16:15 local time, while flying over the South China Sea on a heading of 136 degrees and at a position of 25 miles (40km) south-east of Vung Tau, (South) Vietnam, the rear cargo door and loading ramp blew off. This resulted in a rapid decompression that in turn ejected several victims out of the fuselage. In the process, the aircraft's torque deck was ruptured, its rudder and elevators cables severed and two of its hydraulic systems rendered inoperative, resulting in a loss of pitch control. The crew was only able to maintain control using their flight spoilers, starboard aileron and engine thrust.

Having turned back towards its point of departure, 68-0218 began an approach to Runway 25L. In order to effect alignment with the runway, a left turn was initiated, but at this time the nose of the aircraft dropped. At that point, the pilot levelled out and set down in a rice paddy about 2.5 miles (4km) short of the runway. Touching down at an approximate speed of 310mph (500kmh) with its undercarriage extended and left wing slightly low, the wide-bodied jet transport became airborne briefly, and after the second impact with a dike on the western bank of the Saigon River, broke apart and burst into flames. Killed in the tragedy were 155 of the 330 persons aboard, including about 100 children and five members of the aircraft's crew of 16 air force personnel; most

A Lockheed C-5A Galaxy wide-bodied jet transport, the largest fixed-wing aircraft in the US Air Force fleet and the type involved in the Vietnamese 'Babylift' disaster. (Lockheed Martin)

of the survivors suffered injuries, some of them related to the in-flight decompression.

The flight crew, who escaped serious injury, were later commended for displaying 'great ingenuity and professionalism' in coping with a critical situation which, as noted in the investigative report, was not covered in any flight manual. Two significant actions of the pilot were the increase of power after the initial loss of pitch control to arrest the descent of the aircraft and the levelling of the aircraft during the turn on to the final approach course, which probably prevented a complete loss of control. It was determined that the first three latches on the right side of the ramp became unlocked, resulting in the structural failure after the C-5A had ascended to just above 23,000ft (7,000m). An investigative board was unable to conclusively determine the specific reason for this because a significant number of parts were not recovered.

The ramp and part of the cargo door were later found by the US Navy, and a sequence of events was established leading up to their detachment. Following the loss of support provided by the first three locks, the load was dynamically transferred through the ramp structure to the fuselage hinges and the four remaining locks of the right side, leading to a partial or complete failure of the tie rod between locks 3 and 4. Ultimately, the ramp was torn from right to left and both it and the pressure door separated from the aircraft. The entire failure sequence was believed to have occurred in less than a second. The weather conditions at Saigon at the time of the accident, with scattered clouds at around 2,500ft (750m) and broken layers at higher altitudes, a visibility of 7 miles (11km) and a 15-knot wind from a direction of 120 degrees, were

Despite the almost complete break-up of the C-5A following a crash landing in a rice paddy, more than half of the 330 persons aboard survived. (US Air Force)

not considered a contributing factor. Prior to recommended changes in its locking system, the rear cargo door on all aircraft in the C-5A fleet would not be used for loading or unloading, and never again would one of the giant Lockheed transports be used to carry a large load of passengers.

13 MAY 1975 (c.21:15)

Location	*Near Sakon Nakhon, Thailand*
Operator	*US Air Force*
Aircraft type	*Sikorsky CH-53C (68-10933)*

Participating in a special operations mission to rescue the crew of the *Mayaguez*, an American cargo ship captured by Cambodian military forces, the turbine-engine helicopter crashed about 40 miles (65km) west of Nakhom Phanom Air Base, from where it had taken off earlier. All 23 American servicemen aboard the aircraft (19 passengers and a crew of four) perished.

Bound for Utapao Air Base, also in Thailand, the CH-53 had been cruising in darkness on an almost due westerly heading and at an approximate height of 9,000ft (2,700m) when it was observed by eyewitnesses to go into a descending, uncontrollable spiral before it slammed to earth in an inverted attitude, exploded and burned. The aircraft's main rotor head assembly and main gearbox were found a

considerable distance from the crash site, indicating they had separated in mid-air. The tail rotor and tail gearbox then separated as part of the break-up sequence.

The suspected cause of the accident was the failure due to cracking of a rotor sleeve/spindle assembly, which on a helicopter mates the main blade with the rotor head. The fracture in the threaded area of the sleeve started internally and propagated to its surface. Though its age could not be determined, the crack had undoubtedly existed before the fatal flight. The separation of the corresponding blade created an imbalance in the main rotor assembly, which in turn tore off the main gearbox and the five other blades. The local meteorological conditions at the time, with a visibility of 7 miles (11km) and a 15-knot wind from a direction of 150 degrees, were not considered as contributory to the accident.

3 AUGUST 1975 (c.19:30)

Location	*Near Amapala, Valle, Honduras*
Operator	*Fuerza Aérea de Nicaragua (Nicaraguan Air Force)*
Aircraft type	*Douglas C-47 (412)*

The twin-engine transport, its passengers comprising a group of Mexican performers, plunged into the Pacific Ocean about 1,000ft (300m) from shore and some 150 miles (250km) south of San Salvador. There were no survivors among the 20 persons aboard the aircraft, including a crew of three Nicaraguan military personnel. Subsequently, all the victims' bodies were recovered from the water.

During a flight originating at Veracruz, Mexico, with an

ultimate destination of Managua, Nicaragua, the aircraft had encountered adverse weather conditions and as a result was unable to land for refuelling at Ilopango, El Salvador. It was last seen flying over the water at a low altitude, apparently trying to land, before it crashed around sunset and in conditions of bad visibility due to the storm. Though not officially reported, fuel exhaustion and/or a loss of air speed may have factored in the accident.

27 OCTOBER 1975 (c.06:45)

Location	Near Caranavi, La Paz, Bolivia
Operator	Fuerza Aérea Boliviana (Bolivian Air Force)
Aircraft type	Convair 440 (TAM-44)

Operated by the military airline Transportes Aéreos Militares (TAM) and carrying as passengers mostly military personnel but also some civilians, the twin-engine aircraft crashed in the Cerro Colorado region of the Andes Mountains some 50 miles (80km) north-east of the capital city of La Paz, which was the destination of this internal flight that had departed minutes earlier from Tomonoco. All 67 persons aboard were killed, including a crew of four servicemen.

Following its take-off on the north/south runway, the transport had reached a height of only about 300ft (100m) above the ground, which was insufficient to clear the high terrain surrounding the airport. The weather at the time was neither bad nor 'optimal', according to a military official. Having seats for less than 50 passengers, TAM-44 was apparently overloaded at the time of the accident, and this could have been a significant factor in its crash. However, no official findings were released.

25 NOVEMBER 1975 (c.18:50)

Location	Near Bir Lahfan, Egypt
Operator	Israel Defence Force Air Force
Aircraft type	Lockheed C-130H (011)

The four-engine turboprop transport crashed on the Israeli-occupied Sinai Peninsula, some 25 miles (40km) south of El 'Arish, and all 20 military personnel aboard (nine passengers and a crew of 11) perished. Flying in darkness, the aircraft struck cloud-obscured Jebel Halal, which rises to nearly 3,000ft (1,000m), only about 15ft (5m) below the summit of the mountain. Apparently due to a navigational error, the pilot had assumed a course that took it directly into, instead of around, the high terrain.

20 JANUARY 1976 (c.07:15)

Location	Near Loja, Azuay, Ecuador
Operator	Fuerza Aérea Ecuatoriana (Ecuadorean Air Force)
Aircraft type	Hawker Siddeley 748 Series 2A-246 (FAE-683)

Operated by the military airline Transportes Aéreos Militares Ecuatorianos (TAME) and on a scheduled domestic service to Guayaquil, the twin-engine turboprop crashed at an approximate elevation of 9,000ft (2,700m) in the Chillacocha mountain range. Thirty-four persons aboard were killed, including the crew of six military personnel; the eight surviving passengers suffered various injuries. For reasons that were not determined, the aircraft lost height and slammed into a wooded area some 10 minutes after it had taken off from Loja's La Toma Airport. The meteorological conditions were reportedly good and apparently not a factor in the accident.

9 MAY 1976 (c.16:30)

Location	Near Carrascosa del Campo, Cuenca, Spain
Operator	Imperial Iranian Air Force
Aircraft type	Boeing 747-131F (5-283)

All 17 persons aboard, including a crew of ten Iranian and US service personnel, perished in the fiery crash of the wide-bodied jet transport, which took place about 60 miles (100km) east-south-east of Madrid. Some of its seven passengers were American civilians. The 747 had been on a military logistics flight originating at Tehran, Iran, with an ultimate destination of McGuire Air Force Base, in New Jersey, USA, when it plummeted into farmland after an explosion shattered its left wing.

The accident occurred during a landing approach to Barajas Airport, near the Spanish capital, an intermediate stop. The last radio transmission from 5-283 was the acknowledgement of clearance, which the crew had requested, to proceed on a heading of 260 degrees, or to the left of the direct course, to avoid adverse weather conditions, and for descent from 10,000ft to 5,000ft (3,000m to 1,500m). As confirmed by the pattern of wreckage, which was scattered along a south-westerly heading over an area some 5 miles (10km) long and approximately 2.5 miles (4km) wide, and by the reading of an electric altimeter, which remained fixed to the moment of power cessation, the break-up had occurred shortly after that message, when the cleanly-configured aircraft was at an altitude of around 6,000ft (1,800m) above the ground.

Due to the circumstances of the accident and because it involved an American-built jet transport used widely in commercial airline operations throughout the world, the US National Transportation Safety Board (NTSB) requested and was granted permission to assist in the investigation, and its findings were published in a report released some two years later. Since the aircraft's flight data recorder (FDR) had been inoperative at the time of the crash, the probe concentrated on information obtained from the cockpit voice recorder (CVR) and through examination of the wing itself, which was found to have broken into 15 major pieces. The remains of the wing were re-assembled in a mock-up at the National Aviation Facilities Experimental Centre of the US Federal Aviation Administration (FAA), in Atlantic City, New Jersey.

Comments of the crew transcribed by the CVR and eyewitness reports confirmed the presence of severe

The world-famous Boeing 747 wide-bodied jetliner, one of which, flown by the Imperial Iranian Air Force and virtually identical to this aircraft, crashed in Spain. (Boeing)

thunderstorm activity at the time and location of the accident. An electrical transient heard on the CVR tape was interpreted as an indication that the 747 had been struck by lightning in flight. An explosion took place a fraction of a second afterwards; shortly thereafter, the pilot-in-command

A diagram of the wing section indicating the pattern of break-up of the Iranian military Boeing 747 apparently struck by lightning. (National Transportation Safety Board)

was heard to say, 'The flight control is not working', and the gear warning horn started to sound. Nearly a minute elapsed between the transient and the end of the recording. As further indication of such a strike, pitting and localised burning areas typical of lightning attachment damage were found on the left wing tip and on the vertical stabiliser, at the location of the very-high-frequency antenna.

Following an analysis of the available evidence, it was concluded that the most probable sequence of events culminating in the multiple structural failures, which ended with the separation of the wing, began with the lightning-induced ignition of vapours, produced by the mixture of JP-4 and kerosene with which 5-284 had been fuelled, and which were present in the No. 1 wing tank. The damage to the structure in the area of the tank provided positive indications of an explosion. The most convincing evidence of such 'over-pressure' was the symmetry of damage and the direction of the forces applied to closure ribs, spars and skin, as indicated by the directions of the fractures, bends and fastener hole deformation; the collapse of the fuel jettison tube located within the tank; and the pattern of heat damage and soot on the structure adjacent to the tank. In line with this theory, the explosion would have caused the failure of the fasteners that held the stringers to the ribs and the skin to the spars, resulting in the loss in the integrity of the aft wing box, which greatly reduced the torsional strength of the wing itself; support of the No. 1 power plant in the pitch plane was also lost. The outer wing then began to oscillate, with lateral loads being generated by the vibrating engine, ultimately leading to the failure of the outer wing section.

Evidence indicated that lightning first entered a forward part of the aircraft, perhaps on top of the flight deck section, and exited from a static discharger on the left wing tip. The flash 'hung on' to the initial attachment point as the 747 progressed forward until its vertical stabiliser reached that location, whereupon it re-attached to the fin and continued to exit from the left wing tip. The conductive path of the lightning current to the static discharger at the tip was through a bond strap along the trailing edge. Concentration of current at the riveted joint between this strap and a wing rib caused melting and the release of molten metal and gasses, which were sufficiently conductive to cause the flash to re-attach to this rivet and to leave the discharger.

A careful examination was made to establish how and where fuel vapour ignition might have occurred, with an electrical spark at one of the fuel line couplings considered one possibility. Most likely, however, was that the point of ignition centred in the immediate area of a motor-driven fuel valve, whose connecting drive shaft may have provided a path for an electric current to enter the tank and cause a spark.

It was noted in the investigative report that lightning-induced ignition of vapours had occurred in a few previous aircraft accidents, but only under a rare combination of circumstances, in accordance with the following scenario: an intermittently conductive path was available that closed and opened an electrical 'loop'; a lightning-induced current of sufficient intensity flowed in this path and formed a spark, and a flammable vapour surrounded this spark.

Specialists from the US National Aeronautics and Space Administration (NASA), which participated in the inquiry, concluded that the wing failure resulted simply from the imposition of loads produced by the turbulence within the thunderstorm that exceeded the designed strength of the structure. According to the NTSB, however, this theory was not supported by the physical evidence, i.e. the condition and dispersal of the wreckage, the comments of the crew transcribed by the CVR and eyewitness accounts. Since this accident, the FAA has issued a number of airworthiness directives to prevent such in-flight explosions, such as improvements in the lightning protection design of the fuel system of the 747, and means to assure a clear path in the vents between fuel tanks.

28 AUGUST 1976 (c.12:40)

Location	*Near Peterborough, Cambridge, England*
Operator	*US Air Force*
Aircraft type	*Lockheed C-141A (67-0006)*

Operated by the Military Airlift Command (MAC), the jet transport crashed and burned in a field while preparing to land at RAF Mildenhall, near Bury St Edmunds. All 18 American service personnel aboard, including four passengers in addition to the crew of 14, perished. The C-141 had been on an airlift training mission from McGuire Air Force Base, New Jersey, USA, to Torrejon de Ardoz Air Base, Spain, when it broke up in flight and plummeted to earth about 25 miles (40km) north-west of the RAF facility, which was an en-route stop.

Prior to the accident, 67-0006 had requested radar vectors around an area of severe thunderstorm activity, to which the ground controller replied, 'There's no way I can get you around it.' As the aircraft's weather radar was inoperative, the crew attempted to navigate visually between storm cells, and in their last radio transmission, they reported turning back towards the base, on to a heading of 140 degrees, and requested a precision radar (PAR) approach to Runway 11. At the moment it suffered structural failure, the cleanly-configured transport was at an approximate height of 9,000ft (2,700m) and flying in a south-south-easterly direction, with all four engines, its starboard wing, horizontal stabiliser and upper half of its vertical tail fin separating from the aircraft.

Some 15 miles (25km) south-south-west of the crash site, it was raining, with a broken overcast at 4,000ft (1,200m), scattered stratus clouds down to about 1,000ft (300m) and maximum cloud tops at 26,000ft (8,000m). The thunderstorm itself was capable of extreme turbulence. Its radar track

A US Air Force Lockheed C-141A Starlifter jet transport, two of which crashed fatally during a single day in August 1976. (Lockheed Martin)

indicated that the C-141 had intercepted the leading edge of the storm, actually the inflow or up-draught area, which would create the greatest turbulence potential. Significantly, 67-0006 had a history of trouble with its weather radar, but the crew did not realise that the unit was inoperative until after their departure on the transatlantic flight. It was noted in the investigative report that due to the lack of evidence, a lightning strike apparently did not factor in the break-up sequence.

28 AUGUST 1976 (c.12:40)

Location	Near Holsteinborg, Greenland
Operator	US Air Force
Aircraft type	Lockheed C-141A (67-0008)

The second fatal MAC C-141 crash within about three hours occurred at Sondrestrom Air Base, following an airlift mission by the jet transport from Thule Air Base, also located on Greenland. Twenty-three persons aboard the aircraft were killed in this second accident, including eight Danish civilians; two of the victims succumbed within a three-day period about two weeks later. Three passengers and one of the eight crewmen assigned to 67-0008, all US Air Force personnel, survived with various injuries.

Following a precision radar (PAR) approach, the aircraft touched down slightly 'long' on Runway 11 on its extended undercarriage and with flaps fully deployed, but after a ground roll of approximately 2,000ft (600m), a go-around was initiated. Lifting off in a steep attitude, the C-141 stalled, after which its left wing tip contacted the ground. After a second impact with the ground, it departed the runway off its right side and some 2,400ft (730m) short of the departure end.

The aftermath of the Venezuelan Air Force C-130 crash on Terceira Island, in the Azores, which wiped out a college choir on their way to Spain. (UPI/Corbis-Bettmann)

The aircraft was destroyed by impact forces and by fire, which had erupted when the wing first scraped the ground. At the time, the weather consisted of a high, broken overcast, with a visibility of 10 miles (15km) and a light, north-westerly wind.

There was no evidence of material failure in the aircraft's engines, flight controls or flight instruments. Of considerable significance was the lack of experience of the flight crew, with the captain possessing less than 100 hours in the command position. The specific factor leading to the accident was believed to have been the upwardly sloping terrain, which could have produced an optical illusion and created the impression of there being insufficient runway on which to continue the landing.

3 SEPTEMBER 1976 (c.21:45)

Location	Azores Islands, Portugal
Operator	Fuerza Aérea Venezolana (Venezuelan Air Force)
Aircraft type	Lockheed C-130H (7772)

All 68 persons aboard were killed, including a crew of ten military personnel, when the four-engine turboprop transport crashed and burned on Terceira Island as it was attempting to land at the Lajes Air Base, near Praira da Vitoria. Most of the passengers of the aircraft, which was on a transatlantic flight originating at Simon Bolivar Airport, serving Caracas, belonged to a Venezuelan college choir due to perform in Barcelona, Spain.

During its approach to Runway 16, in darkness and adverse meteorological conditions consisting of little or no visibility, heavy rain and winds of up to around 30 knots, the C-130 slammed into a hill approximately a mile (1.5km) from its threshold. Reportedly, it had not been properly aligned with the runway at the time of impact. The bad weather, which was associated with the passage of hurricane Emmy, was considered as the primary causative factor in the accident. The control tower had reportedly tried unsuccessfully to correct the erroneous flight path of the aircraft in the final seconds before the crash.

3 MARCH 1977 (c.15:00)

Location	Near Cascina, Toscana, Italy
Operator	Aeronautica Militare Italiana (Italian Air Force)
Aircraft type	Lockheed C-130H (MM61996)

The four-engine turboprop transport, carrying 38 naval cadets on an 'orientation flight' with an officer accompanying them, plus a crew of five air force personnel, crashed on Mount Serra some 10 miles (15km) north-east of Pisa. All 44 Italian servicemen aboard perished.

Having taken off about 5 minutes earlier from Runway 04 at San Giusto Airport, serving Pisa, the aircraft was observed by eyewitnesses to initiate an evasive manoeuvre, pulling up and banking to the right, just before it slammed into the wooded terrain at an approximate elevation of 2,600ft (800m), or about 600ft (180m) below the top of the mountain, bursting into flames on impact. The local meteorological conditions at around the time of the accident consisted of a low overcast that obscured the terrain surrounding the airport, with 5/8 strato-cumulus at around 2,500ft (750m) and 4/8 altocumulus down to 800ft (250m), and a visibility of about 3.5 miles (6km) in haze. The wind was calm.

Although no official cause was given, released information indicated that the highly experienced pilot at the controls of the C-130 had deviated from the assigned flight path. There had been no distress message from MM61995, and sabotage or any other type of in-flight explosion was definitely ruled out by military authorities after an initial examination of the wreckage.

19 APRIL 1977 (time unknown)

Location	*Near Tapa, Estonia, USSR*
Operator	*Soviet Air Force*
Aircraft type	*Antonov An-24*

The twin-engine turboprop transport, its passengers comprising military fighter pilots, crashed and burned while attempting to land at the Tapa air base. All 21 persons aboard the aircraft, including the six members of its crew, were killed in the accident. Having nearly completed a flight from Parnu, also in Estonia, the An-24 reportedly descended below a safe altitude while on the final approach, whereupon it struck the chimney of a factory, the crash occurring in conditions of poor visibility in falling snow.

10 MAY 1977 (c.20:30)

Location	*Near Jericho, Jordan*
Operator	*Israel Defence Force Air Force*
Aircraft type	*Sikorsky CH-53D (360)*

All 54 Israeli servicemen aboard were killed when the turbine-engine helicopter crashed and exploded in a sandy desert region of the occupied West Bank, approximately 5 miles (10km) west of the River Jordan. The victims included a crew of four; most of the passengers were army paratroopers participating in a joint exercise with the air force. Occurring a few minutes after the aircraft had taken off, the accident was attributed to pilot error, specifically, flight in darkness below a safe height. Additionally, the commanding officer of the unit to which 360 belonged was faulted for allowing his aircraft to fly below authorised minimum altitudes.

21 JUNE 1977 (c.22:30)

Location	*Off Wake Island*
Operator	*US Navy*
Aircraft type	*Lockheed EC-130Q (156176)*

The airborne command and control aircraft, with a crew of 16 military personnel aboard, crashed in the Pacific Ocean moments after taking off from Wake Island Naval Air Station, on an operational mission. Searchers found only one body; there were no survivors. Also recovered were two power plants, a portion of one wing and some other debris, but the main wreckage of 156176 was lost at sea.

Climbing to no higher than 400ft (120m), the four-engine turboprop slammed into the water approximately 1 mile (1.5km) from the end of Runway 10, which it had used, exploding on impact and creating a fire that burned for a while on the surface of the ocean. The accident occurred in moonlit darkness and weather conditions consisting of a 2,000ft (600m) ceiling and winds out of the east at 17 knots, gusting to 22. For unknown reasons, the EC-130 had failed to follow the normal climb-out profile.

One possible explanation for the crash was that the pilots had lost their visual and peripheral references immediately after passing over the departure end of the runway. One endorsement in the navy investigative report expressed the opinion that the absence of control tower personnel on duty at the time of the take-off, who could have monitored the climb-out of the aircraft, deprived the crew of an additional safeguard.

14 JULY 1977 (c.12:30)

Location	*Near Cuangar, Cuando Cubango, Angola*
Operator	*Força Aérea Popular de Angola (Angolan Air Force)*
Aircraft type	*Antonov An-26 (T-20)*

The Soviet-built twin-engine turboprop transport was reportedly shot down by rebels near the border of Namibia, and all 30 persons aboard were killed. According to witnesses, the aircraft appeared to have been hit at an approximate height of 150ft (50m) above the ground immediately after it had taken off from an airstrip.

24 JULY 1977 (c.19:00)

Location	*Near Puerto Montt, Los Lagos, Chile*
Operator	*Fuerza Aérea de Chile (Chilean Air Force)*
Aircraft type	*Douglas DC-6B (FAC-989)*

As it was attempting to land in darkness and during a heavy rain, the four-engine transport slammed into a swamp and burst into flames. Killed in the accident were 38 of the 82 persons aboard the aircraft, including its entire crew of seven military personnel; many of the surviving passengers suffered injuries. The crash occurred approximately 3 miles (5km) east of the runway during an instrument approach to El Tepual Air Base, an en-route stop during a domestic service originating at Punta Arenas, with an ultimate destination of Santiago. Offering no specific details, military authorities attributed the accident to the adverse weather conditions.

25 JULY 1977 (c.08:00)

Location	*Near Yoro, Honduras*
Operator	*Fuerza Aérea Hondurena (Honduran Air Force)*
Aircraft type	*Douglas C-47 (301)*

Apparently overloaded with public employees and their families, the twin-engine transport crashed and burned in a mountainous region shortly after taking off from the Yoro

*The remains of the US Air Force EC-135K that ploughed into the
rising terrain shortly after taking off from Kirtland Air Force Base.
(US Air Force)*

airport, bound for the Honduran capital of Tegucigalpa, some
80 miles (130km) to the south. The accident claimed the
lives of 25 persons aboard the aircraft, while the 15 survivors
suffered various injuries. According to unofficial reports, the
left power plant of the C-47 had 'exploded' in flight.

14 SEPTEMBER 1977 (23:48)

Location	*Near Albuquerque, New Mexico, USA*
Operator	*US Air Force*
Aircraft type	*Boeing EC-135K (62-3536)*

Operated by the Tactical Air Command as an airborne
command and control platform, the modified jet tanker
crashed about 2½ minutes after taking off from Kirtland Air
Force Base, and its entire crew of 20 perished. The scene of the
accident was in the Manzano Mountains, some 5 miles (10km)
beyond the departure end of Runway 08, which the aircraft
had used, and at an approximate elevation of 6,500ft (1,980m).

Climbing on a heading of 125 degrees, the cleanly-
configured EC-135 was in a right bank of approximately
30 degrees when it struck a peak just 30ft (10m) below its
summit. Examination of a recovered air speed indicator
revealed a reading that correlated to around 185mph
(300kmh) at the moment of the crash. Initial contact was with
its right wing and No. 4 power plant, and in the subsequent
impact the aircraft exploded and disintegrated. It was dark at
the time, but the meteorological conditions were otherwise
good, with a broken overcast at 11,000ft (3,400m), a visibility
of 15 miles (25km) and a south-easterly wind of 4 knots.

The investigation found no evidence of in-flight fire,
explosion or structural, electrical, instrument, engine or flight
control failure prior to impact. It was reported that before the
crash, 62-3536 had been observed on radar to be flying too
low, and that a ground controller unsuccessfully instructed it
to turn right and climb. Fatigue may have contributed to the
crew's failure to follow the proper departure flight profile.

21 OCTOBER 1977 (c.10:30)

Location	*Near Paluan, the Philippines*
Operator	*US Marine Corps*
Aircraft type	*Sikorsky CH-53D (157139)*

The turbine-engine helicopter, carrying a load of troops and
also lifting with an external sling an empty water trailer, or
'bull', crashed and burned in mountainous terrain on the
island of Mindoro, some 80 miles (130km) south-west of
Manila. Killed in the accident were 24 of the 37 American
servicemen aboard the aircraft, including the entire crew
of four, while the 13 surviving passengers and a US Navy
corpsman who came to the scene to help suffered injuries.

After it began to lift the water trailer off the ground, the
rotorcraft yawed to the right, whereupon the crew released
the container. At that point, the CH-53 appeared to stabilise
momentarily, but then continued with increasing speed in
its clock-wise rotation, while in a nose-high attitude. During
this time, a number of occupants were ejected from the
rear cargo door. Still spinning, the aircraft descended until
it struck the terrain approximately 300ft (100m) below the
saddle from which it had picked up the water trailer, the
impact shearing off its tail rotor and a large portion of the tail
assembly. It finally nosed down and slammed to earth, rolling
over at least twice before coming to rest generally upright. At
around the time of the accident, the local weather consisted
of scattered cumulus and strato-cumulus at 2,000ft (600m)
and greater cloud coverage at higher altitudes, and a visibility
of 15 miles (25km) in light haze. The wind was out of the
north at 8 knots, gusting to almost twice that velocity.

It was the opinion of the officer in charge of the
investigation that the high gross weight of the aircraft
and the density altitude conditions in which it had been
operating, requiring high power while both hovering and
lifting an external load, exceeded the authority of the tail
rotor to counter the torque effect of the main rotor and thus
maintain directionally controlled flight. The external load
was jettisoned in an unsuccessful attempt to regain control,
and it appeared that the crew then lowered the collective
pitch, reducing the power applied to the rotor system, and
further tried to fly down the slope of the hill in order to effect
recovery, without success. There was no evidence of any
mechanical failure factoring in the accident.

The investigating officer further expressed the opinion
that with proper restraint, all of those killed except the
two pilots would have survived the crash, and a number of
serious injuries would have been prevented. Though highly
experienced, the flight crew was considered negligent in

The crash of the Philippine Air Force Fokker F.27 wreaked havoc in a residential area near Manila International Airport. (UPI/ Corbis-Bettmann)

trying to lift a load under the prevailing conditions, and the crew chief for not requiring the passengers to use the seat belts that were available; the pilots apparently also failed to supervise him in this respect. With regard to the latter factor, one of the recommendations made in the accident report was that marine personnel wear helmets and use seat belts when riding as passengers aboard rotary-wing aircraft.

26 NOVEMBER 1977 (c.02:30)

Location	Near Beziers, Languedoc-Roussillon, France
Operator	L'Armée de l'Air (French Air Force)
Aircraft type	Nord Noratlas (182)

The twin-engine transport, which was carrying as passengers members of a military band, crashed on a mountain slope and exploded north of the city. Including a crew of three, all 34 French military personnel aboard were killed in the accident, which occurred in early-morning darkness and adverse weather conditions, with fog and gusty winds. No distress message was transmitted prior to impact, casting doubt on some eyewitness accounts of an in-flight fire. However, no official findings pertaining to the cause of the crash were disclosed by military authorities.

10 FEBRUARY 1978 (c.11:20)

Location	Near Artigas, Uruguay
Operator	Fuerza Aérea Uruguaya (Uruguayan Air Force)
Aircraft type	Douglas C-47A (T511)

Operated by by the military airline Transporte Aéreo Militar Uruguayo (TAMU) and on a domestic passenger service originating at and ultimately bound for Montevideo, the vintage twin-engine transport crashed in a field while attempting an emergency landing at Artigas Airport, from where it had taken off moments earlier. All 44 persons aboard, including a crew of four military personnel, were killed.

The aircraft had just become airborne when one power plant apparently malfunctioned, and its pilot then requested clearance to return to the airport, but following a steep turn it plummeted to the ground on a ranch and burst into flames approximately 1 mile (1.5km) from the end of the runway. The weather at the time was clear, with little or no wind, and was not considered to be a factor in the accident.

14 SEPTEMBER 1978 (c.14:50)

Location	Paranaque, the Philippines
Operator	Philippine Air Force
Aircraft type	Fokker F.27 Friendship Mark 200 (10328)

The twin-engine turboprop transport crashed in a residential section near Manila International Airport, where it was to have landed. Killed in the accident were 21 of the 28 persons aboard the aircraft, including the entire crew of four military personnel, as well as 12 others on the ground. The seven surviving passengers and 20 persons on the ground suffered injuries.

Following a domestic flight from Laoag, the F.27 had begun its approach to Runway 06 in the midst of a thunderstorm, with heavy rain, wind gusts of around 35 knots and a visibility of ½–2 miles (0.8km–3km). Its undercarriage extended, the transport slammed to earth to the left of the runway centreline, exploded and burned, destroying ten houses. Reports of a pre-impact lightning strike were never confirmed officially as a factor in the crash; other possible causes were wind shear, the low visibility at the time and adverse affects on the aircraft's flight instruments by the poor atmospheric conditions.

A Soviet-built and operated Antonov An-12, similar to the Indian Air Force transport involved in the disastrous crash in November 1978. (Martin Bowman)

19 NOVEMBER 1978 (c.11:00)

Location	*Near Leh, Kashmir, India*
Operator	*Indian Air Force*
Aircraft type	*Antonov An-12*

The four-engine turboprop transport crashed and burst into flames while attempting to land at the city's airport, the elevation of which is about 10,000ft (3,000m). Killed in the accident were all 77 Indian military personnel aboard the aircraft, including a crew of seven, and a woman who was apparently in a hut struck by the An-12. The passengers were all army soldiers on their way back from home leave. Having completed an internal flight from Chandigarh, Punjab, the aircraft spiralled to the ground approximately 1.2 miles (2km) short of the runway after reportedly experiencing a power plant malfunction during the approach.

7 JUNE 1979 (c.11:00)

Location	*Near Leh, Kashmir, India*
Operator	*Indian Air Force*
Aircraft type	*Hindustan Aeronautics HAL 748-2M (H2178)*

All 27 Indian military personnel aboard lost their lives, including seven air force personnel, when the twin-engine turboprop transport crashed about 10 minutes after it had taken off from the city's airport, bound for a forward area. The passengers of the aircraft were army soldiers. No further details are known about the accident or its possible cause.

22 DECEMBER 1979 (c.14:00)

Location	*Near Puerto Esperanza, Ucayali, Peru*
Operator	*Fuerza Aérea del Perú (Peruvian Air Force)*
Aircraft type	*de Havilland DHC-5D Buffalo (FAP-348)*

During a domestic service from Pucallpa to Puerto Esperanza, the twin-engine turboprop transport crashed in a jungle region some 20 miles (30km) from its destination, and all 29 persons aboard were killed. The victims included the five-member crew of the aircraft, all of whom were military personnel. A severe thunderstorm associated with a hurricane and containing strong down-draughts was believed responsible for the accident.

25 DECEMBER 1979 (c.19:30)

Location	*Near Qarah Bagh, Kabul, Afghanistan*
Operator	*Soviet Air Force*
Aircraft type	*Ilyushin Il-76M (SSSR-86036)*

At the beginning of the Soviet invasion of Afghanistan, the Soviet jet transport crashed some 25 miles (40km) north of the city of Kabul. All 44 persons aboard the aircraft, including its crew of seven, were killed; the passengers were army paratroopers. Having nearly completed a flight from Tashkent, Uzbek SSR, the Il-76 struck a mountain while approaching to land at Bagram Air Base. The accident occurred in darkness during an attempted landing at an airfield that lacked navigational facilities and with which the crew was not familiar.

24 JANUARY 1980 (c.06:20)

Location   Near Mandalay, Burma (Myanmar)
Operator   Union of Burma Air Force
Aircraft type Fairchild Hiller FH-227B (5003)

The twin-engine turboprop transport crashed and burned, killing all but one of the 44 persons aboard. Due to reported power plant trouble, the pilot had requested clearance to return to Annisaton Airport, serving Mandalay, from where it had taken off shortly before, but the aircraft struck the top of a building during the attempted emergency landing.

22 FEBRUARY 1980 (time unknown)

Location   Near Agra, Uttar Pradesh, India
Operator   Indian Air Force
Aircraft type Fairchild C-119G

Loaded with paratroopers who were to have made a training jump, the twin-engine transport crashed and burned about 120 miles (190km) south-south-east of New Delhi as it was taking off from Kheria Airport. All but one of the 47 Indian servicemen aboard the aircraft and one person on the ground were killed. The latter victim was a bicyclist riding on the runway, who, in trying to avoid, may have led the pilot to initiate a premature lift-off, possibly resulting in a stall.

28 FEBRUARY 1980 (time unknown)

Location   Northern Guatemala
Operator   Fuerza Aérea Guatemalteca (Guatemalan
              Air Force)
Aircraft type Douglas C-47

The twin-engine transport, carrying as passengers Guatemalan servicemen and their dependants on a tour of Mayan ruins, crashed in a mountainous area near the town of Sabanetas, in Peten, some 300 miles (480km) north of the capital city, and all 21 persons aboard were killed. The afternoon accident occurred in adverse weather conditions, which may have been a primary or contributing causative factor.

14 MARCH 1980 (c.15:00)

Location   Near Yenice, Cilicia, Turkey
Operator   US Air Force
Aircraft type Lockheed C-130H (74-2064)

The four-engine turboprop transport plummeted into hilly terrain some 25 miles (40km) south-west of Adana and about 15 miles (25km) due west of Incirlik Air Base, which was the point of origin and ultimate destination of a logistics mission in which the aircraft had been engaged, in support of US military installations throughout Turkey. All 18 persons aboard perished, including a crew of six US Air Force personnel.

Last observed on radar at a height of around 5,000ft (1,500m), the C-130 had been descending, as cleared, to 3,000ft (1,000m) and on a south-south-easterly heading when an explosion occurred in its left wing. The weather in the area at the time of the crash consisted of light rain, with a broken layer of cumulus clouds at 4,000ft (1,200m) and solid altostratus at 10,000ft (3,000m), and a visibility of around 5 miles (10km). The wind was calm. Although the combustible material was identified as fuel, the source of its ignition and the underlying material failure that led to the explosion remain a mystery.

Wreckage distribution chart showing the wide dispersal of debris following the in-flight explosion of a US Air Force C-130H. (US Air Force)

15 SEPTEMBER 1980 (c.00:00)

Location	*Near Medina, Saudi Arabia*
Operator	*Royal Saudi Air Force*
Aircraft type	*Lockheed C-130E (453)*

All 89 Saudi military personnel aboard (81 passengers and a crew of eight) perished in the flaming crash of the four-engine turboprop transport, which occurred shortly after its departure from Prince Bin Abdulaziz Airport, serving Medina. The aircraft plummeted into the desert in early-morning darkness, shortly after midnight, reportedly after a fire had erupted and then spread from the cockpit area.

17 SEPTEMBER 1980 (time unknown)

Location	*Near Kindu, Kivu, Zaire*
Operator	*Force Aérienne Zairoise (Zairean Air Force)*
Aircraft type	*de Havilland DHC-5D Buffalo (9T-CBA)*

The twin-engine turboprop transport crashed immediately after it had taken off, killing all 36 persons aboard the aircraft. No specific details about the accident, including the possible cause, were made available.

30 SEPTEMBER 1980 (time unknown)

Location	*Badakshan, Afghanistan*
Operator	*Soviet Air Force*
Aircraft type	*Antonov An-12V (SSSR-11104)*

The four-engine turboprop transport, which belonged to the Soviet airline Aeroflot, was apparently shot down by Afghan guerrilla forces while approaching to land at an unknown airfield, and all 45 persons aboard the aircraft were reportedly killed.

12 NOVEMBER 1980 (23:53)

Location	*Near Cairo, Egypt*
Operator	*US Air Force*
Aircraft type	*Lockheed C-141A (67-0030)*

Operated by the Military Airlift Command (MAC) and completing a cargo flight from Ramstein Air Base, in (West) Germany, the jet transport crashed, disintegrated and burned in the desert as it was attempting to land at Cairo West Airport. All 13 American service personnel aboard (seven passengers and six crewmen) perished.

Cleared for a visual approach to Runway 34, 67-0030 flew over the airport and then initiated a left turn near the mid-field point at an approximate height of 2,000ft (600m) and while descending. According to its flight data recorder (FDR) read-out, the C-141 continued down with its left-banking attitude, speed and descent rate increasing dramatically until it struck the ground about a minute after starting the left turn. Impact occurred some 2 miles (3km) north-west of the assigned runway at an indicated air speed of around 290mph (465kmh), with the cleanly-configured aircraft on a west-south-westerly heading. It was dark at the time of the accident, with no moon and little ground illumination, but the meteorological conditions were good, with a broken overcast at about 20,000ft (6,000m), a visibility of more than 5 miles (10km) and a north-easterly wind of 8 knots.

The cause of the crash was not disclosed, but releasable findings revealed that the engines of the C-141 had been operating properly, and also there was no evidence of flight control system failure prior to impact. Considered as a contributing factor were the British Calvert System approach lights used at the airport. It was further noted in the investigative report that 67-0030 had been equipped, as are airliners, with a ground-proximity warning system (GPWS), but because of its dependence on the aircraft's radar altimeter, it would not have provided timely warnings at extreme bank angles.

7 FEBRUARY 1981 (c.18:00)

Location	*Near Pargolovo, Russian Soviet Federated Socialist Republic, USSR*
Operator	*Soviet Navy*
Aircraft type	*Tupolev Tu-104A (SSSR-42332)*

Three high-ranking officers were among 51 Soviet military personnel killed in the crash of the twin-jet transport, which occurred approximately 10 miles (15km) north of

Little remains of the US Air Force C-141A jet transport that crashed in the desert during an attempted landing at Cairo West Airport. (AP/Wide World Photos)

Leningrad shortly after it had taken off on an internal flight to Khabarovsk. The victims included the aircraft's six-member crew; there were no survivors. Immediately after becoming airborne, and at an approximate height of 150ft (50m), the Tu-104 entered a right bank and plunged to earth, crashing in an inverted attitude and erupting in flames. Occurring in darkness, the accident was attributed to the shift of improperly secured cargo, combined with the inappropriate seating of the passengers, which placed the aircraft's centre-of-gravity behind the authorised limit. Subsequent to this disaster, the remaining aircraft in the Soviet military Tu-104 fleet were removed from use.

26 FEBRUARY 1981 (c.05:25)

Location   South China Sea
Operator   US Air Force
Aircraft type   Lockheed MC-130E-1 (64-0564)

The four-engine turboprop aircraft crashed around 15 miles (25km) west-north-west of Subi Point Naval Air Station, from where it had taken off about an hour earlier, on a tactical exercise. Among the 24 servicemen aboard, all but one member of the crew of nine assigned to 64-0564 lost their lives. The seriously injured survivor was rescued by local fishermen, and the bodies of six victims were also recovered. The passengers consisted of American, Australian, Filipino and New Zealand military personnel. Local fishermen reported seeing the C-130, which had been flying at a low altitude in pre-dawn darkness and visual meteorological conditions, strike the surface of the water in a shallow descent, explode, burn and sink. No further information about the crash was released by the US Air Force.

10 MARCH 1981 (c.05:00)

Location   Comoro Islands
Operator   Aéronavale (French Naval Aviation)
Aircraft type   Dassault-Breguet Atlantique (29)

Shortly after it had taken off from the airport at Moroni, on Grande Comoro, the twin-engine turboprop patrol aircraft crashed into a hillside and exploded, killing all 18 French military personnel aboard. The victims included four maintenance workers riding as passengers in addition to the regular crew. Climbing to an approximate height of 500ft (150m), the Atlantique suddenly plummeted to earth after fire, which, according to unofficial sources, had erupted in one power plant, the accident occurring in pre-dawn darkness at the beginning of an aerial surveillance mission.

6 MAY 1981 (c.10:50)

Location   Near Frederick, Maryland, USA
Operator   US Air Force
Aircraft type   Boeing EC-135N (61-0328)

Originally designed as an astronaut relay and satellite tracking station, the modified jet transport, which was on a navigational training flight from Wright-Patterson Air Force Base, in Ohio, crashed approximately 2 miles (3km) north-north-east of the town of Walkersville, located some 40 miles (65km) north-west of Baltimore. All 21 persons aboard perished; with the exception of two dependants and one other civilian, the victims were all American military personnel, including the 17 designated crew members. One of the dependants, the wife of the aircraft's commander, had apparently been seated in the pilot's position at the start of the accident sequence.

The EC-135 had been cruising at an altitude of 29,000ft (9,000m) and an indicated air speed of around 550mph (885kmh) when, for undetermined reasons, its pitch trim moved to the full nose-down position, which was evident from post-impact examination of the cockpit indicator and the horizontal stabiliser mechanism itself. As a result, 61-0328 rapidly pitched down, most likely upon the release of the autopilot, which should have been able to overcome its trim except when near the full nose-down position. This attitude would have induced sufficient negative gravitational forces to trip off line the generators, causing a total loss of electrical power and, in turn, preventing the pitch trim from being moved electrically. While unusual, this condition could have easily been controlled with prompt corrective action, within 8 seconds, according to simulator tests, but in this case recovery was delayed, for reasons that could not be determined. (The pilot had apparently activated the stabiliser cut-out switch in an attempt to stop the trim from going into a more extreme position.) Under the circumstances, the pitch angle and the air speed of the aircraft would increase until the pitch trim is moved to the neutral position. Without electrical power, this must be accomplished manually with the control wheel on the console between the pilots' seats, which, in this situation, would have required about 35 revolutions to return the trim to zero.

The four-engine jet was seen to emerge from a low overcast in a nose-down attitude of 20 to 30 degrees and at an air speed in excess of 460mph (740kmh). It was around that time, and while at an approximate height of 1,500ft (500m) above the ground, that an explosion occurred in the pressurised compartment of the aircraft, resulting in the break-up of its fuselage and the separation of the wings. Around 90 seconds elapsed from the beginning of the descent until the final impact. Wreckage was strewn in an elliptical shape some 2,400ft (730m) long by about 1,800ft (550m) wide, with all debris being found within approximately 2.5 miles (4km) of the main crash site. The surface weather in the area at the time was characterised by light rain, a slight breeze from a south-south-westerly direction, and a visibility of around 2.5 miles (4km), but had been clear at the cruising altitude, with cloud tops at about 20,000ft (6,000m).

The investigation found no evidence that the presence of passengers on the flight deck caused or contributed to the disaster, nor of any explosion or structural failure prior to the uncontrolled descent. No previous problems had been

A chart indicating the numerous break-up points of the US Air Force EC-135 that disintegrated during an uncontrolled dive. (US Air Force)

reported with 61-0328, and although the cause of the pre-impact explosion could not be determined, the accident report concluded that by that time recovery from the dive would not have been possible and the crash was thus inevitable.

24 MAY 1981 (c.15:00)

Location	*Near Guachala, Zamora-Chinchipe, Ecuador*
First aircraft	
Operator	*Fuerza Aérea Ecuatoriana (Ecuadorean Air Force)*
Aircraft type	*Beechcraft Super King Air 200 (FAE-723)*
Second aircraft	
Operator	*Fuerza Aérea Ecuatoriana (Ecuadorean Air Force)*
Aircraft type	*de Havilland DHC-6 Twin Otter Series 300 (FAE-457)*

Both operated by the military airline Transportes Aéreos Militares Ecuatorianos (TAME), the two twin-engine turboprop executive/transport aircraft, on internal flights from Quito to Macara, crashed and burned in mountainous terrain about 10 miles (15km) from the Peruvian border. A total of 27 persons were killed in the separate accidents, with no survivors from either aircraft. The nine occupants aboard the Super King Air included Ecuadorean President Jaime Roldos Aguilera and his wife, plus a crew of three.

The separate accidents occurred as they were proceeding in formation in good weather conditions under visual flight rules (VFR) procedures. However, the weather deteriorated

as they approached their destination, as confirmed by the pilot in the last communication with the Twin Otter. At Loja, which was the nearest reporting point, the conditions were reported as partly cloudy, with 3/8 coverage at 1,200ft (350m) and a visibility of around 20 miles (30km). The mountains in the area were apparently shrouded in cloud.

26/27 MAY 1981 (c.00:00)

Location	*North Atlantic Ocean (USS Nimitz)*
Operator	*US Marine Corps*
Aircraft type	*Grumman EA-6B (159910)*

This crash and resulting explosions and fire wreaked havoc aboard the American nuclear-powered aircraft carrier USS *Nimitz* (CVN-68), which at the time was operating off the coast of Florida, USA, some 80 miles (130km) east of Jacksonville. Launched earlier in the evening from the navy ship, on an electronic counter-measures training flight, the twin-jet aircraft involved in the accident had been waved off in one unsuccessful landing attempt and as a result, was designated 'fuel critical'. Following a fuel-consuming interval, 159910 began a second approach, using the carrier's automatic landing system for guidance. After it crossed the centreline with a continuing right drift, power was applied at the order of the landing signal officer (LSO), but the EA-6B nevertheless crashed on top of the vessel, careering across the flight deck and ploughing into aircraft parked towards its forward part. The initial accident, at approximately 23:50 local time, was followed about half an hour later by the detonation of a Sparrow air-to-air missile that had been knocked off an F-14 jet fighter.

Fourteen navy personnel were killed in the aviation/marine disaster, including the three crewmen of 159910, one of whom was lost at sea. Among the flight deck crew member casualties, two of those killed and more than half of the 42 injured were victims of the missile explosion. Eleven other aircraft were destroyed or damaged, with monetary costs exceeding US$50 million.

It was dark at the time of the crash, with scattered clouds at 3,500ft (1,050m) and broken layers estimated at 10,000ft (3,000m) and 25,000ft (7,500m), respectively, a visibility of around 5 miles (10km), and a relative wind (due to the 165-degree true heading of the ship) of 16 knots from a north-north-westerly direction. The horizon was not visible. There was also thunderstorm activity and rain in the area, which the carrier began to encounter within an hour of the crash.

The accident was primarily attributed to the failure of the EA-6B to maintain proper alignment during the landing. The primary contributing factor was the failure of the LSO to make a 'line-up' call and his faulty instructions to the pilot, 'Nice and easy, fly it down'. Also contributing to the error by the pilot were several psycho-physiological factors, most significantly, his use of a decongestant medication and of aspirin for treatment of a head cold from which he had been suffering. These were coupled with the stress associated with a night carrier landing, with which his experience was limited, in conditions of poor visibility that were conducive to vertigo and while facing a low-fuel situation due to the earlier 'boltered', or missed, pass. With regard to the first issue, the pilot had removed himself from the flight schedule on the morning of the accident, but in the afternoon reported feeling better. Although there was no record of him being prescribed a drug containing brompheniramine, an unusually high concentration of this element and also salicylates, found in aspirin, were found in his body in the subsequent autopsy. The side effects of the former include dizziness, lethargy and vision problems. A bottle of nasal spray was also found in a pocket of his flight suit. Additionally, the position of 159910 above the glide slope and viewed against a featureless background significantly impaired the ability of the LSO to see its starboard wing drop and increasing drift to the right of the centreline. There was no indication of a flight control system malfunction in the aircraft prior to impact.

The revelation that six of the flight deck personnel killed were found to have used marijuana was considered more of a public relations dilemma for the navy than a factor in their deaths, though the possible use of illegal drugs by emergency crews raised questions as to how it could have affected the post-crash fire-fighting efforts. As it was, their actions were considered 'commendable'.

Among the recommendations made in the investigative report were to return to operational status on the *Nimitz* a centreline flasher system, which might have averted the crash, and for a review of procedures to ensure aircraft fuel conservation in flight operations. With regard to the latter, it was noted that the EA-6B involved in the accident had apparently flown in a highly fuel-consuming configuration, i.e. with its undercarriage and flaps extended, following the boltered pass.

22 SEPTEMBER 1981 (c.12:00)

Location   *Near Babaeski, Turkey*
Operator   *Turk Hava Kuvvetleri (Turkish Air Force)*
Aircraft type   *Northrop F-5A*

The jet fighter crashed and exploded in a bivouac area some 110 miles (175km) west of Istanbul, killing 40 military personnel, including the pilot of the aircraft. Another 72 personnel on the ground were injured. According to a military source, the accident occurred during a practice diving run, possibly after the fighter experienced a mechanical failure.

29 SEPTEMBER 1981 (c.19:00)

Location   *Kahrizak, Tehran, Iran*
Operator   *Islamic Republic of Iran Air Force*
Aircraft type   *Lockheed C-130H (5-8552)*

Four of the nation's top military leaders were among the estimated 80 persons killed when the four-engine turboprop transport crashed in Tir Square approximately 15 miles (25km) south of the city of Tehran, where it was to have landed. Some of the victims may have been on the ground. The aircraft was reportedly carrying dead and wounded service personnel from Ahvaz, in Khuzestan, when the disaster occurred, in darkness.

14 JANUARY 1982 (time unknown)

Location   *Near Addis Ababa, Ethiopia*
Operator   *Ethiopian Air Force*
Aircraft type   *Antonov An-12*

All 73 persons were killed when the four-engine turboprop transport was shot down by Eritrean rebel forces. The victims consisted of Ethiopian, Cuban and Libyan military personnel.

Heavy casualties and damage resulted from the crash of the US Marine Corps EA-6B atop the flight deck of the aircraft carrier USS Nimitz. (UPI/Corbis-Bettmann)

3 FEBRUARY 1982 (c.07:30)

Location	*Djibouti*
Operator	*L'Armée de l'Air (French Air Force)*
Aircraft type	*Nord 2501 Noratlas (140/88-JA)*

The twin-engine transport, carrying 29 members of the Foreign Legion plus a naval officer, crashed on a desert mountain before a planned paratroop drop. All 35 French military personnel aboard the aircraft lost their lives in the accident, including the five members of its crew. The cause of the accident was not disclosed.

5 FEBRUARY 1982 (c.15:00)

Location	*Island of Cheju, South Korea*
Operator	*Republic of Korea Air Force*
Aircraft type	*Fairchild C-123J*

The twin-engine transport, carrying as passengers army troops participating in a training exercise, crashed into Mount Halla while it was approaching to land. All 53 South Korean servicemen aboard, including a crew of six, were killed. The accident occurred in adverse weather conditions, and may have resulted from an encounter with severe down-draughts.

7 FEBRUARY 1982 (time unknown)

Location	*Near Srinagar, Jammu and Kashmir, India*
Operator	*Indian Air Force*
Aircraft type	*Fairchild C-119G*

The crash of the twin-engine transport, which occurred in drizzle and falling snow during an internal flight to Leh from Pathankot, in Punjab, claimed the lives of all 23 persons aboard the aircraft.

A muddy crater marks the impact site of the KC-135 that crashed following an unexplained mid-air explosion near Chicago. (AP/ Wide World Photos)

19 MARCH 1982 (c.21:10)

Location	*Near Woodstock, Illinois, USA*
Operator	*US Air Force*
Aircraft type	*Boeing KC-135A (58-0031)*

Operated by the Illinois Air National Guard, the jet tanker crashed, exploded and burned some 40 miles (65km) north-west of Chicago's O'Hare International Airport, where it was to have landed. All 27 American military personnel aboard perished, including four crewmen.

The aircraft had earlier in the evening been on a training mission and making practice landing approaches to K.I. Sawyer Air Force Base, in Upper Michigan, then landed there to pick up a load of passengers, all of whom were stranded by the grounding of a C-130 transport due to mechanical trouble. After being cleared for descent from 22,000ft to 8,000ft (6,700m to 2,500m), and seconds after acknowledging a request for a speed reduction, the KC-135 disintegrated, its fuselage breaking apart and vertical and horizontal stabilisers and all four engines separating. At the moment of its structural failure, the cleanly-configured aircraft had been descending on an almost due southerly heading at a true air speed of around 360mph (580kmh) and was at an approximate height of 13,700ft (4,200m), and it then plummeted almost vertically into the wooded, marshy terrain. Wreckage was scattered over an area about 5 miles (10km) long and 2 miles (3km) wide. It was dark at the time of the accident, and the weather conditions in the area consisted of light to moderate rain showers, a ceiling of around 500ft (150m) and a surface visibility of 1–3 miles (1.5–5km). Winds at the approximate height of the break-up were about 30 knots from a south-westerly direction.

According to the investigative report, the probability of thunderstorm activity being in the vicinity of the crash site at the time appeared 'extremely low'. Following a thorough examination of the wreckage, no conclusive evidence was found pinpointing what caused the disintegration of the aircraft. Considered as 'most probable', based on the findings of the inquiry, was an over-pressurisation under the cargo floor, an area that houses fuel and other potential sources of ignition. An explosion caused by the ignition of accumulated combustible vapours occurring in that area could, in fact, rapidly propagate to adjacent areas where fuel is present. There was also 'strong evidence' of explosive over-pressures in the forward, aft and upper fuel tank areas. Significantly, investigation showed that were the walls or fittings of the rubber bladder cells containing the volatile liquid to fail, fuel or vapour could be released into the tank cavity and in turn migrate to other parts of the aircraft.

Although there was no evidence of a lightning strike, and no definite factor could be identified, the report noted that there would have been many potential sources of ignition throughout the KC-135. Among these were hot surfaces, such as boost pumps or bleed air lines; electrical arcing or chafing of electrical power lines. One recommendation was for the thorough examination of electrical wiring and antenna

COCKPIT

MAIN LANDING GEAR — CENTER WING

EMPENNAGE

EXT FUEL TANK

CARGO RAMP

NOSE WHEEL
#3 ENGINE

#2 ENGINE

RIGHT ELEVATOR

MAIN GEAR WHEEL

#2 PROP

RIGHT WING

LEFT WING

N

A wide view of the US Air Force C-130 crash site following the in-flight break-up of the transport over Turkey. (US Air Force)

routeing to ensure proper clearance in order to prevent chafing, especially in areas where fuel vapours are present. Subsequent testing, however, showed that the ignition of fuel vapours through chafing of the very-high-frequency antenna lead – one early concern – was 'not probable'.

13 APRIL 1982 (c.14:40)

Location	*Near Erzincan, Turkey*
Operator	*US Air Force*
Aircraft type	*Lockheed C-130H (74-01678)*

All 27 persons aboard perished in the crash of the four-engine turboprop transport, which occurred about 100 miles (150km) east of Sivas. Four of the victims were American civilians riding as passengers, the rest US service personnel, including the eight crewmen assigned to the aircraft. Operated by the Military Airlift Command (MAC), the C-130 was on an internal Turkish flight from Erzurum to Incirlik Air Base, near Adana, where the mission had originated earlier in the day, when it suffered catastrophic structural failure.

Last reported cruising at a height of 20,000ft (6,000m), 74-01678 transmitted a Mayday distress message before it fell in flames into mountainous terrain. Visual meteorological conditions prevailed in the area at the time of the accident. When considering their rotational markings and the fact that portions of their blades were found a distance from the main crash site, it was concluded that the two right propellers had come in contact with other parts of the aircraft and possibly each other. The break-up sequence apparently began with the failure of the No. 4 engine support structure. The No. 3 propeller and gear assembly also separated from the corresponding power plant and sliced into the wing structure, the first strike being against the nose of the

starboard external fuel tank. Ultimately, the right outer wing experienced an 'over-pressure' and its outer portion was blown forward, resulting in an in-flight fire. The aerodynamic forces produced by this condition led to the failure of the left outer wing through overloading.

According to the investigative report, there were indications that one of the two primary attachment bolts in the No. 4 power plant support had not been installed at the time of the crash, and that the left quick engine change (QEC) longerons, or longitudinal supports, had failed in tension and inboard bending. The QEC right upper attachment bolt had also failed, and the diagonal brace aft attachment fitting was sheared. The underlying reasons for these conditions were not disclosed.

19 MAY 1982 (c.19:15)

Location	*South Atlantic Ocean*
Operator	*Royal Navy*
Aircraft type	*Westland Sea King HC. Mark 4 (ZA294)*

During the war between England and Argentina over the Falkland Islands, the turbine-engine helicopter crashed while transporting members of the elite Special Air Service (SAS) fighting unit between ships, from HMS *Hermes* to HMS *Intrepid*. Killed in the accident, which occurred in darkness north of East Falkland, were 21 of the 30 British servicemen aboard the aircraft; the rescued survivors included both pilots. Following a loss of power, the Sea King plummeted into the water, rolled over and sank. Searchers recovered

A Royal Navy Westland Sea King helicopter, the type involved in a fatal crash at sea during the Falklands War in the South Atlantic. (Westland Helicopters)

none of the victims' bodies or the main wreckage of ZA294, preventing a determination of the cause of the crash. Possible causes were a bird strike or major systems failure.

1 JUNE 1982 (c.14:40)

Location	Near Songnam-si, Kyonggi-do, South Korea
Operator	Republic of Korea Air Force
Aircraft type	Fairchild C-123 (56-4391)

The second major South Korean C-123 disaster in less than four months, which resulted in the same number of fatalities as the February crash, occurred about 10 miles (15km) south-east of Seoul, shortly after the twin-engine transport, carrying army paratroopers as passengers, had taken off. All 53 South Korean servicemen aboard were killed, including a crew of four. The accident took place in adverse meteorological conditions, which were probably a primary or contributing factor.

14 AUGUST 1982 (c.09:00)

Location	Near Managua, Nicaragua
Operator	Fuerza Aérea Sandinista (Nicaraguan Air Force)
Aircraft type	Israeli Aircraft Industries Arava 201 (223)

The twin-engine turboprop transport crashed and burned on take-off from the city's Augusto Cesar Sandino International Airport, and all 20 Nicaraguan servicemen aboard were killed outright or died later of their injuries. Carrying a load of medicine and bound for the town of El Rodeo, located on the nation's Atlantic coast, the aircraft rolled to the left and plummeted to earth about 500ft (150m) from the airport immediately after becoming airborne. Although no causative factors were given, the aircraft may have been overloaded.

11 SEPTEMBER 1982 (c.12:50)

Location	Near Mannheim, (West) Germany
Operator	US Army
Aircraft type	Boeing/Vertol CH-47C (74-22292)

Loaded with mostly French but also German and British civilian sky-divers, who were to have jumped over Neuostheim Airport as part of the city of Mannheim's 375th birthday celebration, the turbine-engine helicopter crashed after experiencing catastrophic mechanical and ensuing rotor failure. All 46 persons aboard perished in the disaster, including the four members of the aircraft's crew and four other US military personnel.

The rotorcraft had ascended to an altitude of about 10,000ft (3,000m) before it began to descend without dropping the parachutists. Asked the reason for this, the pilot announced to another pilot who was on the ground, 'We had some noise in the aft and got a flicker on the master caution panel.'

In preparation for landing at the airport, 74-22292 continued in a circling descent and appeared to enter the traffic pattern, turning right and proceeding approximately due south at an estimated air speed of 80–90mph (130–145kmh). After it had reached an approximate height of 500ft (150m) above the ground and while completing a right turn on to the down-wind leg of the circuit for Runway 09, the aft rotor unit, transmission and pylon were seen to separate from the aircraft. The CH-47 then rotated about 180 degrees to the right and fell first in a tail-down attitude, levelling off in an uncontrolled, vertical descent before finally hitting the ground on its belly and lower starboard side, with its nose slightly low and in an estimated right bank of 45 degrees. Impact was on the median of a four-lane autobahn 1,500ft (500m) south of the airport, whereupon the aircraft exploded and burned. At the time, the local weather was hazy but otherwise good, the crew of 74-22292 having taken off under visual flight rules (VFR) procedures.

The crash was blamed on bearing failure in the forward transmission pack, which had caused the No. 1 synchronising drive shaft to rotate in an eccentric manner and come

*The in-flight break-up of the US Army CH-47C is captured on film,
preceding the crash that killed all 46 persons aboard the helicopter.
(UPI/Corbis-Bettmann)*

in contact with the forward pylon structure. As a result,
the forward and aft rotor systems lost synchronisation
and meshed, leading to the blade and structural failures.
Investigation revealed the pinion pack lubricator jets to
be clogged with a combination of grease and walnut shell
particles, which led to the bearing failure through lack of
lubrication, with faulty design the underlying factor. The US
Army's entire fleet of CH-47 helicopters was temporarily
grounded for inspection in the wake of the disaster, and a
modification of the lubrication system ordered.

9 DECEMBER 1982 (c.14:30)

Location	Near Bocay, Jinotega, Nicaragua
Operator	Fuerza Aérea Sandinista (Nicaraguan Air Force)
Aircraft type	Mil Mi-8 (265)

In this disaster, which may have been a combat loss, 84
persons aboard were killed when the turbine-engine
rotorcraft crashed and burned in mountainous terrain some
200 miles (320km) north-east of Managua. The victims
included 75 children; the rest were the mothers of some of
them. The eight survivors included the pilot, co-pilot and

*The scene of the Nicaraguan Mil Mi-8 helicopter disaster, which
claimed the lives of 84 persons, nearly all of whom were children.
(UPI/Corbis-Bettmann)*

the aircraft's other two military crew members. Nicaragua claimed that the Mi-8 had been shot down by anti-Sandinistan rebels, with small-arms fire.

19 APRIL 1983 (c.07:20)

Location	Near Toba, Mie, Japan

First aircraft

Operator	Japan Air Self-Defence Force (JASDF)
Aircraft type	Kawasaki C-1 (58-1009)

Second aircraft

Operator	Japan Air Self-Defence Force (JASDF)
Aircraft type	Kawasaki C-1 (68-1015)

The two twin-jet transports, which were members of a six-aircraft formation flying between two Japanese air bases, from Komaki, in Aichi, to Iruma, in Saitama, crashed on the island of Suga. All 14 Japanese servicemen aboard the two aircraft lost their lives, eight on 58-1009 and six on 68-1015. According to unofficial reports, the group had been proceeding in instrument meteorological conditions consisting of rain and fog at a very low altitude, i.e. around 700ft (200m), when the lead pilot instructed the group to initiate an immediate 90-degree right turn. The two aircraft involved in the accident, which had been flying in tandem, subsequently slammed into the north side of a hill, while a third C-1 brushed the treetops but managed to remain airborne.

5 MAY 1983 (c.10:20)

Location	Near Nakhon Sawan, Thailand
Operator	Royal Thai Air Force
Aircraft type	Fairchild C-123K (L4K-12/18)

All 30 Thai servicemen aboard (24 passengers and a crew of six) were killed when the transport crashed and exploded in a rice field some 70 miles (115km) north of Bangkok. The aircraft had been approaching to land at the Ta Khli Air Base when instructed by the control tower to execute a missed approach because the runway was not clear. Subsequently, the C-123 plummeted to earth approximately 700ft (200m) from the runway. According to a military source, a power plant malfunction, presumably involving at least one of its two piston engines rather than its two auxiliary jets, was suspected as the cause of the accident.

6 JUNE 1983 (c.12:40)

Location	Off Quemoy, Taiwan
Operator	Republic of China Air Force
Aircraft type	Fairchild C-119G

The twin-engine transport, which was carrying civilian passengers, crashed in the Formosa Strait. Among the 47 persons aboard the aircraft, including a crew of eight military personnel, nine survivors were rescued. The C-119 had taken off from the island about 2 minutes before it plummeted into the water, reportedly after its starboard power plant malfunctioned, apparently resulting in a stall.

16 FEBRUARY 1984 (time unknown)

Location	Near Debre Zelt, Shewa, Ethiopia
Operator	Ethiopian Air Force
Aircraft type	Antonov An-12 (1506)

During an attempted hijacking, the four-engine turboprop transport crashed some 25 miles (40km) south-east of Addis Ababa after the air pirate detonated a hand grenade when it tried to land at the Debre Zelt air base. Killed in the explosion or subsequent crash were 26 of the 38 persons aboard the aircraft.

A Kawasaki C-1 jet transport, two of which, flown by the Japan Air Self-Defence Force, crashed simultaneously on Suga Island. (Martin Bowman)

19 FEBRUARY 1984 (time unknown)

Location	*Near San Gerardo, San Miguel, El Salvador*
First aircraft	
Operator	*Fureza Aérea Salvadoreña (Salvadoran Air Force)*
Aircraft type	*Bell UH-1H*
Second aircraft	
Operator	*Fuerza Aérea Salvadoreña (Salvadoran Air Force)*
Aircraft type	*Bell UH-1H*

The two turbine-engine helicopters, carrying soldiers as passengers, collided in mid-air and crashed about 75 miles (120km) north-east of San Salvador, apparently after one of them was hit by guerrilla mortar fire and went out of control. All 28 military personnel aboard the two aircraft, including two pilots assigned to each one, were killed in the combat-related incident.

28 FEBRUARY 1984 (c.19:30)

Location	*Near Borja, Aragon, Spain*
Operator	*US Air Force*
Aircraft type	*Lockheed C-130E (68-10944)*

Operated by the Military Airlift Command (MAC), the four-engine turboprop transport was on an aerial delivery training mission and had been cleared for a low-level supply drop before it crashed and burned some 30 miles (50km) north-west of Zaragoza Air Base. All 18 servicemen aboard lost their lives. With the exception of a Spanish officer, the victims were American personnel, including the aircraft's nine-member crew.

The C-130 had struck the south face of a mesa at an approximate elevation of 2,200ft (670m), or less than 200ft (60m) from the top, at a comparatively low air speed of around 150mph (250kmh), while on a north-north-westerly heading, with its wings level, nose slightly raised and flaps extended to 50 degrees. The crash occurred in darkness, and the local weather was overcast, with a ceiling of 1,200ft (350m) and a visibility of approximately 3.5 miles (6km). There was little or no wind. Although the causative factors were omitted in the investigative report on the accident, releasable findings did not reveal any evidence of pre-impact structural, instrument or electrical failure, or propeller/power plant malfunction in the aircraft.

24 MARCH 1984 (c.04:00)

Location	*Near Hunghae, Kyongsang-Pukdo, South Korea*
Operator	*US Marine Corps*
Aircraft type	*Sikorsky CH-53D (157132)*

All 29 servicemen aboard were killed in the crash of the turbine-engine helicopter, which occurred some 200 miles (320km) south-east of Seoul. The majority of the victims were Americans, including the crew of four, but the passengers also included 11 South Korean personnel.

A later model Sikorsky CH-53 Sea Stallion, similar to the US Marine Corps helicopter that crashed in South Korea. (Sikorsky)

The aircraft involved in the accident was one of eight helicopters engaged in a night assault mission between two air bases, from Pohang to Kannung. It was assigned to the number three position in the second of three groups. As the aircraft were proceeding in the pre-dawn darkness, operating under visual flight rules (VFR) procedures, 157132 slammed into a wooded mountainside at an approximate elevation of 1,300ft (400m) and about 30 miles (50km) north-north-west of its departure point, bursting into flames on impact and sending wreckage tumbling down the steep terrain. The crash occurred some 50ft (15m) below the ridgeline and while the CH-53 was banked approximately 45 to 60 degrees to the left, longitudinally level or in a slight nose-down attitude and on a heading of between 210 and 240 degrees, with its undercarriage retracted and rear loading ramp closed.

Investigation revealed no evidence of mechanical failure or maintenance error as causing or contributing to the accident. One possible factor was the presence in the second division's lead aircraft of a marine air wing division commanding general, which could have influenced the decisions of both its pilot and the mission commander, flying the lead aircraft in the first division, increasing their desire to complete the mission successfully.

Primarily, the crash was believed to have resulted from pilot error attributable to one of three possible causes:

1. Following a left turn by the lead aircraft, 157132 responded similarly, leading to the impact with the unseen high terrain.
2. In attempting to catch up with the group, using a higher rate of speed, the CH-53 initiated a turn to port to avoid over-running them.
3. The aircraft involved in the accident lost sight of the leader, and in an attempt to re-establish visual contact, a 360-degree turn to the left was begun.

Contributing to the crash was the failure of the second division's lead pilot to take off without wearing night-vision goggles and having to order a control change when he put them on, his continuation into deteriorating weather and ambient light conditions, deviation from the proper course, and ultimate disorientation with regard to his position. As the use of night-vision goggles apparently factored in the accident, it was recommended that there be greater emphasis in training on the use of the vision-enhancement devices, as well as on flight in such conditions and in cockpit coordination.

8 MAY 1984 (time unknown)

Location	*Elbet Beni Salama, Egypt*
Operator	*Egyptian Air Force*
Aircraft type	*McDonnell F-4E Phantom II*

Both crewmen and 19 persons on the ground lost their lives when the jet fighter crashed into the village located about 80 miles (130km) from Cairo.

11 JULY 1984 (time unknown)

Location	*Near Buenavista, Marinduque, the Philippines*
Operator	*Philippine Air Force*
Aircraft type	*Bell UH-1H*

The turbine-engine helicopter crashed at sea approximately 2 miles (3km) offshore from the island of Marinduque, and all 30 persons aboard were killed.

5 AUGUST 1984 (time unknown)

Location	*Near Nawabshah, Pakistan*
Operator	*Soviet Air Force*
Aircraft type	*Antonov An-12BP (SSSR-10232)*

All 24 persons aboard (15 passengers and a crew of nine) were killed when the four-engine turboprop transport crashed some 125 miles (200km) north-east of Karachi while en route from Aden, Yemen, to Tashkent, Uzbek SSR. The aircraft had encountered severe hail at 18,000 ft (5,500m), which reportedly damaged the engine radiators and caused a loss of power. During a subsequent emergency descent, which was apparently carried out in heavy rain, the An-12 must have been overstressed, resulting in structural failure.

18 DECEMBER 1984 (c.14:00)

Location	*Near Denomindao El Valor, Amazonas, Peru*
Operator	*Fuerza Aérea del Perú (Peruvian Air Force)*
Aircraft type	*de Havilland Twin Otter Series 300 (FAP-307)*

The twin-engine turboprop transport, which was flying between two stations of the Peruvian oil duct, crashed in flames approximately 2 minutes after taking off from El Valor Airport, serving Bagua. All 21 persons aboard the aircraft lost their lives, including a crew of three military personnel; the passengers were all civilians. According to unofficial reports, the aircraft 'exploded' in the air.

22 JANUARY 1985 (c.09:35)

Location	*Near Puerto Castilla, Colon, Honduras*
Operator	*US Air Force*
Aircraft type	*Lockheed C-130A (56-0501)*

Flown by an air force reserve unit, the four-engine turboprop transport crashed in the Caribbean Sea approximately 8 miles (13km) north-west of Trujillo airport, where it was to have landed. This was an en-route stop during a scheduled re-supply mission originating at Howard Air Force Base, in the Panama Canal Zone, and ultimately bound for Comayagua, also in Honduras. All 21 American military personnel aboard, including a crew of five, were killed. The bodies of about half of the victims were found.

During the initial phase of the approach, the C-130 was observed to turn right towards the open sea, and examination of recovered debris indicated that it struck the surface of the ocean in a left wing-low attitude, with its undercarriage and flaps still retracted. Despite the retrieval of a considerable amount of wreckage, its prolonged immersion in the salt water, which was some 100ft (30m) deep at the site of the accident, had corrosive effects that greatly hindered its evaluation. No evidence could be found of in-flight fire, explosion, or of any deficiencies in the aircraft's flight controls, instruments or power plants. There was an indication of a structural failure in the starboard wing and horizontal stabiliser, but if this occurred, it must have been almost simultaneous with, or resulted from, impact.

At the time, the local weather was overcast, with a ceiling of 1,500ft (500m), and a visibility of 1.5 miles (2.5km). The wind was estimated at 20 to 25 knots from a north-north-westerly direction.

28 MARCH 1985 (c.09:50)

Location	*Near Maracaibo, Caqueta, Colombia*
Operator	*Fuerza Aérea Colombiana (Colombian Air Force)*
Aircraft type	*Fokker F.28 Fellowship Mark 3000 (FAC-1140)*

Operated by the military airline Servicio de Aeronavegación a Territorios Nacionales (SATENA) and on a scheduled domestic passenger service that had originated at Bogotá, with en-route stops at Neiva and San Vicente del Caguan, the twin-jet transport crashed about 10 miles (15km) north of Florencia, where it was to have landed. All 46 persons aboard, including a crew of six military personnel, were killed. In its last radio message, the aircraft was reported to be at 3,600ft (1,100m); less than 10 minutes later, while apparently turning on to the final approach leg, it struck a mountain at an approximate elevation of 1,200ft (350m) and just to the right of the extended centreline of the airport runway, exploding on impact.

The accident occurred in rain and fog accompanied by a low overcast, meteorological conditions that were, according to press reports, below the airport minima. According to an unconfirmed report, the crew had initiated a premature descent during the non-directional beacon (NDB) procedure let-down, possibly while trying to maintain visual contact with the ground in the rapidly deteriorating weather.

24 JULY 1985 (c.17:00)

Location	*Near Leticia, Amazonas, Colombia*
Operator	*Fuerza Aérea Colombiana (Colombian Air Force)*
Aircraft type	*Douglas DC-6B (FAC-902)*

The four-engine transport, which was providing a scheduled domestic passenger service owing to a strike by airline pilots in Colombia, crashed and burned in the Amazonian jungle. All 80 persons aboard, including a crew of four, were killed in the accident. About 5 minutes after the aircraft had taken off from Leticia Airport, bound for the capital city of Bogotá, the pilot reported a fire in the No. 3 power plant and that he was returning to land. The crash occurred moments later, in a rainstorm and after he had radioed, 'We're falling.'

22 SEPTEMBER 1985 (time unknown)

Location	*Afghanistan*
Operator	*Soviet Air Force*
Aircraft type	*Antonov An-12*

All 26 Soviet military personnel aboard lost their lives when the four-engine turboprop transport was shot down by Afghan rebels.

A Colombian Air Force Fokker F.28 jet transport, essentially the same as the aircraft operated by the military airline SATENA that crashed during a passenger flight. (Philip Jarrett)

25 NOVEMBER 1985 (time unknown)

Location	*Near Luassingua, Cuando Cubango, Angola*
Operator	*Soviet Air Force*
Aircraft type	*Antonov An-12BP (SSSR-11747)*

During an internal Angolan flight to Luanda from Cuito, the four-engine turboprop transport was reportedly shot down by a shoulder-launched surface-to-air missile fired by National Union for the Total Independence of Angola (UNITA) rebels, and all 22 Angolan and Soviet military personnel aboard the aircraft (16 passengers and a crew of six) were killed.

30 DECEMBER 1985 (time unknown)

Location	*Near Dhangarhi, Nepal*
Operator	*Nepalese Army Air Service*
Aircraft type	*Shorts SC.7 Skyvan 3-100 (RAN-23)*

The twin-engine turboprop transport, on an internal flight from Kathmandu to Dhangarhi, crashed in a forest near its destination, located some 300 miles (480km) north-west of the capital city, and all 25 Nepalese military personnel aboard the aircraft were killed.

27 MARCH 1986 (time unknown)

Location	*Bangui, Ombella-Mpoko, Central African Republic*
Operator	*L'Armée de l'Air (French Air Force)*
Aircraft type	*Sepecat Jaguar A*

Apparently developing mechanical trouble immediately after it had taken off, the jet fighter crashed into a school and nearby residential area. Many of the 35 persons killed were children, while about 40 others suffered injuries, including the pilot (and sole occupant) of the Jaguar, who had ejected from the stricken aircraft.

A Sepecat Jaguar A jet fighter, identical to the French Air Force aircraft that crashed in Africa, resulting in heavy loss of life on the ground. (E. Moreau)

30 MARCH 1986 (c.10:15)

Location   Pemba, Cabo Delgado, Mozambique
Operator   Força Popular Aérea de Libertação de
                  Moçambique (Mozambique Air Force)
Aircraft type   Antonov An-26 (042)

The crash of the twin-engine turboprop transport killed 49 persons aboard, including the aircraft's three Soviet crewmen. Five others survived the accident, but were seriously injured. A member of the crew reported power plant trouble just after the aircraft had taken off, but as it was

A Dassault-Breguet Atlantique, similar to the French Naval Aviation aircraft involved in a 19-fatality accident in Djibouti. (Dassault-Breguet)

attempting to return for an emergency landing it slammed to earth near the airport runway, bounced, cartwheeled and burst into flames.

1 MAY 1986 (c.04:30)

Location   Near Planes del Pino, El Salvador
Operator   Fuerza Aérea Salvadoreña (Salvadoran
                  Air Force)
Aircraft type   Douglas DC-6B (FAS302)

Bound for Panama City, Panama, the four-engine transport struck a hill and burst into flames some 10 miles (15km) north of San Salvador and about 2 minutes after taking off from Ilopango Air Base. All 37 Salvadoran military personnel aboard (33 passengers and a crew of four) perished in the crash, which occurred in pre-dawn darkness. According to official sources, the accident resulted from 'mechanical failure', which may have led to a power plant fire.

3 MAY 1986 (time unknown)

Location   Northern Taiwan
First aircraft
Operator   Republic of China Air Force
Aircraft type   Bell UH-1H
Second aircraft
Operator   Republic of China Air Force
Aircraft type   Bell UH-1H

The two turbine-engine helicopters collided in mid-air and crashed in a rice paddy about 20 miles (30km) south-west of Taipei, killing 22 Taiwanese military personnel aboard both aircraft and injuring both survivors of the accident.

18 MAY 1986 (c.08:30)

Location   Djibouti
Operator   Aeronavale (French Naval Aviation)
Aircraft type   Dassault Breguet Atlantique (19)

All 19 French servicemen aboard were killed, five of them passengers, when the twin-engine turboprop patrol aircraft crashed some 25 miles (40km) north of the city of Djiboubti. The accident occurred in adverse weather conditions, with heavy rain and low clouds that obscured the surrounding mountainous terrain, but no further details were disclosed.

19 JULY 1986 (c.16:00)

Location	Near La Cruz, Zelaya, Nicaragua
Operator	Fuerza Aérea Sandinista (Nicaraguan Air Force)
Aircraft type	Mil Mi-8 (269)

Shortly after taking off on an internal flood relief flight to Bluefields, the turbine-engine helicopter plunged into the Matagalpa River, approximately 80 miles (130km) north-west of its destination. Among the 23 persons aboard, only the co-pilot, who was one member of the aircraft's crew of eight military personnel, survived the crash.

14 AUGUST 1986 (c.11:30)

Location	Near Wampusirpi, Gracias a Dios, Honduras
Operator	Fuerza Aérea Hondurena (Honduran Air Force)
Aircraft type	Lockheed C-130D (556)

The four-engine turboprop transport, on an internal flight from Tegucigalpa to Durzana Air Base, crashed in a jungle area near its destination. All 59 persons aboard perished, including 11 civilian passengers and the aircraft's crew of six. The accident occurred in adverse weather conditions, which may have been a primary or contributing factor.

19 OCTOBER 1986 (c.21:20)

Location	Near Nelspruit, Transvaal, South Africa
Operator	Força Popular Aérea de Libertação de Moçambique (Mozambique Air Force)
Aircraft type	Tupolev Tu-134A (C9-CAA)

Mozambique's President Samora Machel was among 34 persons killed when the jet transport crashed about half a

A Soviet-built Mil Mi-8 helicopter, extensively used by Nicaraguan military forces and the type that crashed during a flood relief flight. (Philip Jarrett)

mile (0.8km) inside the South African border and some 40 miles (65km) west of Maputo, Mozambique, where it was to have landed at the end of a flight from Lusaka, Zambia. Ten others aboard, including the pilot, who was one member of its crew of nine, survived with various injuries.

At a point approximately 60 miles (100km) from its destination, and while it was descending from flight level 190 to its clearance limit of 3,000ft (1,000m), the Tu-134 turned right from a magnetic heading of 184 degrees on to a direction of 221 degrees magnetic, continuing down until it struck the ground at an elevation of around 2,200ft (670m), its undercarriage down and flaps extended until the moment of impact. Despite the break-up of the aircraft, there was no major fire. The accident occurred in darkness and cloudy weather conditions, with thunderstorm activity reported in the area. The navigator had erroneously executed the premature 37-degree turn, using the aircraft's autopilot, due to a very-high-frequency omnidirectional range (VOR) indication that most probably resulted from the inadvertent selection of the wrong ground station.

Although the pilot questioned the turn, no effort was made to verify the new heading using available navigational aids. Confusion on the part of the crew was attributed to a misunderstanding between them and the air-traffic controller over the operation of the instrument landing system (ILS) and the runway lighting, with the former having mistakenly assumed that a power failure had occurred at the airport. Despite the disorientation of the crew, the pilot continued to descend without having made visual contact with Maputo airport; he also completely ignored a warning from the ground-proximity warning system (GPWS), which had begun to sound about half a minute before impact.

30 OCTOBER 1986 (c.17:00)

Location	Near Wamblan, Jinotega, Nicaragua
Operator	Fuerza Aérea Sandinista (Nicaraguan Air Force)
Aircraft type	Mil Mi-17 (294)

The turbine-engine helicopter plummeted to earth some 125 miles (200km) north of Managua as it was approaching to land, and 21 Nicaraguan servicemen aboard were killed. A soldier riding as a passenger and the aircraft's pilot, who was one member of its crew of three, survived. Different accounts attributed the crash to mechanical failure and to the local weather, with conditions of poor visibility, although Contra rebels claimed to have shot down the Mi-17.

2 NOVEMBER 1986 (c.19:25)

Location	Near Zahedan, Baluchestan va Sista, Iran
Operator	Islamic Republic of Iran Air Force
Aircraft type	Lockheed C-130

The four-engine turboprop transport struck a mountain near the Pakistani border about 10 miles (15km) east of Zahedan, where it was to have landed at the end of an internal flight from Bakhtaran. All 103 Iranian military personnel aboard, including a crew of seven, were killed in the accident, which occurred in darkness. Failing to follow the instructions of the control tower, the aircraft had not maintained the minimum altitude of 6,500ft (1,980m) during the approach, with an altimeter error or defect given as the reason for the disaster.

Shown in civilian livery, this CASA 212 Aviocar is similar to the Spanish military aircraft that crashed at sea off Equatorial Guinea. (Philip Jarrett)

25 NOVEMBER 1986 (time unknown)

Location	Near Sarowbi, Laghman, Afghanistan
Operator	Afghan Republican Air Force
Aircraft type	Ilyushin Il-18

The four-engine turboprop transport was shot down, reportedly by Afghan rebels using an anti-aircraft missile, some 50 miles (80km) east of Kabul, killing all 40 Afghan and Soviet military personnel aboard.

2 JANUARY 1987 (c.16:30)

Location	Off Bata, Equatorial Guinea
Operator	Ejército del Aire (Spanish Air Force)
Aircraft type	CASA 212-100 Aviocar (T.12B-32)

The twin-engine turboprop transport crashed in the Atlantic Ocean immediately after it had taken off from Bata Airport on a passenger service to Malabo, on the island of Bioko, after transmitting a distress message. Searchers subsequently recovered the bodies of the 22 persons killed in the accident, which included a crew of Spanish military personnel; there were no survivors. Prior to the crash, the pilot's request for permission to land had been denied because another aircraft was on the same runway. Subsequently, the Aviocar plummeted into water that ranged from 5–15ft (1.5–5m) deep and about 700ft (200m) offshore. According to one source, there were indications that its right power plant was stopped at the moment of impact, a further sign of a mechanical failure.

13 JANUARY 1987 (c.13:30)

Location	Near Asmara, Eritrea, Ethiopia
Operator	Ethiopian Air Force
Aircraft type	Antonov An-12

All 54 Ethiopian military personnel aboard were killed when the four-engine turboprop transport crashed a few minutes after taking off from Johannes IV Airport, serving Asmara, on an internal flight to Addis Ababa. The accident reportedly resulted from a 'technical malfunction', with a loss of control apparently occurring after the aircraft had turned back and was attempting an emergency landing.

9 FEBRUARY 1987 (c.11:30)

Location	Near Khowst (Matun), Paktia, Afghanistan
Operator	Afghan Republican Air Force
Aircraft type	Antonov An-26

The twin-engine turboprop transport was reportedly shot down by Afghan guerillas, who apparently used a Stinger missile, about 25 miles (40km) from the Pakistani border and shortly after it had taken off from Khowst, on an internal flight to Kabul. According to Afghan government radio, all 36 persons aboard lost their lives, including a crew of six; a number of the passengers were civilians.

30 MARCH 1987 (c.11:00)

Location   *Near Samkani, Paktia, Afghanistan*
Operator   *Afghan Republican Air Force*
Aircraft type   *Antonov An-26*

The twin-engine turboprop transport was shot down by a Pakistani F-16 jet fighter, firing an air-to-air missile, and crashed in flames while on an internal flight from Kabul to Khowst, Paktia. All 40 persons aboard were killed; the passengers included some civilians. Pakistan identified the An-26 as a 'warplane', and claimed it had intruded into its own airspace.

18 JUNE 1987 (c.10:00)

Location   *Near Montelillo, San Martin, Peru*
Operator   *Fuerza Aérea del Perú (Peruvian Air Force)*
Aircraft type   *Antonov An-26 (FAP-392)*

Operating on a domestic civil passenger flight to Saposoa, with an ultimate destination of Iquitos, the twin-engine turboprop transport crashed in a gorge about 370 miles (600km) north of Lima, from where it had taken off earlier. All 46 persons aboard the aircraft, including a crew of six military personnel, were killed in the accident, which occurred in adverse weather conditions. In its final radio transmission, the An-26 was reportedly about 10 minutes from its destination, but no specific details about the crash or possible cause were released.

29 SEPTEMBER 1987 (time unknown)

Location   *Near Da Lat, Vietnam*
Operator   *Vietnamese People's Army Air Force*
Aircraft type   *Unknown*

The crash of the aircraft, possibly a twin-engine turboprop Antonov An-24 or An-26, which occurred about 125 miles (200km) north-east of Saigon, claimed the lives of 50 persons.

8 DECEMBER 1987 (c.22:30)

Location   *Near Santa Rosa, Lima, Peru*
Operator   *Fuerza Aviación Naval del Perú (Peruvian Naval Aviation)*
Aircraft type   *Fokker F.27 Troopship Mark 400M (AE-560)*

The twin-engine turboprop transport, carrying as passengers members of the nation's top soccer team, crashed in the Pacific Ocean approximately 3 miles (5km) offshore and 5 miles (10km) north-west of Jorge Chavez International Airport, serving the city of Lima, where it was to have landed following an internal flight from Pucallpa. Among the 43 persons aboard, including a crew of six military personnel, only the pilot was rescued alive, having remained afloat for about 10 hours.

The accident occurred in darkness and fair weather conditions after the pilot had reported an instrument indication that the undercarriage had not been properly extended, although this must have resulted from a faulty light, as the control tower reported seeing the gear down as the aircraft circled the airport. Searchers had recovered 21 bodies within ten days of the crash, the wreckage having sunk in water that was around 120ft (35m) deep. No information as to the possible cause of the accident was released by Peruvian military authorities.

14 DECEMBER 1987 (c.21:30)

Location   *Off north-eastern Brazil*
Operator   *Força Aérea Brasileira (Brazilian Air Force)*
Aircraft type   *Lockheed C-130H (2468)*

All 29 persons aboard perished when the four-engine turboprop transport crashed in the Atlantic Ocean about 10

A Soviet-built Antonov An-26, shown in civil livery, but otherwise similar to the Afghan military transports lost to hostile action during a four-month period in 1987. (Martin Bowman)

miles (15km) off the island of Fernando de Noronha, where it was to have landed following an internal flight from Recife. The victims included the crew of six military personnel; the passengers were civilians. The crash of the aircraft occurred in darkness during its landing approach, for reasons that, if known, were not disclosed.

8 MARCH 1988 (c.21:45)

Location	Near Clarksville, Tennessee, USA
First aircraft	
Operator	US Army
Aircraft type	Sikorsky UH-60A (85-24462)
Second aircraft	
Operator	US Army
Aircraft type	Sikorsky UH-60A (87-24605)

The two turbine-engine helicopters collided in mid-air, then crashed and burned at the Fort Campbell military reservation, and all 17 American servicemen aboard both aircraft were killed. Involved in the accident were the leader of a flight of three rotorcraft (85-24462), which altogether had just picked up some 36 soldiers and was itself carrying ten passengers plus a crew of three, and the individual UH-60 (87-24605), which had been on a training flight with four crewmen aboard. The group had just taken off and was climbing when the pilots of the two other aircraft observed, in the darkness, the navigation lights of the lone helicopter at their 3 o'clock position, and successfully initiated evasive action. However, the flight leader was struck by 87-24605, the impact shearing off the aft section of the former's tail boom and two of the latter's four main rotor blades. The collision occurred at an above-ground height of approximately 150ft (50m), in visual meteorological conditions, with a ceiling of 8,000ft (2,500m) and a visibility of 7 miles (11km).

In a brief statement, military authorities attributed the accident to 'pilot error, to wit, a reasonable mistake in judgement'. Considered as contributory were restrictions to vision due to door posts and structural components of the aircraft and the limited field of view of the night-vision goggles being used by both crews, which also hampered their ability to see each other.

16 MARCH 1988 (time unknown)

Location	Afghanistan
Operator	Afghan Republican Air Force
Aircraft type	Antonov An-32

The twin-engine turboprop transport was shot down, killing 42 persons aboard the aircraft.

17 MARCH 1988 (time unknown)

Location	Laos
Operator	Lao People's Liberation Army Air Force
Aircraft type	Mil Mi-6

The Laotian deputy defence minister was among 24 persons killed in the crash of the turbine-engine helicopter,

which occurred near the Laotian/Thai border. There were no survivors.

10 APRIL 1988 (c.15:10)

Location	Near Mazar-e Sharif, Balkh, Afghanistan
Operator	Afghan Republican Air Force
Aircraft type	Antonov An-26

The twin-engine turboprop transport was shot down near the Soviet border by Afghan guerillas, using an anti-aircraft missile, while on an internal flight from Maymaneh, Faryab, to Mazar-e Sharif, Balkh. All 29 persons aboard the aircraft were killed, including a crew of six; the passengers included at least some civilians.

27 APRIL 1988 (time unknown)

Location	Near Tchahutete, Angola
Operator	Fuerza Aérea Revolucionaria (Cuban Air Force)
Aircraft type	Antonov An-26 (14-27)

The twin-engine turboprop transport was reportedly shot down accidentally by friendly ground fire some 300 miles (480km) south-east of Lobito and while approaching to land. All 29 military personnel aboard the aircraft, including a crew of three, lost their lives; among the passengers were a number of officers.

16 JUNE 1988 (time unknown)

Location	Near Khost, Afghanistan
Operator	Afghan Republican Air Force
Aircraft type	Antonov An-26

The twin-engine turboprop, bound for Khost, was reportedly shot down by Afghan guerrillas approximately 100 miles (150km) south-south-east of Kabul, and all 35 persons aboard the aircraft were killed.

18 JUNE 1988 (time unknown)

Location	Central Mozambique
Operator	Força Popular Aérea de Libertação de Moçambique (Mozambique Air Force)
Aircraft type	Mil Mi-8

The turbine-engine helicopter crashed in the province of Zambezia, killing 21 military personnel aboard. Four members of the aircraft's crew survived with injuries.

15 AUGUST 1988 (time unknown)

Location	Northern Afghanistan
Operator	Afghan Republican Air Force
Aircraft type	Antonov An-32

All 39 military personnel aboard lost their lives when the twin-engine turboprop transport, on an internal flight to Kunduz, was shot down by rebels, using a surface-to-air missile.

17 AUGUST 1988 (c.16:30)

Location	*Near Bahawalpur, Punjab, Pakistan*
Operator	*Pakistan Air Force*
Aircraft type	*Lockheed C-130B (23494)*

Pakistan's President Mohammed Zia ul-Haq was among 30 persons killed when the four-engine turboprop transport plunged to earth some 60 miles (100km) from the Indian border and about 10 minutes after it had taken off from the Bahawalpur airport, on an internal flight to Islamabad. Also among the victims were the American ambassador to Pakistan, a US general, and five top Pakistani officers and other military personnel, the latter including the aircraft's crew of 13; there were no survivors.

A Pakistani investigation revealed that the crash apparently resulted from an act of criminal sabotage, which led to a loss of control. Speculation on the possible methods ranged from a low-intensity explosive device to interference with or incapacitation of the pilots. With regard to the former theory, a chemical analysis of the wreckage revealed high levels of phosphorous, antimony and sulphur. Another theory advanced was the contamination by brass and aluminum particles of the aircraft's elevator boost system, leading to control difficulties. There was no evidence of a high-intensity explosion or missile strike, and an in-flight fire or structural failure, power plant malfunction or an encounter with adverse atmospheric conditions were all ruled out. No suspects were ever apprehended or identified in connection with the crash.

A fireball marks the collision of three members of the Italian Air Force Frecce Tricolori aerobatic team during the Ramstein air show. (AP/Wide World Photos)

One of the MB.339PAN jets plunges into the crowd at Ramstein Air Base, in (West) Germany, resulting in heavy loss of life among spectators. (AP/Wide World Photos)

28 AUGUST 1988 (c.16:00)

Location	*Near Kaiserslautern, (West) Germany*
Operator	*Aeronautica Militare Italiana (Italian Air Force)*
Aircraft types	*Aermacchi MB.339PAN (x3) (MM54474); (MM54481) and (MM54483)*

A demonstration by the Frecce Tricolori ('Tricolour Arrows') at an air show being held on this Sunday afternoon at Ramstein Air Base ended in the worst peacetime military aviation disaster in the history of Western Europe when three of the precision flying team's ten jet aircraft collided during a low-altitude manoeuvre. One jet was making a loop perpendicular to the other two looping groups when it struck the leader of a five-aircraft formation at an approximate height of 200ft (60m) above the ground, who in turn hit the No. 2 aircraft. The singleton then crashed and exploded in a crowd of spectators, while the second aircraft fell at the airfield and the third into a forest area.

Killed in the tragedy were all three pilots and 67 persons on the ground, the latter including the crew of a US Army UH-60 turbine-engine helicopter standing by their aircraft. More than 500 other persons suffered injuries. The collision was attributed to 'misjudgement' on the part of the solo pilot. Military air displays over German soil were banned after this tragedy, pending a review and modification of safety procedures.

19 NOVEMBER 1988 (c.20:30)

Location	*Near Miram Shah, Waziristan, Pakistan*
Operator	*Afghan Republican Air Force*
Aircraft type	*Antonov An-26*

The twin-engine turboprop transport was shot down in darkness, apparently accidentally, by Pakistani anti-aircraft fire about 100 miles (150km) south-west of Peshawar, after it reportedly experienced a mechanical malfunction during an internal flight from Kabul to Jalalabad and strayed out of Afghan air space. All 34 persons aboard the An-26 were killed.

10 DECEMBER 1988 (c.20:00)

Location	*Eastern Afghanistan*
Operator	*Afghan Republican Air Force*
Aircraft type	*Antonov An-32*

All 25 persons aboard lost their lives when the twin-engine turboprop transport was shot down by a Pakistani jet fighter while on an internal flight to Kabul from Khost. The warplane had reportedly violated Afghan air space, downing the An-32 in darkness.

11 DECEMBER 1988 (time unknown)

Location	*Near Leninakan, Armenia, USSR*
First aircraft	
Operator	*Soviet Air Force*
Aircraft type	*Ilyushin Il-76M (SSSR-86732)*
Second aircraft	
Operator	*Soviet Air Force*
Aircraft type	*Mil Mi-8*

The four-engine jet transport, which had been on an earthquake relief flight and was approaching to land in evening darkness, collided with the turbine-engine helicopter and the fixed-wing aircraft then crashed and burned. Seventy-seven Soviet military personnel aboard the Il-76 were killed, including the nine members of its crew, and the sole surviving passenger, who had been seated in a truck being carried in its cargo compartment, was seriously injured. All five occupants of the rotorcraft survived.

31 JANUARY 1989 (c.12:10)

Location	*Near Abilene, Texas, USA*
Operator	*US Air Force*
Aircraft type	*Boeing KC-135A (63-7990)*

The jet tanker, operated by the Strategic Air Command (SAC), crashed and burst into flames seconds after taking off from Runway 16 at Dyess Air Force Base. All 19 persons aboard lost their lives, including a crew of seven military personnel; among the passengers were four civilian dependants. Only seconds after becoming airborne, the KC-135 slammed to earth approximately half a mile (0.8km) beyond the end, and some 600ft (180m) to the right, of the extended centreline of the runway, its undercarriage retracted and flaps set at 30 degrees at the moment of impact.

The accident occurred in visual meteorological conditions, but gusty winds were blowing from a due westerly direction at the time, with a crosswind component alone of 20 knots or greater. There was no evidence of failure in the aircraft's instruments or flight controls, but eyewitness accounts of smoke or vapour emanating from an engine could have been an indication of trouble in its water injection system. Improper piloting technique was probably an additional factor in the crash.

20 MARCH 1989 (c.07:00)

Location	*Near Hunghae, Kyongsang-Pukdo, South Korea*
Operator	*US Marine Corps*
Aircraft type	*Sikorsky CH-53D (157140)*

The turbine-engine helicopter was participating in a troop lift mission when it crashed and burst into flames in a

A Strategic Air Command KC-135 jet tanker lifts off from Dyess Air Force Base in a slight wing-low attitude. . . .

mountainous region along the nation's south-eastern coast about 15 miles (25km) north-west of Pohang, and some 250 miles (400km) south-east of Seoul. Killed in the accident were 19 of the 34 American servicemen aboard, including both pilots; the other two members of its crew and the 13 surviving passengers suffered various injuries.

Flying on a north-westerly heading in the second position of a two-aircraft formation, 157140 initiated a right turn at an approximate altitude of 350ft (105m) above the ground in preparation for setting down at the designated landing zone, with its undercarriage extended. During this 180-degree turn, the banking angle of the helicopter increased, as did its rate of descent, until the moment of impact, which was on an almost due southerly heading. Just before the crash, control of the aircraft was passed from the second pilot to the pilot-in-command, and the CH-53, which had initiated a flare at an unknown height, struck the ground with its tail rotor and aft pylon, coming to rest in a drainage ditch, its air speed indicator frozen on a reading of around 50mph (80kmh). The crash site was in a ravine approximately half a mile (0.8km) wide and at an elevation of around 250ft (75m). The weather conditions were not considered a factor, and there was no evidence of pre-impact mechanical failure.

The accident apparently resulted from an error in judgement and insufficient coordination on the part of the flight crew, combined with an absence of 'situational awareness' during the initial turn and subsequent approach. The pilots may not have been thoroughly briefed as to the intention of the flight leader or as to the intended destination, possibly resulting in confusion. It was further noted in the investigative report that under the circumstances, a 'highly-aggressive, relatively-inexperienced' pilot could have been lulled into a sense of complacency regarding the performance characteristics of the aircraft

. . . seconds later, its crash is marked by a cloud of dust. (US Air Force)

when operating at a high gross weight, at which time it would handle differently. The low-altitude manoeuvre, called an 'overhead break', had been routinely practised by pilots returning from a mission, when an aircraft's gross weight is much less. Furthermore, the published course procedure at the Pohang base required a higher altitude, 1,000ft (300m) above ground level and 500ft (150m) while on the down-wind leg.

Contributing to the number of fatalities was the fact that none of the passengers had been wearing head protection and some were not using seat belts, both of which violated existing regulations. The fact that none had been wearing helmets, which in this case was to allow for the differentiation of personnel during the force-on-force segment of the exercise, proved particularly tragic in this instance, as some of those killed may have been knocked unconscious in the crash and succumbed to the effects of the post-impact fire. Further insistence on the use of headgear was recommended in the report on this accident. Additionally, high banks by aircraft in this squadron were officially suspended.

21 JUNE 1989 (c.17:40)

Location	*Near Urcubamba, Junin, Peru*
Operator	*Fuerza Aérea del Perú (Peruvian Air Force)*
Aircraft type	*de Havilland DHC-5D Buffalo (FAP-329)*

All 62 persons aboard perished, including a crew of five military personnel, when the twin-engine turboprop transport crashed and burned in the Andes Mountains about 20 miles (30km) north-west of Tarma and some 100 miles (150km) east of Lima. The aircraft slammed into a slope at an approximate elevation of 15,000ft (5,000m) around 10 minutes after it had taken off from San Ramon, which was an en-route stop during a domestic civil passenger flight originating at Pucallpa, with an ultimate destination of Lima. Although no official cause was given, one source indicated that the Buffalo had been considerably overloaded with

A de Havilland DHC-5 Buffalo turboprop transport, the type flown by the Peruvian Air Force that crashed during a commercial flight. (de Havilland/Boeing Canada)

passengers, animals and freight at the time of its departure from San Ramon, and in his last radio transmission, the pilot reported losing altitude.

8 JULY 1989 (time unknown)

Location	Near Cam Ranh, Vietnam
Operator	Soviet Air Force
Aircraft type	Antonov An-12BP (SSSR-11875)

The four-engine turboprop transport crashed while reportedly attempting an emergency landing, and all 20 persons aboard the aircraft were killed.

23 JULY 1989 (time unknown)

Location	Near Jalalabad, Nangarhar, Afghanistan
First aircraft	
Operator	Afghan Republican Air Force
Aircraft type	Mil Mi-8
Second aircraft	
Operator	Afghan Republican Air Force
Aircraft type	Mil Mi-8

The mid-air collision between the two turbine-engine helicopters, which occurred some 60 miles (100km) east-south-east of Kabul, claimed the lives of all 30 persons aboard both aircraft, 15 in each.

23 JULY 1989 (time unknown)

Location	Near Chana, Moxico, Angola
Operator	Força Aérea Popular de Angola (Angolan Air Force)
Aircraft type	Antonov An-26

The twin-engine turboprop transport, which had been on an internal flight from Luena to Cazombo, was shot down near the Zambian border, about 25 miles (40km) from its destination, either by rebels or accidentally by government forces. Among the 48 personnel aboard the aircraft, including a crew of four, 42 were killed and all six survivors suffered serious injuries. After a missile had reportedly struck one power plant, the An-26 crashed while attempting a forced landing.

21 SEPTEMBER 1989 (time unknown)

Location	Central Afghanistan
Operator	Afghan Republican Air Force
Aircraft type	Mil Mi-8

All 26 persons aboard were killed, apparently most of them military personnel, when the turbine-engine helicopter crashed and burned while on an internal flight to Kabul from Baghran, Helmond.

21 SEPTEMBER 1989 (time unknown)

Location	Near Baghran, Helmond, Afghanistan
Operator	Afghan Republican Air Force
Aircraft type	Mil Mi-17

The crash of the turbine-engine helicopter, which occurred about 250 miles (400km) south-west of Kabul, claimed the lives of all 24 military personnel aboard the aircraft.

18 OCTOBER 1989 (time unknown)

Location	Off Azerbaijan, USSR
Operator	Soviet Air Force
Aircraft type	Ilyushin Il-76MD (SSSR-76569)

The four-engine jet transport, carrying paratroopers and a crew of seven, crashed in the Caspian Sea while attempting an emergency landing at the airport from where it had just taken off. All 57 Soviet military personnel aboard were killed. The aircraft had turned back after fire erupted in its port outer power plant, but before it could land the engine separated from the wing, whereupon the Il-76 plunged into shallow water some 1,500ft (500m) offshore.

27 OCTOBER 1989 (time unknown)

Location	Near Yelizovo, Russian Soviet Federated Socialist Republic, USSR
Operator	Soviet Air Force
Aircraft type	Antonov An-26

All 36 persons aboard lost their lives when the twin-engine turboprop transport crashed into a mountain about 20 miles (30km) north of Petropavlovsk-Kamchatsky as it was attempting to land in adverse meteorological conditions. The victims of the accident included both military personnel, among them the aircraft's crew of six, and civilian dependants, who were travelling as passengers.

23 NOVEMBER 1989 (time unknown)

Location   Albania
First aircraft
Operator   Albanian People's Army/Air Force
Aircraft type   Mil Mi-4
Second aircraft
Operator   Albanian People's Army/Air Force
Aircraft type   Mil Mi-4

The two helicopters, which were transporting medical personnel and some of the survivors of a bus accident, collided in mid-air and crashed. Killed in the second tragedy were all 24 persons aboard both aircraft, 12 in each. No further details about the collision were available, including its exact location.

21 DECEMBER 1989 (c.14:00)

Location   Near Guayaramerin, Beni, Bolivia
Operator   Fuerza Aérea Boliviana (Bolivian Air Force)
Aircraft type   Lockheed C-130A (TAM-62)

The four-engine turboprop transport crashed in a jungle area some 370 miles (600km) north-east of La Paz shortly after its departure from Guayaramerin Airport, on an internal flight to Santa Cruz, and all but four of the 28 persons aboard were killed. Among the passengers were women and children; the survivors included two of the aircraft's crew of ten military personnel. It was reported that the C-130 had taken off with one power plant inoperative, but no details were given regarding the suspected cause of the accident.

23 JANUARY 1990 (c.07:45)

Location   Near Sabaneta, Federal District, Venezuela
Operator   Armada Venezolana (Venezuelan Navy)
Aircraft type   CASA 212-200 Aviocar (ARV-0210)

The twin-engine turboprop transport crashed and exploded on El Junquito Hill, approximately 15 miles (25km) west of Caracas and about 5 minutes after it had taken off from that city's Simon Bolivar International Airport, on an internal communications flight to Puerto Ayacucho, Amazonas. All 24 persons aboard lost their lives in the accident, including nine civilian passengers; the rest were military personnel, including the aircraft's crew of three. A probable primary or contributing factor were the conditions of reduced visibility, with rain and a low overcast, in which the crash occurred.

27 JANUARY 1990 (c.17:30)

Location   Near Kinkala, Pool, Congo
Operator   Force Aérienne Congolaise (Congolese
                Air Force)
Aircraft type   Nord 262C-66 (TN-230)

All 23 persons aboard were killed when the twin-engine turboprop transport, on an internal flight from Pointe-Noire to Brazzaville, crashed some 50 miles (80km) south-east of its destination. The victims included some civilians; the rest of the passengers and the aircraft's crew of four were military personnel. The crash was probably related to the bad weather conditions encountered by TN-230, with rain and winds of more than 40 knots.

17 FEBRUARY 1990 (c.19:30)

Location   Near Ngwerere, Likouala, Zambia
Operator   Zambia Air Force
Aircraft type   de Havilland DHC-5D Buffalo (AF-315)

The twin-engine turboprop transport, which was on an internal flight to Lusaka from M'bala, Likouala, crashed in darkness about 5 miles (10km) north of the capital city. All 28 persons aboard perished, most of whom were

An Ilyushin Il-76 jet transport, similar to aircraft flown by the Soviet Air Force that crashed in the Caspian Sea. (Philip Jarrett)

military personnel, including the crew of five. Last reported descending in preparation for landing at Lusaka International Airport, the aircraft subsequently plummeted into a field.

1 MARCH 1990 (time unknown)

Location	*Near Meerut, Uttar Pradesh, India*
Operator	*Indian Air Force*
Aircraft type	*MiG-23*

After its pilot had successfully ejected from the stricken aircraft, the jet fighter crashed into two tanker trucks on a road about 70 miles (110km) north-east of Delhi, killing 50 persons on the ground.

27 MARCH 1990 (time unknown)

Location	*Near Kuito, Bie, Angola*
Operator	*Força Aérea Popular de Angola (Angolan Air Force)*
Aircraft type	*CASA 212-300 Aviocar (T-410)*

The twin-engine turboprop transport, on an internal Angolan flight, was shot down by a rocket fired by National Union for the Total Independence of Angola (UNITA) forces about 20 miles (30km) from Kuito. All 25 persons aboard the aircraft were killed, including a crew of five.

20 APRIL 1990 (time unknown)

Location	*Near Kinshasa, Zaire*
Operator	*Force Aérienne Zairoise (Zairean Air Force)*
Aircraft type	*Lockheed C-130H (9T-TCG)*

The four-engine turboprop transport, which was on an internal flight to Gbadolite, Equateur, crashed about 3 minutes after it had taken off from N'dola Airport, serving Kinshasa. All but four of the 24 persons aboard the C-130

were killed in the accident, some of them military personnel; among the survivors was a 2-year-old girl, one of its civilian passengers. Reportedly, one blade had separated from the aircraft's No. 3 propeller and then struck the No. 4 power plant, resulting in serious damage and leading to the crash.

10 AUGUST 1990 (time unknown)

Location	*Near Shindand, Farah, Afghanistan*
Operator	*Afghan Republican Air Force*
Aircraft type	*Antonov An-12*

The four-engine turboprop transport crashed and exploded some 120 miles (190km) south of Herat shortly after it had taken off from the military base at Shindand, killing all 83 persons aboard (78 passengers and a crew of five). According to an unofficial report, the disaster resulted from 'mechanical failure'.

29 AUGUST 1990 (00:34)

Location	*Near Kaiserslautern, Germany*
Operator	*US Air Force*
Aircraft type	*Lockheed C-5A (68-0228)*

The wide-bodied jet transport, operated by the Military Airlift Command (MAC), crashed and burned in a field immediately after taking off from Ramstein Air Base, killing 13 of the 17 American military personnel aboard. The survivors, who included one member of the aircraft's crew of eight, suffered various injuries.

Bound for Rhein-Main Air Base, also in Germany, with an ultimate destination of Saudi Arabia, the C-5 had just lifted off from Runway 27 when it began to drift to the left, initially clipping a number of trees with its port wing. Ultimately, it struck the ground approximately half a mile (0.8km) from the end of the runway and some 500ft (150m) south of its extended centreline. The accident occurred in darkness, and there was thunderstorm activity in the area at the time, with broken layers of cumulonimbus and altocumulus clouds at 5,000ft (1,500m) and 10,000ft (3,000m), respectively.

An analysis of the wreckage showed 'four fully extended thrust reverser actuators' in the area of the No. 1 and 2 engines, and an industry official further confirmed that they belonged to the former. According to a procedural warning, the operation of a thrust reverser at take-off speed and while the flaps are deployed can cause a loss of lift, and such a condition on one side of the aircraft can result in a loss of speed and altitude. Reportedly, 68-0228 had stopped accelerating at a velocity of around 185mph (300kmh) and stopped climbing at a height of around 50–100ft (15–30m) above the ground. Subsequent to this accident, C-5 flight crews were instructed to stop performing pre-flight reverser checks.

A section of the aircraft's fuselage is still recognisable following the crash of the US Air Force C-5A near Ramstein Air Base. (US Air Force)

5

1991–2009

The end of the Cold War, which could perhaps best be symbolised by the tearing down of the Berlin Wall in 1989, marked not only a shift in the world diplomatic scene but also in strategic military policy. The USA and USSR began dismantling nuclear bombers and missiles once held in large numbers under what became known as the Balance of Terror. Other weapons were aimed away from population centres. The worth of tactical air power was well illustrated during the Persian Gulf War in 1991, where it enabled American-led western forces to drive the occupying Iraqis from Kuwait in a matter of days, with remarkably few casualties. The war also saw the first large-scale use of such high-tech weaponry as 'smart' bombs, cruise missiles, and the revolutionary Stealth jet fighter.

The unrecognisable remains of the Chinook helicopter that crashed in Scotland, resulting in the worst rotary-wing disaster in the history of the RAF. (PA News)

Technology can also receive credit for a general improvement in the military safety record, with the exception perhaps of the forces of the former Soviet Union, which were in considerable disarray following the break-up of the nation into a number of independent countries. As with commercial aviation, however, safety improvements often come only after tragedy. It took the mid-air crash between American and German military transports to bring about the installation by both countries of collision-avoidance systems, as were already in use aboard airliners. As military aviation moved into its second century of heavier-than-air flight, it can look back at its past with pride and look ahead to its future, aware of its responsibilities – and its risks.

10 JANUARY 1991 (c.18:00)

Location   Near Paramo Mucuti, Merida, Venezuela
Operator   Armada Venezolana (Venezuelan Navy)
Aircraft type   CASA 212 Aviocar 200 (ARV-0209)

The twin-engine turboprop transport, which had been on an internal flight from Caracas to the city of Merida, crashed into a mountain some 35 miles (55km) south of its destination. All but one of the 22 persons aboard lost their lives, including the crew of three, and the sole survivor was seriously injured. Most of the victims were Venezuelan military personnel. Initially diverting to Santa Barbara due to adverse meteorological conditions, the aircraft had proceeded on towards Merida, but about half an hour later the crew reported being unable to land due to the weather and declared an emergency, with the accident occurring shortly thereafter, around dusk. Ironically, ARV-0209 had been transporting a funeral party with the body of a navy aviator killed a few days earlier, and the passenger who survived this crash had also survived the previous one. The victims of the second accident also included family members of the pilot killed earlier.

5 FEBRUARY 1991 (c.12:50)

Location   Near Nea Ankhialos, Magnesia, Greece
Operator   Hellenic Air Force
Aircraft type   Lockheed C-130H (748)

All 56 Greek military personnel aboard (51 passengers and a crew of five) were killed when the four-engine turboprop transport struck Mount Othris about 100 miles (150km) north-west of Athens and approximately 25 miles (40km) from Nea Ankhialos Air Base, where it was to have landed at the end of an internal flight from Elefsira. The crash occurred as the aircraft was letting down in instrument meteorological conditions, but no further details were made available.

14 FEBRUARY 1991 (time unknown)

Location   Near Taisha, Morona Santiago, Ecuador
Operator   Fuerza Aérea Ecuatoriana (Ecuadorean
                Air Force)
Aircraft type   de Havilland DHC-6 Series 300 (FAE-447)

Operated by Transportes Aéreos Militares Ecuatorianos (TAME) and on a non-scheduled domestic passenger service of the military airline to Taisha from Macao on behalf of a missionary group, the twin-engine turboprop crashed and burned at an approximate elevation of 5,000ft (1,500m) on Mount Paso Macuna, only about 100ft (30m) below its summit. All 22 persons aboard, including a crew of three military personnel, were killed in the accident, which occurred in adverse weather conditions, some 20 miles (30km) from the aircraft's destination.

22 FEBRUARY 1991 (time unknown)

Location   Near Cazombo, Moxico, Angola
Operator   Força Aérea Popular de Angola (Angolan
                Air Force)
Aircraft type   Antonov An-26

The twin-engine turboprop transport was shot down some 250 miles (400km) east of Luena by UNITA rebel forces, using a Stinger surface-to-air missile, and all 47 persons aboard lost their lives, including a crew of four military personnel. Most of the passengers were civilians.

21 MARCH 1991 (time unknown)

Location   Near Ras-al-Mishab, Saudi Arabia
Operator   Royal Saudi Air Force
Aircraft type   Lockheed C-130H (469)

The four-engine turboprop transport, its passengers all Sengalese soldiers returning from duty in the Persian Gulf War, crashed about 15 miles (25km) south of Khafji as it was attempting to land at Ras-al-Mishab, in conditions of poor visibility due to oil fires in nearby Kuwait. Killed in the accident were 98 military personnel aboard the aircraft, including its six Saudi Air Force crewmen; three soldiers survived with serious injuries.

21 MARCH 1991 (c.02:15)

Location   Off Southern California, USA
First aircraft
Operator   US Navy
Aircraft type   Lockheed P-3C (158930)
Second aircraft
Operator   US Navy
Aircraft type   Lockheed P-3C (159325)

This disastrous mid-air crash occurred during an anti-submarine warfare training exercise. Designated as the 'on-station' aircraft, 159325 was being relieved by 158930, having provided sonobuoy contact as part of the operation. The two four-engine turboprop patrol aircraft collided at an approximate altitude of 3,000ft (1,000m) and some 60 miles (100km) south-west of San Diego, and both then plummeted into the Pacific Ocean. All 27 crewmen from both aircraft, 14 aboard 158930 and 13 aboard 159325, lost their lives. Searchers recovered a small amount of debris, but none of the victims' bodies.

Both aircraft had been based at the Moffett Field Naval

Air Station, located near San Jose, California. The altitude separation to be used in the turnover had been established in pre-flight briefings by their crews. Though both were operating under visual flight rules (VFR) procedures, horizontal separation at the scene would have been afforded through air-to-air tactical air navigation (TACAN) facilities. In addition, the aircraft were in radio contact with each other.

According to radar transcripts, 158930 had, prior to the accident, descended from its en-route altitude, and was maintaining its height, while 159325 had ascended an estimated 300–1,000ft (100–300m). Just before impact, the former was headed generally north, the latter generally east. The crew of a navy helicopter observed the fireball produced by the collision. It was dark at the time, and the meteorological conditions consisted of intermittent rain, with the cloud level down to around 2,000ft (600m) and a visibility of between 5 and 10 miles (8 and 16km). There was also thunderstorm activity in the area. The weather was considered a possible contributing factor.

Although the exact sequence of events could not be determined, the accident apparently occurred after one crew either misunderstood the other's intentions, lost situational awareness at a critical time, or violated a previous understanding or agreement made in radio communications as to how each P-3 would shift altitudes in order to effect the turnover. Significantly, the flight of 159325 had been marked by equipment failures, an inoperative autopilot system, and extended time in turbulent weather conditions, which reportedly caused airsickness among some of its crewmen. These factors, combined with the added distractions of reported interference on its crew intercom system and fatigue associated with the length of time on station and the night-time duty, could have contributed to the accident had this crew been at fault.

As previously mentioned, 159325 was the aircraft that deviated from the self-assigned swap height of 2,500ft (750m), although this could have been agreed upon between both crews by radio. Despite a recommendation for such, the investigative report noted no plans to retrofit the US Navy's P-3 fleet with crash-survivable flight data recorders.

25 MARCH 1991 (c.08:15)

Location	Near Bangalore, Karnataka, India
Operator	Indian Air Force
Aircraft type	Hindustan Aeronautics HAL 748 Series 2 (H-1513)

The twin-engine turboprop transport, which was on an air-experience flight, its passengers comprising trainee engineers and cadets, crashed and burned shortly after take-off from Yellahanka Air Base. All 28 Indian service personnel aboard were killed, including the crew of three. Climbing to an approximate height of 150ft (50m), the aircraft began to lose height until it slammed to earth about half a mile (0.8km) from the airfield. The accident may have been related to power plant failure.

26 JULY 1991 (time unknown)

Location	Near Maymaneh, Faryab, Afghanistan
Operator	Afghan Republican Air Force
Aircraft type	Mil Mi-8

All 30 persons aboard lost their lives, including an estimated crew of five military personnel, when the turbine-engine helicopter was shot down by rebel forces. Most of the passengers were civilians.

5 OCTOBER 1991 (c.15:00)

Location	Condet, Java, Indonesia
Operator	Tentara Nasional Indonesia Angkatan Udara (Indonesian Air Force)
Aircraft type	Lockheed C-130H (A-1324)

A total of 148 Indonesian military personnel were killed in the flaming crash of the four-engine turboprop transport in a south-eastern suburb of Jakarta. The victims of the accident included a guard on the ground; there were no survivors among the occupants of the aircraft (135 passengers and a crew of 12). Reportedly, one power plant of the C-130 had caught fire, and the crash occurred during an attempted emergency landing at Perdonakusuma Halim Airport, from where it had taken off shortly before, on an internal flight to Bandung.

The scene of devastation where the Indonesian Air Force C-130H transport crashed on Java, with a loss of nearly 150 lives. (AP/Wide World Photos)

1 NOVEMBER 1991 (time unknown)

Location	*Near Karakent, Azerbaijan, USSR*
Operator	*Azerbaijan Air Force*
Aircraft type	*Mil Mi-8*

The turbine-engine helicopter was shot down by rebel forces, and all 40 persons aboard lost their lives.

20 NOVEMBER 1991 (time unknown)

Location	*Nagoro-Karabak, Azerbaijan, USSR*
Operator	*Soviet Air Force*
Aircraft type	*Mil Mi-8*

The turbine-engine helicopter slammed into a cloud-obscured hill and exploded after its pilot reported being unable to see anything. All 23 persons aboard the aircraft, including a crew of three military personnel, were killed in the crash. There was another report that the aircraft had been shot down.

28 JANUARY 1992 (c.16:20)

Location	*Azerbaijan, Commonwealth of Independent States*
Operator	*Azerbaijan Air Force*
Aircraft type	*Mil Mi-8*

All 47 persons aboard were killed, including a military crew, when the turbine-engine helicopter was shot down about 5 miles (10km) south of Stepanakert. The aircraft had been en route from Agdam to Shusha when it was hit by a surface-to-air missile, exploding in mid-air.

6 FEBRUARY 1992 (c.10:00)

Location	*Evansville, Indiana, USA*
Operator	*US Air Force*
Aircraft type	*Lockheed C-130B (58-0732)*

Operated by the Kentucky Air National Guard, the four-engine turboprop transport struck a motel and then crashed into a restaurant and exploded. The five military crewmen (and only occupants) of the aircraft and 11 persons on the ground were killed, while nine others suffered injuries. Additionally, a police officer who assisted in the post-crash rescue effort, and who was among those hospitalised, succumbed more than a week later. The impact and resulting fires also destroyed eight vehicles and damaged some 20 others.

During the approach phase of a touch-and-go practice routine being conducted at Evansville Regional Airport, the aircraft was advised by the control tower to return to its home base, Standiford Field, at Louisville, in neighbouring Kentucky. Abandoning the approach, it then climbed to an approximate height of 1,700ft (520m) above the ground before going into a rapid descent. Subsequently, the C-130 slammed to earth approximately 1 mile (1.5km) south of the departure end of Runway 22, its undercarriage retracted but flaps extended to 50 degrees. Although the cause was not officially reported, an unnamed military source attributed

Military personnel search through the remains of the Air National Guard C-130 that crashed into a motel and restaurant in Evansville, Indiana, USA. (AP/Wide World Photos)

the crash to the failure of the pilots to maintain sufficient air speed during a simulated engine failure due to distractions with air-traffic control instructions and their check-list routine, resulting in a stall.

16 APRIL 1992 (time unknown)

Location	Nairobi, Kenya
Operator	The 82 (Kenyan) Air Force
Aircraft type	de Havilland DHC-5 Buffalo (214)

Soon after it had taken off from Eastleigh Air Base, the twin-engine turboprop transport crashed in the Nairobi suburb of Kaloleni. Killed in the morning accident were all 46 persons aboard the aircraft, two of whom were civilian dependants and the rest Kenyan military personnel, including the crew of four, plus six others on the ground. About half-a-dozen others suffered injuries.

The aircraft's left power plant had failed and the corresponding propeller consequently autofeathered following the aircraft's departure from Runway 06, and the pilot initiated a left turn in an attempt to return to the airfield. But while turning on to the final leg of the circuit, 214 entered a low overcast, and the pilot apparently lost sight of the runway, causing him to overshoot the approach course. As he tried to effect realignment, the aircraft stalled and plummeted to the ground with its undercarriage down and flaps extended, then skidded into a block of apartment buildings and exploded. No determination could be made as to the reason for the engine malfunction.

26 APRIL 1992 (c.12:20)

Location	Near Saveh, Markazi, Iran
Operator	Islamic Republic of Iran Air Force
Aircraft type	Fokker F.27 Troopship Mark 400M (5-8815)

Operated by the carrier Saha Air Lines, which is owned by the Iranian Air Force, and on a domestic non-scheduled service to Tehran from Bandar-e Mah Shahr being conducted on behalf of the National Iranian Oil Company (NOIC), the twin-engine turboprop crashed in adverse weather conditions some 60 miles (100km) south-west of its destination. All 39 persons aboard, including an estimated crew of four, were killed.

5 JULY 1992 (c.17:00)

Location	Near Iyakochchi, Sri Lanka
Operator	Sri Lanka Air Force
Aircraft type	Shaanxi Y-8D (CR872)

All 19 military personnel aboard were killed, including a crew of six, when the four-engine turboprop transport, basically a Chinese-built Antonov An-12, crashed and burned approximately half a mile (0.8km) from the Elephant Pass Army Garrison. The aircraft was apparently shot down by rebel forces while approaching to land at the military installation.

14 JULY 1992 (time unknown)

Location	Near Nakhichevan, Azerbaijan, Commonwealth of Independent States
Operator	Russian Air Force
Aircraft type	Antonov An-12V (SSSR-11111)

The four-engine turboprop transport crashed and burned immediately after it had taken off from the Nakhichevan airport, bound for Rostov-na-Donu, Russian Federation, killing 29 Russian military personnel. Five others aboard, including two members of the aircraft's crew of seven, survived with serious injuries. There was one report that the aircraft had experienced fuel exhaustion.

14 JULY 1992 (time unknown)

Location	Near Bir Fadl, Yemen
Operator	Unified Yemen Air Force
Aircraft type	Antonov An-12

The four-engine turboprop transport crashed and exploded about 5 miles (8km) from the Aden airport, where it was to have landed at the end of a flight from the island of Socotra. All 58 persons aboard lost their lives, including a crew of six military personnel; most of the passengers were civilians. The aircraft had been held for a time in a traffic pattern because of reduced visibility associated with a sandstorm, and the accident occurred after the pilot announced he was diverting to San'a.

26 SEPTEMBER 1992 (c.18:00)

Location	Near Lagos, Nigeria
Operator	Federal Nigerian Air Force
Aircraft type	Lockheed C-130H (NAF-911)

The four-engine turboprop transport crashed in a swamp, killing all 152 persons aboard. Other than four civilians, the victims were military personnel, mostly Nigerian, including three air force crewmen, but also from Ghana, Tanzania, Zimbabwe and Uganda. The accident occurred about 3 minutes after the aircraft had taken off from Murtala Muhammed Airport, serving the capital city, on an internal flight to Kaduna. Two of its power plants had malfunctioned initially, followed by a third, possibly as the pilot-in-command was attempting to ditch the C-130 in a canal, with the resulting crash occurring around dusk and in clear weather conditions. Fuel contamination was mentioned as the cause of the multiple engine failure.

5 NOVEMBER 1992 (time unknown)

Location	Near Anapa, Russian Federation, Commonwealth of Independent States
Operator	Russian Air Force
Aircraft type	Mil Mi-6

The turbine-engine helicopter crashed while transporting military personnel and their families from Rostov-na-Donu back to their home base, near Krasnodar. All but one of the 29 persons aboard were killed in the accident, including the aircraft's crew of five; the surviving passenger was seriously injured. Although the cause was not officially reported, overloading of personal baggage may have been a factor in the crash.

11 NOVEMBER 1992 (time unknown)

Location	Near Tver, Russian Federation, Commonwealth of Independent States
Operator	Russian Air Force
Aircraft type	Antonov An-22 (SSSR-09303)

The four-engine turboprop transport crashed and burned some 125 miles (200km) north-west of Moscow shortly after taking off from Migalovo Air Base, on a chartered freight service to Yerevan, Armenia. All 23 persons aboard lost their lives, including a crew of seven military personnel; a few of the passengers were civilians. The aircraft had climbed to an approximate height of 800ft (250m) before it lost height and slammed to earth beyond the end of the airport runway. Improper loading and excessive weight were believed to have been factors in the accident. Not explained was the registration of the aircraft, identical to an An-22 reported missing over the North Atlantic Ocean in 1970.

11 NOVEMBER 1992 (time unknown)

Location	Off Bombay, India
Operator	Indian Air Force
Aircraft type	Mil Mi-8

Possibly after its rotor blades struck an oil rig, the turbine-engine helicopter crashed in the Arabian Sea, and 20 persons aboard the aircraft were killed.

30 NOVEMBER 1992 (c.21:20)

Location	Near Harlem, Montana, USA
First aircraft	
Operator	US Air Force
Aircraft type	Lockheed C-141B (65-0255)
Second aircraft	
Operator	US Air Force
Aircraft type	Lockheed C-141B (66-0142)

The two jet transports, operated by the Military Airlift Command (MAC), collided in mid-air some 150 miles (250km) north-east of Great Falls, and both then crashed and burned. All 13 crewmen of both aircraft, seven in 65-0255 and six in 66-0142, were killed. The collision occurred at a height of around 25,000ft (7,500m) in darkness and meteorological conditions consisting of scattered clouds at lower altitudes, a visibility of 7 miles (11km) and moderate turbulence.

The two involved in the accident were among four transports engaged in a training mission, and had just completed mid-air refuelling from a KC-135 tanker. Proceeding on a west-south-westerly heading at the time of the collision, both aircraft then suffered catastrophic structural failure, and wreckage was scattered across the open terrain over an area of approximately 8 miles (13km) long by about 3 miles (5km) wide. It was reported that after completing refuelling, 66-0142 had remained at an unusually close position behind the tanker, and after 65-0255 was refuelled, it 'backed away' and turned to the left, whereupon it struck the other aircraft, its crew unaware of the former's location.

14 DECEMBER 1992 (time unknown)

Location	Near Lata, Georgia, Commonwealth of Independent States
Operator	Russian Air Force
Aircraft type	Mil Mi-8T

The turbine-engine helicopter was shot down by Georgian rebel forces, using a surface-to-air missile, some 25 miles (40km) east-north-east of Sukhumi, and all 61 persons aboard were killed.

10 FEBRUARY 1993 (time unknown)

Location	Near Daraim, Badakhshan, Afghanistan
Operator	Afghan Republican Air Force
Aircraft type	Mil Mi-8

The turbine-engine helicopter, which was reportedly overloaded and poorly maintained, crashed some 200 miles

The front fuselage section of 66-0142, one of the two US Air Force C-141B jet transports involved in the mid-air collision over Montana, is pictured where it came to rest. (US Air Force)

(320km) north-east of Kabul while on a flight to Daraim, about 20 miles (30km) south of Faisabad, where it had taken off from earlier. All 30 persons aboard were killed.

27 APRIL 1993 (time unknown)

Location	*Near Kholm (Tashqurgan), Samangan, Afghanistan*
Operator	*Afghan Republican Air Force*
Aircraft type	*Antonov An-32*

All 76 Afghan military personnel aboard were killed, including an estimated crew of five, when the twin-engine turboprop transport, which was on an internal flight from Kabul to Mazar-i-Sharif, crashed into a hill some 40 miles (65km) east of its intended destination. The accident occurred in evening darkness, with low clouds and fog.

27 APRIL 1993 (c.22:45)

Location	*Off Libreville, Gabon*
Operator	*Zambia Air Force*
Aircraft type	*de Havilland DHC-5D Buffalo (AF-319)*

The twin-engine turboprop transport, which was carrying the Zambian national soccer team, its manager and support staff, plummeted into the Atlantic Ocean about five minutes after its departure from the Libreville airport, an en-route refuelling stop during a service originating at Lusaka, Zambia, with an ultimate destination of Dakar, Senegal. All 30 persons aboard the aircraft, including a crew of five military personnel, were killed in the accident, which occurred in evening darkness. An investigation revealed that after the aircraft's left power plant had failed, the pilot may have inadvertently shut down the right engine, whereupon the Buffalo lost altitude and finally crashed approximately 1,500ft (500m) offshore. Fatigue was a probable factor in the suspected error by the pilot.

6 JULY 1993 (time unknown)

Location	*Near Ochamchire, Georgia, Commonwealth of Independent States*
Operator	*Georgian Air Force*
Aircraft type	*Mil Mi-8*

The turbine-engine helicopter was shot down by Abkhazi forces some 30 miles (50km) south-east of Sukhumi, and all 23 persons aboard were killed.

4 OCTOBER 1993 (time unknown)

Location	*Near Svanetia, Georgia, Commonwealth of Independent States*
Operator	*Georgian Air Force*
Aircraft type	*Mil Mi-8*

The turbine-engine helicopter crashed during an internal refugee flight to Svanetia from Abkhazia, killing all 60 persons aboard.

15 DECEMBER 1993 (time unknown)

Location	*Near Libmanan, Camarines Sur, Philippines*
Operator	*Philippine Air Force*
Aircraft type	*Lockheed C-130H (4761)*

All 29 persons aboard perished, including a crew of six military personnel, when the four-engine turboprop transport struck a wooded mountainside and exploded about 20 miles (30km) north-west of Naga City, where it was to have landed at the end of an internal flight from Manila. The afternoon accident occurred in adverse weather conditions, with heavy rain and zero visibility, reportedly after the aircraft had descended below a safe altitude during its landing approach.

17 MARCH 1994 (c.22:30)

Location	*Near Nagornyy Stepanakert, Karabakh, Azerbaijan, Commonwealth of Independent States*
Operator	*Islamic Republic of Iran Air Force*
Aircraft type	*Lockheed C-130H (5-8521)*

The four-engine turboprop transport was shot down by Armenian forces while en route to Tehran from Moscow, Russian Federation, and all 32 persons aboard were killed, including a crew of 13 Iranian military personnel. Its passengers comprised the families of the Iranian embassy staff on their way home. The aircraft was hit by a missile while flying in darkness.

23 MARCH 1994 (c.14:30)

Location	*Near Fayetteville, North Carolina, USA*
First aircraft	
Operator	*US Air Force*
Aircraft type	*General Dynamics F-16D (88-0171)*
Second aircraft	
Operator	*US Air Force*
Aircraft type	*Lockheed C-130E (68-10942)*
Third aircraft	
Operator	*US Air Force*
Aircraft type	*Lockheed C-141B (66-0173)*

The jet fighter and the turboprop transport collided in mid-air as both were approaching to land at Pope Air Force Base, and the former then crashed and skidded across the tarmac into a staging area where some 500 army paratroopers were preparing to board parked aircraft, including the C-141. Hit by debris, the jet transport was destroyed in a fiery explosion. The disaster claimed the lives of 23 military personnel on the ground and injured 100 others. Both airmen in the F-16 ejected and parachuted to earth, while the damaged C-130 landed safely without injury to its five-member crew.

An official inquiry regarded as a major factor in the collision confusing instructions given to the F-16 by a civilian tower controller at Fayetteville Regional Airport, who first issued a traffic advisory concerning the C-130, then cleared 88-0171 for a straight-in approach to Runway 23 at the

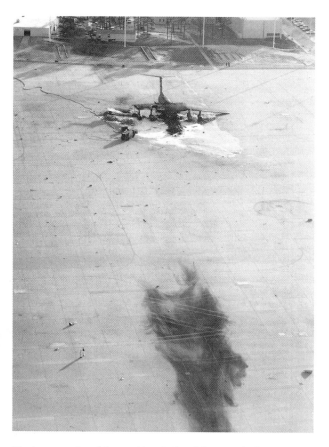

The impact point of the crashing F-16 jet fighter (in the foreground) and the destroyed C-141 transport following the disaster at Pope Air Force Base. (US Air Force)

military base during a simulated engine failure. After the advisory, the fighter pilot did not ask the tower about the position of the transport, and did not break off the simulated flame-out. A trainee controller tried to alert the fighter pilot regarding the presence of 68-10942, but used the wrong call sign. The collision occurred in visual meteorological conditions at an approximate altitude of 300ft (100m), with the F-16 striking the stabiliser of the C-130. Camouflage painted, 68-10942 had been nearly impossible to see against the forested terrain in the background.

14 APRIL 1994 (c.09:35)

Location	*Northern Iraq*
First aircraft	
Operator	*US Army*
Aircraft type	*Sikorsky UH-60 (87-26000)*
Second aircraft	
Operator	*US Army*
Aircraft type	*Sikorsky UH-60 (88-26060)*

Following the end of the Persian Gulf war and occupation of Kuwait by Iraqi forces three years earlier, the US National Command Authority instituted Operation Provide Comfort.

With the intention of protecting the Kurdish population in an area of Iraq designated as a security zone, American, British and other coalition military aircraft began patrolling in what was known as a Tactical Area of Responsibility (TAOR), north of the 36th Parallel. Iraqi aircraft were prohibited from entering this area, but had nevertheless tested coalition forces on numerous occasions, leading to several skirmishes.

The sequence leading up to this tragedy began with the departure of the two turbine-engine helicopters from Zakhu, bound for the towns of Irbil and Salah ad Din, also in Iraq. They were carrying as passengers the Turkish and US co-commanders of the Military Co-ordination Center (MCC) and their party to a scheduled meeting with UN representatives and officials of the Kurdish Democratic Party. In accordance with prescribed procedures, the flight contacted an Airborne Command and Control System (AWACS) aircraft, actually an American Boeing E-3B jet flying above, informing the en-route controller of their intended destination. Also on patrol in the area were two US Air Force F-15C jet fighters.

About 2 minutes after the fighters had entered northern Iraq, the lead pilot reported radar contact with a low-flying target. At the time, the helicopters had been proceeding on a course of about 100 degrees at a speed of around 150mph (250kmh). The TAOR controller, also aboard the E-3, acknowledged the radio transmission, responding with a 'clean there', indicating no such contacts. Attempts by the F-15 pilots to identify the rotorcraft by electronic means were unsuccessful, so the fighters then made one pass in an attempt to identify them visually.

It was at that point that the lead pilot misidentified the UH-60s as Soviet-built, Iraqi-operated Mi-24 Hind helicopters; his wing man saw them but could not make positive identification. The F-15s then attacked the two friendly helicopters, which at the time were flying through a valley in a staggered left trail formation at a height of 100–200ft (30–60m) above the ground, shooting down both. The lead fighter brought down the trailing helicopter with an AIM-120 air-to-air missile fired from behind at a range of approximately 5 miles (10km). In what may have been an escape manoeuvre, the lead UH-60 turned on to a north-easterly heading and entered a narrow, steep gorge, but seconds later it was hit with a Sidewinder air-to-air missile fired by the second F-15, also from behind and at a distance of around 2 miles (3km). The two rotorcraft burst into flames when struck, then crashed some 30 miles (50km) north-north-east of Irbil and about 10 miles (15km) from the Turkish border. Including eight US military crewmen divided evenly between them, all 26 persons aboard both helicopters lost their lives, 13 in each one.

This tragedy was attributed to a chain of events that began with the break-down of clear guidance from the Combined Task Force, which oversaw the entire operation, to its component organisations. The result was a lack of coordination between helicopter flights and other air operations within the TAOR. Additionally, personnel were found to have been lacking in consistent, comprehensive training, and in some cases possessed an over-simplified understanding of the proper Rules of Engagement. Still another factor was the high degree of independence given to MCC personnel in helicopter operations, without sufficient consideration being given to the potential threat of engagement with coalition combat aircraft operating in the area.

Information about these flights was not adequately communicated to the task force staff. The AWACS surveillance section had assigned the helicopter flight a 'friendly general' track symbology and an 'H' character programmed to appear at its location whenever an identification friend or foe (IFF) Mode I 'squawk', or reply, was detected. (This code is designed to confirm the friendly status of an aircraft and in this case would be used outside the TAOR.) There was no evidence that the en-route controller performed a Mode IV IFF check on the helicopters, which, though not directed, is an implied duty. (This code is used to differentiate between friend and foe, and its use would be important within the TAOR.)

The helicopter crews were apparently not aware that a different Mode I code was to be used when flying within the no-fly zone. Neither the en-route controller nor the senior director had instructed the helicopter crews to switch to the TAOR clear frequency, nor had they advised them that they were still emitting the incorrect Mode I Code. Both IFF and radar contact with the helicopters were lost when they entered a mountainous region at a low altitude. As a result, the AWACS computer continued to move the 'H' symbol based on the last available heading and air speed information from the helicopters. However, the en-route controller failed

This Sikorsky HH-60 helicopter is similar to the two US Army aircraft misidentified and shot down over Iraq by two US Air Force F-15 jet fighters. (Sikorsky)

The position of the two F-15 fighters and the two UH-60 Black Hawk helicopters shortly before the 'friendly fire' disaster. (US Air Force)

to note this information, and never transferred control of the flight to the individual monitoring the TAOR.

Although the air surveillance officer had marked the helicopters' last known position with a computer-generated 'attention arrow', the blinking alert light was automatically dropped after 60 seconds. Minutes later, the en-route controller dropped the symbology representing the helicopters from the radar scopes, the only visual reminder of their presence in the area.

It could not be ascertained why the F-15 pilots were unsuccessful in identifying the UH-60s through their IFF Mode IV interrogation system (despite an initial, momentary, friendly response). This probably resulted from one or a combination of factors, namely, both fighter pilots selecting the wrong interrogation code; the incorrect processing of the transponder signals from the helicopters by the fighters' air-to-air interrogators; improper loading of both UH-60 IFF codes; possible garbling of the helicopters' friendly IFF responses caused by the use of the same code by both army crews in close proximity to each other; or an intermittent loss of the 'line-of-sight' radar contact between the fighters and the helicopter flight due to the mountainous terrain and the latter's low altitude, which could have precluded a successful Mode IV interrogation.

Significantly, the American Secretary of Defence regarded the IFF system as a back-up rather than a primary means of identifying aircraft. The F-15 pilots themselves were found to have had only limited recognition training during the previous four months, and neither had ever seen a UH-60 Black Hawk in the configurations of these two, i.e. with sponsons and external fuel tanks. Their identification pass was made at a speed of around 520mph (840kmh), and at an altitude and distance from which it would have been unlikely for them to detect the markings on the helicopters, despite the daylight and good weather conditions in the area, with unlimited visibility.

Investigation also revealed that the en-route controller on duty at the time of the tragedy had previously received three 'unsatisfactory' ratings in simulated flights in the areas of safety, airspace coordination and aircraft positioning. However, he had performed well in two recent training exercises. He would later be acquitted by a military court of charges stemming from his actions on the day of the shoot-down.

The friendly-fire incident spurred a sweeping review of command and control procedures in joint US military air operations, and led to significant changes in the air force AWACS programme, including the addition of more crews and improvements in their training.

2 JUNE 1994 (c.18:00)

Location	Near Campbeltown, Strathclyde, Scotland
Operator	Royal Air Force
Aircraft type	Boeing/Vertol Chinook HC. Mark 2 (ZD576)

The worst helicopter disaster in the history of the RAF occurred during a flight that had originated at Aldergrove Air Base, near Belfast, Northern Ireland. The passengers included a number of anti-terrorist specialists from the Royal Ulster Constabulary, who were on their way to a security conference at Fort George, near Inverness, Scotland. Observed at a height of under 500ft (150m) over the North Channel, the turbine-engine rotorcraft was seen to change its direction, towards Corran, then began to ascend and finally disappeared into a low cloud base. Subsequently, it slammed into Beinn Na Lice (The Mountain of the Stone Slab), only about half a mile (800m) from the lighthouse on the Island of Kintyre, at an approximate elevation of 800ft (250m), bursting into flames on impact, which was at a speed of around 170mph (270kmh). All 29 persons aboard were killed, including a four-man military crew.

An investigative report attributed the accident to what it described as the 'grossly negligent' action of the flight crew in proceeding towards the high ground in a heavy fog below a safe altitude. The pilots then selected an inappropriate rate-of-climb in order to clear the rising terrain. In addition, the route of the Chinook was slightly displaced to the east of the correct course due to the actual position of a waypoint selected into its navigational system and possibly due to an error in the system itself related to the wind speed. Significantly, the helicopter's newly-installed power plant control system may have been susceptible to icing, which in this case could have necessitated flight below the clouds, rather than in them, in order to avoid such conditions.

In 2002, a report issued by the House of Lords concluded that the reviewing officers who conducted the first investigation were 'not justified in finding that negligence on the part of the pilots' caused the accident. And subsequent to the crash of ZD576, the RAF announced plans to install its rotorcraft with flight data recorders and cockpit voice recorders to aid in accident investigations.

29 JUNE 1994 (time unknown)

Location	Near Logar, Afghanistan
Operator	Dostum-Galboddin Militia
Aircraft type	Antonov An-32

The twin-engine turboprop transport was shot down by Afghan ground troops, and 50 of the 70 persons aboard the aircraft were killed.

5 AUGUST 1994 (c.08:50)

Location	Near Boda, Russian Federation, Commonwealth of Independent States
Operator	Russian Air Force
Aircraft type	Antonov An-12

All 47 persons aboard were killed when the four-engine turboprop transport crashed and burned on a hillside in Eastern Siberia while attempting to land. Most of the victims were military personnel, including the crew of six. The accident occurred in conditions of poor visibility due to heavy rain and fog approximately 3 miles (5km) from the aircraft's destination, near the end of an internal flight from Dzhida, and was reportedly precipitated by a power plant fire.

14 OCTOBER 1994 (c.22:00)

Location	Near Formoso do Araguala, Tocantins, Brazil
Operator	Força Aérea Brasileira (Brazilian Air Force)
Aircraft type	Lockheed C-130E (2460)

The four-engine turboprop transport, on an internal flight from Rio de Janeiro to Belem, Para, crashed in darkness some 250 miles (400km) north-north-west of Brasilia, and all 21 military personnel aboard were killed. It was considered possible that the load of munitions being carried by the aircraft had exploded in the air.

26 OCTOBER 1994 (time unknown)

Location	Near Cuito Cuanavale, Cuando Cubango, Angola
Operator	Força Aérea Popular de Angola (Angolan Air Force)
Aircraft type	Mil Mi-8MTV (H-534)

The turbine-engine helicopter was shot down by rebel forces, about 250 miles (400km) south-south-west of Luena, killing all 22 military personnel aboard the aircraft.

25 NOVEMBER 1994 (time unknown)

Location	Near Cuito Cuanavale, Cuando Cubango, Angola
Operator	Força Aérea Popular de Angola (Angolan Air Force)
Aircraft type	Mil Mi-17 (H-584)

During a medical evacuation flight, the turbine-engine helicopter was shot down by UNITA rebel forces and 22 military personnel aboard were killed. The aircraft's four crewmen survived.

17 JUNE 1995 (time unknown)

Location	Near Cuvela, Benguel, Angola
Operator	Força Aérea Popular de Angola (Angolan Air Force)
Aircraft type	CASA 212 Aviocar 200 (T-401)

The twin-engine turboprop transport, which was on an internal flight from Ondjiva to Catumbela and carrying as passengers members of a local soccer club, crashed some 10 miles (15km) east of its destination, while approaching to land. Forty-eight persons aboard the aircraft, including its three military crew members, were killed; the five survivors suffered various injuries. The primary factor in the crash was believed to have been adverse weather conditions, though in addition to that the transport reportedly had been overloaded.

18 JULY 1995 (time unknown)

Location	Near Antananivo (Tananarive), Madagascar
Operator	L'Armée de l'Air Malgache (Madagascan Air Force)
Aircraft type	Douglas C-47A (525)

Having been chartered to carry a French medical team back from Maintirano, the vintage twin-engine transport crashed while preparing to land at Ivato Airport, serving Antananivo. The accident claimed the lives of 34 persons aboard the aircraft, including the five members of its military crew. Six passengers survived with serious injuries. It was unofficially reported that both engines of the C-47 had malfunctioned during the landing approach, with the resulting crash occurring some 1,500ft (500m) from the end of the runway.

9 SEPTEMBER 1995 (c.07:15)

Location	Near La Macarena, Meta, Colombia
Operator	Fuerza Aérea Colombiana (Colombian Air Force)
Aircraft type	CASA 212 Aviocar 200 (FAC.1152)

Operated by the military airline Servicio Aeronavegación a Territorios Nacionales (SATENA) and on a scheduled domestic flight from Villavicencio to the resort town of La Macarena, the twin-engine turboprop crashed and burst into flames in a tropical forest region near its destination and about 70 miles (110km) south-east of Bogotá. All 22 persons aboard the aircraft were killed, including its crew of four military personnel; one passenger was found alive but later succumbed to injuries. The Aviocar slammed into a hillside during rain and fog approximately 5 miles (10km) from the local airport as it was trying to land after initiating a missed approach procedure, the second of two unsuccessful landing attempts.

13 SEPTEMBER 1995 (c.07:20)

Location	Gulf of Mannar
Operator	Sri Lanka Air Force
Aircraft type	Antonov An-32B (CR-861)

All 75 persons aboard perished, including five military crewmen, when the twin-engine turboprop transport crashed some 25 miles (40km) north-west of Colombo, Sri Lanka. Bound for Palay, in the Tamil region of the nation, the aircraft had taken off from Ratmalana Airport, near the capital city, before it plunged into the sea from an approximate height of 8,000ft (2,500m). The pilot had radioed that he had an instrument problem and that he was returning to his departure point, and may have lost control during the 180-degree turn. At the time of the accident, the meteorological conditions in the area were adverse, with thunderstorm activity and a heavy overcast.

A US Air Force Boeing E-3B AWACS aircraft, identical to the one that crashed after taking off from Elmendorf Air Force Base in Alaska. (Boeing)

22 SEPTEMBER 1995 (c.07:45)

Location	*Near Anchorage, Alaska, USA*
Operator	*US Air Force*
Aircraft type	*Boeing E-3B (77-0354)*

The modified Boeing 707-320B jet, used as an Airborne Warning and Control System (AWACS) aircraft, crashed and exploded shortly after taking off from Elmendorf Air Force Base, on a routine training mission. All 24 crewmen aboard perished.

Investigation revealed that a flock of 100 or more Canada geese, which had been roosting on the grass adjacent to the runway, rose into the air and were ingested into the two port

A swath cut in the forest marks the site of the E-3B crash, which was attributed to a bird strike. (US Air Force)

engines of the E-3, five seconds after the commander was heard to call 'rotate' on the cockpit voice recorder (CVR) tape. This resulted in the immediate, uncontained and catastrophic failure of the No. 2 power plant and severe compressor stalls in the No. 1, leading to an asymmetrical thrust condition. The aircraft began a slow left-hand climbing turn before it initially struck the ground with its port wing tip and then slammed into the hilly, wooded terrain approximately 1 mile (1.5km) north-north-east of the departure end of Runway 05, which it had used, its undercarriage still down and flaps partially extended at the moment of impact. The local weather at the time consisted of scattered clouds down to about 1,500ft (500m) and layers at higher altitudes, a visibility of 7 miles (11km) and light to moderate turbulence.

Only 2 minutes before the crash, a C-130 transport had disturbed the birds that would bring down 77-0354, but while this had been observed by the tower controller, he did not inform either the AWACS crew or Airfield Management. Also cited were the procedures employed to reduce the bird hazard at the base, including preparations for the migration season, which were described as 'inadequate'. Four officers assigned to the base received 'administrative discipline' for their failure to provide leadership in this area.

8 NOVEMBER 1995 (c.21:00)

Location	*Near Luyaba, Córdoba, Argentina*
Operator	*Fuerza Aérea Argentina (Argentine Air Force)*
Aircraft type	*Fokker F.27 Friendship Mark 500 (TC-72)*

Operated by the Argentine military airline Lineas Aéreas del Estado (LADE) and on a domestic flight to the city of Córdoba from Comodoro Rivadavia, Chubat, the twin-engine turboprop transport crashed at an approximate elevation of 8,000ft (2,500m) in the Sierra Grande range of mountains, some 10 miles (15km) from Villa Dolores. All 53 persons aboard, including a crew of five, were killed. The passengers on the flight consisted of military personnel and their dependants, including about 20 children,

A Soviet-built Antonov An-32 turboprop transport, the type flown by the Sri Lanka Air Force and involved in two major crashes in the latter half of 1995. (Philip Jarrett)

who were on their way to the 25th anniversary of a flight academy graduation.

At the time of the accident, which occurred in darkness and adverse weather conditions consisting of thunderstorm activity, accompanied by heavy rain, strong winds and turbulence, TC-72 had been on the direct course between Villa Reynolds and Córdoba. However, it was also observed to be very low before it slammed into the mountain about 1,000ft (300m) below the summit, exploding on impact.

22 NOVEMBER 1995 (c.19:00)

Location	Off Jaffna Peninsula, Sri Lanka
Operator	Sri Lanka Air Force
Aircraft type	Antonov An-32B (CR-862)

The twin-engine turboprop transport, which was on an internal flight from Colombo, its passengers mostly soldiers, crashed in the Indian Ocean while attempting to land at Palaly Air Force Base. All 63 persons aboard the aircraft, including a crew of six, were killed. The last contact with the An-32 was when the pilot asked for the approach lights to be switched on; the subsequent accident occurred in darkness.

22 JANUARY 1996 (c.12:00)

Location	Off Point Pedro, Sri Lanka
Operator	Sri Lanka Air Force
Aircraft type	Mil Mi-17 (CH-587)

The turbine-engine helicopter was shot down by Tamil rebels and plummeted into the Indian Ocean, killing all 39 military personnel aboard the aircraft.

11 FEBRUARY 1996 (time unknown)

Location	Near Kandahar, Afghanistan
Operator	Taliban Militia
Aircraft type	Helicopter

All 20 occupants lost their lives in the crash of the rotorcraft, which was probably a turbine-engine Mil Mi-8.

26 FEBRUARY 1996 (c.19:00)

Location	Near Jabal Awliya, Khartoum, Sudan
Operator	Silakh al Jawwiya as Sudaniya (Sudanese Air Force)
Aircraft type	Lockheed C-130H

The four-engine turboprop transport, which had been on an internal flight from Al-Ubayyid, crashed and burned some 25 miles (40km) south-west of the city of Khartoum while attempting an emergency landing due to an in-flight fire. All 91 military personnel aboard (85 passengers and a crew of six) were killed in the accident, which occurred in darkness and good weather conditions.

9 MARCH 1996 (time unknown)

Location	Near Mesones Muro, Amazonas, Peru
Operator	Aviación del Ejército Peruana (Peruvian Army Aviation)
Aircraft type	Mil Mi-17 (EP-561)

The turbine-engine helicopter, which was on an internal flight from Condorcanqui to Bagua, crashed into a mountain ridge and exploded north of its destination, killing all 23 persons aboard. Nearly half of the victims were civilian passengers, the rest Peruvian military personnel, the latter including the aircraft's crew of four. The heavy fog in which it occurred was probably a significant factor in the accident.

A US Air Force Boeing T-43A – similar to the Boeing 737 derivative that crashed in Croatia. (Boeing)

3 APRIL 1996 (c.16:00)

Location	*Near Dubrovnik, Croatia*
Operator	*US Air Force*
Aircraft type	*Boeing CT-43A (73-1149)*

This mission of economic revitalisation of a war-torn nation would end in tragedy on a rocky mountainside due to a series of errors by an experienced flight crew and flaws reaching into the upper levels of the air force command structure. The aircraft involved had been converted from a navigational trainer so as to have passenger-carrying capability. Having taken off earlier from Tuzla, on the next to last segment of a five-leg flight to various locations within Bosnia-Herzegovina and Croatia, the twin-engine jet was to have landed at Cilipi Airport, serving Dubrovnik, but it crashed and burned during the final phase of a non-directional beacon (NDB) instrument procedure approach to Runway 12. All 35 persons aboard, including a crew of six military personnel, were killed; the

The charred rear fuselage section of the aircraft on which US Secretary of Commerce Ron Brown and 34 others were killed. (AP/ Wide World Photos)

other occupants consisted of a contingent of American business officials, headed by US Secretary of Commerce Ron Brown. Searchers found one passenger in the wreckage showing signs of life, but she was pronounced dead after being taken to a hospital.

With its undercarriage extended and flaps set at 30 degrees, the CT-43 had slammed into St John Hill at an approximate elevation of 2,200ft (670m), only about 100ft (30m) below its summit, some 2 miles (3km) to the left of the runway threshold. Impact speed was calculated to have been around 170mph (270kmh). At the time, the meteorological conditions in the area consisted of a low overcast, with broken clouds at 400ft (120m) and solid coverage at 2,000ft (600m), and a visibility of about 5 miles (10km) in light rain. The wind at ground level was from a direction of 120 degrees at 12 knots.

The investigation of the accident was conducted without the use of either a flight data recorder (FDR) or a cockpit voice recorder (CVR), which normally would have been installed on an equivalent civil jet transport, relying instead on examination of the wreckage and reconstruction of the aircraft's flight path. Although the flight of 73-1149 from Tuzla was actually slightly ahead of schedule, this was somewhat disrupted when the crew attempted to take a course through restricted air space, which resulted from improper planning on their part. This mistake was corrected by an air-traffic controller in an E-3 Airborne Warning and Control System (AWACS) aircraft, but the re-routeing of the flight added some 15 minutes to the trip.

During its descent in preparation for landing, the aircraft's air speed was too high for the application of the correct flap setting, as required by air force directives, but instead of entering a holding pattern in order to effect such stabilisation, the pilots began their approach to the runway without clearance from the controlling air-traffic facility, also in violation of prescribed procedures. Clearance was obtained following passage of the final approach fix (FAF), but its speed at the time remained around 90–115mph (145–185kmh) above the norm.

From the FAF to the point of impact, 73-1149 maintained a heading of 110 degrees, a deviation from the correct course of 119 degrees. When considering the 25-knot wind blowing from a south-easterly direction at the flight altitude, a course correction of 6 degrees would have been required, with the crew using the aircraft's radio magnetic indicator and setting the heading 'bug' on its horizontal situation indicator to 125 degrees. The 'bug' was in fact set at 116 degrees, and the pilot's course select window also indicated the wrong bearing.

Whereas the NBD procedure at Dubrovnik required two automatic direction finder (ADF) receivers, examination revealed the single unit with which the CT-43 was equipped to be tuned to the FAF beacon, designated 'KLP'. The crew could not have identified the missed approach point without a second ADF, and the tuning of the same receiver to different beacons during the final approach would not have been allowed under air force regulations. Examination of the ground-proximity warning system (GPWS) installed on 73-1149 indicated that it did not activate at any time prior to impact, this because it was not designed to respond to the particular combination of terrain profile, aircraft configuration and flight path. The system would in fact have been desensitised when the aircraft's undercarriage and flaps were extended, so as to avoid false alerts. (It was noted in the accident report that a newer, enhanced GPWS would have provided nearly 40 seconds of early warning to the crew of the CT-43.)

The fact that both engines were at higher-than-normal power settings at the time of the crash indicated that the crew may have been initiating a missed approach procedure or pulling up after making visual contact with the ground. That the aircraft had even attempted to land at Dubrovnik Airport represented a failing by the air force command to comply with governing directives from higher headquarters, as the non-precision approach procedure being used there had not been authorised. These directives required a review of all instrument approach procedures not approved by the US Department of Defense to consider the overall safety of the procedure, including the accuracy of navigational facilities and obstacle clearance. A waiver had been requested, but was denied by higher authorities.

The approach at Dubrovnik was found to be improperly designed with regard to obstacle clearance and featured an excessively low minimum descent altitude. Nor was radar monitoring available there. In an effort to reduce controlled-flight-into-terrain type accidents, the US Air Force distributed 100 video tapes on the subject to various flying wings, and also announced the development of a greatly-improved terrain avoidance system for use in some of its aircraft.

12 JUNE 1996 (c.19:00)

Location	Near Rollingstone, Queensland, Australia
First aircraft	
Operator	Australian Army Aviation Corps
Aircraft type	Sikorsky S-70 (A25-113)
Second aircraft	
Operator	Australian Army Aviation Corps
Aircraft type	Sikorsky S-70 (A25-209)

The two turbine-engine helicopters collided in mid-air and crashed some 35 miles (55km) west of Townsville, killing 18 Australian servicemen. Among the ten injured survivors of the accident were nine of the 15 aboard one aircraft; only one of the 13 aboard the other escaped with his life.

Six helicopters were engaged in a night counter-terrorist exercise, flying in an abreast formation, and approaching their drop zone, when the lead aircraft banked to the right. The others failed to follow, however, and when the former's pilot, perhaps fearing a collision, tried to turn back, the main rotor of his aircraft struck the No. 2 helicopter. Following the collision, the No. 1 exploded and slammed to earth in an inverted attitude, while No. 2 crashed and burned during an autorotative landing.

According to the investigative report on the accident, the pilots involved may have been stressed, fatigued and inadequately prepared, and just prior to the accident were flying some 700ft (200m) lower than required in order to see the designated target. Other factors may have been confusion as to the location of the drop zone, a possible course deviation by the group and limitations in the night-vision goggles being used, including a lack of peripheral vision, acute fluctuations in light gain and limited depth perception.

15 JULY 1996 (c.18:00)

Location	Near Eindhoven, North Brabant, The Netherlands
Operator	Belgische Luchtcomponent (Belgian Air Force)
Aircraft type	Lockheed C-130H (CH-06)

The four-engine turboprop transport crashed and burned at Eindhoven Airport, located about 50 miles (80km) south-east of Rotterdam. Thirty-four military personnel aboard, including the four Belgian crew members assigned to the aircraft, lost their lives. The passengers consisted of a Dutch Army band returning from Villafranca, Italy, seven of whom survived with serious injuries. Numerous bird carcasses were found at the accident site, indicating that the C-130 had collided with large flocks of lapwings and starlings despite an attempt by the crew to abandon the visual landing approach to Runway 04, to which they had been cleared. The ingestion of the birds caused, in sequence, the failure of its Nos 1 and 2 power plants. And for unknown reasons, the No. 3 engine was apparently shut down intentionally and the corresponding propeller feathered. The resulting loss of power and asymmetrical thrust condition led to a loss of directional control, making it veer to the left during the attempted go-around manoeuvre. Its port wing then hit the ground, and the transport finally came to rest adjacent to the runway. The accident occurred in fair weather conditions, with scattered clouds at around 5,000ft (1,500m) and good visibility. The wind was from a direction of 10 degrees at 10 knots.

Contributing to the heavy death toll was the failure of the base air-traffic control officer to inform rescue workers of the passengers on CH-06. As a result, the fire-fighters concentrated on extinguishing the blaze, assuming the crew was already dead and that there were no other occupants. They did not gain entry to the cabin for more than half an hour after the crash, even though most or all of those aboard had probably survived the impact. Subsequent to the accident, the Belgian

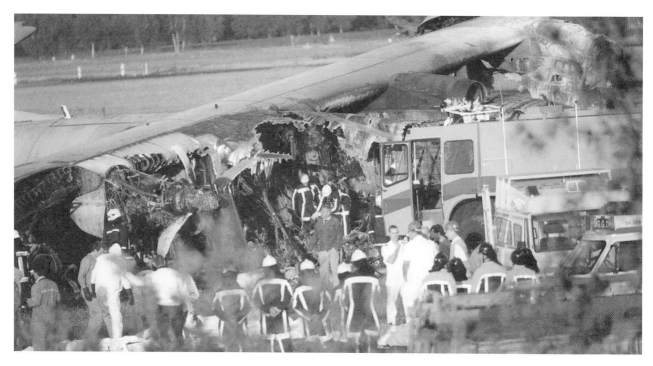

The burned-out hulk of the Belgian Air Force C-130H transport that crashed at an air base near Eindhoven, Holland. (Associated Press)

and Dutch governments asked the International Civil Aviation Organisation (ICAO) to modify its flight plan procedures to ensure that destination airports are aware of the number of passengers aboard an arriving aircraft.

27 NOVEMBER 1996 (c.23:50)

Location	*Near Mokhovo, Russian Federation, Commonwealth of Independent States*
Operator	*Russian Air Force*
Aircraft type	*Ilyushin Il-76MD (RA-76804)*

Operating on an internal cargo flight to Petropavlovsk-Kamchatsky, the jet transport crashed into a mountain and exploded about 10 miles (15km) from Abakan, itself located in Siberia some 2,500 miles (4,000km) east of Moscow, and from where it had taken off shortly before. All 23 persons aboard (13 passengers and a crew of ten) perished. Overloading was believed to have been a factor in the accident, which occurred in darkness.

24 DECEMBER 1996 (c.15:40)

Location	*Near Nellore, Andhra Pradesh, India*
Operator	*Indian Air Force*
Aircraft type	*Hindustan Aeronautics HAL 748 Series 2 (H1032)*

All 22 Indian military personnel aboard (18 passengers and a crew of four) were killed when the twin-engine turboprop transport crashed in a field about 100 miles (150km) north of

Madras, Tamil Nadu. The aircraft had been on an internal flight from Tambaram Air Force Station, located near Madras, to Hyderabad, Andhra Pradesh, and the accident occurred after its left power plant separated from the wing, leading to the loss of the wing itself. Cracks were reportedly found in the same engine, which had not been detected during maintenance.

2 FEBRUARY 1997 (c.17:30)

Location	*Near Quibaxe, Cuanza Norte, Angola*
Operator	*Força Aérea Popular de Angola (Angolan Air Force)*
Aircraft type	*CASA 212-200 Aviocar (T-400)*

All 37 military personnel aboard were killed, including a crew of three, in the crash of the twin-engine turboprop transport. The aircraft had been on an internal flight from Luanda to Cafunfo, but prior to the accident was seen heading in the opposite direction, i.e. towards the south, and appeared to be in difficulty.

4 FEBRUARY 1997 (c.19:00)

Location	*Northern Israel*
First aircraft	
Operator	*Israel Defence Force Air Force*
Aircraft type	*Sikorsky CH-53D (357)*
Second aircraft	
Operator	*Israel Defence Force Air Force*
Aircraft type	*Sikorsky CH-53D (903)*

In the worst military aviation disaster in the history of Israel, the two turbine-engine rotorcraft collided, crashed and exploded near She'ar Yeshuv, in the Galilee panhandle. All 73 servicemen aboard them were killed, including two four-member crews assigned to each aircraft.

The two helicopters had taken off shortly before from a landing strip in Israel and were ferrying ground troops into southern Lebanon. The subsequent collision occurred in darkness, but otherwise good meteorological conditions, at an approximate altitude of 300ft (100m) above the ground and about 10 miles (15km) from the border of the two countries, with the rear aircraft, 357, striking 903 with its main rotor blades, the impact tearing off the former's entire rotor head and the aft fuselage of the latter. After they hit, one CH-53 fell onto some unoccupied houses and the other into a cemetery.

Although the cause of the disaster could not be determined, possible contributing factors were a lack of knowledge by both aircraft commanders as to who was to be the flight leader and inexperience by both as lead pilots. Also, there were no clear instructions when pilots were to turn off their lights, for security reasons, when crossing into Lebanon. Included among the recommendations of the investigative report was allowing helicopters entering Lebanese airspace to fly separately in most cases, and that a flight leader must be designated in operations involving more than one aircraft.

13 MARCH 1997 (c.18:00)

Location	*Near Mirabad, Khorasan, Iran*
Operator	*Islamic Republic of Iran Air Force*
Aircraft type	*Lockheed C-130H*

The four-engine turboprop transport, carrying as passengers servicemen and their dependants, crashed in mountainous terrain some 25 miles (40km) west of Mashhad, where it was to have landed during an internal flight from Dezful, Khuzestan. All 88 persons aboard, including a military crew, were killed in the accident, which occurred around dusk and was reportedly related to power plant failure.

The Luftwaffe Tu-154M jet transport (11+02), the aircraft lost in a mid-air collision with a US Air Force C-141B over the South Atlantic Ocean. (AP/Wide World Photos)

23 APRIL 1997 (time unknown)

Location	*Afghanistan*
Operator	*Afghan Republican Air Force*
Aircraft type	*Antonov An-26*

The twin-engine turboprop transport crashed into a mountain in the province of Konduz, killing all 36 persons aboard.

6 JULY 1997 (time unknown)

Location	*Near Saravena, Meta, Colombia*
Operator	*Ejército de Colombia (Colombian Army)*
Aircraft type	*Mil Mi-17*

Chartered from the civilian company Helicol Colombia and carrying as passengers Colombian soldiers who were to protect workers at the scene of a sabotaged oil pipeline, the turbine-engine helicopter was shot down by rebels some 220 miles (350km) east of Bogotá. Among the 25 persons killed were the four members of the aircraft's civilian crew; four soldiers survived. The Mi-17 was reportedly hit at an approximate height of 300–600ft (100–180m) above the ground, then crashed and exploded.

13 SEPTEMBER 1997 (c.17:10)

Location	*South Atlantic Ocean*
First aircraft	
Operator	*Luftwaffe (German Air Force)*
Aircraft type	*Tupolev Tu-154M (11+02)*
Second aircraft	
Operator	*US Air Force*
Aircraft type	*Lockheed C-141B (65-9405)*

The two jet transports collided in mid-air and crashed about 75 miles (120km) off the coast of Namibia. Among the 33 persons aboard both of them, the body of only one victim – a flight attendant from the German aircraft – was recovered; there were no survivors. Pieces of wreckage were also found in the water, which was some 3,000ft (1,000m) deep in the area.

Both aircraft had been flying at an approximate height of 35,000ft (10,500m), their crews apparently unaware of each other's presence, at the time of the collision. The Tu-154, carrying 12 German marines and two civilian passengers plus a crew of 10, had been en route from Cologne, Germany, to Cape Town, South Africa, with a planned refuelling stop at Windhoek, Namibia, from where the C-141 had taken off, bound for the US via Ascension Island, with nine crewmen aboard.

According to a US Air Force investigative report, the German transport had not been flying at the altitude requested in its flight plan, 39,000ft (12,000m). In fact, neither its requested nor its actual height conformed with guidelines for an aircraft flying on this particular south-easterly heading. German authorities issued a statement acknowledging the error of its crew. The American transport had been at its assigned cruising altitude when the collision occurred. Inadequacies in the Angolan air-traffic control service responsible for flights in its air space and poor communications between controlling agencies, the latter attributed to the 'complicated and sporadic operation' of the Aeronautical Fixed Telecommunications Network (AFTN), were considered as contributing factors.

Neither transport had been equipped with an airborne collision-avoidance system, which should have prevented the accident. Subsequently, both the US Air Force and the Luftwaffe announced plans to install the safety systems on some of their large aircraft.

6 DECEMBER 1997 (c.14:45)

Location	*Irkutsk, Russian Federation,*
	Commonwealth of Independent States
Operator	*Russian Air Force*
Aircraft type	*Antonov An-124-100 (UR-82005/08)*

The four-engine wide-bodied jet transport, on an internal flight to Vladivostok and carrying two Sukhoi Su-27 jet fighters, crashed into a block of apartment buildings and burned only about 20 seconds after it had taken off from

An Antonov An-124 heavy-lift jet transport, shown in the colour scheme of the Russian airline Aeroflot but otherwise similar to the military aircraft that crashed at Irkutsk. (Douglas Green)

the Irkutsk aircraft factory. Killed in the disaster were all 23 military personnel aboard the transport (17 crew members and six passengers), and 44 other persons on the ground. About a dozen others suffered injuries.

All four of the aircraft's power plants had failed, the No. 4 first, followed in succession by 3, 2 and 1, reportedly due to the use of warm-weather fuel in below-freezing temperatures that lead to the clogging of the fuel filters by ice crystals, with defective design a possible contributing factor. The An-124 fleet would be grounded for six months after this accident.

13 JANUARY 1998 (c.22:30)

Location	*Near Chaman, Quetta-Pishin, Pakistan*
Operator	*Afghan Taliban Militia*
Aircraft type	*Antonov An-12*

The four-engine turboprop transport, carrying as passengers Taliban soldiers and originally on a flight within Afghanistan, from Kandahar to Herat, crashed and burned near the Khojak Pass some 75 miles (120km) north of Quetta and about 10 miles (15km) from the Afghan border. All 51 persons aboard the aircraft, including the six members of its crew, were killed.

Unable to land in the adverse meteorological weather conditions at either Herat or Shindand, the An-12 proceeded back to Kandahar, but the weather there had also deteriorated, preventing a safe landing. It then flew back to Quetta, but the aircraft may have run out of fuel after receiving initial landing clearance. The accident occurred in darkness and conditions of reduced visibility, with heavy rain and snow, which were accompanied by strong winds.

3 FEBRUARY 1998 (c.15:15)

Location	*Near Cavalese, Trentino-Alto Adige, Italy*
Operator	*US Marine Corps*
Aircraft type	*Grumman EA-6B (163045)*

This tragedy, which would create some diplomatic rancour between two NATO allies, began as a low-level training flight out of the Aviano Air Base, near Vittorio in Italy. On at least two of the six legs of the mission, the maximum speed and minimum altitude restrictions were exceeded, culminating in the twin-jet electronic counter-measures aircraft striking and severing two cables, one about 370ft (110m) above the ground and the other 6ft (2m) lower, which were suspending an aerial tram at the Cermis ski resort, some 30 miles (50km) north-east of the city of Trento. The gondola then plummeted about 300ft (100m) to earth, and all 20 occupants were killed. The aircraft sustained substantial damage, but nevertheless returned safely to the base, its four-man crew escaping injury.

The disaster was attributed to error by the crew of 163045, who, according to the Marine Corps investigative report, 'aggressively' manoeuvred their aircraft, flying above the speed limit of approximately 520mph (840kmh) and well below the prescribed minimum height in the area of the accident of 2,000ft (600m), and even below the altitude at which the flight had been planned, and the crew briefed, of 1,000ft (300m).

Though not considered directly contributory to the tragedy, this discrepancy between the briefed and actual minimum altitudes was attributed to a squadron supervisory error, specifically, the failure to ensure a 'read-and-initial' programme of providing vital information to flight crews. Significantly, it was learned that while several documents distributed to the squadron stipulated the fact, all but 3 of the 18 crew members assigned to the squadron were unaware of the 2,000ft minimum in the area of the accident, which had been imposed as a noise-abatement measure. The No. 1 electronic counter-measures (ECO) officer of 163045, who would also have been responsible for navigation and was positioned in the front right seat beside the pilot, later stated that the crew was neither aware of the minimum height nor the ski resort itself. Nevertheless, three separate copies of a kneeboard card containing that information were found in the accident aircraft. The meteorological conditions in the area at the time consisted of a few clouds at around 20,000ft (6,000m) and a visibility of 7 miles (11km). The wind was from almost due south at 4 knots.

The pilot of the EA-6B, who had not flown a low-level mission in six months and may have experienced an optical illusion with regard to his height, saw the cables at the last moment, and tried to dive below them. Rolled approximately 45 degrees to the left and in a nose-down longitudinal

Shown in US Navy markings, this Grumman EA-6B is otherwise the same as the Marine Corps aircraft involved in the accident at an Italian ski resort. (Northrop Grumman)

attitude, the aircraft struck the 2¼in (57mm) load-bearing cable, which supported the gondola, and the 7/8in (20mm) drive cable beneath it with its starboard wing, vertical stabiliser and station 5 jamming pod.

The Naval Air Training and Operating Procedures Standardisation (NATOPS) manual states that pilots shall utilise their radar altimeter at low altitudes to maximise safety. The system on 163045 was found to have been functioning properly, although the aural height alert was not reported by the crew. No other technical failures were found in the aircraft that could have been a factor in the disaster.

The investigative board found no pattern of 'unprofessional or reckless' attitudes within the squadron that could have contributed to the accident. Although the US Marine Corps chain of command was found to be 'cumbersome and complicated', this was not considered to be a factor. It was noted in the accident report that during

The flattened gondola car in which 20 persons lost their lives when the American military jet cut its support and drive cables while flying at extremely low altitude. (AP/Wide World Photos)

the 18 months before the tragedy, minimum training altitudes were in a constant state of flux, resulting in some confusion, but had been fixed at 1,000ft about six months before it actually occurred.

Subsequently, the squadron commander to which 163045 belonged was relieved of his duty and re-assigned, while both the pilot-in-command and the navigator were convicted in a US military court of conspiracy and obstruction of justice for hiding and later having destroyed a videotape recorded in the cockpit of the EA-6B, which could have provided crucial evidence in determining exactly how it brought down the gondola. The latter two were dismissed from the marines, the pilot after serving most of a six-month prison term. The families of the victims received a settlement of nearly US$2 million each, with most of the cost being borne by the American government. Additionally, the US military announced that it would look elsewhere for areas to practise low-level flight operations due to Italy's restrictive rules.

12 FEBRUARY 1998 (c.08:30)

Location	*Near Nasir, Sobat, Sudan*
Operator	*Al Quwwat al Jawwiya As Sudaniya (Sudanese Air Force)*
Aircraft type	*Antonov An-26*

Sudan's First Vice-President, Lt Gen Al-Zubeir Mohammad Saleh, was among 27 persons killed when the twin-engine turboprop transport overshot the runway while landing in a heavy fog at a small airfield and ploughed into the River Sobat. Most of the 30 survivors were reported injured.

29 MARCH 1998 (c.09:30)

Location	*Near Piura, Peru*
Operator	*Fuerza Aérea del Perú (Peruvian Air Force)*
Aircraft type	*Antonov An-32 (FAP-388)*

The twin-engine turboprop transport, which was evacuating civilians from areas of flooding, crashed in a canal about 1 mile (1.5km) from Capitan Guillermo Concha Iberico Airport, serving Piura, killing 28 of the 61 persons aboard and 1 on the ground. Among the survivors, who included the five members of its crew, 20 suffered injuries. Reportedly, the aircraft had experienced a loss of power in one engine, then stalled during its landing approach.

20 APRIL 1998 (c.16:44)

Location	*Near Bogotá, Colombia*
Operator	*Fuerza Aérea Ecuatoriana (Ecuadorean Air Force)*
Aircraft type	*Boeing Advanced 727-230 (FAE-560)*

Operated by the military airline Transportes Aéreos Militares Ecuatorianos (TAME) as Flight 422, a scheduled passenger service being conducted on behalf of the civilian carrier Air France, and bound for Quito, Ecuador, the jet transport crashed in the Andes some 5 miles (10km) south-east of El

Dorado International Airport, serving the capital city, from where it had taken off about 4 minutes earlier. All 53 persons aboard (43 passengers and a crew of ten) perished.

Following its departure from Runway 13, the aircraft failed to make a right procedural turn of approximately 90 degrees upon reaching an above-ground height of 400ft (120m) or the Romeo radio beacon, whichever came first, and took no action despite a ground controller's warning that it was off course. Subsequently, FAE-560 struck the mountain Cerro el Cable at an elevation of around 10,000ft (3,000m), only about 150ft (50m) below its summit, and while on a south-easterly heading, exploding on impact. At the time of the accident, the weather conditions in the area consisted of thunderstorm activity, with a broken overcast at 1,700ft (520m) and scattered clouds at 8,000ft (2,500m), and a visibility of slightly less than 1.5 miles (2.5km) in rain showers. The wind was at 5 knots from a direction of 220 degrees. Significantly, the mountain struck by the 727 was shrouded in cloud. The crash was attributed to 'a loss of situational awareness' on the part of the flight crew.

5 MAY 1998 (c.21:30)

Location	*Near Tintiyacu, Loreto, Peru*
Operator	*Fuerza Aérea del Perú (Peruvian Air Force)*
Aircraft type	*Boeing Advanced 737-282 (FAP-351)*

Chartered by the American firm Occidental Peruana to carry oil workers to a company camp, the jet transport crashed and burned in a swamp about 3 miles (5km) north of Andoas Airport, where it was to have landed, and some 700 miles (1,100km) north of Lima. Killed in the accident were 75 of the 88 persons aboard; one member of the aircraft's crew of seven and 12 passengers survived with serious injuries. Having nearly completed a domestic flight from Iquitos, the 737 slammed into a swamp during the final phase of a non-directional beacon (NDB) procedure approach to Runway 12, the crash occurring in darkness and light rain.

12 MAY 1998 (c.19:30)

Location	*Near Nema, Mauritania*
Operator	*Force Aérienne Islamique de Mauritanie (Mauritanian Air Force)*
Aircraft type	*Xian Y-7H-500 (5T-MAG)*

The twin-engine turboprop transport crashed during a sandstorm shortly after it had taken off, killing 39 persons aboard. There were three survivors. Other than seven civilians, the fatalities were military personnel.

25 MAY 1998 (c.10:20)

Location	*Near Longtiang, Laos*
Operator	*Lao People's Liberation Army Air Force*
Aircraft type	*Yakovlev Yak-40 (ZPX 01)*

All 26 persons aboard were killed when the jet transport, which was carrying a Vietnamese delegation on an internal

Laotian flight from Vientiane to Xiang Khoang, crashed during a heavy rainstorm. The aircraft struck a jungle-covered mountainside at an approximate elevation of 6,000ft (1,800m) and exploded, possibly after a premature descent as it was preparing to land.

2 SEPTEMBER 1998 (time unknown)

Location	*Near Kafunfo, Lunda Norte, Angola*
Operator	*Força Aérea Popular de Angola (Angolan Air Force)*
Aircraft type	*Antonov An-26B (RA-26028)*

Chartered from the Russian carrier Permtransavia PM and reportedly carrying military personnel, the twin-engine turboprop transport crashed some 50 miles (80km) north-east of Luanda, from where it had taken off earlier, on an internal flight within Angola. All 24 persons aboard the An-26, including a crew of four, were killed. The pilot had earlier reported a power plant fire and that he would attempt an emergency landing, first at Malange and then 'straight ahead'. At the moment of impact, the aircraft's undercarriage was retracted and its flaps were set at 25 degrees. There were reports that the RA-26028 had been shot down by UNITA rebels, although the organisation denied responsibility.

21 JANUARY 1999 (c.08:00)

Location	*Near Bluefields, Atlantico Sur, Nicaragua*
Operator	*Fuerza Aérea de Nicaragua (Nicaraguan Air Force)*
Aircraft type	*Antonov An-26 (152)*

During an internal flight to Bluefields from Managua, the twin-engine turboprop transport crashed into a hillside some 10 miles (16km) south of its destination. All 28 persons aboard the aircraft, including a crew of 4 military personnel, were killed in the accident. The victims included 15 civilian dependants travelling as passengers.

5 MARCH 1999 (time unknown)

Location	*Near Hakkari, Turkey*
Operator	*Turk Kara Kuvvetleri (Turkish Land Forces)*
Aircraft type	*Sikorsky S-70A*

All 20 occupants were killed when the turbine-engine helicopter crashed in the Cilo Mountains in the vicinity of the Iraqi border. Kurdistan guerrillas claimed to have shot down the aircraft.

7 MARCH 1999 (c.08:30)

Location	*Near Delhi, India*
Operator	*Indian Air Force*
Aircraft type	*Antonov An-32 (K-2673)*

As it was approaching to land at Indira Gandhi International Airport, serving the Indian capital city, the twin-engine turboprop transport crashed and exploded, smashing through several brick huts at a water tank construction site. Killed in the accident were all 18 Indian military personnel aboard the aircraft and six persons on the ground. At least a dozen others suffered injuries.

The An-32 had been on an internal flight from Agra to Allahabad, with two en-route stops. During an instrument landing system (ILS) approach to Runway 10, the An-32 descended considerably below the proper glide path, and the crash occurred after its extended undercarriage reportedly clipped overhead wires. It was foggy in the area at the time of the accident, with a visibility of around 1,500ft (500m). Two possible causes of the crash were disorientation of the crew, or their attempt to proceed visually in the adverse weather conditions.

3 JUNE 1999 (time unknown)

Location	*Near Wad Hassuna, Khartoum, Sudan*
Operator	*Al Quwwat al-Jawwiya As-Sudaniya (Sudanese Air Force)*
Aircraft type	*Lockheed C-130H Hercules*

The four-engine turboprop transport, on an internal Sudanese flight from Kassala to the city of Khartoum, crashed some 50 miles (80km) east of its intended destination. All 50 military personnel aboard the aircraft were killed in the accident, which was reportedly attributed to 'mechanical failure'.

10 SEPTEMBER 1999 (time unknown)

Location	*Afghanistan*
Operator	*Afghan Republican Air Force*
Aircraft type	*Helicopter*

The rotorcraft crashed while on an internal flight from Kabul to Kandahar, killing at least 20 persons.

29 OCTOBER 1999 (c.12:00)

Location	*Near Pasni, Baluchistan, Pakistan*
Operator	*Pakistan Navy*
Aircraft type	*Lockheed P-3C (83)*

The four-engine turboprop patrol aircraft crashed in the Arabian Sea some 200 miles (320km) west of Karachi, the accident occurring during an air/sea exercise, and all 21 members of its crew were killed. Searchers recovered some wreckage and at least one body not long after the crash.

5 FEBRUARY 2000 (time unknown)

Location	*Near Lubango, Huila, Angola*
Operator	*Força Aérea Popular de Angola (Angolan Air Force)*
Aircraft type	*Mil Mi-8*

All 30 persons aboard lost their lives when the turbine-engine helicopter crashed at Lubango Air Force Base, from where it had just taken off, the accident apparently resulting from the overloading of the aircraft.

30 MARCH 2000 (time unknown)

Location	*Near Anuradhapura, Sri Lanka*
Operator	*Sri Lanka Air Force*
Aircraft type	*Antonov An-26 (UR-79170)*

Chartered from a private Ukrainian company, Avialinii AAR, and carrying as passengers troops, some of them wounded, the twin-engine turboprop transport was shot down by Tamil Tiger rebels approximately 10 miles (15km) south of Anuradhapura. All 40 persons aboard the aircraft were killed, including its crew of four. The An-26 was struck by a surface-to-air missile during an internal Sri Lankan flight to Colombo from Palaly Air Base, near Jaffna.

8 APRIL 2000 (c.20:00)

Location	*Near Marana, Arizona, USA*
Operator	*US Marine Corps*
Aircraft type	*Bell/Boeing MV-22B Osprey (165436)*

The turbine-engine vertical take-off and landing (VTOL) aircraft crashed and burned while preparing to land at Marana Regional Airport, located some 20 miles (30km) north-west of Tucson. All 19 American military personnel aboard, including a crew of four, lost their lives in the accident.

The crash occurred during a night-training exercise, in which 165436 was one of two aircraft of the same type that were participating. According to the investigative report, the sequence of events began with both aircraft arriving at their final approach initiation point 2,000ft (600m) above the height for which the crews had been briefed. The MV-22 that was leading attempted a rapid descent into the landing zone,

A Bell/Boeing MV-22 Osprey vertical take-off and landing aircraft, the type involved in the 19-fatality crash in Arizona. (US Marine Corps)

followed by 165436. Unbeknown to the pilots of the latter, the tail wind of 10 to 15 knots had reduced their indicated air speed. This combined with the high rate of descent and the crew's control inputs induced a 'vortex ring state', or rotor blade stall, leading to an asymmetrical loss of lift of the twin propeller/rotor units. Subsequent control inputs exacerbated the condition, resulting in a total loss of control.

Among the actions of the Marine Corps in the wake of this accident were the continued evaluation of the MV-22 to help better understand the flight characteristics of this unique aircraft, and the possible development and installation of a warning system that would recognise low air speeds and an unsafe rate of descent.

19 APRIL 2000 (time unknown)

Location	*Near Pepa, Katanga, Congo*
Operator	*Rwanda Air Force*
Aircraft type	*Antonov An-8 (TL-ACM)*

Chartered from Centralafrican Airlines and bound for Kigali, Rwanda, the twin-engine turboprop transport crashed and exploded near the southern tip of Lake Tanganyika, killing all 24 persons aboard. The victims included several Rwanda military officers and four Russian crew members. Reportedly, the An-8 experienced a bird strike immediately after taking off, leading to the failure of a power plant, and the aircraft subsequently lost height while apparently attempting to return to the Pepa airstrip.

19 OCTOBER 2000 (time unknown)

Location	*Near Dabeiba, Antioquia, Colombia*
Operator	*Ejército de Colombia (Colombian Army)*
Aircraft type	*Sikorsky UH-60L Black Hawk (EJC-152)*

The turbine-engine helicopter crashed some 80 miles (130km) north-west of Medellin, killing all 22 Colombian servicemen aboard, including a crew of four. According to military authorities, its main rotor may have struck the ground as the aircraft was landing, although rebel forces claimed to have shot down the Black Hawk.

25 OCTOBER 2000 (c.18:15)

Location	*Near Bat'umi, Georgia*
Operator	*Russian Air Force*
Aircraft type	*Ilyushin Il-18D (SSSR-74295)*

The four-engine turboprop transport, carrying as passengers service personnel and their dependants, crashed and burned about 10 miles (15km) east of Chorokh Airport, serving Batumi, where it was to have landed. All 83 persons aboard the aircraft, including 11 crew members, were killed. Having nearly completed a flight from Chkalovskiy Air Base, near Moscow, Russia, SSSR-74295 had made its approach from the north-east, instead of the normal track from the west, and after initiating a descent from 10,000ft (3,000m) it slammed into a mountain at an approximate elevation of 4,000ft (1,300m), the accident occurring in darkness and adverse weather conditions, with clouds and rain.

The deviation from the proper track was considered to have been the primary causative factor. Contributing factors were a navigational error by the crew during the final approach phase; the failure of the air-traffic controller properly to identify the aircraft and notify the crew of the deviation; the failure of the crew, with the controller's input, to proceed to an alternate airport under the prevailing conditions; and technical failures in the ground facilities at the Batumi airport.

4 JANUARY 2001 (c.12:45)

Location	*Xianrenzhuang, Henan, China*
First aircraft	
Operator	*People's Liberation Army Air Force*
Aircraft type	*Shaanxi Yunshuji Y-8 (31242)*
Second aircraft	
Operator	*People's Liberation Army Air Force*
Aircraft type	*Shaanxi Yunshuji Y-8 (31243)*

The two four-engine turboprop transports crashed either separately due to tailplane icing or after a mid-air collision as they were approaching to land at Zhengzhou Air Base, with one of them striking a house. Killed in the accident were all 16 crew members of both aircraft, eight in each, plus six persons on the ground.

3 MARCH 2001 (c.09:55)

Location	*Near Unadilla, Georgia, USA*
Operator	*US Army*
Aircraft type	*Short C-23B Sherpa (93-1336)*

Operated by the Florida Army National Guard, the twin-engine turboprop transport crashed and burned in a ploughed field about 100 miles (150km) south-south-east of Atlanta. All 21 American servicemen aboard the aircraft,

A US Army Short C-23B Sherpa, identical to the aircraft that crashed in Georgia after encountering a severe thunderstorm. (US Army)

including a crew of three, perished; the passengers were members of the Virginia Air National Guard.

The accident occurred in an area of severe thunderstorm activity, accompanied by strong turbulence, heavy rain and a low ceiling, as the Sherpa had been on a US domestic interstate flight from Hurlburt Field, near Pensacola, Florida, to Oceana Naval Air Station, near Virginia Beach, Virginia. Some 40 minutes before their departure, the crew of 93-1336 had been briefed by a weather forecaster to fly 'as far east as possible before turning north' to avoid the adverse meteorological conditions along their route. During the flight, air-traffic control personnel informed them that they had observed the Sherpa on the edge of level 3 to 4 thunderstorm activity and level 5 build-ups embedded within. Nevertheless, the plotted route and their conversation transcribed on the aircraft's cockpit voice recorder (CVR) tape clearly indicated that the pilots made 'conscious decisions' to remain close to their filed flight plan, with no evidence that they discussed the weather warnings received or devised an option to alter their course away from what was a 'significant' storm system. The transport was observed on radar at its assigned cruising height of 9,000ft (2,700m) before it began to descend. Its last recorded altitude was just under 5,000ft (1,500m).

According to the investigative report, 93-1336 was overweight and improperly loaded at the time of take-off, and its cargo apparently shifted when the pilot got out of his seat to use the lavatory. Following a loss of control, the aircraft suffered structural failure. (The occupants were believed to have been incapacitated by the high gravitational forces prior to the break-up of the Sherpa). However, the chief investigator expressed the opinion that the crash resulted from an encounter with extreme turbulence and wind shear, with weight imbalance and poor route selection considered as contributing factors. He also said that the aircraft's autopilot may not have been functioning properly.

The investigative board noted that the weather radar installed on 93-1336 was not giving the crew accurate information, but that this did not factor in the accident, since the pilots had been warned of their proximity to the thunderstorm activity. Among the recommendations made by the board were more checks to ensure proper functioning of weather radar units and improved training of pilots in their use. More restrictive centre-of-gravity requirements in the C-23 were also implemented pending further testing.

16 MAY 2001 (c.13:15)

Location	*Near Arapkir, Malatya, Turkey*
Operator	*Türk Hava Kuvvelteri (Turkish Air Force)*
Aircraft type	*CASA/IPTN CN.235M-100 (86)*

The twin-engine turboprop transport crashed in a field some 150 miles (250km) north-west of Diyarbakir, from where it had taken off earlier, on an internal Turkish flight to Ankara. All 34 military personnel aboard the aircraft lost their lives in the accident, including a crew of six; the passengers were all special forces commandos. According to unconfirmed reports, the CN.235 experienced a loss of control at 17,000ft (5,200m), possibly due to icing. Additionally, the transport was reportedly overloaded.

2 DECEMBER 2001 (c.06:00)

Location	*Near Novaya Inya, Russia*
Operator	*(Russian) Federal Border Guard Aviation Command*
Aircraft type	*Ilyushin Il-76TD (RA-76839)*

The jet transport crashed approximately 65 miles (105km) east of Okhotsk while on an internal Russian flight from Moscow to Bratsk, and all 18 persons aboard were killed. While cruising in predawn darkness at around 30,000ft (10,000m), the crew reported an in-flight fire in its cargo hold before the aircraft slammed into a forest after an emergency descent had been initiated.

2 JUNE 2002 (time unknown)

Location	*Near Ndalatando, Angola*
Operator	*Força Aérea Popular de Angola (Angolan Air Force)*
Aircraft type	*Mil Mi-17*

The turbine-engine helicopter crashed in adverse weather conditions some 125 miles (200km) east of Luanda, from where it had taken off earlier, bound for a demobilisation camp at Mussabo. Killed in the accident were 20 persons aboard the aircraft, while five others survived with various injuries.

27 JULY 2002 (c.13:00)

Location	*Near L'viv, Ukraine*
Operator	*Ukrainian Air Force*
Aircraft type	*Sukhoi Su-27UB Flanker (42)*

In history's worst air show disaster, 77 persons on the ground were killed, including some two dozen children, when the jet fighter crashed in a crowd of spectators at

The flaming crash of the Ukrainian Air Force Sukhoi Su-27 jet fighter at the L'viv airport resulted in history's worst air show disaster, claiming the lives of 77 persons on the ground. (Yuri Rura/AP/Press Association Images)

L'viv International (Skryliv) Airport. Both of its crewmen, who ejected before the main impact of the aircraft, were among the approximately 120 persons injured in the tragedy. Additionally, a L'viv Airlines Ilyushin Il-76MD jet transport was struck by debris and damaged.

The pilots had not been properly briefed as to what they were supposed to do during the aerial display, and during the performance they deviated from the flight plan and descended too low. After an apparent loss of control, the Flanker hit the runway, then slid into the spectator area and exploded. Other military personnel were blamed for not ordering a change of course. The local weather conditions at the time were good and apparently not a factor in the accident.

As a result of the disaster, the commander of the Ukrainian Air Force and three other high-ranking officers were prosecuted for what an official statement referred to as 'serious errors in organising, preparing and conducting flights, in particular demonstration flights at L'viv'. The two crewmen flying the fighter were subsequently sentenced to prison for violating safety rules during their aerobatic performance. The investigative commission recommended restructuring of the Ukrainian armed forces.

19 AUGUST 2002 (c.16:50)

Location	*Near Groznyy, Chechnya, Commonwealth of Independent States*
Operator	*Russian Ground Forces*
Aircraft type	*Mil Mi-26T (89)*

This first helicopter disaster to claim more than 100 lives occurred when the turbine-engine rotorcraft was shot down by Chechan rebels as it was approaching to land at the Russian military headquarters at Khankala. A total of 127 persons lost their lives, including at least two civilians; 25 others aboard survived, including the five members of its crew, and all but seven of the latter were injured. The Mi-26 was carrying mostly servicemen when hit by a surface-to-air missile at an approximate height of 1,000ft (300m). It then plummeted into a field that was possibly filled with mines and burned. As a result of this disastrous combat loss, operations using this type of aircraft were stopped in Chechnya. The fact that the 89 had been used in a troop operation violated a defence ministry decree issued five years earlier.

19 FEBRUARY 2003 (c.18:30)

Location	*Near Balbuyeh, Kerman, Iran*
Operator	*Islamic Revolutionary Guard Corps Air Force*
Aircraft type	*Ilyushin Il-76MD (15-22)*

In history's worst military aviation disaster, the jet transport crashed some 500 miles (800km) south-east of Tehran and about 20 miles (30km) south-east of the city of Kerman, which was its destination at the end of an internal Iranian flight from Zahedan. All 276 Iranian military personnel aboard the aircraft were killed, including a crew of 18; the passengers were members of the nation's Revolutionary Guards corps.

During the descent in darkness and adverse meteorological conditions, with strong winds reported, 15-22 struck Sirach Mountain only about 300ft (100m) below its peak and at an approximate elevation of 11,500ft (3,500m). According to one report, the pilot had in his last radio transmission stated his intention to 'get closer' to the airport, where, presumably, the weather was better, while another indicated that the aircraft had descended below a safe height during the initial approach phase.

20 FEBRUARY 2003 (c.08:30)

Location	*Near Gambat, Pakistan*
Operator	*Pakistan Air Force*
Aircraft type	*Fokker F.27 Friendship Mark 200 (10254)*

All 17 persons aboard were killed when the twin-engine turboprop transport, on an internal Pakistani flight to Kohat from Islamabad, some 150 miles (250km) to the south-east, struck a cloud-obscured mountain about 20 miles (30km) east of its destination. Other than the wife of a Pakistan Air Force commander who was aboard, the victims were all military personnel, including the aircraft's crew of eight.

In violation of standard operating procedures, the pilot had initiated a premature descent in an apparent attempt to make visual contact with the ground, resulting in the impact at an approximate elevation of 3,000ft (1,000m). Despite the low overcast, the conditions were within the operating minima, and no technical anomalies in the F.27 were identified that could have factored in the crash.

26 FEBRUARY 2003 (c.06:30)

Location	*Near Pailiatas, Cesar, Colombia*
Operator	*Ejército de Colombia (Colombian Army)*
Aircraft type	*Sikorsky UH-60L Black Hawk (EJC-163)*

The turbine-engine helicopter crashed around 300 miles (480km) north-east of Bogotá, killing all 23 military personnel aboard (17 passengers and a crew of six). One of three aircraft on an internal Colombian flight from Loma to Curumani, EJC-163 flew into the side of a hill after the formation had split up when it encountered adverse weather conditions, in which the accident apparently occurred.

28 OCTOBER 2003 (time unknown)

Location	*Umm Saiyala, Northern Kordofan, Sudan*
Operator	*Al Quwwat al-Jawwiya As-Sudaniya (Sudanese Air Force)*
Aircraft type	*Helicopter*

All 20 persons aboard lost their lives when the rotorcraft, possibly a turbine-engine Mil Mi-8, crashed some 150 miles (250km) south-west of Khartoum after an apparent technical malfunction. Other than one of the passengers who was a civilian, the victims were military personnel, including the crew of eight.

15 NOVEMBER 2003 (c.18:30)

Location   *Mosul, Iraq*
First aircraft
Operator   US Army
Aircraft type   *Sikorsky UH-60L Black Hawk (93-26531)*
Second aircraft
Operator   US Army
Aircraft type   *Sikorsky UH-60L Black Hawk (94-26548)*

During the occupation of Iraq by Western military forces, the two turbine-engine helicopters collided in mid-air, and both then crashed into the city of Mosul. A total of 17 American military personnel were killed in the incident, although five of the 12 aboard one aircraft survived. There were no reported casualties on the ground. The two rotorcraft had been flying together in darkness at an approximate height of 400ft (120m), reportedly in the pursuit of insurgents, when one was apparently struck by a rocket-propelled grenade, after which it flew into the other Black Hawk. The wreckage of at least one of the helicopters burned after its impact with the ground.

29 NOVEMBER 2003 (c.16:00)

Location   *Near Boende, Equateur, Congo*
Operator   *Force Aérienne Congolaise (Congolese*
                  Air Force)
Aircraft type   *Antonov An-26 (9T-TAD)*

The twin-engine turboprop transport crashed into a market and caught fire after an aborted take-off at Boende airport, some 500 miles (800km) north-east of Kinshasa, which was its destination. A total of 37 persons lost their lives in the accident, including the five crew members and all but four passengers among the 26 aboard 9T-TAD; the rest were on the ground. The survivors suffered serious injuries. One of its tyres had reportedly failed during the take-off run, and the aircraft could not be brought to a safe stop on the unpaved runway.

21 AUGUST 2004 (c.16:15)

Location   *Near Maracay, Aragua, Venezuela*
Operator   *Fuerza Aérea Venezolana (Venezuelan*
                  Air Force)
Aircraft type   *Shorts 360-300 (FAV-1652)*

The twin-engine turboprop transport crashed approximately 40 miles (65km) south-west of Caracas and some 15 miles (25km) from El Libertador Air Base, where it was to have landed at the end of an internal Venezuelan flight from the island of La Orchila. All 30 persons aboard lost their lives in the accident, including a crew of three; among the passengers were five children. The aircraft was last reported having descended through 9,500ft (2,900m) during the approach using very-high-frequency omnidirectional range (VOR) instrument procedures before it slammed into Mount El Perico, presumably in poor weather conditions.

11 SEPTEMBER 2004 (c.11:00)

Location   *Near Karyes, Peloponnisos, Greece*
Operator   *Hellenic Army*
Aircraft type   *Boeing/Vertol CH-47SD (ES-916)*

The turbine-engine helicopter, whose passengers included Patriarch Petros VII of Alexandria, the spiritual leader of the Greek Orthodox Church in Africa, who was on a pilgrimage to the Mount Athos community of monasteries at Kariai, plummeted into the Aegean Sea some 20 miles (30km) from its destination. Among the 17 persons aboard the aircraft, who included a four-man military crew, the bodies of 11 victims were recovered, but there were no survivors. The wreckage of ES-916 was later found at a depth of around 2,850ft (870m). Having taken off earlier from Pahi Air Base, located near Athens, ES-916 crashed approximately 5 miles (10km) off the Halikdiki Peninsula after the pilot reported that he was losing altitude. The weather in the area was good and apparently not a factor in the accident.

13 JANUARY 2005 (c.00:20)

Location   *Near Tumaco, Narino, Colombia*
Operator   *Ejército de Colombia (Colombian Army)*
Aircraft type   *Sikorsky UH-60L Black Hawk*

All 20 Colombian military personnel aboard (16 passengers and a crew of four) were killed when the turbine-engine helicopter crashed around 340 miles (550km) south-west of Bogota while on a counter-narcotics operation. The accident occurred in darkness and heavy fog.

26 JANUARY 2005 (c.01:20)

Location   *Near Ar Rutbah, Al Anbar, Iraq*
Operator   *US Marine Corps*
Aircraft type   *Sikorsky CH-53E (164536)*

In the worst US military aviation disaster to occur during its Iraq operation, all 31 American servicemen aboard (27 passengers and a crew of four) were killed when the turbine-engine helicopter crashed some 220 miles (350km) west of Baghdad, during a troop transport operation. The accident occurred in early-morning darkness and poor atmospheric conditions, with the visibility having been reduced by blowing dust. It was believed that the pilots became disorientated and failed to realise that the aircraft had begun banking to the left. The CH-53 must have struck the ground approximately 3 seconds after activation of the ground-proximity warning alert.

Other factors identified in the investigation were possible over-confidence on the part of the pilots as to their ability to see using night-vision goggles, and the failure of the pilot of an accompanying aircraft to provide the crew of 164536 with updated weather information. (The former was later taken off flying status.) As both helicopters were low on fuel, they had to continue on to their destination and could not turn back despite the prevailing conditions.

6 APRIL 2005 (c.13:45)

Location	*Near Ghazni, Afghanistan*
Operator	*US Army*
Aircraft type	*Boeing/Vertol CH-47D (88-0100)*

The turbine-engine helicopter crashed and burned in the desert some 80 miles (130km) south-west of Kabul, killing all 18 persons aboard. With the exception of three American civilians, the victims were US military personnel, including the aircraft's crew of five. Designated as Chalk 1, the CH-47 was one of two Chinook rotorcraft engaged in a general support mission, carrying a mixed passenger/cargo load and flying between unspecified forward operating bases. Following six previous en-route stops, the flight encountered an area of reduced visibility, probably down to only about 1 mile (1.5km), which was associated with blowing dust, with wind gusts of up to 35 knots. At the time of the encounter, 88-0100 was believed to have been at an approximate above-ground height of 100ft (30m).

After reporting having inadvertently entered instrument meteorological conditions, the crew of Chalk 1 announced that they were turning on to a heading of 50 degrees, while the accompanying helicopter also turned and initiated a climb. Shortly afterwards, the latter's crew heard over the external radio frequency the pilot of the former state three times 'Level the wings!' He was then heard to say twice, 'Nose it over!' It was suspected that after the pilots of 88-0100 had lost their outside visibility, and while transitioning to instrument flight, they experienced spatial disorientation, causing them to over-control the helicopter, which then flew into the ground in a steep, inverted attitude. There was no evidence of prior failure in the aircraft's power plants or other major systems.

16 AUGUST 2005 (c.11:30)

Location	*Near Herat, Afghanistan*
Operator	*Ejército de Tierra (Spanish Army)*
Aircraft type	*Eurocopter AS532UL Cougar (ET-657)*

The turbine-engine helicopter crashed and burned in a field, killing all 17 Spanish military personnel aboard. Strong winds were blamed for the accident, and may have been responsible for the crash-landing of a second aircraft, in which five soldiers suffered injuries.

6 DECEMBER 2005 (c.14:00)

Location	*Near Tehran, Iran*
Operator	*Islamic Republic of Iran Air Force*
Aircraft type	*Lockheed C-130E (5-8519)*

The third Iranian military aviation disaster in less than 20 years to claim more than 100 lives involved an aircraft whose passengers comprised journalists being taken to view naval exercises in the Persian Gulf. Shortly after the four-engine turboprop transport had taken off from Mehrabad International Airport, on an internal Iranian flight to Bandar Abbas, in Hormozgan, the pilot reported trouble in its No. 4 power plant and that it needed to return to its point of departure. During an instrument landing system (ILS) approach to Runway 29-Left, the C-130 struck a ten-storey apartment building and burst into flames. The disaster claimed the lives of 128 persons, including all 94 aboard the aircraft, among them its ten military crew members, and the rest on the ground. Approximately 90 others suffered injuries.

19 JANUARY 2006 (c.20:30)

Location	*Near Telkibanya, Hungary*
Operator	*Air Force of the Armed Forces of the Slovak Republic*
Aircraft type	*Antonov An-24B (5605)*

The twin-engine turboprop transport crashed and burned about 10 miles (15km) from the Kosice-Barca air base, across the border in Serbia, where it was to have landed. All but one passenger among the 43 persons aboard the aircraft lost their lives in the accident, including the 8 members of its crew; the survivor was seriously injured. Most of the passengers were peace-keeping troops returning home. Having nearly completed a flight from Pristina, Kosovo, the An-24 slammed into Borso Hill at an approximate elevation of 2,300ft (700m) during a visual approach to Runway 01. The accident occurred in darkness but good weather conditions, with a visibility of around 5 miles (10km) and no clouds below 5,000ft (1,500m). Reportedly, the crew had initiated a premature descent over the unlit terrain.

11 FEBRUARY 2006 (c.08:00)

Location	*Aweil, Northern Bahr el Ghazal, Sudan*
Operator	*Al Quwwat al-Jawwiya As-Sudaniya (Sudanese Air Force)*
Aircraft type	*Antonov An-24*

All 20 persons aboard (13 passengers and a crew of seven) lost their lives when the twin-engine turboprop transport crashed some 600 miles (970km) south-west of Khartoum as it was landing at the local airport. Reportedly, one of its tyres burst after the aircraft had touched down, resulting in a loss of control. The An-24 then slammed into a building and burst into flames.

25 FEBRUARY 2006 (time unknown)

Location	*Near Barra de Dande, Bengo, Angola*
Operator	*Força Aérea Popular de Angola (Angolan Air Force)*
Aircraft type	*Mil Mi-17*

The turbine-engine helicopter crashed in the Atlantic Ocean some 30 miles (50km) north-north-east of Luanda, killing 20 of the 32 persons aboard the aircraft, including the two members of its crew.

3 JUNE 2006 (c.15:00)

Location	Near Yaocun, Anhui, China
Operator	People's Liberation Army Air Force
Aircraft type	Shaanxi KJ-200

The four-engine turboprop, a Chinese-built version of the Soviet Antonov An-12 transport designed for early-warning and control system (AEWCS) operations, crashed into a bamboo-covered hill some 120 miles (190km) south-west of Shanghai. All 40 persons aboard lost their lives, including a crew of five; the passengers were technicians. Reportedly, the aircraft encountered icing conditions at an approximate height of 26,000ft (8,000m), apparently resulting in a stall condition. The unrestrained passengers were probably hurled to the rear of the aircraft, leading to a complete loss of control.

18 JULY 2006 (time unknown)

Location	Near Gabo Gabo, Qorahay, Ethiopia
Operator	Ethiopian Air Force
Aircraft type	Helicopter

The rotorcraft, probably either a turbine-engine Mil Mi-8 or Mi-17, was shot down by rebel forces some 45 miles (70km) north-east of the city of Qabri Dahar, and all 26 Ethiopian military personnel aboard the aircraft were killed.

2 SEPTEMBER 2006 (c.15:50)

Location	Near Gondigan, Kandahar, Afghanistan
Operator	Royal Air Force
Aircraft type	Hawker Siddeley Nimrod MR.2 (XV230)

All 14 British servicemen aboard perished when the four-engine reconnaissance jet crashed approximately 12 miles (20km) west of the city of Kandahar. Except for two victims, those killed were RAF personnel. Minutes after it had completed a mid-air refuelling, the crew of XV230 transmitted a Mayday distress message, reporting a fire warning indication. The Nimrod broke apart at an above-ground height of 1,000ft (300m) or lower after it had initiated an emergency descent, scattering wreckage over a wide area.

The accident was believed to have been precipitated by either overflow from the No. 1 fuel tank or a fracture in a fuel line somewhere near the computerised control unit designed to steady the flow of fuel into the wing tanks and which is located in the lower fuselage, either of which must have occurred during or shortly after the refuelling process. Subsequently, fuel and vapour that had leaked into the bottom of the aircraft's fuselage, in the area of the starboard wing root, ignited, possibly as a result of an electrical fault. The break-up followed an apparent loss of control related to damage to its hydraulic system or flight controls, combined with a series of explosions and the depressurisation of the cabin.

Considered as contributing factors were the age of the aircraft's components; the lack of a flame detection and suppression system within its No. 7 tank dry bay, as well as the failure to recognise the fire threat there; the incorporation of mid-air refuelling capability into the Nimrod without the realisation of the effects on its fuel system; and RAF maintenance policy. There was no evidence that the crew had been aware of the fuel leak that led to the fire. Subsequent to the accident, procedural changes were implemented in Nimrod operations, including the cessation of air-to-air refuelling. In following recommendations made in the wake of the crash, the RAF Nimrod fleet was modified with replacement fuel seals and engine bay hot air ducts.

The Royal Air Force Nimrod MR.2, serial number XV230, the actual aircraft that crashed in Afghanistan after an in-flight fire. (PRM Aviation)

A CASA/IPTN C-295M twin-engine turboprop of the type flown by the Polish Air Force that crashed during an attempted landing.

27 NOVEMBER 2006 (c.07:00)

Location	*Near Tehran, Iran*
Operator	*Islamic Revolutionary Guard Corps Air Force*
Aircraft type	*Antonov An-74T-200 (15-2255)*

The Russian-built twin-jet transport crashed on take-off from Mehrabad International Airport. All 39 military personnel aboard the aircraft, including its crew of six, were killed. Reportedly, one power plant failed seconds after 15-2255 had become airborne from Runway 29-Right, and after the corresponding wing struck the ground, the aircraft broke apart and burst into flames.

23 JANUARY 2008 (c.19:00)

Location	*Near Miroslawiec, Pila, Poland*
Operator	*Polish Air Force*
Aircraft type	*CASA/IPTN C-295M (019)*

The twin-engine turboprop transport crashed around 70 miles (110km) north-north-west of Poznan and in the vicinity of Miroslawiec Air Base, where it was to have landed during an internal flight originating at Warsaw, with an ultimate destination of Krakow. All 20 Polish military personnel aboard the aircraft (16 passengers and a crew of four) were killed.

After being cleared for a precision radar (PAR) approach to Runway 30, the C-295 banked steeply to the left, then slammed into a forest approximately 1 mile short of its threshold and some 1,000ft (300m) to the left of its extended centreline. Impact was at a speed of 170mph (270kmh) and on a heading of 220 degrees, with its undercarriage extended and flaps set at 15 degrees, whereupon the aircraft disintegrated and burned. The accident occurred in darkness and adverse meteorological conditions, with a ceiling of 300ft (100m) and a visibility of 2 miles (3km) in mist.

Spatial disorientation and the inadvertent loss of situational awareness during the final approach phase were blamed for the crash, resulting in the extreme bank angle and a loss of altitude while the pilots were apparently trying to establish visual contact with the runway and approach lights.

Considered as secondary factors were poor crew coordination, including the failure of the pilots to monitor their flight instruments and radio altimeter; the failure of the crew to set the latter instrument to the minimum descent altitude; possible misinterpretation of the barometric altimeters; improper procedures that led to the pilot's and co-pilot's altimeters being set differently, the former to the given airfield elevation (QFE) and the latter to the above sea level height (QNH); the fact that the ground-proximity warning system (GPWS) had been inhibited, which prevented an audio alert pertaining to excessive bank angle, sink rate and height; improper analysis of the weather by the pilot prior to departure; and faulty monitoring of the aircraft by the PAR controller, who also failed to compensate for the 20-knot crosswind and used poor technique when providing advisories to the crew.

Factors considered as contributory were the improper selection of the crew for the flight, with the pilot lacking any previous experience in this version of the C-295 or in PAR approaches with the weather close to the prescribed minima and the co-pilot not rated in the type in night and/or instrument flight operations; the use by the crew of a hand-held global positioning system (GPS) receiver; improper vectoring procedures by the controller, who had no previous experience in PAR operations except those involving Su-22 jet fighters; the inoperative status at the base of the instrument landing system (ILS), which had never worked properly since its installation and which could have provided the crew with precision approach guidance; the use of different units of height measurement, with the aircraft's altimeters scaled in feet and the controller using metres; and the more general issue of instrument approach procedures at military airports in Poland not meeting the standards of the International Civil Aviation Organisation (ICAO) and, specific to the Miroslawiec base, the improper dissemination of information pertaining to minimum weather conditions and available navigational aids.

31 MAY 2008 (c.15:00)

Location	*Near Wenchuan, Sichuan, China*
Operator	*People's Liberation Army Air Force*
Aircraft type	*Mil Mi-171 (LH92734)*

The turbine-engine helicopter, which had been transporting injured survivors of an earthquake, crashed on a mountain north-west of Chengdu. The accident occurred in adverse weather conditions, with fog and severe turbulence. All 19 persons aboard the aircraft, including the five members of its crew, were killed in the accident.

26 JUNE 2008 (c.15:00)

Location	*Java, Indonesia*
Operator	*Tentara Nasional Indonesia Angkatan Udara (Indonesian Air Force)*
Aircraft type	*CASA 212-200M (A-2106)*

The twin-engine turboprop transport crashed in a forest near Salak Mountain, some 25 miles (40km) south of Djakarta, from where it had taken off earlier, on an internal flight to Bogor, with the purpose of testing a new digital mapping camera. Its wreckage was located two days later with no survivors among the 18 persons aboard; six of the victims were civilians.

6 APRIL 2009 (c.12:30)

Location	*Bandung, Java Barat, Indonesia*
Operator	*Tentara Nasional Indonesia Angkatan Udara (Indonesian Air Force)*
Aircraft type	*Fokker F.27 Troopship Mark 400M (A-2703)*

All 24 Indonesian military personnel aboard lost their lives when the twin-engine turboprop transport crashed and burst into flames at Husein Sastranegara Airport, serving Bandung. In addition to the crew of six, the victims were comprised of special forces trainees and their instructor. The aircraft was landing in a heavy rain and a reported 20-knot crosswind when it struck a hangar near the threshold of Runway 29.

20 MAY 2009 (c.06:30)

Location	*Geplak, East Java, Indonesia*
Operator	*Tentara Nasional Indonesia Angkatan Udara (Indonesian Air Force)*
Aircraft type	*Lockheed 100-30 Hercules (A-1325)*

In the third major Indonesian military air disaster in less than a year, the four-engine turboprop transport, carrying as passengers service personnel and their dependants, crashed and burst into flames while attempting to land at Iswahyudi Airport, serving Madiun. Killed in the accident were 94 of the 112 persons aboard the aircraft and three others on the ground; many of the 18 survivors suffered serious injuries. Having nearly completed an internal flight from Jakarta, some 325 miles (525km) to the west, A-1325 appeared to lose height during its approach, after which its starboard wing struck a tree and was sheared off. The aircraft then ploughed into a residential area and skidded to a stop in a rice field, the accident occurring in clear weather conditions.

3 JULY 2009 (time unknown)

Location	*North-western Pakistan*
Operator	*Pakistan Army*
Aircraft type	*Mil Mi-17*

All 26 military personnel aboard were killed when the turbine-engine rotorcraft crashed some 10 miles (15km) from Peshawar during a troop transport flight, reportedly after experiencing a 'technical fault'.

The most disastrous of three Indonesian Air Force accidents occurring in less than a year was this Hercules crash in East Java. (PA Images PA-7330851)

References

Books

Craig, Gary; Freeman, Roger A.; Hutchinson, Paul;
  Middlebrook, Martin; Price, Alfred; and Steel, Rodney,
  Target Germany (Marshall Cavendish, 1974)
Airclaims Loss Record (Ascend Worldwide)
Bowers, Peter M., *Boeing Aircraft Since 1916*
  (Putnam Books, 1989)
British Aerospace 748 (Air-Britain, c.1986)
Brookes, Andrew, *Crash* (Ian Allan, 1991)
Burden, Rodney; Draper, Michael; Rough, Douglas; Smith,
  Colin; and Wilton, David, *Falklands, The Air War* (Arms
  and Armour Press, 1986)
Cornelius Cotter, *Jet Tanker Crash* (The University Press of
  Kansas, 1968)
Eastwood, A., and Mitchell, S., *Military Aircraft Serials of
  North America* (The Aviation Hobby Shop, 1991)
Eastwood, Tony, and Roach, John, *Airliner Production Lists*
  (The Aviation Hobby Shop, 1994)
Ethell, Jeffrey, and Price, Alfred, *Target Berlin* (Jane's
  Publishing, 1981)
Freeman, Roger, *Mighty Eighth War Diary*
  (Jane's Publishing, 1981)
Gunston, Bill, *Jane's Aerospace Dictionary*
  (Jane's Publishing, 1986)
Hastings, Max, and Jenkins, Simon, *The Battle for the
  Falklands* (W. W. Norton, 1983)
Hopkins III, Robert, *Boeing KC-135 Stratotanker*
  (Midland Publishing, 1997)
Jane's All the World's Aircraft (Jane's Publishing)
Major Loss Record (Airclaims, 2009)
Matricardi, Paolo, *The Concise History of Aviation*
  (Arnoldo Mondadori Editore Spa, 1984)
McClement, Fred, *The Anvil of the Gods*
  (J. B. Lippincott, 1964)

Middlebrook, Martin, and Everitt, Chris, *The Bomber
  Command War Diaries* (Viking Press, 1985)
Olausson, Lars, *Lockheed Hercules Production List*
  (Lars Olausson, 1993)
Oliver, David, *British Military Aircraft Accidents*
  (Ian Allan, 1990)
Hillman, Peter; Jessup, Stuart; and Ottenhof, Guus, *Soviet
  Transports* (The Aviation Hobby Shop, 1996)
Piekalkiewicz, Janusz, *The Air War* (Historical Times, 1978)
Read, Piers Paul, *Alive: The Story of the Andes Survivors* (J.B.
  Lippincott, 1974)
Stewart, Stanley, *Air Disasters* (Ian Allan, 1986)
Taylor, Michael, and Mondey, David, *Aircraft Facts and Feats*
  (Guinness Superlatives, 1984)
The Times Atlas of the World
The World Book Encyclopedia (World Book Inc.)
Weingarten, Arthur, *The Sky is Falling*
  (Grosset and Dunlap, 1975)
World Aircraft Accident Summary (Airclaims, 2009)
World Airline Accident Directory (Civil Aviation Authority/
  Airclaims)

Newspapers and periodicals

Air Forces (New Jersey and Great Britain)
Aviation Letter (Ruislip, Middlesex)
Aviation Week and Space Technology (New York City)
Flight International (Sutton, Surrey)
Hadley, Christopher, 'The Mystery of Flight F4J40',
  Esquire (July/August 1996, London)
La Opinion (Los Angeles, California)
Lloyd's List (London)
Los Angeles Times
New York Times
The Times (London)

Index